ALSO BY BARRY SIEGEL

Fiction

The Perfect Witness

Actual Innocence

Lines of Defense

Nonfiction

A Death in White Bear Lake

Shades of Gray

Claim of Privilege

MANIFEST INJUSTICE

MANIFEST INJUSTICE

The True Story of a
Convicted Murderer
and the Lawyers Who
Fought for His Freedom

BARRY SIEGEL

Henry Holt and Company
New York

Henry Holt and Company, LLC
Publishers since 1866
175 Fifth Avenue
New York, New York 10010
www.henryholt.com

Henry Holt® and ® are registered trademarks of Henry Holt and Company, LLC.

Distributed in Canada by Raincoast Book Distribution Limited

Library of Congress Cataloging-in-Publication Data

Siegel, Barry.
  Manifest injustice : the true story of a convicted murderer and the lawyers
who fought for his freedom / Barry Siegel.
      p.   cm.
  ISBN 978-0-8050-9415-2
  1. Macumber, William, 1935–   2. Trials (Murder)—Arizona—Maricopa County.
3. Judicial error.   4. Arizona Justice Project.   I. Title.
  KF224.M18S54 2012
  364.152'3092—dc23   2012028986

Henry Holt books are available for special promotions and premiums.
For details contact: Director, Special Markets.

First Edition 2013

Designed by Meryl Sussman Levavi

Printed in the United States of America

1   3   5   7   9   10   8   6   4   2

To my father, who showed me the way.
With much love and admiration

Contents

PART TWO ■ QUEST FOR JUSTICE

PART THREE ■ LAST CHANCE

Author's Note

In the summer of 2010, a scattering of news accounts drew my attention to the case of William Wayne Macumber, a seventy-five-year-old man who by then had served thirty-five years of a life sentence in Arizona State Prison for a double murder he very possibly did not commit. The case, rife with extraordinary irregularities, had attracted the sustained decade-long involvement of the Arizona Justice Project, one of the first and most respected of the nonprofit groups that now represent victims of manifest injustice throughout the country. By reputation, I knew of the Justice Project's founding director, Larry Hammond, a celebrated criminal and civil liberties attorney who had just been named winner of the prestigious 2010 Morris Dees Justice Award, given annually to a lawyer "who has devoted his or her career to serving the public interest and pursuing justice, and whose work has brought about positive change in the community, state or nation." We arranged a phone conference and, on a Saturday morning late that June, talked for two hours. What I heard then, and subsequently discovered from my research, aroused in me an interest to write this book. I asked for Hammond's cooperation, and he readily agreed.

So began my unique relationship with the Justice Project team and, eventually, Bill Macumber. Without anyone saying so directly, it seemed clear that the Justice Project lawyers and I shared certain values and a mutual respect. Yet I was not on their defense team, and they weren't my coauthors. As always between journalists and subjects, each party had its own goals and interests; there was a kind of unavoidable, collegial, unspoken maneuvering. The Justice Project associates naturally hoped to shape the narrative in a way favorable to their client, while I wanted access—intimate, authentic access. As a result, we found ourselves in a friendly yet careful kind of dance.

Larry Hammond, by nature impulsive and forthcoming, nonetheless gave careful thought to what he'd reveal, openly telling me when he was "thinking as a lawyer." His estimable Justice Project colleague Bob Bartels, a distinguished law professor at Arizona State University's Sandra Day O'Connor College of Law, nicely but frankly informed me that if it were up to him, he wouldn't share anything. Yet eventually both did share and tell, in a series of enlightening conversations. So did a journalist turned private investigator, Rich Robertson, and a group of extraordinarily committed former law student volunteers, chief among them Karen Killion, Sharon Sargent-Flack and Jen Roach, who regularly rushed to assist the Macumber team long after they'd launched their own careers.

Each time I returned to Arizona, the door swung wider and the piles of documents on the counters of my home office grew higher. Yet the more I researched, the more I came to realize that my trove derived almost entirely from public documents chronicling events set well in the past. What I lacked was a detailed inner look at the Justice Project's ten-year effort on Macumber's behalf, started not long after Larry Hammond founded the organization. Good reason existed for this deficiency, of course: The case remained ongoing, with the Justice Project still serving as Macumber's lawyer. So barriers of confidentiality and attorney-client privilege stood between me and an understanding of the more recent efforts.

All the same, if I were to tell the story I had in mind, I needed both to chronicle the present and reconstruct the past. This I explained to Larry Hammond during a marathon four-day session we held in late February 2011 at his Phoenix law office, four days in which we talked constantly, morning to night, about the legal system, the Justice Project and the Macumber case—except when we stopped on a balmy Saturday afternoon to sneak in three innings of a spring training game between the Dodgers and Giants, baseball being Larry's other great passion besides social justice. Even there, with Hammond keeping a detailed scorecard, unabashed about his statistical fanaticism, I pressed him about my needs as he explained the fine points of legal confidentiality. I could tell he was at least listening and considering. "Renegade" might be too strong a word for Hammond, but he did seem a lawyer inclined to think outside the box. What's more, he had his own compelling reasons for me to tell Macumber's story.

Our visit would prove pivotal. Days later, Hammond sent a message to his Justice Project team members, urging their "full cooperation" with me, even if that involved divulging client confidences and disclosing in detail some of the "awkward reasons" it had taken the project so long to file a petition on Macumber's behalf. "I think we have a good story to tell," he explained. Bill Macumber "has been briefed extensively on this question and he is in full accord and wants to waive the privilege."

With that, the locks came off the file cabinets. Three young, talented Justice Project attorneys, Katie Puzauskas, Lindsay Herf and Sarah Cooper, gathered around, excitedly offering accounts of their recent months out in the field, a "girl team" of lawyer-detectives going to the ground to track down witnesses from long ago. Katie, a vivacious twenty-seven-year-old of chiefly Italian descent; Lindsay, a sunny thirty-year-old college track and swim team jock; Sarah, an intense twenty-four-year-old wunderkind barrister with a strong British accent—together they walked me through their still fresh investigation, spreading their reports on a conference room table, recalling details, setting scenes, building a chronology. The earlier Macumber team volunteers, the former law students Karen Killion, Sharon Sargent-Flack and Jen Roach, provided their accounts as well, along with piles of their notes and reports. Bill Macumber contributed, too, in a major way. After I spent a singular weekend visiting him at his Arizona State Prison home, a full Saturday and Sunday together from 9:00 A.M. to 4:00 P.M. each day, he decided to provide me with a thick file of personal letters and his entire four-hundred-page journal, a chronicle spanning his early life, arrest, conviction, and decades behind bars.

In this fashion, my understanding of the Macumber case and the

Justice Project's efforts kept expanding. Inevitably, so did my evolving sense of ambiguity: The more I could see, the more complicated matters appeared. The complexities only deepened when I finally had the chance to meet with Macumber's ex-wife, Carol Kempfert. This case certainly involved a long list of strikingly dubious elements, as well as a convicted killer whose wit, erudition, calm decency and exemplary conduct (in prison and out) had inspired many to support him. Yet the record also included what seemed to be some quite damaging evidence against Bill Macumber—his own lawyer at trial had warned that the jury might not believe him because, though true, his account did sound "fishy." So why Larry Hammond's passion and the Justice Project's unflagging decade-long commitment? By its nature, the cash-strapped Justice Project, with limited resources and manpower, had to be highly selective. The group's manifesto assigned to its staff only cases involving innocence or "manifest injustice" (obvious unfairness), and in reality, that alone wasn't enough: The Justice Project associates had to choose just those few cases where they could have an impact, where they could win. That they'd even selected the Macumber case was telling. That they'd stuck with it for more than a decade spoke volumes.

Larry Hammond, after all, knew from the start how hard it would be to ever convincingly prove Macumber's innocence. This because they had no DNA evidence—no physical or biological evidence of any sort remained in the Macumber file. DNA exonerations by then had become a familiar story, many of them won by Barry Scheck and Peter Neufeld's renowned Innocence Project at Yeshiva University in New York. But such outcomes were the exception, since most cases didn't include DNA, making it far harder to win post-conviction relief—in fact, so hard that Scheck and Neufeld's Innocence Project wouldn't touch non-DNA cases. Larry Hammond's Justice Project did all the time.

The deeper I plunged into the record, the more I wanted to understand the Justice Project's ceaseless, quixotic campaign to free Bill Macumber.

Prologue

On June 10, 1998, in the Arizona State Prison at Douglas, an isolated
border town in the far southeast corner of Arizona, a fellow inmate handed
Bill Macumber an article from that day's newspaper. Macumber carried
it back to what he called his "home"—a small cubicle in the prison's flat,
single-story Mohave Unit. He wasn't feeling well, as he'd been having
trouble getting his heart medication from the prison's medical staff. He
knew one nice lady on the prison staff who treated him like a human
being. That helped. But the temperature in Douglas had suddenly dropped
by twenty degrees, the nights falling into the low forties, and there'd be
no heat for at least another week. Two light blankets and his sluggish
circulation made for chilly nights. He stood a lanky and angular six foot
seven, so he needed a special bed. It filled most of his ten-by-seven-foot
stall, set in a large dorm room with twenty-eight other such cubes, each
divided by low partitions. Even in such a crowd, he remained alone, being
decades older than the other prisoners.

In his cubicle, he read the article, written by an *Arizona Republic*
columnist, Steve Wilson. Its subject, a case just then before the U.S.
Supreme Court, involved the suicide of deputy White House counsel
Vince Foster. The justices had heard oral argument two days before.

Wilson's local interest: "A controversial decision by the Arizona Supreme Court two decades ago might figure in the outcome."

Macumber kept reading. Yes, he could see what the reporter meant. At the Supreme Court hearing, an old Arizona murder case indeed had haunted the conversation: his murder case. *Arizona v. Macumber.*

He recalled Vince Foster's suicide. Facing possible scandal, Foster had shot himself in the head. A legal battle had ensued, the independent prosecutor Kenneth Starr trying to get access to notes taken by Foster's lawyer at their last meeting. Did attorney-client privilege survive the death of a client? That's what they were arguing at the Supreme Court. The very same issue they'd argued at Macumber's murder trial.

He read on. How interesting—Justice Sandra Day O'Connor, being from Arizona, knew his case well. At the oral hearing, she'd posed a question to Vince Foster's lawyer: "Mr. Hamilton, you take the position that there can be no compelled testimony by someone in your circumstance, even if the information would be essential to show that a third person was not guilty of a crime, such as in the Macumber case in Arizona?" Faced with *Macumber*, Hamilton conceded that disclosure of a dead client's confession might have been appropriate there—but that such a "singular situation" didn't warrant wholesale overriding of the attorney-client privilege.

Steve Wilson agreed with Hamilton. Macumber's case, he told his readers, involved a lovers' lane double homicide. Bill Macumber had been "an unlikely suspect" with "no known motive and no prior record." What's more, "someone else admitted to the killings." Ernest Valenzuela, on trial for another rape and murder, had confessed to his attorney, Thomas O'Toole, now a prominent Maricopa County Superior Court judge. So both the Foster and the Macumber cases involved attorney-client privilege. Yet the two differed. "For the privilege to be breached," Wilson concluded, "the circumstances should be extremely compelling. They were in 1974 when an Arizona man stood trial for murder. They aren't in 1998 when Starr is fishing for evidence."

To Macumber, this column told a familiar story. He knew of his case's notoriety, that it had been the subject of multiple law review articles, symposium panels, textbook chapters. He knew that to certain critics, his case had become a symbol of just how seriously the legal system places attorney-client privilege over the search for truth. What did it matter? He didn't see how any of it had done any good. Still, maybe this time. Macumber could only try. The next morning, he mailed the column to his closest friend and ally, his cousin Jackie Kelley.

Jackie and Bill had grown up together back in Iowa, more like brother and sister than cousins. Ever since his conviction, she'd been endlessly battling for his release. Sixty-seven years old, five years Bill's senior, she and her husband lived on a remote 160-acre spread in northwest New Mexico. Sitting at her kitchen counter in late June, she read and reread the newspaper piece. Her eyes kept traveling back to the name Thomas O'Toole. "If Valenzuela was lying, he was very convincing," Judge O'Toole had told Wilson. "He had details about the crime that were only known to police."

On June 27, Jackie turned to her typewriter. "I am writing to you concerning the attached article from the Arizona Republic," she began a letter addressed to Judge O'Toole. "This article was sent to me by my cousin, William Wayne Macumber...."

Bill has always been like a brother to me. Bill did not, at the time of his arrest, have a great deal of money, nor did his family. For this reason he could rely only on the services of a public defender.... I have the same problem as does Bill—no access to a great deal of money. I am also quite ignorant in the ins and outs of our legal system. Actually, about all I have is determination! Is it possible for either you, or someone in your office, to give me any suggestions, any assistance in gaining my dear cousin's freedom? For the life of me I cannot understand how the rights of a dead, confessed killer can supersede those of a living, innocent man! We are God-fearing people, as is my cousin. If there is any assistance or suggestions you could give to me, I would be eternally grateful.

Judge O'Toole, who preferred the cool air of Flagstaff during the blazing hot Phoenix summers, did not immediately attend to Jackie's letter. When he did pick it up, he stiffened: *Ernest Valenzuela*. Back in

1967, O'Toole had been a young federal public defender. He'd represented thousands of clients since then. Most were a blur now. But he'd never forgotten Ernie Valenzuela. Valenzuela had scared the wits out of him. As the years went by, even after he became a judge in 1984, and then the Maricopa County presiding criminal department judge, O'Toole would regularly reflect about Valenzuela and how he'd confessed to the lovers' lane killings—not bragging, not running his mouth, not huffing and puffing, just talking, his eyes flat and cold. So eerie, like a wild animal. The way he recalled the murders with obvious relish, savoring and cherishing the memory. O'Toole had never stopped thinking about this case, had never managed to shake it. He *knew* Ernie was a hardened killer, he knew Ernie liked to prey on couples in lovers' lanes. He'd absolutely believed Valenzuela's confession. So he'd tried to testify at Macumber's trial. The judge wouldn't let him. That had been hard, watching Bill Macumber get convicted.

Finally, though, it had not been his case, his concern. Life went on. Until now—until he opened Jackie Kelley's letter. *If there is any assistance or suggestions you could give to me, I would be eternally grateful.* He couldn't again let it go, Judge O'Toole decided. This time he had to push harder.

He could think of only one person to call: Larry Hammond. O'Toole knew him mainly by reputation. Hammond was a legend, having battled zealously for years on behalf of the wrongly accused. He'd collected all sorts of lustrous awards—and a fair amount of resentment—for fighting to correct systemic injustice in the legal system. He sat on indigent-defense task forces, human rights committees, capital representation agencies. Most important, he'd recently launched the Arizona Justice Project. Hammond had no funding, no office, no staff, no structure—just volunteer lawyers and law students. Yet if anyone could help Macumber, O'Toole reasoned, it would be Hammond.

O'Toole reached him in the early afternoon on September 18, 1998. Hammond didn't field many such calls from judges. Though he'd served as law clerk for two U.S. Supreme Court justices (Hugo Black and Lewis Powell), his dealings with judges in more recent years had usually involved arguing before them in courtrooms or fuming at their authority behind their backs. Now here was O'Toole, urging the Justice Project to look at

Macumber. If there's any case you should take, O'Toole told Hammond, it's this one. O'Toole pointed to the Vince Foster litigation. Reassess *Macumber* in light of Foster, O'Toole advised. Foster might apply. The judge openly pled: *I am aware of this case. I have known of it for years. I represented a man who confessed to the murders. Larry, I represented the killer.*

That's how it began. That's how Bill Macumber played a card he didn't think he had, and that's how Larry Hammond heard the siren call of an impossible obsession. At his urging, the Arizona Justice Project would embark on the tenacious pursuit of questions that offered no clear answers: What happened all those years ago on a remote lovers' lane north of Scottsdale? And what happened at Bill Macumber's home on West Wethersfield Road in the workaday corner of Phoenix known as Deer Valley?

PART ONE

CRIME AND CONSEQUENCES

CHAPTER 1

Why Oh Why

In the spring of 1962, the greater Phoenix area had not yet sprawled hap-
hazardly across the high desert floor. To the northeast, where luxury
resorts would later rise in Scottsdale, open reaches of barren sandy land
rolled on for miles and miles. Yet the Scottsdale desert had its inhabi-
tants, at least at night, when young people from all over Maricopa County
would arrive to party, drink and build bonfires—or park in isolated lovers' lanes. There might have been one thousand teenagers in the vicinity
on any night. Sometimes one party would be romping just two hundred
feet away from another. Little trails crisscrossed the desert, created by
cars driving off-road, which they did for good reason. If you circled your
cars and started drinking right on the edge of the desert, twenty-five feet
from Scottsdale Road, the cops would catch you. So everyone drove deeper
in, at least two hundred feet. Despite that act of caution, most of the kids
would then go ahead and build a bonfire, only to wonder later how the
cops managed to find them. By dawn, everyone would be gone, the desert abandoned to the heat of the day.

Out there, where the pavement gave way to sand, a school bus full of students drove by at 7:30 A.M. on May 24, 1962, a Thursday. The students, from the small town of Cave Creek, were on their way to Paradise Valley High, two miles north of Phoenix. They were laughing and talking until, looking east out at the desert, they saw a car parked some three hundred feet off Scottsdale Road, just north of Bell Road. Near the car, they saw two people—bodies?—lying on their backs. The students rushed to tell the bus driver, who at a stop sign called out to a state highway crew foreman, Joe Armos, asking him to notify the sheriff's department. Armos instead flagged down two deputies on their way to target practice at the sheriff's range. It had been their day off, but now Joe Duwel and Don Spezzano turned and drove into the desert. They reached the car—a 1959 Chevy Impala, white with a red stripe—at 7:54 A.M. It sat under a palo verde tree, some thirty-eight feet up one of the many desert trails. Beside it lay the body of a young man, his head facing the car, and, six feet south, the body of a young woman, on her back with her legs pointed toward his. Both were fully and neatly dressed, he in Levi's and a short-sleeved striped shirt, she in yellow capri pants and a checked yellow blouse. Both still had their wallets, money and jewelry, with her purse untouched in the car, a man's class ring on her left index finger. Both also had holes in their heads—her right temple, his left. They had each been shot twice. Deputy Duwel called his supervisor. Within twenty minutes, Sergeants Jerry Hill and Lester Jones arrived at the scene, summoned from their breakfast at Helsing's Coffee Shop.

It did not take the sheriff's detectives long to identify the victims. Tim McKillop and Joyce Sterrenberg, both twenty—he six foot four, 180 pounds, blond hair and blue eyes, she five foot nine, 125 pounds, brown hair, blue eyes—had been employed by Mountain States Telephone. They'd been engaged, with plans to marry. They had left Joyce's home near 8:00 P.M. the previous evening, after celebrating her dad's birthday over ice cream and cake, saying they were going to look at model homes in a new development. Their parents had wakened in the early morning to find Tim and Joyce's beds made up and empty—they'd never come home. Tim's father, Jim McKillop, had called the Sterrenberg home at 5:30 A.M. Cliff Sterrenberg had filed a missing person report and cruised the neighborhood. Back home, near 9:30 A.M., both he and McKillop heard the same news report on their kitchen radios: two bodies, a young couple, found shot to death in the desert north of Scottsdale. McKillop just knew it was Tim and Joyce. Sterrenberg braced himself and called the sheriff's department.

At the murder scene, Sergeants Hill and Jones took notes, shot photos and collected evidence. They found four spent .45 reloaded gun casings (new bullets in old cartridges), one live shell, one mutilated slug, tire tracks, Joyce's purse, Tim's wallet, a handkerchief and a thatch of hair— the last recovered some sixty feet from the car. They noted that the front passenger door was locked, suggesting that both victims had gotten out on the driver's side. Tire marks told them that another car had backed up and sped out to Scottsdale Road, the tires digging into the desert floor as a car does when it accelerates rapidly from a dead stop. According to Hill and Jones's initial report, they marked, tagged and placed all items of evidence in envelopes labeled MARICOPA COUNTY SHERIFF'S OFFICE PROPERTY.

Yet it can't be said that the deputies ran a sophisticated operation. They didn't identify the type of blood at the murder scene. They didn't make casts of the tire tracks. They didn't secure the site—on the morning of May 24, journalists and TV crews joined investigators in tromping around the area. Stranger still, the deputies didn't lift fingerprints off the car out in the desert. Instead, they had the Chevy Impala towed to a sheriff's department lot in downtown Phoenix, without monitoring the route taken or the departure and arrival times. Once there, the car sat in an open, unsecured area before being moved into a garage.

Shortly after noon, a sheriff's fingerprint technician, Sergeant Jerry Jacka, arrived at the garage to start his process of photographing, dusting and lifting latent prints off the Impala. In all, he came up with fifteen latents, but most were either the victims' or unintelligible. Two weeks later, he sent just one latent lift to the FBI's fingerprint section; he'd taken it from the bottom of the left front door handle, thinking it the best possible for a match. When that yielded nothing, Jacka sent the FBI three more lifts, apparently the remaining intelligible ones, noting that "these latent impressions are the only physical evidence that we have at this time." Again, nothing.

*　*　*

By then, the Maricopa County Sheriff's Office was in a frenzy. The pressure had been on from the first day, when news of the murders claimed front-page banner headlines ("Authorities Sift Slender Clues in Savage Slaying of Young Pair"), supplanting news that astronaut Scott Carpenter had landed after three orbits of the earth in the *Mercury-Atlas 7* rocket. On the second day, a renowned Arizona State University psychologist told reporters that the killer either knew and had been rejected by Joyce or was a sadist who would strike again. In an interview at his home, Jim McKillop sobbed and pounded his thigh with a fist. "What is there to say," he asked, "when you learn your only son and the girl he was going to marry have been shot to death by a madman? Why oh why? Is there anyone in the world who had anything against either one of those kids? They were good kids who wanted to get married. Neither had ever hurt anyone." McKillop seemed to be in a state of semishock as he rose to show the reporter bowling trophies he and Tim had won together in a church league. "My pal, my hunting and fishing partner, that fine boy gave me a lot of proud moments, the little fella I watched grow into a real man. We fished, we camped, we'd go everywhere together. It made me glad when I learned my boy had met a girl he wanted to marry. He had planned a big wedding for next April."

Cliff Sterrenberg also spoke to a reporter: "You read about these things in the newspapers. You think it can't happen to you. . . . They'd been going steady since they were introduced last October. They were buying things as they planned their wedding." He recalled the last time he'd seen his daughter: She at the door, leaving to get gas in her car, saying, "We won't be long."

Sheriff L. C. Boies soon had seventeen investigators assigned full-time to the Scottsdale lovers' lane murders, working twelve-hour days in five separate teams, helped by 110 other deputies ordered to funnel information to a coordinating captain. Officers spread through the Phoenix area, canvassing citizens and gun dealers, collecting and test-firing many dozens of .45-caliber pistols, focusing on people known to use hand-reloaded .45 shells. They questioned informers, visited pawnshops, talked with parolees and crackpots—anyone with an idea or a theory. Hundreds of telephone tips began flooding the department, the numbers rising along with the growing total of reward money contributed by businesses and community groups—$1,000 became $5,000, then $7,000, finally $10,000.

Theories abounded. The investigators variously thought the murders the work of a jealous suitor, a robber, a madman or an enraged driver. Some in the sheriff's office believed the killer had certainly known his victims. But Sergeant Lester Jones suspected a gang of roving thrill seekers. "This was a spur of the moment slaying," he told reporters. "It is the type committed by a bunch of punks driving around looking for trouble." Sergeant Jones said he had a number of reasons to believe there was more than one person in the killer's car, "but I'm not ready to release this evidence for publication. It could hurt our case." Also: "There's a possibility there are two or three teen-agers that witnessed the crime and are now reluctant to come forward with their accounts because they fear the gunman who fired the fatal shots."

What "number of reasons" did Sergeant Jones have? What evidence that he was "not ready to release?" The Macumber file never yielded answers to these questions. Not a single sheriff's report—at least not a single surviving report—addressed or documented this possibility. Whatever the deputies' theories, the investigators appeared to still have no solid clues or leads when Joyce and Tim went to their graves together at a double funeral held on Monday afternoon, May 28, in the Memory Chapel of A. L. Moore and Sons Mortuary. Two gray caskets rested end to end in a dimly lit room, draped in flowers, with more than three hundred mourners attending—including a team of plainclothes detectives, watching for a possible killer among them.

"To those who love God all things can work together for good," the Reverend Philip A. Gangsei reminded the mourners. "Blessings can come, and usually do, from trouble and difficulty." He knew everyone was asking why this young couple had been so brutally murdered. The young pastor could only say, "We live in a world where men's minds sometimes become twisted."

In the ensuing weeks, the Maricopa County Sheriff's Office continued to search frantically but vainly for clues and leads. Sheriff Cal Boies issued a public appeal for assistance, as did Cliff Sterrenberg. "We'll continue to check out every lead including crank calls," Captain Ralph Edmunson vowed. "We can't pass up one because you never know when the right tip will come in. . . . Neither I nor all the men who have been working this have been able to get it off our minds. None of us will rest until it's over. Someday we'll get the guy."

In time, though, every tip started feeling like a crank call. A local attorney thought a former client he'd represented years before in Montana on a grand theft charge might be the killer. A man reported that he'd been getting annoying phone calls from a stranger in the middle of the night, someone talking about "the deal out on Scottsdale and Bell Road." A priest reported a boy who was "acting abnormal" and rambling on about the double slaying. Women at bars tried to turn in ex-lovers, ex-husbands and anyone who'd done them wrong. Others thought their next-door neighbors had been acting oddly. An alcoholic ex-con fingered his brother, with whom he'd been arguing all night. A woman jailed on a drunk driving charge loudly accused her husband, who when contacted by investigators said, "She sure must be mad at me." Another wife, deep into a custody dispute with her estranged husband, insisted that he'd killed the couple in the lovers' lane. A disturbed young man tried to confess so he could be committed to the Arizona State Hospital and get help. Jim McKillop even had some suspicions about Cliff Sterrenberg.

In issuing his fiscal year report at the end of June 1962, some five weeks after the Scottsdale murders, Sheriff Boies could claim a generally high crime-solution rate—they'd solved 59 percent of all felony cases, more than twice the national average. During that year, they'd arrested fifteen persons in connection with ten homicides. They'd solved nine of those murder cases—all but one: the double slaying of Timothy McKillop and Joyce Sterrenberg on May 24.

Then, amid all the crank calls and false leads, came another tip. On August 25, three months after the Scottsdale killings, an informant advised sheriff's investigators that a seventeen-year-old girl confined at the Maricopa County Detention Ward had told a matron a story that seemed to place her at the scene of the murders.

The tip went to the chief investigators, Sergeants Jerry Hill and Lester Jones. They tried to interview the girl, Linda Primrose, who was temporarily in the detention center over a stolen car charge, her usual domicile being the Good Shepherd Home for Girls, where she'd been placed by her mother. But Primrose wouldn't cooperate with Hill and Jones. Despite what she'd told the matron, she now resolutely denied any knowledge of the homicides.

Hill decided to try again with another deputy sheriff, Sergeant Tom Hakes. On September 9, Hakes visited Primrose at the Good Shepherd Home and found her much more cooperative. She told him her story: On the night of May 23, she'd been picked up near her home by a man named "Ernie Salazar," a girl known as "Terry" or "Theresa," and two other men. They were all drinking and smoking pot, and she was skin-popping, too. While driving north on Scottsdale Road, they spotted the Sterrenberg Impala at a gas station. They followed the Impala up Scottsdale, being on their way to pick up a "stash" out in the desert. About a half mile north of Bell Road, the Impala turned onto a dirt road. Ernie drove his car past the dirt road for a tenth of a mile, then made a U-turn and came back. He pulled his car almost parallel with the Impala and stopped. He got out of his car and walked over to the Impala, where he started talking to the couple inside. Primrose heard Ernie shout some profanities, then saw him return to his car and get something from under the driver's seat. Everyone was outside of their cars by now. Primrose heard a shot, turned, and saw the young man lying on the ground. She saw Ernie shoot the young woman—once, then again while she was lying on the ground. The girl named Terry or Theresa began to scream and yank at her own hair in a fit of sorts. Primrose pushed Terry back into Ernie's car, and they quickly drove off.

Six days later, Sergeant Hakes met Primrose again, along with two other deputies. During a two-hour interrogation, Primrose once more told of being at the scene of the murders and seeing "Ernie" kill Tim and Joyce. This time, the deputies took shorthand notes and transcribed her statement. Primrose offered a revised version: Now they'd initially come across the Impala in the desert, while looking for their "stash," rather than at a gas station. Otherwise the details remained much the same, though Primrose at moments appeared somewhat confused. The interrogators kept asking this teenage addict to be precise, and she kept telling them she couldn't remember and didn't care: *I didn't notice. . . . Like I said, I was high. No, I can't think of her name because I don't give a damn about her name.*

Yet she did remember the victims' car: a white Impala with a stripe. And she remembered the murders: *We couldn't pick up our stash because those people were there. Ernie was mad. Bang. There was a shot. When I heard the shot, I looked up. The girl was running. Bang. They came up close to her head. Bang again.*

Deputy county attorney Joe Shaw did not regard this one as a crank lead. Two days after Primrose testified, he arranged for her to take a polygraph test. Shortly past noon on September 18, a team of deputies brought Primrose to John McCarthy at the Arizona Polygraph Laboratory. There he interviewed and tested her. She resisted and tried to evade, taking long, deep breaths while answering questions. Yet McCarthy offered the deputies an unequivocal conclusion: "Primrose was present at the time of the homicide and does have firsthand knowledge of the crime and other persons involved."

Joe Shaw next arranged for Primrose to visit Dr. Milton Erickson, a prominent psychiatrist. He spoke to her for three hours on September 20, then for another hour on September 26. Again she resisted, flaring angrily at the doctor. Yet Dr. Erickson thought that what she told him confirmed her previous statements. She talked to him of being present at the murder scene. She described how she'd stood over Joyce's body. Dr. Erickson ended up firmly convinced that she was telling the truth. He believed "she could give further good information on all subjects present at the scene of the crime."

Another day that September, Hakes and a second officer put Primrose in a car and invited her to direct them to the scene of the murder. She took them straight there and accurately described the layout—the position of the cars and the bodies—in detail not available in the newspapers. "She led us by direction," Hakes later testified. "She knew where she was going. She knew what the area was."

Then came investigative roadblocks. Hours after Primrose first saw Dr. Erickson, deputies took her to the southeast section of Phoenix, where together they vainly searched for "Terry" or "Theresa," the woman who'd pulled her hair at the murder site. Two days later, a team of investigators spent all day and night in the Deuce area, prowling the streets in an attempt to locate "Ernie," "Terry," and the others who populated Primrose's story. That same night, Hakes and several colleagues spent three hours in and around the area of Second Street and Madison, Third Street and Jefferson, and Third Street and Washington. "Numerous subjects were questioned," Hakes noted, "but very little information was obtained."

The last line of his report: "Investigation continues." It did not. Here the Primrose file ends. Unable to locate "Ernie" or "Terry," the investigators didn't follow up. They never connected "Terry" tearing her hair with the thatch of hair found at the scene. They never tested that thatch of hair.

As time went by, the unsolved Scottsdale lovers' lane murders hung heavily over the Maricopa County Sheriff's Office. Yet the case no longer consumed the public's attention. By early June, the story had disappeared from the local newspapers' front pages, and then it left even the inside pages. After their encounter with Primrose, sheriff's investigators added just a few scant reports to their own file—they had nowhere left to go. Only on anniversaries did the case recapture attention. "Year Passes Since Desert Killing of Engaged Couple; Clues Meager" read a headline in the *Arizona Republic* on May 23, 1963. His office, Sheriff Boies reported, had conducted more than three hundred investigations into leads. They had test-fired more than seven hundred pistols. They had questioned burglars, armed robbers, sex perverts and dozens of gun owners. They had given lie detector tests to all known rapists and other men with records of violent crime in the area. Yet they'd come up empty. Boies couldn't believe that the $10,000 reward hadn't brought the hoped-for results.

In October 1963, the sheriff's department released to the news media copies of the four latent fingerprints they had earlier provided to the FBI, and sent flyers featuring the prints to law enforcement agencies across the country. "Double-Murder," read the banner atop the flyer. "Information Wanted. $10,000 Reward Posted." This, too, yielded nothing.

In May 1964, newspaper headlines recognized the second anniversary: "Still a Mystery; Sweethearts Murdered in Desert 2 Years Ago." By then, deputies had conducted ballistics checks on more than eight hundred guns. They'd talked to yet another group of informers, mental patients and barroom drunks. They'd written jurisdictions nationwide, whenever word came of a murder in another state that resembled the Scottsdale lovers' lane killings. "Today the case still remains open and periodically officers go over the file looking for any little detail they may have overlooked," reported one newspaper account that May. "Every large community seems to have a murder that plagues the police. In Boston there is a strangler at large, in Los Angeles the 'Black Dahlia' is still unsolved. In each instance the police never close their files. They never forget and the killer or killers will never really be safe from apprehension."

Less than three months later, another intriguing lead emerged. On August 13, 1964, Sergeant Ralph Anderson of the Maricopa County Sheriff's Office received a phone call from an Officer Shaver of the Scottsdale Police Department. Shaver was just then booking a twenty-year-old man on a charge of joyriding—a man who believed "he was the one who committed the double homicide north of Scottsdale." The subject's name: Ernest Valenzuela. *Ernie.*

Sergeant Anderson drove to the Scottsdale Police Department to interview Valenzuela. It turned out Valenzuela had confessed once before to the Scottsdale lovers' lane killings. In early 1963, while serving ninety days in a Phoenix jail on a burglary charge, he'd told a fellow inmate, Richard Green, that he'd killed Joyce Sterrenberg and Tim McKillop. Green had relayed this information to authorities, who'd arranged for a psychologist to examine Valenzuela. Nothing more came of that incident, other than a note in Valenzuela's file. Now here he was, again volunteering a confession.

Valenzuela grew worried and nervous, he explained to Sergeant Anderson, every time he heard or thought about these murders north of Scottsdale. He wanted to clear up his mind about this murder. He'd been drinking heavily and smoking marijuana that night—not unusual for him—so his memories were hazy. As he recalled, the murders took place in the desert north of Scottsdale. There were two victims, a male and a female. He killed them, he believed, because he saw this good-looking gal with this man and wanted to prove to her that he was a better man than her guy. He believed he used a .45-caliber automatic he'd borrowed from his nephew.

Sergeant Anderson, knowing the evidence, asked: Did the female attempt to run or resist? Yes, Valenzuela said. He thought she attempted to back away or run, and then he shot her.

One more thing: Valenzuela thought that "an unknown girl" was with him that night.

He stared at Sergeant Anderson, his tone even and uninflected. He was of Native American heritage—a Pima Indian—with close-cropped hair and an impassive manner. Though not big, at five foot nine and 156 pounds, he looked well muscled, in good shape. His record, just in the past year, included a string of burglaries, a grand theft auto and an assault with a deadly weapon. He'd been in and out of trouble since the age of eleven. He'd recently traveled to Oklahoma with a pistol, aiming to kill a former girlfriend who'd ratted him out on a burglary, but instead ended up being arrested for carrying a concealed deadly weapon. Sergeant Anderson, weighing all this, decided to take him to the sheriff's office for further questioning. There, deputies made arrangements for a psychiatrist, Dr. Maier Tuchler, to interview Valenzuela.

They met the next day at 2:50 P.M. Before beginning, Tuchler warned Valenzuela that he, though a doctor, might be subpoenaed to testify in a courtroom about this communication. Tuchler advised Valenzuela of his legal rights and explained that he didn't have to continue with the interview if he didn't wish to. Valenzuela said he understood and wanted to keep going. They talked for one hour, in the presence of Anderson and a second sheriff's investigator. Five days later, Dr. Tuchler wrote a report of this encounter, addressed directly to Sheriff Cal Boies. Valenzuela, he began, is "a very dangerous and impulsive young man who is capable of homicide for justification and reasons which appear to him adequate." Tuchler continued:

He gives a long history of a pattern of aggressive behavior involving carrying a gun and disturbing lovers in various lover's lanes in this area. For example, he carried a .22 rifle to a lover's lane in Laveen, held the gun to a chap and a girl who were involved in some romantic act, found himself quite enjoying the confusion that ensued. He did not at this time shoot. He reports on another occasion having his cousin's pistol or revolver and aimlessly wanting to shoot someone. This suggests a rather cold blooded and emotionless individual with little concept or value for human life. Needless to say the officer who apprehended [Valenzuela] and reported this statement to [me] recognizes the potential homicide capacity in this individual. [I] emphatically agree.

In the end, on the basis of a limited one-hour interview, Tuchler felt unable to rule out, with certainty, the possibility that Valenzuela was just fantasizing or projecting. The doctor nonetheless had a definite judgment of Ernest Valenzuela: "This is an exceedingly dangerous young man and whatever possible legal means are available to keep him under observation, such means should be evoked. . . . [If] released on bond, we are dealing with a potential homicide in a lad who is rather devoid of conscience and feels little or no remorse. This case deserves intensive investigation."

Despite this warning, authorities—on the very day Tuchler wrote his letter—released Valenzuela after just five days in jail. The records document no follow-up or evidence that detectives ever connected Valenzuela with the statements made by Linda Primrose two years earlier.

As the months passed, investigators still chased odd tips, always in vain. In May 1969, seven years after the killings, another clue of sorts emerged. The Sterrenberg and McKillop families notified the sheriff's office that at times when they visited Tim and Joyce's side-by-side graves, they found roses placed on them. For a while, deputies staked out the cemetery to see if they could catch a remorseful killer, and the lovers' lane killings became known as the Rose Petal Case. Journalists once again came to interview Tim's and Joyce's parents. "Neither Cliff nor I bear any malice against whoever did it," Jim McKillop told them. "We'd just like to know why. That's the question: Why?"

CHAPTER 2

Memories of Days
Now Gone

AUGUST 1935–AUGUST 1974

When Bill Macumber thinks back to his years of freedom—to what he calls "memories of days now gone"—his mind fills mainly with images of his three young sons and the fun things they did together. The ball fields, the lakes, the forests, the desert. Hunting and fishing, hiking and climbing, swimming across ponds, the boys tied to inner tubes, his youngest tiring and rolling over so that Bill had to pull him the rest of the way. One summer, he built them a full replica of the *Apollo* space capsule, right in their backyard, and wired a remote-control panel in the house. The boys had space suits and knew all the stages of liftoff. Bill liked to say, *Being a dad—ain't nothing like it.*

He came from Davenport, Iowa, born there at Mercy Hospital in August 1935. He had one brother, Robert, two years younger, and a first cousin, Jackie, who was always at their house, living with them at times. The extended family—Grandma and Grandpa, Grandma's sister, uncles and aunts—took driving trips together. Tomahawk Lake, the Black Hills of South Dakota, Mount Rushmore, Wild Bill Hickok's saloon and a whole bunch of fishing cabins that quickly filled with pounds of bluegill, bass, walleye, northern pike and pickerel. The year after Pearl Harbor, Jackie came down from Cedar Rapids for an extended stay, and Bill's father, Harold, bought all the children silver World War I–type helmets with American flags painted on the front. Harold went to work at the Rock Island Arsenal around then and joined its marching band. On weekends, he also played in a small dance band, handling the sax, clarinet and banjo, and the whole family would accompany him to performances—at the Lions and Elks Clubs, Turner Hall, all over Scott County during the Christmas season. Bill and his brother would sometimes get up and dance, and one or both together would often sing with the band. On V-J Day in 1945, Harold's band set up at Third and Harrison in Davenport and played all afternoon and night, the streets barricaded, everyone wildly celebrating, beer and liquor flowing, drunks everywhere but no one arrested. Bill, age ten, watched with wide-eyed wonder.

The Macumbers, like everyone else they knew in the Midwest heartland, were avid hunters. Bill's dad began taking him pheasant hunting when he was six years old. For his twelfth birthday, Harold bought him the finest present he'd ever received: his own, brand-spanking-new Stevens 16-gauge shotgun. The gun kicked like a Missouri mule, but Bill never said a word, despite his black-and-blue shoulder. That October, when squirrel season opened, his dad took him to the Sanger farm, which featured two large patches of timber chock-full of fat juicy fox squirrels. Bill bagged four of them, his dad six. The next month, at the start of pheasant season, Harold took the whole family to Fred Wessles's farm outside of DeWitt, Iowa, where Bill brought down his first ring-necked pheasant. Back home, Harold bragged to all the neighbors, and his dad's pride meant the world to Bill.

By junior high school, he already stood six foot seven, which served him well on the basketball and football teams but set him apart from his classmates. In high school he continued to play despite a crowded schedule—he also was on the student council and had a job at the new service station his father had opened in the spring of 1950, a forty-five-minute bus commute from school. On weekends Bill worked fourteen-hour days there alongside his dad. Despite their efforts, the station, really a twenty-four-hour truck stop, did not do well, and they struggled to keep it going. Together they traveled to Lincoln, Nebraska, to woo large trucking companies, but the only one they won over, a produce operation, ran up large charges it couldn't pay. In the fall of 1952, when Bill was seventeen, Harold filed for bankruptcy. You have to accept the bad with the good, he reminded his son. Harold quickly landed a fine job with a car dealership in Davenport, and Bill began working nights at a dairy company, where he washed the delivery trucks, rarely finishing before 11:00 P.M. Both also joined the Ground Observer Corps, which, as part of the country's national civil defense system, watched the skies for large multi-engine aircraft.

The next summer, the Macumber clan drove to Arizona to visit relatives. Bill loved the high desert and the mountains, the smell of orange blossoms, the sway of real palm trees, and he celebrated when his father decided to move the family to Phoenix. There Harold found work as a mechanic and—with Bill's contribution—bought a home on West Highland Avenue. Bill could not land a job, though, so after searching for half a year, he decided to enlist. On Valentine's Day 1955, he was sworn into the U.S. Army and sent off to Fort Ord for basic training. There he got to shake hands with the commanding general after becoming one of only eight men ever to fire a perfect score on rifle qualification. They offered him the chance to attend Officer Candidate School, but he declined, not sure he wanted to enlist for another two years. In the spring of 1957, his tour of duty over, he returned to his parents' home in Phoenix. He and Harold began working together at Firestone Tire on North Central Avenue, where they ran the brake and front end department. In May 1960 they once again went into business for themselves, opening a new filling station on the corner of Twelfth Street and Missouri.

That year Bill met the woman who would become his wife. Carol Kempfert was dating his brother Robert at the time, Bob still in the army then, stationed down at Fort Huachuca. Bob Macumber and Carol Kempfert were part of a group: four servicemen and their high school girls, teenagers infatuated with men in uniform. They all liked to party and drink—sometimes running liquor up from Mexico—but Bob quickly realized that he didn't click with Carol. She felt like flypaper to him—too close, too demanding. When he told her they were done, she started dating Bill, still living at his parents' house. He was twenty-five and not overly experienced with women. Growing up, he'd worked most of the time, rarely going out on dates. Even his brother had to allow that Bill, gangly and angular, wasn't real handsome. Being so tall didn't help, either. Back in Iowa during his senior year at high school, there'd been one girl Bill truly loved, an accomplished pianist who often accompanied him when he sang somewhere. They once made a record together, of "The Lord's Prayer" and "Bless This House." And one year, they performed "The Lord's Prayer" and "The Holy City" over WOC radio for Easter sunrise services. But she didn't feel the same about him; she just wanted to be friends. When she dropped him, he was devastated.

Bob Macumber warned his brother about Carol's nature and later tried to dissuade him from marrying her, but Bill had fallen very much in love with this outgoing, vivacious young woman. They got married on July 20, 1961, in his parents' backyard. She was eighteen, he about to turn twenty-six. After a three-day honeymoon in Yosemite, they moved into a new home Bill had bought at 3317 West Wethersfield Road—the first house he owned and the first he'd occupied apart from his parents. Not long after, Bill and his father leased a second gas station, this one at Seventh and Missouri, and began working long hours, from 7:00 A.M. to 10:00 P.M. or later. In May 1962, Carol learned she was pregnant.

Their first son, Scotty, was born in January 1963; their second, Steven, in April 1965; their third, Ronnie, in December 1967. By then Bill had gone to work at Honeywell as an assembler and inspector of computers; he and his dad had closed their last gas station in October 1964, the victim of repeated gas wars in the Phoenix area. With three young boys to support, Bill needed to make more money, and to do that, he needed more education. In the spring of 1967, he enrolled at Glendale Community College, taking night classes while working full-time. Two years later he transferred to Arizona State University, where he earned his bachelor's degree in business management in 1973. At Honeywell, he soon won promotion to a position as process-control engineer, his salary $12,000 a year.

His three boys—he invariably called them his three "wonderful boys"—were, by all accounts, the joy of his life. Those who knew their family in those years, friends and neighbors who visited their home, would recall his devotion to his sons, the many hours he spent with them. In the spring of 1971, when Scotty became eligible to play, Bill volunteered with their local Deer Valley Little League, ending up as team manager, coaching his son. The next year the community elected him president of the Deer Valley Little League. Under his supervision the league solicited donations, upgraded the playing field, improved the bleachers, put in lights and built food stands. Two or three days a week, he'd be out at the ball field, dragging screens to clean the base paths. He'd become a leader in the neighborhood, recognized and respected, always talking about how to get things done, how to make things better.

That same year, 1972, Bill decided to form a volunteer search-and-rescue team, the Desert Survival Unit, in association with the Maricopa County Sheriff's Office. He'd been haunted by a tragedy near Bartlett Lake two years before, when four young children and their grandmother died out in the desert after getting lost. Bill thought the sheriff's department had responded a little too slowly. He took his idea to the department and received approval, though little direct support. On his own he sent out notices to local companies—among them Honeywell, Sperry, and AiResearch—seeking funding and volunteers. Within two months he had nearly one hundred recruits to train. Besides ground searchers, he organized a mounted search unit, an air search unit, a radio operation and a medical staff. Under his command the Desert Survival Unit participated in dozens of searches, more than once preventing loss of lives, and collected an "Operational Excellence" award from the sheriff's department.

Neighbors in the community came to Bill regularly with their concerns, turning to him as a sounding board. They found him open and friendly, full of suggestions, always willing to help. Years later, what they mostly remembered was his presence. Paul Bridgewater, who lived nearby, had a strong sense that Bill would never speak falsely to him. He stood by his words.

Boxes of court records can only suggest how Bill and Carol's marriage started to founder. As usual in unhappy marriages, there are competing narratives. In Carol's version, Bill was possessive and jealous, wanting to shut her off from all friends; in Bill's version, Carol grew selfish, particularly about caring for the boys. Their troubles apparently deepened in 1971, when she began attending night classes at Glendale Community College in criminology and law enforcement, including two courses on the detection, classification and lifting of latent fingerprints. She soon befriended the various recruits and officers sitting alongside her, some from the Phoenix Police Department, some from the Maricopa County Sheriff's Office. After class, she'd go out with them. Other evenings, she'd sign up to do ride-alongs with officers on patrol. In this way, she met a good number of men wearing the uniform of law enforcement. Among them: Dennis Gilbertson of the Phoenix Police Department and Sergeant Ed Calles, head of the Maricopa County Sheriff Office's detective section.

Carol took classes with Ed Calles over three semesters. They seemed to become fairly well acquainted, for she listed him as a reference, and he provided a recommendation, when she applied in January 1973 for a position in the sheriff's office. She landed a job as a clerk in the department's identification section, then transferred eight months later to the detective section, working for Calles as a secretary in a detail he supervised. There, she took to browsing through old case files. "Carol's work and her studies in police work dominated almost all her time," Bill would later testify. "Even when she was home she would spend her time going through old case files that she would bring from work. She had little or no time for me and the most minimal time for the boys. This latter fact was the basis for many very heated arguments between us."

Tensions mounted. Testifying in January 1976, Carol said of Bill: "Many times he accused me of having affairs or wanting to have affairs with friends that we knew—it was just about any man that I came in contact with." Also testifying that month, Bill said of Carol: "She began staying out later and later every night. The class would end at 9:30, 10. She'd sometimes be an hour or two late, sometimes five or six hours. . . . It wasn't too long before I understood what was going on."

Just how and when Carol left their home remains unclear. After a particularly intense argument—or perhaps without any argument at all— the Macumbers' marriage finally ruptured and Carol packed up. "The night prior to my wife leaving," Bill later testified, "she informed the boys that she would be leaving, and I have three children. They are 7, 9, and 11 years old. And my nine-year-old cried and begged his mother to stay. And she never even shed a tear."

With the boys under Bill's care, Carol, in late May or early June 1974, rented an apartment on North Fifty-eighth Avenue, sharing it with another clerk in the sheriff's department, Frieda Kennedy. Carol was thirty-one then, Frieda twenty. Divorce and custody proceedings began, along with all the familiar claims.

The catalyst for what might be called Bill Macumber's week of hell came in August 1974. During the first half of that month, he and his parents took his sons on vacation to Oregon. A few days after returning, just past midnight on Thursday, August 22, while home with his sons, Macumber made an emergency 911 call. There'd been a shot fired into his home, he reported.

He'd been in his living room watching television, he told W. H. Rice, the Phoenix police officer who first responded to his call. He went to the kitchen to answer the phone. An instant later, from the alley at the back of the house, someone fired a shot through the kitchen window, narrowly missing him, the bullet slamming into a cabinet just inches from his head. Bill dropped to the floor, grabbed his handgun off a shelf, then stood and ran out the kitchen door. He saw someone climbing over the fence at the rear of the yard. He sank to one knee, braced himself, and shouted "Stop!" before firing one shot. He thought he heard a female voice in the alley cry, "Oh no."

Rice was dubious—he saw no evidence of blood or disruption in the alley, and the fence seemed too rickety to climb over. He took note that Macumber was in the midst of a divorce and custody battle, though Macumber, he reported, "does not think his wife would do anything like this."

By the next day, Friday, August 23, Rice's report had made its way from the Phoenix Police Department to the Maricopa County Sheriff's Office, apparently because Macumber, as commander of the Desert Survival Unit, carried a sheriff's badge. For reasons never entirely clear, the file went immediately to the sheriff's internal investigation unit. When a Phoenix police detective, Joe Rieger, came to retrieve the initial police report that day, he found it there, on Corporal Richard Diehl's desk. Diehl, in fact, was at that moment interviewing Bill Macumber. Yet this remained a Phoenix Police Department case, so Rieger went in search of Carol— he considered her a suspect and wished to know her whereabouts on Wednesday night, August 21.

Carol, he soon learned, had been at a cocktail party that evening at the Casa Bell Hotel, along with various Phoenix police and Maricopa County sheriff's officers and employees. The party later moved to Room 715. At around 9:00 or 9:30, the party moved again, this time to Nobo Jones for dinner; then, at around 10:30, it continued at Mr. Lucky's on Grand Avenue—eight miles from the Macumber home. Carol didn't hear about the shooting, she told Rieger, until her roommate, Frieda Kennedy, called her from the sheriff's office near 8:00 A.M. the next morning. She didn't believe Bill's story. Bill had told her wild tales in the past; here was another. He'd done this shooting himself. Their marital problems went back at least five years. They were in the midst of a divorce.

Rieger's interview with Carol took place late in the afternoon on August 23. From her apartment, he went next to the Macumber home. There he studied the trajectory of the bullet fired through the window— Bill had a string tied from the kitchen cabinet to a stake at the rear of the backyard. The kitchen light rays were almost in a line with the path of the bullet. Rieger noted that a right-handed shooter would have been positioned in the dark.

Outside, he inspected the back fence. Made of a redwood basket weave, it appeared wobbly, as Officer Rice had noted earlier. Yet Rieger climbed the fence twice, and it did not collapse. And, unlike Rice, he did notice signs of disruption in the alley. He saw a piece of board that matched the fence lying in the alley. He also saw an impression on the ground that appeared to be a heel mark, and a lesser impression of the rest of a foot— size 8. Whoever went over the fence had his or her weight on the heel.

Macumber told Rieger he had no known enemies and did not think his wife was involved. He would be going camping over the weekend and would return Sunday evening. In his report that day, Rieger wrote, "Due to what assigned officer found at the scene, this report could not be unfounded. Investigation is continuing."

It had been near 5:00 P.M. when Rieger left Carol and Frieda's apartment. Carol fumed. Rieger had grilled her, asked for an alibi, and asked to look at her service revolver. Carol believed that Bill was trying to blame her in some direct or indirect way for the shot through the house. "I became angry," she explained later, "and decided they ought to know what kind of a kook they were dealing with."

At 5:45 P.M., Carol picked up the phone and called Corporal Diehl in the sheriff's internal investigations unit. She wanted to talk, she said; she had something to tell him. They made an appointment to meet at the sheriff's department at 6:45 P.M. Frieda came with Carol, and Detective Joe Rieger, from the Phoenix police, joined them. The four were together for one hour. Then Nancy Halas, a sheriff's department stenographer, received a phone call at 7:45 P.M. from Sheriff Paul Blubaum, asking her to come in and take a statement on a sensitive internal investigation. Halas showed up soon after. Carol began to tell her story—this time for the record, Nancy Halas writing it down in shorthand notes.

> Approximately three months ago my husband, William Wayne Macumber, and I were discussing [the two of us] starting the MCSD Reserve Academy. Bill and I were discussing the possibility. At that time he stated to me, as he had on previous occasions, that he could not go through the Academy because it required a polygraph and that he could not take the polygraph. He told me that the reason he couldn't take the polygraph was because he had done things in the Army and had killed people in the Army and that this would be looked on as a crime. . . . I told him that whatever he did in the Army was alright if under Army auspices. He then started to hint that there was more, and finally said he had killed the two kids from Mountain Bell Telephone that they'd found on Scottsdale Road about 10 years ago.
>
> He said that the Army CID [Criminal Investigation Division] had told him there would be two suspects. . . . The army had given him a description of the vehicle and that these two subjects would be at the A&W Root Beer out in Scottsdale. He told me that he went out to Scottsdale to the root beer stand and he saw the suspect car— again it sticks in my mind it was a white pickup that the kids were driving. He saw the car that the Army had described to him, and he followed it out on Scottsdale Road and pulled off into the desert and he followed them with his bright lights on. The car stopped and the guy got out and he made some gesture, like he was reaching for a gun or something, so Bill fired. I think he told me that he fired from

behind—he said he got out of the truck and was standing behind the door firing through the open window. The kid fell, the girl got out and started to scream and run and he shot her.

As Carol gave this statement, Diehl had the Sterrenberg-McKillop case file and photos spread before them. "Did you ever read these case reports over?" Diehl asked her.

"I am sure that at one time or another I had this thing pulled out. . . . It is possible that I did see it."

Carol continued: "I do remember at the time of the killing that the purse had been gone through so I assume from that the door would have to be touched in some way, but that is assumption on my part. I have to be careful about what he actually told me and what I remember about the case. But he did say that he went through the girl's purse to make it look like a burglary."

Carol wasn't finished. She had a second story to tell, about a night Bill left the house to go to a Varmint Callers meeting:

I don't remember the month, but it was warm—he wasn't wearing a coat. He had a .45—said he was going to a Varmint Caller's meeting. He had never been to one before and he was going to go see if he liked it. . . . He got home between 9 and 10 P.M. At that time he was covered with blood and he was white and shaking. He said that he had gone down the freeway to Dunlap, over Dunlap and just on the other side of the freeway there were three kids stopped by the side of the road with the hood up on their truck. He stopped to help them and when he put his head under the hood to see what was wrong, out of the corner of his eye he saw one of the kids lift something to hit him and he came around and hit one of them on the bridge of the nose. . . . He fought all three, according to him. And this is how he got blood on him. At that time I told him, "For God's sake, call the Phoenix Police Department and tell them about it," and he said—no, that they were juveniles and that if he had seriously hit one, we would get sued.

A moment before, Carol had not remembered the month this happened, but now she said: "It was the next day or the day after, I am pretty sure, it was the next day that I heard about the two kids found in the desert near Scottsdale. . . . At that time I began to wonder because Bill comes home the night before covered with blood."

And yet, "we finally let it drop" back in 1962, Carol told her colleagues. She and Bill never discussed the matter again until the spring of 1974. "I had forgotten completely about it until that night that he mentioned it three months ago."

How could Carol forget and "let it drop," going on to bear and raise three sons with Bill Macumber? Forever after, she would hear and try to answer that question.

CHAPTER 3

Interrogation

AUGUST 23–30, 1974

After Carol gave her statement on Friday, August 23, five days passed with Bill Macumber knowing nothing of it. He went camping that weekend, returning on Sunday night and, as usual, going to work at Honeywell on Monday morning. That evening, he sat in the kitchen of his neighbor Paul Bridgewater's home, talking about the window-shooting incident. How he went to answer the phone, how he fell to the floor after the shot, how he ran out to the alley with his pistol. He suspected Carol—he allowed as much to Bridgewater. He looked tired and sounded desperate. I can't believe she'd go to this end, he sighed. Why is this happening?

The next day, Phoenix police detective Joe Rieger visited Macumber at Honeywell to discuss the report he was preparing. Rieger had taken Macumber's gun for testing, to exclude the possibility that he'd staged the shooting, and had just received his crime lab's ballistics analysis. Your gun, he advised Macumber, didn't match the .38-caliber bullet extracted from the kitchen cabinet.

Less can be said about actions in the Maricopa County Sheriff's

Office, given the paucity of reports. For a time during those five days, Carol remained a suspect in the shooting on Wethersfield Road, as did her roommate, Frieda Kennedy. The internal investigation unit called them in more than once. "They were asking questions about it," Frieda recalled in a deposition. "They were asking where we were at and what we were doing. We had to provide an alibi. I know I was with Mike Moreno that night. . . . Carol, I don't know where she was at because I stayed out that night until 4 or 5 in the morning."

Eventually, Carol and Frieda managed to satisfy or divert the deputies' questions. It apparently helped that Carol took and passed a lie detector test on August 27, although polygraphs, given their unreliability, were not admissible in Arizona courtrooms. For whatever the reasons, she and Frieda were suspects for a while, and then they weren't.

At 9:00 A.M. on Wednesday, August 28, Bill Macumber had an appointment at the sheriff's internal investigation office, the stated purpose being to review with Corporal Diehl a six-page Phoenix Police Department report on the shooting at his home. Macumber was thirty-eight then, rail thin with thick eyeglasses, a droopy mustache, and a thatch of brown hair hanging over his forehead. He arrived at the department half an hour early, accompanied by Carl Pace, a close friend, Honeywell colleague and fellow member of the Desert Survival Unit. He'd invited Pace for moral support and because he felt it best to have somebody other than department people present. The window-shooting incident had upset him greatly, as had his separation from Carol. He had not been sleeping much—in fact, he had not slept at all the night before—and he'd been eating irregularly. He had stomach problems, the result of an ulcerated condition in his intestines.

It's not possible to say with certainty what happened during the next sixteen hours at the sheriff's department. Anyone poring through the reports and transcripts later could only speculate, for the deputies did not transcribe or tape-record their extended interrogation of Macumber. Nor did they take notes—at least they never shared any notes. What's known: Around 11:00 A.M., Macumber, after talking to deputies for two hours, agreed to take a polygraph about the window-shooting incident. So they all drove to the Ezell Polygraph Institute, where Tom Ezell questioned Macumber, just as he had Carol the day before. Shortly before

1:00 P.M., Diehl informed Macumber that the results of the polygraph indicated deception.

Diehl then advised Macumber that he wished to talk to him about another allegation, one made against Bill by his wife. After first reciting his Miranda rights, Diehl began to read out loud Carol's statement of August 23. Macumber soon interrupted him, saying he did not understand. So Diehl handed Carol's written statement to Bill. "Upon completion of the reading," Diehl wrote the next day in his brief, two-and-a-half-page report, "Macumber appeared angry and made comments like, 'She is really out to get me.'" Diehl also wrote that Macumber, asked if he'd confessed to Carol, "hung his head for a moment and, looking at the floor, said 'yes.'" Asked why he'd confessed, Diehl wrote, Bill "said it was to keep Carol from leaving him."

Bill's friend Carl Pace would recall it differently. No, he later testified, Bill never told the deputies that he had confessed the killings to his wife. Pressed by the prosecutor, Pace held his ground: He would have remembered that, he insisted. He would have remembered if Bill had made such an admission.

Whatever transpired in these critical unrecorded moments, Sheriff Paul Blubaum already seemed to know the endgame. At midday, with Macumber and the deputies still at the polygraph institute awaiting test results, Blubaum came into the office where Carol worked. "He said that he had called the newspaper people reference this case," Carol later testified, "and that if I wanted to go get the kids that it was fine with him, and I left. Right around lunch time, I guess it would be 12, 12:30, somewhere around there."

Carol continued, explaining: She'd learned "two or three days" before that they'd be questioning Bill, so she had asked Diehl and Calles if she could at that time pick up her kids. After Blubaum gave her the green light, around noon, "I went to the house on Wethersfield Road. They weren't there. I went to a park because Bill had told me that Donna [their babysitter] was going to take them to a park. They weren't there. I finally went to Donna's house and that is where they were. I picked them up and my guess would be 1:30, 2."

A 2:30, back at the sheriff's office, Macumber called Donna and learned from her that Carol had "come and got the boys." Nothing that happened on this day seemed to upset him as much as this. Tears filled his eyes; he began to cry. Carl Pace thought he looked "pretty shook up." Diehl, in his report, quoted Macumber as saying, "You better lock me up if that dirty bitch has the children." Diehl kept assuring Bill that he'd "have the children brought to the Sheriff's Department for him and that he could leave with the children."

But then, at 4:30 P.M., at the deputies' request, Macumber voluntarily let Sergeant Charles Ford take his palm prints (they already had his fingerprints, given when he'd started the Desert Survival Unit). He also voluntarily signed a consent allowing deputies to pick up his Ithaca .45-caliber automatic pistol. In fact, he described where they'd find it on his bedroom dresser, and he called his babysitter to say deputies were on their way. As he saw it, he'd later explain, he was among colleagues, trying to help resolve a perplexing matter. Macumber still had not eaten all day, consuming only cigarettes and coffee. His stomach ached, and he felt exhausted. He kept asking if he could leave when his children arrived.

Within half an hour, Sergeant Ford had compared Bill's palm print with the latent prints lifted from the Chevy Impala. Bill's right palm print, he reported, matched Latent Lift 1, taken from the chrome strip by the window, above the handle, on the driver's door. At 5:00 P.M., Sheriff Blubaum called Robert Stiteler, superintendent of the sheriff department's Support Services Division, asking him to come down and confirm Sergeant Ford's match. As an adjunct faculty member at Glendale Community College, Stiteler had been Carol's teacher in her two courses—Evidence Technology I and II—that involved advanced instruction on how to take, lift, classify, develop, photograph, file and prepare fingerprints. He arrived at the sheriff's department within twenty minutes. Diehl joined him in the lab, leaving Macumber with the other deputies in the internal investigations office. Fifteen minutes later, Diehl returned. "Bill," he said, "I want to read your rights to you again." Then Diehl informed Macumber that one of his palm prints matched a latent palm print from the victims' car. At 5:35 P.M., Diehl snapped handcuffs on Macumber and placed him under arrest on two counts of homicide. As they led him away, Macumber turned to one of the deputies, Jack Barnby, who'd worked with him as liaison to the Desert Survival Unit, and said, "Jack, I have never killed anybody in my life." Barnby's response, as Carl Pace would recall it: "I know Bill, I know."

To Macumber, it would forever remain unclear how Sheriff Blubaum could call the newspapers and dispatch Carol around noon if the palm print didn't match until 5:00 P.M. In his jail cell thirty-eight days after his arrest, writing in his journal well past midnight, Macumber asked, "How did Carol know five hours in advance of my being arrested?"

Macumber's interrogation on August 28 did not end with his arrest at 5:35 P.M. In Room 10 of the Maricopa County sheriff's department shortly before 7:00 P.M., Sergeant Ed Calles, too, read him his rights. The two men would spend the next five hours alone together, Calles interrogating Macumber until midnight about Carol's statement, the palm print match, his .45-caliber gun and his bloody fight with three boys beside the free- way. Bill still ate nothing, instead drinking cup after cup of coffee. His head was swimming, but he kept talking. Even now he thought they'd resolve this matter. He saw no need for a lawyer.

At some point late in the evening, rather than flatly deny the entire document, Macumber began to scribble corrections on a copy of Carol's statement, what he saw as mistakes and discrepancies in her account. According to the brief, three-page report Calles wrote the next day, Mac- umber also again allowed that he "had made a statement to her reference the 'kids on Scottsdale Road,'" but "only to keep her from leaving." Once more, though, anyone poring through the documents later could only speculate, for Ed Calles—like his colleagues during the day—made no record of the five-hour interrogation: No shorthand transcriber, no tape recorder, no notes.

On August 30, two days after the marathon interrogation, Calles signed a murder complaint against Macumber. News that the sheriff's depart- ment had finally cracked the haunting twelve-year-old Scottsdale mur- der case—"one of Arizona's most inexplicable ever"—dominated banner headlines in the local newspapers and prime time on the local TV stations. Quotes from Sheriff Blubaum filled the stories, his comments about the "baffling lack of motive" and the "thousands of hours of investigative work." So did shots of Macumber being led down hallways in handcuffs, his eyes blank and downcast, cameras whirring and clicking, the TV reporters shouting "Did you kill those two kids? . . . How come your fingerprints were all over the car?" A newswire story had Carol explaining that she'd turned in her husband because she "feared for her life," given the divorce proceedings. Another story quoted Tim McKillop's mother crying, "May God have mercy on his soul. . . . I just feel sorry for him," and Joyce Sterrenberg's father saying, "I'd like to know what his state of mind was, why it was so important that he kill two people for nothing?"

But one article on August 30, in a small newspaper serving Macumber's local Deer Valley community, offered a different perspective. "DV Residents Upset with Macumber's Treatment," the headline reported. The story continued: "Deer Valley residents are talking about nothing else since William Wayne Macumber has been charged with the shooting deaths 12 years ago of a young couple north of Scottsdale. The general consensus of Macumber's neighbors is he was a model citizen. . . . The residents of the area in which Macumber lived are concerned about the way Macumber is being treated, both by the police and the media. And they're upset because Mrs. Macumber is familiar with police operations due to her work at the sheriff's department, and she may have access to privileged information. Residents feel she may be using that knowledge in the divorce proceedings the Macumbers are going through." Already, a hint of certain suspicions: "When asked if he felt Macumber was being set up by his wife, a member of the desert survival unit replied, 'No comment.'"

Yet another perspective emerged that same day. An elderly woman named Mildred Lunsford called the sheriff's department to say that she, in effect, had an alibi for Bill Macumber on the night of the Scottsdale murders. Two detectives came to take her statement. The story she told them: That day, May 23, 1962, she'd been headed for Veterans Hospital to visit her very sick husband. Her "little Rambler" started giving her trouble. It would go, it would stop, not moving until she shifted. She called the Macumbers at their gas station. "Mac"—Harold Macumber—

gave her a ride to the hospital, then took her car to their station. She called over there at 7:30 P.M. and talked to Bill, who was still working on the Rambler. She called and talked to Bill again at 8:00 P.M. When she called at 9:30, Harold answered the phone, and Mildred could hear Bill in the background, "yowling because he couldn't figure what was wrong." At 11:00 P.M., she called again and talked to Bill. They were still working. "That's all I know is that they were there, Bill was working on my car the 23rd of May," Mildred told the two deputies. "I talked to Bill at 9:30, then again at 11." She recalled the date clearly because her husband ("Harry J. Grimston, veteran of World War I") moved to the hospital's "dying room" that day and passed away five days later, on May 28. Also, she kept a journal in her glove compartment of all her car repairs, listed by date. She was absolutely certain. She'd talked to Bill that night, right up to 11:00 P.M.

Millie Lunsford's account, of course, didn't fit with the murder complaint signed that day by Ed Calles—or with what the detectives questioning her apparently believed to be Macumber's statements during his August 28 interrogation. So one of the officers now attempted to dissuade Millie.

Detective Heberling: "Mrs. Lunsford, we have explained to you that William Macumber has given a statement and it does not corroborate what you have told us. With this knowledge, do you still claim that William Wayne Macumber was working on your vehicle on the night of the 23rd, May the 23rd, 1962?"

Lunsford: "Well all I know, to my knowledge I know they were working on my car. I mean they were there, both of them. Now, how can he be in two places at once?"

The detectives' conclusion, offered in their written report: "It should be noted that at no time on May 23 did Mrs. Lunsford actually see suspect William Macumber. She only heard someone's voice in the background during a telephone conversation with the suspect's father. Mrs. Lunsford's statement cannot be corroborated. . . . It is the opinion of these officers that no further action should be taken in reference to Mrs. Lunsford's statement." Their closing words, in all caps: "PREVIOUSLY CLEARED BY ARREST."

CHAPTER 4

Maricopa County Jail

AUGUST–OCTOBER 1974

In his cell at the Maricopa County Jail, Bill Macumber began to keep a journal, writing in tablets he bought at the jail commissary. As he told it, he first put pen to paper a week after his arrest, so he reconstructed the first few days and later revised other portions "to convey in better words what took place."

1st Day, Wednesday August 28, 1974.

I have been arrested for murder. I have not killed anyone but no one here will believe me. . . . When I first entered the jail everything seemed unreal but now the reality of it all is setting in and I am afraid. I am also depressed beyond words but thus far my pride will not allow me to show any outward emotion. What about my three small boys? What will they be thinking and where are they? . . . Finally the last door shuts and I am in a cell. There are four bunks in the cell but I am the only occupant. I have not been given a mattress

cover or a blanket but at this point I am just too tired to care. . . .
Without question this has been the very worst day of my life. . . .

2nd Day, Thursday August 29, 1974.

12:15 a.m.: Thoughts concerning my children keep going through
my mind. What is happening to them? Do they still love their father
or has my wife Carol succeeded in making them believe their father
is a murderer? I want to see my boys so bad and to tell them, to make
them believe that everything will be alright. . . .

4:45 a.m.: I am now very afraid, terribly tired and very depressed.

8:45 a.m.: They have come to get me once again for questioning. I
was told I would be able to see my boys but they are not here. . . . I am
terribly disappointed and I tell the officers that I have nothing further to say to them. I am allowed to call my father and he has told me
they are getting a lawyer for me. I know now I should have called
Dad sooner but I honestly thought I could straighten this whole mess
out without getting him or anyone else involved. . . . I am being held
for murder and I won't be going home to my children now and perhaps maybe never. . . . I miss Scott, Steve and Ronnie so much.
Thankfully no one can see me cry right now.

4:45 p.m.: There is an attorney here to talk to me and there is so very
much to talk about if it's not already too late. I have never met this
man before but I have to trust him. . . .

3rd Day, Friday August 30.

3:15 p.m.: There is trouble in the cellblock. The other prisoners have
found out . . . that I was a volunteer member of the Sheriff's Department. They are making no effort to hide their hatred. . . . For the first
time real fear is beginning to set in. My stomach is in knots and the
pain is almost unbearable. . . .

7:30 p.m.: I have asked that I be put in one of the solitary cells
because of the present situation with the other prisoners. . . . It turns
into a very long night filled with jeers, curses and threats. . . . A man

in the next cell to the left of mine has just thrown a roll of burning toilet paper into my cell.

Macumber's fourth day in jail, Saturday, August 31, was his birthday. He wrote, "I would never have believed I would be spending my 39th birthday in a place like this. Never in my life have I ever known fear as I know it right now."

That evening, Bill's father and brother, Harold and Robert, came to see him. Bob Macumber had first heard of his brother's arrest on the radio. Then Carol had called, Carol whom Bob used to date. The news floored him. He broke down crying, right there in the office at Motorola where he worked as a manufacturing engineer. He could not believe this report. It all felt so surreal, so out of the blue, so not fitting. And so hard to understand: When he asked Carol why they'd arrested Bill, she said she had no idea, she didn't know. Only later did Bob and Harold learn about Carol's statement.

Bob immediately called his father. Together they talked to a private defense lawyer, who offered to represent Bill—for $25,000 up front. Vainly, Bob and Harold tried to raise that kind of money from relatives. They would keep looking for someone who charged less, but for the time being, they arranged for a county public defender to handle the case. That's who had visited Macumber on his second day in jail. Talking to Bill now, Bob and Harold assured him that they were doing everything possible on his behalf. They sat before him, separated by bars. They couldn't touch him, couldn't slap him on the back.

Harold had a difficult question for his son: Are you responsible for this? Did you do this?

"Absolutely no," Bill said. "I did not."

That satisfied Harold and Bob. No way would Bill lie to his dad, Bob thought. No way. He'd always been an honest and trustworthy man. It made absolutely no sense that Bill would have killed those two young people in 1962. Newly married, awaiting the birth of his first child, working long hours—he had no reason to be out in the desert late at night following those two people.

Four days later, on September 3, Bill received another visitor—Carol. Her arrival shocked him. "Actually," he wrote in his journal, "she didn't come to see me but rather to tell me she needed money to make the house payment and to pay other bills." Bill asked if he could see the boys. Maybe, she replied, if I get the money. Bill looked at his wife. You misunderstood what I said, he told her. I didn't say I killed those two.

Macumber's preliminary hearing began the next day in Mesa, just outside Phoenix, and continued for one week. Bill entered the courtroom each morning through a phalanx of reporters and photographers. On Wednesday, September 11—after listening to Diehl, Calles and the fingerprint experts testify—Justice of the Peace Lawrence Mulleneaux ordered Macumber held for trial in superior court on two counts of murder. A day later, at a bond hearing, Ed Calles added a new piece of seemingly damning evidence: The sheriff's department, he testified, had just received a telegram from FBI laboratories in Washington, D.C., stating that ejector marks on one of the shell casings found at the murder scene matched the ejector of Bill's .45-caliber gun.

Macumber's defense could only counter with character witnesses. Half a dozen of them testified to Bill's high character and reputation in the community. If released on bond, he would certainly appear for all court hearings, they said. They were convincing; despite it being a murder case, Superior Court Judge Williby E. Case Jr. ruled that Macumber should be bailable and set bond at $55,000.

The Macumber family didn't have that kind of money, though. Bob and Harold put up their homes as collateral and started searching for others willing to do the same. "That's an awful lot of money," Macumber wrote in his journal. "I see no possible way that I can ever raise that much. At the moment I feel so very empty."

For days now, the recurring themes in his journal entries had been his longing for visitors, his insomnia, his burning stomach pain, his missing medications, his mounting fears, and—most of all—his three sons. He hoped they were safe. He wondered if anyone had thought to take them dove hunting, as he would have at that time of year. He pictured them waking in the morning, getting ready for school. He wished he could be with them for just a few minutes. He prayed that they continued to believe in him, to believe him innocent.

On September 7, midway through the preliminary hearing, he had the chance to visit with his sons briefly at the jail. He assured them of his innocence. "This has been the most beautiful day I've had since this whole thing started," he wrote in his journal. "All my questions were answered when I felt their hugs and their kisses. . . . Knowing that they love me and believe in me is the most important thing in the world. I am crying as I write this but it is out of happiness. . . . Everything is going to be alright. I just know it will be after seeing them."

Things weren't all right, though. Jail was like "a world until itself. No sunlight, no sounds other than those made by the doors or the prisoners." He could not imagine how a man might exist over extended time under such conditions, without dying just a little or going partway insane.

His dad and brother came to visit after the bond hearing. They promised they'd try to somehow raise the bail, and they urged him to hang in, to have faith, for God would not forget him. But after they left, Macumber was alone again, without solace. He loved to have people around, he loved the kidding and teasing and normal bantering in life. In jail, however, his interactions with others were few and rarely positive. Once he cadged a sandwich from a corrections officer, another time a piece of steak in exchange for cigarettes. Mostly, all he had were distant noises—a fight going on in 42 Block, another prisoner shouting threats. That was it. Days went by without any visitors or mail. He read books, he played solitaire, he marked dates off on a calendar. He wished "with all his heart" he could say good night to his boys and tuck them into their beds.

On his twenty-fourth day in jail, September 20, his dad and brother came again. They assured him that their efforts to raise bail were "going well." Bill appreciated their report. He valued his brother's support and regretted those times in the past when he'd treated Bob poorly. Always it had been over Carol, how he'd countenanced her hostility to his family. He hoped Bob understood. He hoped Bob would forgive him for being a fool.

Several times, during visits with his lawyer, Bill learned of "some evidence pending" that could be of great benefit but for legal reasons had not yet been released to his attorney. Each day he waited for more word about this. Evidence that could clear a man must surely be given out. Surely. "I have to win," Macumber wrote one day. "There is no other way if I wish to go on living."

On the twenty-sixth day, September 22, he received letters from each of his sons. They'd been written at a neighbor's house. He wept, reading his boys' words, the feeling so bittersweet. He hoped someone could find a way of getting him out of this place. Only that would settle his nerves and end his terrible depression.

Two days later, he woke up shaking and crying and couldn't stop. A nurse at the dispensary gave him a pill, but it didn't help. "I'm afraid I'm not going to make it and I don't know what to do," he wrote. "Dear God help me please."

That same day, September 24, his lawyer from the public defender's office came by with a release for him to sign. He was withdrawing from the case. In his place the Macumber family had hired a private attorney, James Kemper. Bill's uncle—Jackie Kelley's father—had paid Kemper's $5,000 fee. They couldn't afford a $25,000 lawyer, but they hoped Kemper would improve Bill's chances. "I haven't talked with my new attorney enough to have formed any opinion," Macumber wrote two days later. "Everyone says he is very competent and that the change will benefit me. . . . I realize I am not in the correct frame of mind at present to be making those kinds of decisions for myself." In fact, just then the prisoner in an adjacent cell was "doing his very best to drive me out of my mind. Starting about 10:30 at night he bangs on the wall about every three to four seconds. After an hour or so of this I get in such a state that I pray he will stop. When he does finally stop I lay there holding my breath waiting for him to start up again. These are the kinds of things that are pushing me to the breaking point."

Sitting in jail for twenty-four hours a day, Bill found that he could easily slip into a state of depression. He began to wonder about his own soundness of mind. He thought about the fine line between sanity and insanity and feared sliding over the edge. He could not let that happen. He knew that the human mind, such a wonderful machine, could also be a person's worst enemy. Rational could suddenly become irrational, logical become illogical. He had to pay attention to his internal environment, to control and direct his thinking as well as his emotions. He had to exercise extreme positive control over his actions. That was hard to do, Macumber thought. That was difficult.

One day, a correctional officer named Parks stopped by to visit. He told Macumber they had a 20 percent chance of rain that night. Bill thought of how he'd like to see rain. But even more, how he'd like to feel it on his face. Parks, one of the younger guards, was a nice man, rare in that place. He always treated Bill with respect and courtesy, never trying to undermine his dignity. Now Macumber, just in conversation, asked him, Will you have dinner with me when this is all over? Yes, Parks said. He would.

When this is all over. Macumber's mind kept drifting to that prospect. Perhaps he'd go back to Honeywell, if they wanted him. He'd try his best to make up with his brother, mother and father for whatever wrongs he might have done them. Maybe he could resume leadership of the search-and-rescue unit, though that would be up to the sheriff's department; if nothing else, he could serve as an adviser. Maybe, heeding his father's advice, he'd even reestablish communication with his God— he'd distanced himself from Him for too long.

He was not so foolish as to believe that this matter would be over soon. Things might very well go badly for him. Still, he lay awake at night, thinking about walking out of the jail, of going home. At least it provided some light at the end of the tunnel. Light, and a diversion from the sounds around him, the constant clanging of steel against steel—doors being opened, people being brought in or taken out. There were the fights over in 42 Block, and a big fire one night in 43 Block, and that one prisoner who tried to poke out another man's eyes. On the night of his thirty-second day in jail, Saturday, September 28, a near riot had erupted— prisoners trying to break down the 44 Block restraining door, burning rags thrown into cells, fire alarms, smoke and fire, firemen and police, the whole fourth floor evacuated. Macumber stayed in his cell, feeling safest there.

His cell. Compared to others, it was deluxe, he had to admit: twelve feet by six feet, with a bunk bed, a small table, a chair and a very small shower. The solid steel door had a feeding port and a viewing port. In one corner, Macumber had squirreled away a treasure: the three candy bars and three oranges he planned to give his boys when he next saw them. So very little, he knew, but all he had. Perhaps if his case didn't go to trial— some visitors had raised that prospect—he could take the boys squirrel hunting. He imagined Scott watching football on TV, Steve and Ronnie right there with him, probably hassling over one thing or another. When this was over and done, he'd move from their home on Wethersfield and raise the boys in a larger house, what they deserved and needed. These plans took a great deal for granted, he realized—they assumed he'd walk free and be given custody of the boys. He had to believe all this, though. How else to think of the future?

Near the end of September, Macumber learned from his brother that they appeared close to raising the $55,000 bail. Someone in the community had stepped forward, offering to provide a major portion. Bill's neighbors, including Paul and Shirley Bridgewater, had done the rest, agreeing to put up their homes as collateral. On Tuesday, October 1, in anticipation, Macumber packed up his belongings. Waiting, he listened for the elevator, the sound of someone coming for him. No one appeared that day, though, or the next. Bill worried that he'd be out of writing paper by the end of the week—he hadn't ordered more tablets because he'd assumed he'd be released by then.

But on Friday, October 4, Bill's father came to see him, bearing bad news: They had failed to raise the full bail. One of those involved had backed out. Bill could not hide his dismay. Harold promised that he would keep trying. Again he urged his son to hang in there.

That same day, later in the afternoon, Macumber received another visitor: John Thomas, the civil attorney representing him in his divorce proceedings. Thomas, too, had disturbing news for Bill, of an entirely different sort: He'd just heard that years before, someone else had confessed to the Scottsdale murders. But neither the county attorney nor the sheriff's department, Thomas told Macumber, will allow the use of this information in your case. In fact, they will fight to keep it out of the courtroom.

This was how Macumber first learned of Ernest Valenzuela. In his journal, he vented: "If I knew I was going to die tomorrow I doubt I could or would feel any worse. I've been charged with the crime of murder. A crime I did not commit. I have sat here for the last 39 days and been questioned, lied to and who knows what else. . . . Men from this department have taken the stand and outright lied in an effort to make a better case. The media has done their very best to put me in the worst possible light. . . . I've lost my children, my home, my possessions, my income and my freedom. . . . I've been subjected to every possible indignity and have faced letdown after letdown. After all of this I find that someone else confessed to the crime and that the powers that be choose to ignore that confession. If there is anything more that can possibly happen it lies beyond my imagination."

CHAPTER 5

Valenzuela's Confession

SEPTEMBER–OCTOBER 1974

Word of Ernest Valenzuela's confession had not emerged just then by accident. In September, Thomas O'Toole—still a federal public defender, not yet a judge—had followed the news about Bill Macumber's arrest with mounting unease. O'Toole felt certain that he'd represented the true killer. But what could he do? The question haunted him. He couldn't shake the memory of Ernest Valenzuela, couldn't shake the image of that man's eyes. Valenzuela, he knew, had not remained free for long in 1964, following his confessions to the cops and Dr. Tuchler. Soon after being released that August, he'd been arrested again on a second-degree burglary charge, drawing a four-to-five-year prison sentence. Released once more in the summer of 1967—despite a "very poor conduct record" in the state prison at Florence—he'd waited just ten days before kidnapping a couple, killing the husband and raping the wife. Because the murder and rape occurred on the Gila River Indian Reservation, Valenzuela needed a federal public defender.

That's how O'Toole came to represent him, appointed by a magistrate. Valenzuela wrote O'Toole a note the very next day: "Dear Sir, I want to know how the case looks. I also would like to talk to you. . . . Please let me know how the case looks." The case, in truth, looked awful to O'Toole. Late on the evening of August 9 and on into the early morning of August 10, Valenzuela had been drinking at a bar in Phoenix with Lamson and Salina Nelson, both Apache Indians. At his request, the couple started to drive Valenzuela to the reservation. Once there, Valenzuela pulled a gun, shot the husband, ordered him into the trunk of the car, drove a ways, then stopped to shoot the man several more times, killing him. Then he held his gun on Salina Nelson while raping her in the front seat of the car. She eventually snuck away and sought help at the Gila Crossing Presbyterian Church. Police found Valenzuela nearby, asleep in the Nelsons' car.

The state had an easy case, O'Toole had to admit. His client was toast. He started visiting with him regularly. Valenzuela, a fit and wiry twenty-three-year-old Pima Indian, looked like an Apache or Hispanic. Sharp features, piercing eyes. Early on, Valenzuela started talking about the double murder north of Scottsdale. He flat out said he killed those two. He identified the victims by name, Joyce Sterrenberg and Timothy McKillop. He said he came upon them in the desert while high on booze and grass. In a matter-of-fact way, he said, "One was running. I shot 'em like a rabbit." As Valenzuela recalled the killings, his eyes lit up. He appeared possessed—O'Toole thought him bloodcurdling. Valenzuela was clearly a homicidal person who enjoyed killing people. He told O'Toole that he liked to get into fights, liked to get hit. He also told O'Toole that he liked to fantasize about women, that he would go to Arizona State University to watch the girls on campus. He would follow them around and imagine having relations with them. O'Toole had never met anyone like Valenzuela. A shocking man, really—evil personified. O'Toole and his supervisor, Tom Karas, decided to never meet with him alone. They'd only visit Valenzuela together.

All told, they saw him eight or nine times, an hour at a time, in the U.S. marshal's office on the eighth floor of the Federal Building in Phoenix. The Scottsdale murder confession came up more than once, and O'Toole took fairly detailed notes, though this was not the focus of their conversation; they had their own murder-rape charge to defend. O'Toole didn't need or want to know all the details on how Valenzuela killed the young couple. Even so, he couldn't help but notice that this murder on the Indian reservation looked rather similar to the Scottsdale lovers' lane murders. Booze and marijuana, a couple in a car, a gun, random violence.

O'Toole's job had made him fairly skeptical. Dealing with all sorts of people, he'd learned to smell out the bullshit, but he sensed truth here. He had no reason to doubt—Valenzuela had the persona of a cold-blooded killer.

O'Toole wasn't the only lawyer to reach this conclusion. Because of a scheduling conflict, the federal public defender's office had to withdraw from Valenzuela's case in December 1967. The court appointed a private attorney, Ron Petica, to replace O'Toole. Over the next six months, preparing for trial, Petica visited with Valenzuela at least once a week, accumulating a number of clear impressions. Valenzuela appeared physically strong, cold, and unsmiling. Petica did not think he had the capacity to be friendly, or to like or dislike other people. One day, sitting at a table together discussing the murder and rape on the Indian reservation, Valenzuela said, "This is not the first person I have killed." He started talking about the couple he'd shot north of Scottsdale. As he spoke, he looked directly at Petica, holding his gaze, his eyes suggesting cold steel. Like O'Toole, Petica felt scared. Again, Valenzuela was just talking, not boasting, discussing the murders as if killing were part of living to him, his modus operandi. He had no reason to lie. Petica believed him.

So did a psychiatrist, Dr. Leo Rubinow, brought in by Petica to administer Sodium Pentothal—at the time considered a kind of truth serum. After testing and interviewing Valenzuela twice in March 1968, Rubinow wrote a letter to the judge presiding over Valenzuela's case, conveying his assessment: "He is extremely dangerous with severe homicidal tendencies. He has a tremendous amount of uncontrollable hostility and resentment. He demonstrates marked disturbance of thought processes with delusional thinking and paranoid ideations plus tremendous amount of fantasy. . . . In my opinion he is insane. I strongly recommend that he be committed immediately to an appropriate facility. His prognosis is very poor." Rubinow's diagnosis: "Schizophrenic reaction, paranoid type, severe with strong homicidal tendencies."

The same day he wrote this letter to the judge, Rubinow, deeply concerned, called the U.S. marshal's office in Phoenix. Valenzuela, he wanted personnel there to know, is "in an extremely dangerous condition and could kill at any time."

After eventually pleading guilty to second-degree murder, Valenzuela ended up bouncing from one federal penitentiary to another, no one wanting him, everyone finding him "highly rebellious" with "poor institutional adjustment" and "homicidal thoughts." He refused to work, got caught with contraband knives, threatened guards and broadcast his intention to kill fellow inmates. He spent most of his time in administrative segregation, prison officials unable to justify releasing him into the general population. By early 1973, he was in segregation at Leavenworth, where authorities vainly tried to transfer him elsewhere because of his "violent background" and "threatening, hostile behavior." Despite a special plea from the Leavenworth warden, who expressed concern both about "safety" issues and the "general morale" of his institution, no other penitentiary would take Valenzuela. Leavenworth finally returned him to the general population in June 1973. There—as they'd all feared—Valenzuela engaged in one last fight. On November 8, 1973, he arrived at the prison hospital with multiple stab wounds. The duty medical officer declared him dead at 8:40 P.M.

Bill Macumber's arrest for the Scottsdale murders came ten months later. Thomas O'Toole, hearing the news and learning of Valenzuela's death, went to talk to his supervisor, Tom Karas. Tom, he said, Macumber's defense team needs to know. *They need to know.*

They both understood the obstacle: Despite Valenzuela's death, what he'd told O'Toole remained protected by attorney-client privilege, part of the even broader ethical duty of confidentiality, among the most fundamental tenets of the legal system. Lawyers, as advocates, have to keep confidential what they hear from clients. Clients have to be able to disclose everything, good or bad, without fear of retribution, even if that means a lawyer will sometimes obscure the truth; the privilege by its nature at times protects wrongdoing. Trade-offs abound, of course. O'Toole knew that lawyers and judges regularly carved out exceptions to confidentiality—such as when an attorney believes his client is going to kill someone. (Also when the attorney's own interests are at stake:

Lawyers are allowed to reveal confidences to defend their reputation or collect a fee.) Yet no such exception existed when it came to helping a potentially innocent defendant in a murder case, not even if the client has died. The dead client's interest in keeping his disclosures private trumps the defendant's constitutional right to present his defense.

Still—the law has always allowed multiple interpretations. O'Toole felt compelled to explore his options. In late September 1974, he and Tom Karas presented a hypothetical question to the State Bar of Arizona's standing ethics committee: In a situation where an attorney has heard a murder confession from a client who later died, and has since learned that another person has been charged with that murder, may the attorney disclose the information to the prosecutor and defense attorney?

In a written opinion ("Arizona Ethics Opinion No. 74-30") delivered on October 2, the state bar's ethics committee ruled that the attorney not only "may" disclose but is obliged to. "We hold that it is the ethical obligation to disclose the confidential information of the past commission of crime by his now deceased client," the committee wrote. "The prosecution of the third party in the fact situation presented may constitute a fraud upon the courts and a gross denial of due process upon one who may be unjustly accused. As such, the failure to disclose the information by the inquiring attorney would constitute the continuing of the client's wrong by the bond of silence.... The attorney as an officer of the Court has an obligation to assist in maintaining the integrity of the Courts and of the legal profession.... A lawyer is bound to disclose such confidential information under those circumstances."

With that opinion in hand, O'Toole on October 8 wrote to Judge Charles Hardy, who would preside at Macumber's trial, copying the letter to the county attorney and Bill's lawyer, James Kemper. "Pursuant to Arizona Ethics Opinion No. 74-30, dated October 2, a copy of which is attached, please be advised that I am in possession of certain information which I am ethically required to disclose to your court or the defendant, or both.... I would greatly appreciate notification by your court regarding what, if any, procedure you desire me to follow in revealing this information to the appropriate parties."

The next day, Judge Hardy wrote back, also copying his letter to Kemper and the prosecutor. "I wish to thank you for your letter of October 8. . . . In my judgment full disclosure of the information should be made to both the prosecutor and defense counsel. If such disclosure is made to both sides, I can see no reason to also make it to the court. I commend you for recognizing the ethical implications involved."

A week later, O'Toole wrote directly to Kemper: "By letter of October 9 . . . Judge Hardy has instructed me to make available to you and the prosecution information in my possession concerning [*State v. Macumber*]. I suggest that you and the prosecutor contact me for the purpose of arranging a meeting to discuss this matter." O'Toole's concluding sentence conveyed his sense of urgency: "I am hopeful that we can meet as soon as possible."

Jim Kemper, through informal channels, likely received advance notice of these letters before they arrived. While visiting Bill Macumber on October 7, he told him about Thomas O'Toole's emergence and Valenzuela's confessions. This officially confirmed what Macumber had heard from his divorce attorney. He did not know what it meant legally, but he believed it had to be beneficial.

That's what his brother thought when he visited later in the evening. Bob Macumber came with his own good news: They'd raised $58,000 for bail, with more neighbors and relatives offering their houses and stock as collateral. They would be going before the judge in two days, on Wednesday morning. If all went well, Bill would be home by Friday, October 11. The guards let him stay out of his cell for almost half an hour as a way to celebrate. He couldn't conceive of being able to sleep that night.

The week unfolded slowly, Macumber imagining when he would see his sons, thinking how great it would be to eat supper with his mom and dad. He battled his mood swings but kept recording them dutifully in his journal. By lunchtime on Thursday, he'd still heard nothing. He played solitaire that afternoon, trying to keep busy. He could see the doors to the elevator from the viewing port in his cell's steel door. Every time they opened, he jumped a little, thinking it might be someone coming for him. Then, just before the swing-shift guards reported for duty, Macumber received a note from downstairs, written by a Lieutenant McKinney: "Bill, your Dad just called and said you will be out on bail tomorrow."

The young guard Mr. Parks, part of the newly arrived shift, already knew. He'd heard it on the radio. Macumber wondered if Carol had also heard ahead of him, and if his sons had learned the news. His cell seemed a whole lot brighter that evening, almost like a room. He hoped his divorce attorney was making the necessary arrangements for him to be with his boys. Right at that moment, he believed himself the happiest and richest man in the entire world.

They came for him at 3:34 the next afternoon. After he signed his release papers, the guards led him outside through a final steel door. It felt like moving from nothing to everything. His dad and brother were waiting there for him. So, too, were a number of reporters and photographers. Bill had not been looking forward to them—he felt the journalists always seemed to put him in the poorest possible light. He'd seen shots of himself on TV the night before; he'd looked like a villain.

That morning's *Arizona Republic* had featured a particularly upsetting article. Under the headline "Estranged Wife Fears Release of Suspect in 1962 Murders," it began, "The estranged wife of a man accused of killing a young Phoenix couple 12 years ago said Thursday she is extremely afraid for her life if her husband is freed on bond today as scheduled. . . . 'I'm living right out in the open. I haven't got the money to run and hide or anything, so I'll just have to keep my fingers crossed and hope.'" Bill thought that funny. In their thirteen years of marriage he had never once seen his wife in a situation that scared her.

From the county jail, Bill's dad and brother drove him home to see his mother, then to his doctor for a thorough checkup. He called friends later that afternoon, and finally sat down with his family for a big steak dinner. He was tired but took comfort in knowing he'd go to bed that night a free man. When he thought about the coming days, his mind fixed on only one thing: Soon, he would see his sons. Soon he would be with his boys.

CHAPTER 6

Days of Freedom

The countdown to Bill Macumber's trial began. Living once again at his parents' home, a small one-bedroom trailer in the Bethany Home Trailer Park, Macumber would have almost three months to think about what was to come. The first days there soothed his nerves. He ran errands with his dad and brother, among other things buying a tape recorder so they could record all phone calls—protection against anyone making claims about what he'd said. He also picked up flowers for his neighbor Shirley Bridgewater, it being her birthday. The young girl running the flower stand clearly recognized him—"Haven't I seen you on TV?"—but smiled anyway, without judgment, and said, "I hope you have a very nice day." Macumber hoped God would be especially kind to her.

Late that first afternoon, he took the flowers to the Bridgewaters' home and sat talking to Shirley and Paul over a beer. They'd met and grown close through the Deer Valley Little League, Shirley the head of the auxiliary when Bill served as league president. Until now, Paul had seen Bill upset about only one thing: his separation from Carol. This murder charge was something else, though. In their living room, Bill looked destroyed. He kept saying, "I can't believe she's doing this to me." He also said, "This is a farce. . . . I'm not going to have a problem because I didn't do it."

That appeared obvious to Paul. Bill's arrest had shocked everyone in the neighborhood. Bill just wasn't a killer—not the guy Paul knew. It seemed incomprehensible, impossible. Why would Bill go out and do something like that? One day so different from the entire rest of his life— what possible motive? And such irony: Carol knew he was a killer for years, then all of a sudden she's scared for herself and the kids? No, things just didn't fit. Pile of crap, Paul thought. He hadn't hesitated to put up his house as bail collateral. He'd needed maybe two minutes to decide.

Macumber looked around their living room. The Bridgewaters' house, like his, was a small, plain wood-frame rambler in a neighborhood of such homes, their community nearly rural, a modest suburb in the far north-west corner of Phoenix. When Paul bought his home, it stood on farm-land. Bill pointed to their unadorned fireplace. "I'm going to build you a hearth," he promised.

So it went at the start. Visits with friends, a picnic in the desert, quiet mornings with his brother, dinners out with his parents. But the tension and despair soon began to build again, not much different from how he'd felt during the endless hours in jail. He tossed and turned at night, sleep-ing on a foldout couch in his parents' small living room. Several times, consumed by fear and uncertainty, he broke down and cried. He knew his anxiety came partly from not yet being able to see or talk to his boys. He'd also not heard from his attorney—not a word. His mood kept dark-ening. He hesitated now to visit with certain people. "No one seems very happy around me right at this moment," he wrote in his journal. "I seem to cast a shadow over everyone and everything."

Then on Friday, October 18—the fifty-second day since his arrest— his divorce attorney called to say Judge Ed Hughes, after holding a hear-ing and talking to Bill's sons in chambers, had ruled that Bill should have adequate visitation rights. Macumber would get to see his boys that Sun-day. He celebrated, the news dulled only by concern over what his boys thought of him now. Without his sons, he had nothing. He wanted them to believe in his innocence.

Sunday, he got the boys at noon rather than 10:00 A.M., at Carol's insistence. No matter. They rushed into his arms, hugging and kissing. Bill and Harold took them to buy motorcycle helmets for their bicycle races. Then they all had lunch together and spent the afternoon just hanging out. "Today has shown me how easy it is for a man to worry himself into the grave needlessly," Macumber wrote. "It has been one of the most beautiful and wonderful days in my life."

Macumber's mood lifted even more when word came, on October 24, that Judge Hughes had granted him regular visitation rights with fixed hours: every other weekend from 3:00 P.M. on Saturday to 5:00 P.M. on Sunday. He could talk to his boys by phone now. He could buy them the off-road racing bike he knew they badly wanted.

That day brought other comforting news. "A very special and very wonderful woman," Bill wrote in his journal, "told me that she was in love with me. . . . She said she is not ashamed of her feelings and told me of them openly and honestly. She cried for me and made me feel very special. She said she knows I am innocent and that nobody will ever be able to convince her differently." They had met through Little League back in the spring of 1971, becoming good friends. By late 1973, they'd sensed an attraction that went well beyond friendship but had said nothing, as both were married. She could see straight into him; she understood him. He wished he'd met her long ago, although then, he reminded himself, he would not have his three beautiful sons. In the early summer of 1974, with Carol gone and this lady also working toward a divorce, they'd happened to cross paths at a Denny's. Over coffee, they'd finally shared their feelings for each other. On occasion in the following weeks, they'd kissed or held each other, nothing more. His arrest that August had cut short their time together but hadn't altered her belief in him. He valued this beyond words, but he cautioned her: If I'm convicted, you must never attempt to see me.

He didn't fear dying, and given the choice between that and spending the rest of his life in prison, he knew what he'd pick. The notion did not depress him, really. For all his efforts to be upbeat, he realized he very possibly could be convicted. He had to face reality, however frightening. People who knew him believed him innocent, but what of all those who didn't know him? They could judge only from the evidence they heard.

Macumber felt that few days of freedom remained. One weekend he played football with his boys on Saturday, then the whole extended family spent Sunday riding dune buggies in the desert. On their next visit he took his sons to the county fair. Two weekends later, in a wave of forced optimism, he took them house hunting—for when "this is all over." Other moments he spent with his "very special woman," who pledged to attend every day of his trial.

On Friday, November 1—the sixty-sixth day since his arrest—Macumber met with his attorney Jim Kemper, who had a great many questions. Bill thought he managed to answer most of them. Yet they still had the palm print and shell casings and Carol's statement. Kemper wasn't terribly encouraging about their chances. He faced the daunting problem of reaching back twelve years, trying to reconstruct events from 1962. At least he had more time now: The trial, scheduled to start in five days, had been postponed until after the holidays. Macumber regretted the postponement, really. The sooner it started, the sooner it would be over.

He'd grown ever more aware of how his dark moods were affecting others. He'd drawn back from everything, becoming almost reclusive, blocking out even his dad, and this, he sensed, hurt his parents a great deal. He'd always been an outgoing and supportive person, so the change was readily apparent to not only his family but his friends. He resolved to hide his fear and loneliness. He started making a point of laughing and joking with those around him. Playing golf with his dad, talking on the phone with Shirley Bridgewater, taking his boys to the movies and agate hunting out in Buckeye—he could see the infectious impact of his high spirits. He'd always been totally honest with everyone, but no longer. He would put on a false front in order to make those he loved happy.

On Tuesday, November 12, the seventy-seventh day since his arrest, Macumber heard bad news from his attorney: The possibility of getting Ernest Valenzuela's confession introduced at his trial looked slim, maybe nonexistent. Because of attorney-client privilege, Jim Kemper explained, Judge Hardy probably would not let it in. Macumber thought it almost beyond belief that a man might end up going to prison because the guilty person's confession could not be used.

As the days passed, he grew increasingly nervous and afraid. His hands shook badly at times. Despite his efforts at a false front, he feared being around people, worrying about how he should act. One Saturday, he spent the entire day walking out on the desert by himself. This normally brought him piece of mind, but not now. He started sitting for hours in front of the television. He was no longer seeing or hearing from many people. He knew he could call the Bridgewaters—they'd gone quarry-rock cutting together a while back, and he'd built them that fireplace hearth—but he didn't want to intrude or force himself on them. When he did go see them, he couldn't be upbeat. This is not looking good, he told them. And I can't do anything about it.

Only the weekends with his sons brought him comfort. Those he savored. Bowling, fishing trips, dinners out, sleeping in Bill's camping trailer—at the end of the visits he always thought himself the most fortunate man in the world. Yet two weeks would then pass without the boys. Despite people being around, treating him well, he felt terribly alone. In truth, he'd been lonely much of his life. He could not deny this fact. He didn't want to be lonely anymore but didn't know how to fix it. One long evening, Macumber stayed home by himself, staring into a mirror, rather than go with his parents to Bob's house for dinner.

Another day, he and his dad drove to Safford, Arizona, in hopes of locating a motel where he and Carol had stayed over a weekend in the late spring of 1962—Bill thought they might have been out there at the time of the murders. They found the motel, but the owners' records didn't go back to 1962, so they had another dead end. One afternoon in late November, his friend Jim Wollum took him out to lunch, concerned about his low spirits. If I were in your shoes, Jim told him, I'd be tempted to up and leave the country. Bill allowed he'd considered that; he'd be a liar to say he hadn't. But he couldn't run from his children and all those who believed in him. Running would be an admission of guilt.

Over the long Thanksgiving holiday, Macumber had his boys with him for a three-day weekend. It was a wonderful interval, just being together with them. By Sunday night, he'd made a decision: For thirty-nine years, he'd lived in a protected dream world, having been raised by parents who taught that truth and justice prevail, that God will always protect you from harm. He'd now been forced to face reality, to exit his dream world. He'd survive but he did not intend to keep writing in his journal, saying the same things day after day. Except for significant or special moments, "this will be the last night in 97 days on which I shall commit my thoughts to paper."

Macumber had his sons again over the Christmas break, from December 23 to January 3, when they returned to school. With his trial due to start in four days, on January 7, he felt panic, fear and the urge to run. He and his boys had spent much of the break out on the desert, where it seemed nothing could ever be wrong. "Yet our world is very possibly coming to an end and I am powerless to stop it," he wrote. "I want to scream and cry and beg but I cannot do that. My boys must remember their father as being a proud man. They must remember me as a father who always loved them. I want them to cherish those thoughts because it is all I have to leave with them."

CHAPTER 7

The Trial

Just ten years old, the Maricopa County East Court Building, on West Jefferson Street in Phoenix, was decidedly utilitarian, a plain ten-story brick-colored box planted on an unremarkable downtown intersection. Bill Macumber's trial unfolded in a compact courtroom on the sixth floor, a windowless chamber featuring eight rows of spectator seating and walls covered by flat pieces of dark wood held together with aluminum. The defense and prosecution teams sat at separate tables, with deputy county attorneys Larry Cantor and Tom Henze nearest the jury, Jim Kemper and Bill Macumber on the far side. At thirty-five, Kemper appeared younger than his years, an impression helped by his preference for sporty sweaters over suits. He and his client offered a study in contrasts: Kemper casually sprawled in his chair, boyishly grinning, talking in a southern drawl; Macumber sitting upright in a coat and tie, always the taciturn cowboy. Kemper had spirit but little trial experience; he'd mainly done appellate work, one of the reasons the Macumber family could hire him to handle a murder case for only $5,000.

On the bench, Judge Charles Hardy had just finished presiding over another notorious Arizona murder case. On January 6, 1975, the very day before jury selection began in Macumber's trial, Judge Hardy had sentenced John Henry Knapp to death, a jury having convicted him of setting a fire that killed his two young daughters. In certain quarters, Hardy had a reputation for falling asleep during trials, perhaps due to narcolepsy, but others believed he just tended to close his eyes as he followed the testimony. Lawyers considered him caring and evenhanded, if not the brightest judge in the state. He let them operate without a lot of close control. Some attorneys, for this reason, thought him easily swayed, but this would not prove to be the case at Macumber's trial.

The state's case, though entirely circumstantial, without proof of a motive, featured extensive testimony over the course of a week from an overwhelming run of investigators and forensic technicians. Carol's statement came in, though because of marital privilege, she did not testify. Sergeant Jerry Jacka linked Macumber's palm print to the victims' Impala. An FBI firearms expert, Robert Sibert, offered his unequivocal conclusion that three of the four shell casings found at the murder scene had markings produced by the ejector in Bill's .45-caliber pistol. Deputies Richard Diehl and Ed Calles recounted their versions of what Macumber said on the day of his arrest; though their memories faltered and evolved at moments under cross-examination, each recalled Bill admitting that he'd told Carol he'd shot the two kids.

After listening to Calles testify on January 16, Macumber wrote in his journal, "Right now I see very little hope that I will not be convicted. The fact that I'm innocent has no bearing on what is about to happen to me. . . . I met with my attorney tonight to go over my testimony. . . . Jim Kemper was very candid when he said that the jury was not likely to believe me because though true it did sound 'fishy.'"

Most striking at this trial was what the jury didn't hear. Kemper had told Judge Hardy he thought his case would take about a day and a half. As it turned out, he wouldn't need even that much time, for Hardy now, after the state ended its case on January 17, ruled that three key witnesses for the defense could not testify.

The first two: Thomas O'Toole and Ron Petica. Both of Valenzuela's former attorneys stood ready to take the stand, O'Toole after writing Judge Hardy in early October. In Hardy's chambers on the morning of January 20, Kemper and the prosecutors discussed that prospect, with Bill Macumber present. They were making a record for appeals more than debating, since Hardy had already decided he would not let the jury hear about Valenzuela's confessions.

Kemper began: "Now the next question is, as you probably recall from that letter that you got from O'Toole, there are two lawyers who represented a guy named Ernest Valenzuela, who told them that he committed this crime. Now, I would like to present . . . what is in the nature of an offer of proof." Moving step by step, he described the extended sequence in which first Tom O'Toole, then Ron Petica heard Ernest Valenzuela's confession on multiple occasions. "All right," he concluded. "Everything that I have related are facts which Mr. O'Toole and Mr. Petica are prepared to testify to. Mr. O'Toole was scheduled to be here at 3:30 this afternoon. And Mr. Petica was scheduled to be here tomorrow. . . . We are offering these confessions as declarations against [penal] interest, as an exception to the hearsay rule. And this is the offer of proof, so that the Appellate Court will know the precise nature of the evidence which the Court is today holding inadmissible."

Judge Hardy, for once, didn't waver. The issue seemed cut-and-dried to him, not even a close call. The attorney-client privilege, such a bedrock principle in the legal system, didn't go away when the client died. Hardy said, "Let the record show the Court has ruled that the proffered evidence isn't admissible. First because the communications to Mr. O'Toole and Mr. Petica were privileged because of the attorney-client relationship. There's been no waiver of the privilege. I said first. That is sufficient."

The next day, Judge Hardy barred yet another key defense witness: Charles Byers, a ballistics expert who would have told the jury that it was impossible to match shell casings to a specific gun on the basis of ejector marks. This represented a central issue at Macumber's trial. Microscopic ejector marks, produced when the cartridge strikes the ejector—a small protrusion that essentially "kicks" the shell casing out of the weapon— were not the normal way to match a bullet and a gun. In fact, the FBI's

Robert Sibert had never before based his analysis solely on ejector marks. He'd done so in this case because he had no other means; the firing pin, breech face and extractor marks—the usual basis for comparisons—did not match Macumber's pistol. Sibert nonetheless had delivered his opinion with certitude: The ejector marks "could have been produced by no other ejector in the world."

Byers didn't think it possible for such a statement to be true. He had been an engineer overseeing production of ammunition and shell casings at Remington Arms Company, where he'd designed rifles and ammunition, and was then president of a company that manufactured .45-caliber ammunition for the U.S. Marine Corps. He'd studied firearms identification and published articles on firearms. He didn't believe ejector marks had a distinct signature. Yet he had never testified as an expert witness in a case like this. On these grounds, deputy county attorney Tom Henze objected to his qualifications before he could take the stand.

Henze had his reasons: He believed the state's ballistics evidence to be the key to Macumber's conviction. Years later, Henze would not remember Carol's statement being the meat of the case. Nor would he recall Bill's palm print being the clincher—that could be explained away even without proving it had been planted. The Impala, after all, had been left unsecured for hours, and before the murders, its driver could have stopped at Macumber's gas station. To Henze, the shell casings made his case. The ejector marks were the tiebreaker. So he wanted to keep Byers off the stand.

Judge Hardy had never before heard of using ejector marks to make a comparison, but he, too, questioned Byers's qualifications. "Mr. Kemper," he said, "I am going to have to sustain the State's objection."

This ruling stunned Kemper. First they'd lost the Valenzuela confession, and now their ballistics expert. "I am not sure I understand you," he told the judge. "Could you explain that to me again."

Hardy tried, though he had some trouble with technical ballistics terms. His explanation didn't satisfy Kemper.

"If Your Honor please, if I may make a couple of comments? . . . The thing I can't understand, that baffles me . . . is the biggest fallacy in this courtroom. I don't believe Your Honor can understand it. Mr. Henze and Mr. Cantor get up here and they tell you what the standards would be of an expert in the first place. And then you say because Mr. Byers doesn't meet what they say is an expert, he can't testify."

"I never said that," Judge Hardy interrupted.

Kemper kept going: "I am still trying to understand the basis of the Court's ruling. May I ask some questions so I can understand? . . . We have got up here some pictures that we know were taken of evidence shells and we have got some pictures over here that we know hit the ejector in that gun, all right? Now, that's what Mr. Sibert had, okay? . . . And he says, 'In my opinion these look like these.' Now, Mr. Byers on the other hand has put the evidence shells and test shells under a microscope, but he has gone one step further. . . . He has taken pictures of them so the Jury can . . . see it with their own eyes. But you say he can't [testify]. . . . I can't fathom that."

Judge Hardy: "You have left out an important step. That is, Mr. Sibert testified that he has been trained and is experienced in comparing hundreds of thousands of ejector marks and he has learned that . . . each ejector mark has a characteristic pattern on the casing. . . ."

Kemper: "Precisely. And we can come in here and tell you they don't make a pattern. And we can show the Jury why they don't make a reproducible pattern. Do you suppose Mr. Sibert was born in a witness chair? He had to testify for a first time at some point in his life. . . . You have to start somewhere. I had to try my first case. What about a court reporter? What about you? Mr. Sibert started somewhere. Mr. Byers has never testified before, but he has done the exact same thing Mr. Sibert has done, except he goes a bit farther and he can prove it to the Jury."

Soon Kemper was beside himself: "Now I understand he is to be excluded entirely from giving any expert testimony. Is that my understanding? . . . I understand he can't testify as to his opinion as to any tests or experiments that he has done. Is that the Court's ruling?"

It was. Judge Hardy would not let the jury hear Byers. The next morning a desperate Jim Kemper continued arguing in the judge's chambers. His agitation was understandable. He did not have other experts to summon—he'd found it hard enough for a cash-strapped defense team to find anyone to testify. Most experts worked for or were paid fees by the state. Kemper had already spent weeks vainly looking all over Phoenix for a fingerprint expert available to the defense. No such person existed.

He'd also called a friend in Los Angeles, who couldn't find anyone there in a three-day search. Kemper explained this problem to Hardy, pleading, "If this ruling stands when there's a technical question which is vital to guilt or innocence, the guilt or innocence is going to be determined by the law enforcement agencies in this country. They're going to have a monopoly on it. They've got the microscopes. They've got the training manuals. They've got all the equipment. They won't let anybody else use them. . . . And anybody who has ever tried a criminal case knows that there aren't any private laboratories where you can get an equivalent examination of evidence. . . . A defense lawyer has to do the best he can. He has to spend hours and hours and hours just to try to find somebody that's qualified. And then when he finds them they really haven't the proper equipment. The practical results of this decision are to foreclose any reasonable possibility that a criminal defendant can properly defend himself on a technical question where it's vital to guilt or innocence."

In fact, Kemper maintained, Judge Hardy's ruling constituted a fundamental violation of due process. "We're talking about due process of law here, and I take the position if we're not allowed to present evidence on this subject through Mr. Byers, we are being denied due process of law in that we are being denied the right to present a defense. . . . We are being denied the right to confront the witnesses against us. . . . There is no way in the world that you can impeach or contradict a witness like Mr. Sibert except to put on another expert witness that says I don't agree with him, I come to the opposite conclusions. So we take the position that if Mr. Byers is not allowed to testify before the jury we are being denied the right to confront the witnesses against us under the Sixth and Fourteenth Amendments to the United States Constitution."

Kemper had one last plea: "And finally I say this to the Court. If the Court does not change its ruling on this subject, I respectfully ask for a two-day continuance of this matter so I can go to the Arizona Supreme Court and file a petition for a special action, and ask for a stay until this question can be resolved."

Judge Hardy still stood firm. He denied Kemper's plea to allow Byers's testimony, and he denied Kemper's request for a recess so he could appeal to the state supreme court.

The defense had no ballistics expert, no fingerprint expert, no Valenzuela confession—and also no Linda Primrose. Though her account to sheriff's deputies back in 1962 seemingly corroborated and dovetailed with Valenzuela's confession, and possibly explained the thatch of hair found at the murder scene, Jim Kemper did not know about Primrose. Nor, apparently, did the prosecution. The Maricopa County Sheriff's Office had never included the Primrose reports in the Macumber case file handed to the lawyers. At this trial, Linda Primrose—and that thatch of hair— just did not exist.

Except for a half dozen character witnesses, in the end the defense had nothing to offer but Bill Macumber himself. He took the stand on Monday, January 20.

Kemper walked Macumber through his personal history, aiming to convey to the jury a full sense of this man. Bill talked of his upbringing, his education, his background with hunting and guns, his time in the army, his employment record, his involvement in the Deer Valley Little League, and his launching of the Desert Survival Unit. He talked also of his marriage and his separation from Carol in the spring of 1974. "She started staying out later and later every night after school," he said. "And I questioned her about it, just asked her more or less why she was out so late, and she always had an excuse, and I guess I just had a feeling—"

The prosecutor objected at this point: "I would like to remind the Court, Your Honor, we can sit here and turn this thing into a tremendous character assassination on Carol Macumber. We can't call anyone else in the world to refute that testimony." Judge Hardy, after considering, allowed testimony about Carol studying fingerprinting at Glendale Community College but not about Carol "running around with someone else, I can't see that has any relevancy."

Kemper eventually asked Macumber about his statements of August 28 to Deputies Diehl and Calles.

KEMPER: You will recall, and this again is from Officer Diehl, that he saw or heard another sheriff's detective named Barnby place his arm around your shoulders and Officer Diehl said that he heard Barnby say to you, "Did you tell Carol you killed those people?" And Officer Diehl testified that he heard you say, "Yes" to Barnby. Now, did Barnby in fact ask you that question?

MACUMBER: No, sir, he did not.

KEMPER: Did he ask any question?

MACUMBER: Yes, he did. . . . He asked me why would I say that to my wife.

KEMPER: And what did you say?

MACUMBER: Well, there was some preliminary—there were other things that went on prior to that, and I said, "I suppose to keep her from leaving us."

It had been, Macumber would forever after explain, a hypothetical answer to a hypothetical question. He didn't regard it as an admission of any sort, so he never disavowed it, here or in subsequent interviews. Minutes later, Kemper asked Macumber to recount his conversation with Deputy Ed Calles. Macumber's unequivocal response: "He asked me first of all, he said, 'Bill did you kill those kids?' And I said, 'No sir, I did not.' And he asked, 'Did you tell your wife that you killed those kids?' And I said, 'No, I did not tell her I killed those kids.'"

On cross-examination, prosecutor Larry Cantor hammered at the notion that Macumber's defense essentially hinged on a claim that everyone in law enforcement was lying, everyone framing him. Macumber struggled to respond, for he would not, could not, point a finger.

Q: Is Sergeant Calles a liar?

A: I would prefer to say Sergeant Calles is mistaken, sir.

Q: Are you telling us that you in no way ever said words to the effect to Sergeant Calles that you told your wife you had shot and killed those kids?

A: No, sir, I did not tell Sergeant Calles that I told my wife I killed those kids.

Q: Now, you say he's very mistaken when he testified to that, is that correct?

A: I didn't say very mistaken, sir. I said I would tend to say that he was mistaken rather than lying.

Q: Does he have any motive to lie?

A: I don't know.

Q: You're saying he may have a motive to lie?

A: Yes, sir, he may have a motive for lying.

Q: What you are saying is, someone tried to frame you?

A: I'm saying something has happened.

Q: Let's get this straight now. Officer Jacka has substituted a phony print, is that your testimony?

A: No, sir.

Q: Who substituted a phony print?

A: I would have to make an accusation on the stand if I was to say that. And without proof, sir.

That night, back home at his parents' home, Macumber wrote in his journal, "Today I was cross-examined by the State and it was not a pleasant thing to have to go through. All I could do was answer the questions as honestly and as accurately as possible. . . . Perhaps I made errors though it was not intentional."

He had his boys with him this evening. "I tried my best to prepare them for what is about to happen. . . . All I was able to do was assure them that I loved them with all my heart and that no matter what happens I shall be with them always in their minds and in their hearts."

Macumber's last entry in his journal came the next evening: "Very little happened in court today. . . . The judge decided to recess until tomorrow morning when the final arguments will be made. . . . When that is done the jury will then deliberate until they arrive at a verdict. I can only pray to God it will be not guilty."

His prayers went unanswered. Two days later, on Friday, January 24, 1975, the jury returned its verdict: guilty on two counts of first-degree murder.

CHAPTER 8
———

Civilly Dead

FEBRUARY 1975–DECEMBER 1976

Bill Macumber's trial occurred during a four-year moratorium on the death penalty brought about by the 1972 U.S. Supreme Court opinion in *Furman v. Georgia,* which declared that the "arbitrary and inconsistent imposition of the death penalty" violated the Eighth and Fourteenth Amendments. So on February 18 Judge Hardy sentenced Macumber to life in prison, under circumstances that essentially meant no possibility of parole. Authorities revoked Macumber's bail and returned him to the Maricopa County Jail. There he wrote two letters to a local newspaper. "Myself, my wife and my God are the only ones that know . . . beyond any doubt that I am innocent . . . ," he began the first one. He continued:

> The jury convicted me because of the evidence that they were per-
> mitted to hear. I believe with all my heart that had they been allowed
> to hear the rest of the evidence, I would have been found not guilty.
> The evidence that we want to present in our defense was not circum-
> stantial. It was hard facts with all of the necessary supportive infor-
> mation. It consists of a confession of the real killer made not to one

but to two reliable and responsible attorneys. We were also ready to present evidence the casings found at the murder scene were not and could not have been fired from my gun. None of this evidence was allowed to go to the jury. . . .

I pray to God that those of you who believe in me will not let this end here. For the first time in my life, I am asking for help. Please write to the media and to those who can help change this terrible mistake.

In his second letter, he expanded on this theme:

Each and every one of us are guaranteed by our Constitution the right to trial by jury and the right to face and confront our accusers. This does not merely mean a face-to-face confrontation, but also to present evidence in our own behalf which may first create a question as to the accuracy of our accusers' evidence altogether. . . .

I am behind bars because I was denied the right to face my accusers and present evidence that would have proven my innocence and let me return to my home and my sons. . . . What has happened to me can happen to any man or woman in this land. . . . It is the people who have the power to right the wrongs and correct the inequities. That is why I am writing this. . . . I'm not asking you to believe in my innocence but I am asking you to help me so that I might have a chance to present my evidence—all the evidence—to a jury. . . . You will be helping me but more importantly you will be helping yourselves by standing up and protecting your rights and privileges as an American citizen.

In a presentencing report, a county probation officer had seen matters differently. Relying on the sheriff's accounts, Basil Wiederkehr thought the evidence "overwhelming," Macumber "guilty beyond a doubt." From what Ed Calles told him, he also thought "no possibility of a frame-up exists." Yet Wiederkehr remained puzzled: "The difficult part of this whole affair is trying to determine a motive for the crime." Robbery or an intended sexual attack seemed unlikely. Macumber "gives the impression of being a calm, composed, articulate, sane person." His parents,

Wiederkehr noted, insist that he has always been so, and his neighbors and colleagues confirm this. Still—Carol had advised Wiederkehr that Bill possessed "a very violent temper" and "told crazy stories about being an executioner for the Army's C.I.D." So perhaps Macumber "just acted out the policeman and executioner roles that he used to talk about." Perhaps he even suffered "temporary insanity" at the time. Perhaps the victims annoyed him in some way and his "violent temper" erupted.

The probation officer relied on Carol's characterizations throughout his report. To keep her, she'd advised Wiederkehr, Bill had also threatened suicide and claimed he had cancer. Then he'd staged that shot through the kitchen window—to her, the final straw. At the time, she didn't believe him truly guilty. She was just annoyed, thinking he was trying to frame her, so she'd gone to the authorities. "She pointed out that she has suffered greatly from the whole affair," Wiederkehr wrote, "and would be much better off if she had never told. For example, she had moved into an apartment and was having the time of her life. Now she is back at home with her three sons and is not earning enough money to support them."

In late February, authorities transported Macumber from the county jail to the state prison at Florence. He heard threats and catcalls from inmates as soon as he passed through the gates, the price paid for his connection to the Maricopa County sheriff's department. His second day there, two inmates jumped and pummeled him at a blind spot near the stairs to the second tier. The next morning, two other inmates stopped by his cell to demand protection payments. He couldn't and wouldn't pay, so he got beaten again. He had blood in his urine now, and pain in his ribs when he breathed deeply. The warden summoned him, demanding to know who'd attacked him, growing angry when Macumber couldn't provide names. Eventually, the warden ordered him into administrative segregation, a form of isolation that Macumber found unpleasant. He had a cell to himself, but he could leave it only twice a week, for a five-minute shower. He ate his three daily meals alone in his cell. He felt like a pariah.

★   ★   ★

In early March, Carol's attorney filed a motion for summary judgment in the divorce proceedings, which apart from division of property had involved the issue of custody and visitation. There remained nothing to contest, Carol argued, for Bill, "being civilly dead," had no standing to appear or oppose her requests. *Civilly dead*—that was the legal term applied in such proceedings to one convicted of murder and sentenced to life in prison. Bill Macumber "is in fact for these proceedings dead," Carol's petition declared. "He has no standing to object to the motion."

But Judge Ed Hughes wasn't inclined to declare him dead, as Macumber's conviction might be "revisited" down the road. In fact, Judge Hughes was willing to consider Bill's request for visitation rights— Macumber wanted his parents to bring his sons to the prison regularly. Judge Hughes thought the request "most unusual," even unprecedented, "the only one I've ever had or ever heard of." All the same, he noted, a convicted felon doesn't lose all his "natural rights or property rights." Before ruling about visitation or custody, Hughes wanted a report prepared by the Conciliation Court, a division of the Maricopa County Superior Court.

That report arrived on March 26, written by Conciliation Court counselor Pat Ferguson, who had interviewed Carol, Bill, the boys and a range of witnesses—neighbors, friends, colleagues and family members, twenty-six in all. "Most of the witnesses," Ferguson reported, "were provided by Mr. Macumber. Mrs. Macumber gave counselor only three witnesses that were not members of her immediate family. Two of the witnesses counselor spoke to. The third did not keep his appointment, nor did he call. Due to the lack of impartial witnesses, many of Mrs. Macumber's allegations regarding Mr. Macumber could not be verified."

Carol's allegations covered the gamut: Contact with Bill negatively affected her sons; Bill was mentally unstable; Bill had interest in hard-core pornography; Bill had taught the boys to hunt "for the love of killing."

Should visitation be granted, Carol told Ferguson, she would have no choice but to leave the state with the boys. Carol wanted Ferguson to know that she, "tired of being the bad guy," had called an *Arizona Republic* newspaper reporter to give her side of the custody-visitation issue ("Involvement Costly Macumber's Wife Says," read the resulting headline. "'I'm Fighting for My Kids'"). She'd learned from the reporter that

Judge Hughes was saying she "runs around with a lot of men." How, Carol asked Ferguson, could the judge have this information?

"Counselor told her that this appeared to be very common knowledge," Ferguson wrote in her report, "that many people had made the same statement unsolicited. . . . Many witnesses made comments regarding a number of men in connection with Mrs. Macumber. Neighbors report that there are three or four men who commonly visit Mrs. Macumber's house in the evening. . . . It is apparent that there is much negative feeling about Mrs. Macumber in the neighborhood."

During her investigation, Ferguson heard allegations that Carol left the boys alone for long periods of time while she rode patrol with the deputies. Ferguson also heard the three boys express "a great desire" to visit with their father. She added, "Not seeing him is apparently very distressing to all of them. . . . It is apparent that in the past, Mr. Macumber was the major parental figure for the boys. Witnesses state that they spent many hours together and seem to be very devoted. . . . [Carol] does confirm that when she and Mr. Macumber had agreed to divorce, she had agreed to give him custody of the children."

Ferguson's conclusion: "It is recommended that the three minor children be allowed to visit Mr. Macumber at the Arizona State Prison according to prison regulations. . . . It is further recommended that the paternal grandfather, Mr. Harold Macumber, be afforded weekly visitation on a one day per week basis." Ferguson also recommended that the three children be afforded counseling "in order to vent their feelings and thoughts to an unbiased, noninvolved individual."

Judge Hughes, accepting Ferguson's first recommendation, granted Macumber visitation rights. One day in April 1975, Bill's parents brought two of his sons, Steve and Ronnie, to the state prison. This would be the boys' one and only visit. True to her word, Carol soon after packed up the family and moved to Colorado. Bill kept writing letters to his boys, more than fifty in all, but the post office returned each one unopened. He lost all contact with his sons after the spring of 1975. Scott was twelve then, Steve ten, Ronnie seven.

* * *

Later that year, Macumber left administrative segregation only to find himself in a block with considerably smaller cells. He had a cellmate now, a youth of about twenty, half Bill's age, and obviously afraid of him. It took Macumber several weeks to assure the boy that he meant him no harm.

Weeks turned into months. In Phoenix, the local newspaper coverage had given way to more extended magazine articles, summing up the case that finally appeared to be closed. In these narratives, reporters cast the sheriff's officers as heroes and reconstructed how deputies diligently pursued thousands of leads, never giving up, never doubting they would capture the killer. The young prosecutor Tom Henze also drew favorable attention, yet he soon left his job for a new one. During Macumber's trial, he'd socialized with Jim Kemper at times, having a drink with the defense attorney after a day in the courtroom—the legal profession, in Phoenix at least, being more civil back then. Kemper had a small two-lawyer practice. If you ever want to join us, he told Henze, if you ever want to switch sides, let us know.

In December 1975, less than a year after Macumber's trial ended, Henze decided to accept this offer. The prosecutor became a defense lawyer in Kemper's law firm. A month later, sitting at his desk there, he heard Jim Kemper bang on the wall. It was January 13, 1976. Kemper came running into Henze's office, waving a piece of paper. "I told you," he shouted. "All because of that stupid move you made. I told you!"

The Arizona Supreme Court that day had reversed Bill Macumber's conviction, ruling that Judge Hardy should have allowed the defense's ballistics expert, Charles Byers, to testify. It was Henze who'd challenged Byers, Henze who'd persuaded Hardy to bar his testimony. At the time, Kemper had told Henze, *If he's convicted, this case is coming back for that.* Kemper, who'd filed the appeal, had been proven right.

The Arizona Supreme Court had almost reversed for another reason, as well: Judge Hardy's decision to bar Tom O'Toole's and Ron Petica's testimony about Valenzuela's confession. In a close, conflicted vote, the justices split three to two on that issue. The majority sided with Judge Hardy, concluding that the attorney-client privilege survives death and can be waived only by the client or "someone authorized by law to do so on his behalf." The two other justices filed a separate concurring opinion, agreeing with the reversal but saying they would have also reversed because of the refusal to admit Valenzuela's confession.

Justice William Holohan, who wrote this concurring opinion, relied heavily on a landmark 1973 U.S. Supreme Court decision, *Chambers v. Mississippi*. *Chambers* would forever hover over the Macumber case, for it concerned third-party culpability—someone other than the defendant confessing to a crime. In Mississippi, Leon Chambers had been convicted of murdering a cop, though another man had confessed three times to three separate people—people who were not allowed to testify at Chambers's trial. The Supreme Court's decision reversing Chambers's conviction, authored by Justice Lewis Powell, ruled that the exclusion of testimony about another party committing the crimes had denied Chambers his fundamental due process rights under the Fourteenth Amendment. Arizona Justice Project founder Larry Hammond, as it happened, had been Powell's law clerk at the time—and Powell had invited him to write an initial draft. Hammond, just twenty-seven then, would come to regard *Chambers v. Mississippi* as the most important case he ever worked on. "*Chambers* is my life," he told people in later years, while poring over the Macumber file with his Justice Project team.

Justice Holohan recognized the *Chambers* issues being replayed in *Macumber*. Boisterous in person but spare in his judicial writings, he had picked up the nickname "Wild Bill" during his years on the bench. Legal observers considered him the court's most conservative member, a hard-line advocate on criminal appeals, yet now he wrote eloquently on behalf of Macumber's cause. The United States Supreme Court in *Chambers*, Holohan pointed out, "has ruled that it is a violation of due process" for a state to bar "reliable hearsay declarations against penal interest when such evidence is offered to show the innocence of an accused." Yes, the attorney-client privilege has been held to survive the death of the client, but "the real problem is whether the privilege can survive the constitutional test of due process." Holohan noted that an accused has the basic right to present a defense to a criminal charge. "The problem of balancing competing interests, privilege versus a proper defense, is a difficult one, but the balance always weighs in favor of achieving a fair determination of the case," he wrote. Again he cited *Chambers*: "A state's rules of evidence cannot deny an accused's right to present a proper defense."

Holohan's conclusion: "When the client died there was no chance of prosecution for other crimes, and any privilege is merely a matter of property interest. Opposed to the property interest of the deceased client is the vital interest of the accused in this case in defending himself against the charge of first degree murder. When the interests are weighed, I believe that the constitutional right of the accused to present a defense should prevail over the property interest of a deceased client. . . . I would allow the defendant to offer the testimony of the attorneys concerning the confession of their deceased client."

Bill Macumber first learned of the Arizona Supreme Court's reversal while sitting in the crowded cell at Florence he'd now shared with another inmate for eight months. Some other prisoners along their hallway had television sets. Hearing reports on the news shows, they began calling out: *You got returned. . . . You got returned.* Macumber had not expected this, despite Jim Kemper's assurances that they would appeal. Waves of joy and relief lifted him. Maybe, he allowed himself to think, this would work out.

Carol Macumber heard the news in Colorado when a local Phoenix reporter called her. "Oh God," she exclaimed. "He's not getting out, is he? . . . I'm terribly frightened." The resulting story in the *Phoenix Gazette* the next day used that line as its headline and continued to quote Carol, who again wanted to tell her side because she was "tired of being the baddie." If Bill gets out, she said, "we'll spend the rest of our lives running. I'm just that scared. From what I've heard from people who had contact with him in prison he's just gone completely off his rocker. . . . I'm practically in shock. . . . If he gets out I'm heading for the hills."

Authorities soon returned Bill Macumber to the Maricopa County Jail. There he found out he'd be represented at his second trial by the Maricopa County public defender's office, since the Macumber family had no money for a private attorney. (Jim Kemper couldn't continue anyway, with Tom Henze now his partner.) At least he'd have a top man in the PD's office, deputy public defender Bedford Douglass, considered one of the best in the state. When they met for the first time, Douglass offered neither high hopes nor pessimistic predictions. He would do his best to help him, he told Macumber. Okay, Bill reasoned. He could not ask for more than that.

His father and brother came to visit, too. They had already started working on his bail. If the judge approved release on bond, they felt certain they could raise the amount needed. Bill asked his father if he'd heard anything from the boys. Harold knew only that they were in Colorado, where Carol worked for a sheriff's department. Bill's divorce attorney, John Thomas, was trying to track them down.

At a hearing on February 19, a magistrate approved Macumber's release on bail, setting bond at $69,000. Again relatives and neighbors put up their houses as collateral. This time the process moved quickly; Bill was out by the end of the month, back home with his parents. After a full year in the state prison, it took him several weeks to adjust. His family worked hard to keep him busy, to keep his mind occupied with matters other than the upcoming trial. They bought a gem-cutting outfit and set it up in Harold's storage shed. Bill spent hours there, carving objects he then sold—his only income. He and his dad played golf twice a week. He went fishing often with both of his parents. He fielded regular invitations to visit the Bridgewaters and other good friends.

He also met periodically with Bedford Douglass. The public defender was quite candid. We have a difficult road ahead of us, he told Macumber, but not an impossible road. He planned to make every effort to get Valenzuela's confession introduced. If that could be accomplished, he said, "it would help us tremendously."

The weeks and months passed, Macumber living at his parents' home for almost all of 1976, once again sleeping on the foldout couch in their small living room. Having no contact with his boys weighed on him, his returned letters to them a huge disappointment. He fought nervous spells and depression, swinging from moments of joy to much darker depths. Yet he felt he had a better grip on reality now than during his first time out on bail—he no longer lived in a dream world. He hoped for the best but expected nothing.

CHAPTER 9

Return to the Courtroom

In early meetings with his new client, Bedford Douglass found Bill Macumber to be an unusual person, quite unlike most he represented as a
Maricopa County public defender. The man he came to know was intelligent, thoughtful, engaged, wry and accomplished—not the type you'd
think would commit two brutal, random murders. In his line of work,
Douglass tried not to make such intuitive judgments, for he had to defend
all clients to the best of his ability. His belief about guilt or innocence, if
he had one, would just get in the way, making his judgments subjective
and his case less convincing. All that said, Douglass believed Macumber
innocent. This forever remained his unqualified position. The state's only
suggested motive—Macumber playing out a one-time posse-authority-
figure fantasy—seemed quite unlikely. And never before or after, just that
one night?

Yet Douglass knew that, on its face, the state's case was strong: the
palm print, the ejector marks, and Carol's statement. He weighed how to
counter. He was aware that Carol had close relationships with various
sheriff's deputies, including Ed Calles, who'd conducted the investigation

and signed the murder complaint. He also knew that she'd had access to the print and shell evidence, as well as to Bill's gun. He'd heard about various irregularities generally in the sheriff's department. All that suggested to Douglass a conspiracy of some sort. They would have to push that theme; they would have to try to prove a frame-up. At the least, they would have to discredit Carol, to show she had motivation to lie. They also would have to suggest that someone else committed the murders—so they had to get Valenzuela's confession admitted. Those would be the two pillars of the defense: fight for Valenzuela's confession; directly attack Carol, Ed Calles and the Maricopa County Sheriff's Office.

Bill Macumber's second trial began on December 13, 1976, in a capacious second-floor courtroom in the Maricopa County Old Courthouse, which stood on Washington Street just south of the East Court Building. Unlike the compact, modern chamber that housed the first trial, this one, built in the 1920s and never refurbished, featured a gracious if shabby older style, with wood paneling, carved posts and windows giving onto the street. This time, Maricopa County was paying all the attorneys: for the state, Deputy County Attorney Larry Turoff; for the defense, Bedford Douglass and Paul Prato. Judge Robert Corcoran presided.

Newly appointed to the bench just months before, Corcoran had progressive roots as a lawyer. Besides several blue-chip law firms, he'd worked with the ACLU in Arizona, including a stint on the landmark *Miranda* case. He had his admirers, who appreciated his "understanding heart" and his firm belief in the role and rule of law in society. Yet there were those who thought Corcoran full of himself and abundantly ambitious. He could be intense and excitable, and he wrote long, heavily explanatory opinions. At age forty-two—one year older than Macumber—Corcoran plainly wanted to rise in the judiciary.

Bedford Douglass, thirty-three then, came from different roots. Born in Mesa, a small community just outside Phoenix, he'd grown up mostly among Mormons. His mother, a Mormon, was deeply conservative religiously and culturally. As a teenager, Douglass had an interest in the conservative politics of Barry Goldwater and William Buckley. Yet he had never been keen on authority and came to dislike both hypocritical politicians and judges who misused power. Over time, he grew more liberal, in part because of his work as a criminal defense attorney. Seeing how the state could abuse its powers, he developed a healthy regard for civil liberties and protections.

Tall and thin, with a polio-crippled left arm in a black sling, Douglass projected a kind of Lincolnesque aura in the courtroom, his manner before Judge Corcoran relentless and unflappable. With an excitable, ambitious judge and a persistently deadpan defense attorney, conflict seemed inevitable.

The state's case followed much the same path as at the first trial, depending on testimony from a long, by now familiar lineup of investigators and forensic experts. For six days they paraded to the witness stand, building an effective case, though on cross-examination Bedford Douglass managed to land some punches not made in the first trial. Under his questioning, Deputies Richard Diehl and Ed Calles again seemed to suffer memory lapses. On the witness stand, Diehl couldn't remember Bill ever denying that he'd committed the murders. Nor could Ed Calles. Calles also didn't remember how he'd come to know Carol Macumber. He "guessed" that he met her "sometime in 1973" when she arrived at the sheriff's department as a clerk in the ID section, before transferring to the detectives detail he supervised. He didn't recall knowing her before she became an employee at the sheriff's department. He didn't recall taking classes with her at Glendale Community College. He didn't recall serving as a reference when she applied for a job at the department. He didn't recall telling the department back then, in January 1973, that he had been "acquainted with Mrs. Macumber now for three semesters."

But all this was merely prelude to the main show: the battle over whether Judge Corcoran would allow the jury to hear about Ernest Valenzuela's confession. On the afternoon of December 21, Bedford Douglass finally threw down the gauntlet, asking permission to present an offer of proof at an evidentiary hearing, without the jury present. He had Tom O'Toole and Ron Petica, among others, waiting to testify.

The prosecutor jumped up to object. He did not want Valenzuela in this trial. "If the Court please," Larry Turoff said, "I think there should be no hearing whatsoever. This matter has already been resolved by the Supreme Court in the appeal of this case, and this is the law of the case. The Justices stated that testimony that [Douglass] now intends to attempt to introduce through these witnesses cannot be introduced, and that was the majority opinion in this case. And I might indicate to the Court that the three Justices who wrote that decision or concurred in that opinion are still sitting on the Supreme Court."

Douglass had an answer to that: The Arizona Supreme Court, in reversing Macumber's conviction, said the attorney-client privilege could be waived only by the client or "someone authorized by law to do so on his behalf." They now had such a person: Valenzuela's mother.

Thomas O'Toole, working with Douglass, had sent an investigator in search of her. They'd finally located Nina Reems in a rest home on the Salt River Pima-Maricopa Indian Reservation, at sixty-two already an aged, worn-down woman. They'd told her of Bill Macumber's arrest, her son's confession and their need for her waiver. She'd listened, then agreed to help. In mid-December, in the presence of her daughter and the rest home's director of nurses, she had signed a notarized affidavit.

"If the Court please," Douglass said, "we plan to present Mrs. Reems, the mother of Ernest Valenzuela, who will waive the privilege if there was one."

"How did this proceed at the last trial?" Judge Corcoran asked. "Did it go by testimony or simply an offer of proof [in chambers]?"

"There was an offer of proof, Your Honor. No testimony."

Corcoran knew little of the matter at this point—the Arizona Supreme Court's opinion the previous January hadn't set out the facts. His own experience, he now told Douglass and Turoff, "is that offers of proof often exceed by a wide margin the facts that they are based upon." But he felt that "the Court should have a full hearing," because "should the defendant be convicted there will be an appeal . . . and there will be no evidence on record relating to exactly what happened." He wanted a hearing "so that a record can be made" for the appeal, a record based on "the facts of this case rather than an offer of proof by an attorney."

Corcoran clearly wanted to avoid another reversal. He knew well that the Arizona Supreme Court had split three to two over admitting

Valenzuela's confession. The switch of a single vote the next time Macumber came before that court could result in yet another reversal if Corcoran didn't at least allow a hearing. He made this plain: "The additional reason I have for having a hearing," he told the lawyers, "is that the Supreme Court decision is three to two." Witnesses' testimony should be preserved "in the event that a reversal of their decision should come about in the Arizona Supreme Court"—or in case "a federal court would take a different position relying on *Chambers v. Mississippi*, decided by the US Supreme Court in 1973." Here was Larry Hammond's handiwork once again, "the most important case" he'd ever worked on.

Bedford Douglass began the evidentiary hearing by calling Thomas O'Toole, but Turoff objected before O'Toole could even state his name, arguing that this witness could not be called, could not testify. So at Corcoran's suggestion, O'Toole stepped down and Nina Reems instead took the witness stand. Ernest Valenzuela's mother wept and struggled with language issues, not making much sense, until Corcoran assumed the questioning. Slowly, he explained the situation to her, as if for the first time. Because her son "may have done something for which another man is charged," he asked, can the lawyers who represented him "tell us what your son said? Would you permit them to do that?"

"Yes," Nina Reems replied.

On came the witnesses. Bedford Douglass, deciding to hold O'Toole back for a moment, first called Maier Tuchler, the psychiatrist who'd seen Valenzuela in 1964. Douglass gambled here, for Tuchler was well known among lawyers (Douglass, Prato and O'Toole included) as a "prosecution whore," a professional witness for the state, always aware of who paid his bills. Yet Tuchler had heard Valenzuela confess, so Douglass wanted him in the record. At first, the gamble appeared to pay off. Yes, Tuchler testified, he'd heard Valenzuela confess, and yes, he'd thought him "exceedingly dangerous." On cross-examination, though, Tuchler, guided by the prosecutor, said he basically didn't believe Valenzuela. Valenzuela spoke in a "dreamy" and "vague" way, a detached drawl that "appeared to be almost unreal." Tuchler thought he was out for recognition, parroting what he'd read in the newspapers. No, Tuchler did not think Valenzuela had actually committed the murders.

Douglass called Thomas O'Toole next. Though not before a jury, O'Toole could finally tell his story in a courtroom. O'Toole vividly described how Valenzuela first brought up the Scottsdale Road murders, saying he "shot 'em like a rabbit" out in the desert north of Scottsdale. To O'Toole, Valenzuela hadn't been anything like the "dreamy" person Dr. Tuchler described; rather, he'd been hard and cold-eyed. Tuchler had seen Valenzuela for one hour, O'Toole for eight or nine hours. O'Toole had "no doubt" that Valenzuela told him the absolute truth.

Yet O'Toole had been representing Valenuzela on an entirely different murder charge, so he had not focused on the Scottsdale Road murders; professionally, he could not. He had a defense to prepare, and attorney-client privilege to honor. On cross-examination, Larry Turoff hammered at this. "Your report then of what he told you reflects no facts whatsoever of how he killed these people? . . . You don't recall him telling you how he got to this area?" Turoff kept pounding on this: *Do you recall . . . do you have anything in your notes?* Judge Corcoran jumped in too, sounding much the same theme: "Now I take it your position was that you had other fish to fry in that you were representing him on a different charge and you were not primarily or even substantially concerned with getting an accurate and complete statement from him relating to the Sterrenberg-McKillop murders? . . . You weren't interested in getting a complete, in effect, police report relating to his statement?"

O'Toole was taken aback. He thought it startling for Corcoran to expect a defense lawyer to construct and document a "complete police report" on a client's confession to an unrelated double murder. It would have been unethical—preposterous—for O'Toole to do so. Surely Corcoran knew this, surely Corcoran had not really imagined he'd get such a police report at this hearing. How possibly to respond?

"That is correct," O'Toole said. "What the client tells you about another crime he has committed you don't spend much time with. . . . We weren't concerned about it."

The prosecutor went at Ron Petica in much the same way when he took the stand. Valenzuela confessed the Scottsdale Road murders to him twice, Petica testified. Sitting in a conference room, Valenzuela had been lucid, cold, matter-of-fact, looking Petica straight in the eye—not at all in the dreamlike state Dr. Tuchler described. Petica "absolutely" believed him. "The way he said it I had no doubt but that he was telling me the truth."

Yet Petica, like O'Toole, had been representing Valenzuela on an entirely different murder case. So no, he did not question his client in detail about the Scottsdale Road homicides. First, because "Ernie was very distrustful . . . and I didn't want him to get the impression that I was trying to secure information on an unrelated case to do damage to him." And second, because he worried about being "subpoenaed to testify against him, even though I recognized the attorney-client privilege did exist." For that reason Petica took no notes: "I was afraid that it could have got out of my hands by some form or means, and could have been used against him in prosecution of those two crimes." Again Judge Corcoran jumped in, pressing that theme: "So I take it your primary interest was in frying the fish you had to fry and not getting a complete statement or report relating to what he was saying about the Sterrenberg-McKillop homicides?"

Petica couldn't disagree: "That is correct, Your Honor."

The next morning, Dr. Leo Rubinow took the stand as the final witness at this hearing. He'd interviewed Valenzuela twice in March 1968, he testified. He'd provided reports to two judges. He did not think Valenzuela had faked or fooled them while confessing. Yet like the lawyers, he could not recount a wealth of precise details about Valenzuela's confession. Rubinow had taken copious notes, but he no longer had them. Facing cardiovascular surgery in 1971, which he thought he would not survive, "I destroyed all psychiatric records so as not to divulge to someone whose hands they may fall, details of personal patient-physician relationships and so forth."

To O'Toole, Petica and Rubinow, Ernest Valenzuela had been a client and a patient, not a suspect subject to police interrogation. This circumstance now appeared to shape Judge Corcoran's evaluation of their testimony. By late that morning, he was referring to the "so-called"

Valenzuela confession. He asked Bedford Douglass, in the first sign of the tension brewing between them, "You presented all of your evidence on the so-called Valenzuela confession?" Yes he had, Douglass allowed.

Judge Corcoran didn't need to ponder for long. At 3:00 that afternoon, out of the presence of the jury, he delivered his ruling: "I find that the testimony of the witnesses relating to the statements made by Valenzuela lack sufficient circumstantial probability of trustworthiness to justify their admission into evidence. . . . I find that statements made to Misters O'Toole and Petica lack any reasonable degree of specificity as to any involvement Mr. Valenzuela would have had in the homicides. . . . They did not interrogate him or ask him any questions." Also: "The statements made to Misters O'Toole and Petica . . . were made after Mr. Valenzuela was expressly advised that whatever he told them was subject to an attorney-client privilege," which "cannot be waived under these circumstances." Mindful of the hugely pivotal impact of his ruling, Corcoran later underscored his reasoning, in chambers: "I want to make clear as to Valenzuela, my ruling and finding of fact is that none of the testimony . . . bore persuasive assurances of trustworthiness. I also ruled that the testimony of Messieurs O'Toole and Petica should be barred by the attorney-client privilege."

Corcoran's comments showed just how much he had his eye on both the U.S. Supreme Court's *Chambers* decision and Justice Holohan's minority opinion in the reversal of Macumber's first conviction. In fact, Corcoran had adopted the very wording of Holohan's opinion—"playing to the dissenters," Bedford Douglass called it. There and in *Chambers,* the judges had recognized a due process right for defendants to have confessions such as Valenzuela's admitted—if the confessions bore "considerable assurance of their reliability" and "persuasive assurances of trustworthiness." Those were Corcoran's words now, exactly. Listening to him, Bedford Douglass concluded that Corcoran—though seemingly amenable at the start—had never intended to admit Valenzuela's confession. He'd allowed the hearing to avoid the chance of reversal, but he had already decided to bar the testimony. Douglass had to hand it to Corcoran—the judge was clever and cunning and knew precisely what he wanted on the record.

The public defender recognized what this meant to their case. The trial, he'd later say, was decided at this hearing. To not let the jury hear Valenzuela's confession, he believed, constituted a major injustice for Bill Macumber. He thought it incredible that the judge blocked evidence central to the defense, evidence that might have had a profound impact on the verdict. Certainly the jurors might doubt the veracity of the confession—but let them decide, let them determine what's "trustworthy." The jurors, after all, define the "facts." The lawyers just tell their stories.

At a conference in chambers days later, Douglass attempted a last assault on the judge's ruling, but Corcoran held firm: "My feeling was . . . Mr. Valenzuela might just have wanted to see Mr. O'Toole's eyes pop . . . knowing that it had no consequence and couldn't be used in any way against him."

Yet that, Douglass pointed out, was only Corcoran's personal feeling. Appellate courts have found it "altogether atypical, extraordinary and improper" for a judge to exclude evidence because he does not believe it. Why not let this evidence come in, let the lawyers argue over it, and let the jury decide?

No, Corcoran said. He had heard of numerous cases where people confessed to crimes that they obviously didn't commit, and he thought he had one here. "It's just a naked statement of 'I did it,' and that's why I think the showing has not been made."

With that, the battle over Valenzuela ended. The jury would never know he had confessed to the Scottsdale murders.

At the trial's start, Douglass had waived giving an opening statement, and now he did so again when it came time for the defense to put on its case. Many years later, he would consider that a mistake. In the moment, though, he simply didn't know what story to tell the jurors. He still—this late in the trial—remained uncertain about what evidence of a frame-up he could get in, how far he could go.

For that matter, he didn't know what he could tell the jury about Linda Primrose. While digging through boxes of documents in preparation for this second trial, prosecutor Larry Turoff had finally discovered the sheriff's reports about Primrose and revealed them to Douglass, who'd promptly subpoenaed her. At first, she'd tried to quash the subpoena, invoking her Fifth Amendment right against self-incrimination; "I will take the Fifth on questions besides my name," she declared at a pretrial hearing, "and I don't belong in the case." After a judge ruled she couldn't invoke the Fifth in this situation—and the state refused to grant her immunity—she wrote directly to Bedford Douglass, pleading with him "to please reconsider and not use me in the trial." Otherwise, she warned him, she would recant rather than again try to invoke the Fifth. She would say she lied to the deputies in 1962.

Douglass called her as a witness anyway, wanting her existence and prior statements on the record. She took the stand at Bill Macumber's trial on the afternoon of December 22. She was then a thirty-two-year-old married woman with two children—no longer a drug-addled teenager joyriding with strangers on the Scottsdale desert. She didn't deny making statements years before about witnessing the murders, though she couldn't remember what she'd said. She knew only that they were false. "I remember that I lied and I made false statements but I can't tell you word for word," she testified. She'd lied to the sheriff's deputies, the polygraph examiner, and the psychiatrist. That's all she recalled—that she had made false statements to everyone. Yes, she had earlier refused to answer questions on the grounds that her answers might tend to incriminate her. Yes, she had only started recanting after she'd failed to quash the defense's subpoena. Yes, her husband and children knew nothing of her past. Yes, she didn't want her husband and children to know about the statements she'd made to Detective Thomas Hakes in 1962. "That's right," Primrose said. "That's right."

The defense had few others to call beyond character witnesses. Like Jim Kemper at the first trial, Douglass had found it nearly impossible to locate qualified forensics experts willing to testify for the defense. To Judge Corcoran's bewilderment, Douglass chose not to call the ballistics expert Charles Byers. Despite the Arizona Supreme Court's finding him qualified and despite his exclusion at the first trial being the sole basis for the reversal, Douglass still worried that he wouldn't come across well as a witness. Byers was available and, in conversations with Douglass, emphatic that the shell casings couldn't be matched to Macumber's gun, but the public defender declined to use him. In the end, Douglass called no ballistics expert at all—he just could not find one, he explained later.

Douglass did put a fingerprint expert on the stand, but this witness— Jerome Steigmann, a former New York police detective and latent-fingerprint examiner—could testify only generally about the ways to forge prints. It's quite possible, he explained, to remove a latent lift from a card and substitute another one, without any sign of tampering. He'd seen many cases where this had happened, and he'd transplanted prints himself, doing "numerous control experiments" to confirm the method. But no, he could not say that Bill Macumber's print had been forged. On cross-examination, Larry Turoff asked him, "You weren't telling the Court and jury, sir, that this fingerprint [Bill's] has been forged, transplanted or transferred?"

"It could have been."

"I'm asking were you telling us that."

"I didn't say it had been. I said it could have been."

"You're not saying it had been?"

"No."

Carol had not testified at the first trial, but now, on December 29, the state called her to the stand as a rebuttal witness. She was thirty-three, a deputy with the Pitkin County Sheriff's Office in Aspen, Colorado. Yes, she said in response to the prosecutor's questions, she had taken courses in fingerprinting at Glendale Community College, one in classification, another in detecting and lifting latent prints. But no, she had never tampered with the latent lifts in the Macumber case file. Here Turoff walked her through the frame-up charges:

Q: Did you ever go to wherever they keep them in the Sheriff's Office and remove that card with the latent liftback on it and replace it with another fingerprint or palm print?

A: No, sir.

Q: Did you ever go to wherever they keep the negatives and remove the negative and replace it with any other negative?

A: No, sir.

Q: Did you ever ask any other individuals at the Sheriff's Department or anybody else to do these things for you?

A: No, sir.

Q: Carol, did you ever take a photograph of the defendant's palm print and place it on a chrome strip of an automobile?

A: No, sir.

Q: Did you ask anybody else to do that?

A: No, sir.

Q: Did you ever go to the property room and remove the shells . . . ?

A: No, sir.

Q: Did you ever ask anybody else to do that?

A: No, sir.

On cross-examination, Bedford Douglass attacked. Yes, Carol allowed, while employed at the Maricopa County Sheriff's Office she'd had access to all the case files. Yes, she'd likely read the Sterrenberg-McKillop file, along with all the others. Yes, she'd had access to all items of evidence kept in the sheriff's department identification section. Yes, she'd taken Bill's prints when he started the Desert Survival Unit. Yes, she'd met Ed Calles at Glendale Community College. Yes, he'd recommended her for employment at the sheriff's department.

Douglass started picking apart her August 23 statement to deputies, identifying inconsistencies, pointing to details that didn't match the crime scene. *It is your claim now . . . You assume . . . Well, didn't you say on August 23rd . . .* On the bench, Judge Corcoran grew annoyed, his face flushing. He thought Douglass was trying to get the jury to draw unfair inferences about Carol, trying to make her look inconsistent and foolish. In his chambers during the afternoon recess, Corcoran told Douglass just that. The judge's admonishment didn't stop the defense attorney. With Carol back on the stand, he kept hammering at inconsistencies and challenging her memory. Then he started asking Carol whether she'd had affairs with various police officers.

Q: Prior to obtaining your divorce, you were dating other men, were you not?

A: No, sir, I was not dating other men.

Q: You know Dennis Gilbertson, don't you?

A: Yes, sir.

Q: You were dating Dennis Gilbertson prior to your divorce, weren't you?

A: I saw him at school. We went out. We were with many other people. . . .

Q: You were having an affair with Mr. Gilbertson?

A: No, sir, I was not.

Bedford Douglass couldn't go much further. At a hearing months before the trial started, he and his deputy Paul Prato had sought Carol's personnel file, telling a judge that "we want to review the internal affairs records to confirm or refute certain information we have regarding Mrs. Macumber." Sheriff's department sources had told them she'd been subject to an internal investigation over "certain relationships with certain deputies" that would give her "perhaps some leverage over these individuals." But Douglass had never found that internal affairs report, never been able to confirm what they'd heard. So he had to remain ineffectively oblique:

Q: After Bill was arrested, you were still working for the Maricopa County Sheriff's Office. . . . You had some concern about your job then, correct?

A: Yes, sir.

Q: Didn't you tell Frieda Kennedy that if I'm fired I'll take 20 or so people with me?

A: No, sir.

Q: You didn't say that to Frieda?

A: No, sir.

Douglass called two witnesses to impeach Carol, both compelled by summons to take the stand: Frieda Kennedy, who testified that yes, Carol had said if fired, she'd "take several people with her . . . around 20"; and Loretta Orenelas, a neighbor, who testified that yes, Carol had acknowledged to her having an affair with Dennis Gilbertson—in fact, Loretta had met Dennis at Carol's home one afternoon when Bill was at work. Beyond that, Douglass could only wave flags in his closing argument.

There he hammered hard and directly at the notion that Carol and others had framed Bill Macumber. The palm print—unclassifiable in 1962, suddenly a good read in 1974—must have been planted. Carol had access to those prints—"the most coincidental part of the whole case." She had the "know-how" as well; she knew how to dust and develop, lift and transfer. She also had access to Bill's .45 automatic—"Carol could have taken it, she could have fired it. . . . Those cartridge casings are easily substituted. . . . Carol Macumber could have done it herself. It requires no expertise." What of the lost reports, all the missing reports? "Carol Macumber had access to those files, she could have combed them for information inconsistent with her own idea."

Carol could have. That's what Douglass hung his argument on, had to hang it on: reasonable doubt. "Reasonable doubt is at the center of this case," he told the jury. "It pervades this case. There is not an aspect of this case you cannot examine without finding it saturated with doubt based on reason."

The jury, limited to what it knew of the case, deliberated for three days. Despite the many competing themes advanced by the lawyers, despite the attack on Carol's reputation and the allusions to her affairs, for these jurors it finally came down to the palm print and shell casings. Years later, one juror could not even remember the emphasis on Carol Macumber's involvement, on the prospect of her tampering and framing. She could only vaguely remember Linda Primrose. She mainly recalled the scientific evidence. The prints and casings put Bill Macumber at the crime scene—and that, this juror believed, convicted him. Just as a frustrated, anguished Jim Kemper foretold in Judge Hardy's chambers at the first trial, the state's unmatched phalanx of expert professional witnesses controlled the narrative.

Yet the jurors, at first, weren't certain or unanimous. On their initial ballot, three of the twelve thought Macumber innocent. On their second and third ballots, four voted for innocence. Then the tide turned. The next ballot split ten to two for guilt. The next, eleven to one. The last holdout finally gave up. At 3:00 P.M. on January 7, the jurors delivered their verdict: guilty on two counts of first-degree murder.

That afternoon, Judge Corcoran addressed the jurors. "You were faced with a great deal of conflicting testimony, a great deal of scientific testimony. . . . You have come up with a verdict which is . . . well within the evidence. . . . I think you came up with a fair verdict and one which you can be proud of." Yet he knew they would "look back on this experience with perhaps some mixed emotions." He also knew they would soon learn about Ernest Valenzuela's confession. Clearly, this concerned Corcoran. "You can go through [the newspaper articles] at this time. I can tell you that, if you do that, you will find that there was testimony during the trial out of your presence which you may consider to be material to the case had you known about it. But you didn't know about it and that information was kept out by me because I felt the rules of law required that it be kept out. I am sure that will be the subject of an appeal in this case so that Mr. Macumber will have a full opportunity to present those matters on an appeal."

With bond revoked, authorities returned Bill Macumber to the county jail. He felt nothing now, as if anesthetized. Bedford Douglass kept fighting for him. First he forced a hearing over a newly emerged witness, then another over a juror who he'd learned had been a heavy user of Percocet and Demerol during the trial. That move particularly enraged Corcoran, especially when Douglass began grilling the juror on the witness stand, characterizing her as an addict. "You are making a direct attack on her integrity, her honesty, and her ability to act as a juror in this case," Corcoran snapped, his face flushed again. Unflappable as always, Douglass disagreed: "What I am doing is presenting the facts that came out to me, which I did not solicit."

By this time, Corcoran was openly seething at the public defender and his mounting claim of a frame-up. He'd fumed as Douglass had attacked first Carol, then the sheriff's department, and now the attorney had gone after a juror. At the sentencing of Bill Macumber on February 17, Corcoran gave vent to his feelings. "In the trial of this matter," he began, "we have seen a number of trials. . . . During the trial itself Mr. Macumber was on trial for two counts of murder, first degree. During that trial also the former Mrs. Macumber was put on trial by Mr. Douglass. At the same time, Mr. Douglass put on trial the Maricopa County Sheriff's Office. After the convictions of guilt, we then had another trial. One of the jurors . . . was put on trial by Mr. Douglass." Corcoran glared at Douglass. "The defendant has had the benefit of the services of the Maricopa County Public Defender's Office, which spared no effort. . . . It even seemed to me the trial went to the point of not only trying to show reasonable doubt but to manufacture it."

Manufacture reasonable doubt. Corcoran's mocking words would make it into headlines and TV news broadcasts, much to Douglass's dismay. He'd never before been attacked like that in a courtroom, and never would again. The judge had publicly accused him of doing something improper, something immoral if not illegal. Yet Douglass had a duty to zealously defend his client; he had an obligation to try his best to establish reasonable doubt. He obviously hadn't succeeded, that was the real problem. And he hadn't succeeded, Douglass believed, because the judge had excluded witnesses who would have created reasonable doubt.

At this sentencing hearing, Corcoran turned on Bill Macumber as well. It began after the judge asked if the defendant had anything to say. Macumber did. He sat erect in his chair, hands on the table. When he spoke, his voice was, as usual, low and steady:

"Yes, Your Honor, I would. I realize that I am going back to prison and that's a fact that I can do nothing about. The fact also remains, Your Honor, that I did not kill these two people. That's another fact that can't be disputed, no matter how many witnesses you put on that stand or what judgment you might make here today. I am not the only one, Your Honor, that knows without a doubt that I did not do that. At least three other people do. Three people sat on that witness stand that know. My wife—former wife, for one . . . and Ed Calles for another . . . even though he sat up there and tried very hard to deny that there was a relationship [with Carol]. I doubt seriously there was anybody in this courtroom that didn't realize the relationship existed. And then there was Linda Primrose Chavez. She, probably more than anyone else, with the exception of myself, knows that I didn't do it because she was there that night and she saw the killer and she knew it wasn't me. . . . My wife in her twisted way, I guess, feels that she has got her revenge on the kind of life she might have had or should have had. And Ed Calles . . . doesn't have to worry about recrimination. . . . And Mrs. Chavez [Linda Primrose] . . . doesn't have to worry about ever being charged with an accessory to murder. Well, I can't do anything about that, and evidently nobody else will. But the fact remains, Your Honor, that there is going to come a day, as it does for all of us, when they have got to meet final judgment. . . . I am innocent before this Court, Your Honor, and I am innocent before God, and there is no way on this earth that you or the jury or anyone else is ever going to change that. . . ."

Corcoran responded: "The one thing that impressed me during the trial was during your appearance on the stand you did not . . . indicate that it was your feeling or belief that your wife was framing you, and I was surprised at that since it was the thrust of Mr. Douglass's defense. . . . This is the first time that I can recognize that you have taken the position that she has framed you. . . ."

"May I answer that, Your Honor?

"You may."

"I sat here. I listened to the evidence, and I grant you, I can't give you any hard fact that my wife framed me. That's true. Neither can Mr. Turoff give you any hard facts that I was out there and killed those two young people that night. . . . The circumstantial evidence . . . that Mr. Turoff has produced convicted me without any consideration of the circumstantial evidence produced that my wife framed me. . . . I believe, Your Honor, that [in] honesty and justice, the two balance themselves."

Corcoran disagreed: "My own conclusion was that the evidence showed you guilty beyond a reasonable doubt. I would not have been shocked had the jury acquitted you. I would have been surprised, however. If the matter were tried to me sitting without a jury, I would have found you guilty on the same evidence. It would have taken me a lot deal shorter in time to do so, inasmuch as I wouldn't have to concur with 11 other people."

Corcoran turned to the matter of sentencing. He ordered that Bill Macumber be incarcerated "for the term of your natural life" on Count 1, the murder of Timothy McKillop, and Count 2, the murder of Joyce

Sterrenberg. He further ordered that the two life sentences "run consecutively"—that is, back to back, one after the other, rather than concurrently.

Douglass instantly rose to object: "Judge Hardy has previously, at the first trial, sentenced the defendant to concurrent terms. The Court by its sentence here would have doubled the sentence imposed by Judge Hardy, which I submit would be contrary to the Constitution." Douglass was right: The judge could impose a harsher sentence only if the defendant had shown "baser mental or moral propensities" than at the first trial. To Corcoran, though, that's just what Macumber had shown by asserting an aggressive frame-up defense.

"Well, I submit that it would be justice," Corcoran told Douglass. "And you can take that up on your appeal also."

For a time, Macumber remained in the Maricopa County Jail, pending appeals—including a motion for change of judge filed by Douglass, vainly seeking to replace Corcoran for all post-trial judgments because his comments and conduct "evidenced a bias toward both defense counsel and the defendant." In his jail cell, Bill kept to his bed, crying for hours on end. He was not a particularly religious person, even though his family and friends had been urging him for many months to have faith in God, to put his life in God's hands. In fact, some years before he had walked away from God, had even denied that God existed. Yet now, days after his second conviction, he wrote to his father, asking Harold to send a minister to see him. Not a particular minister, as he had none, but someone. Macumber also asked a jail guard to bring him a Bible. He began to read, and felt a degree of peace. Then a Pastor Bowers came to talk and pray with him. He asked Macumber if he would accept the Lord Jesus Christ as his Savior. Bill, crying, said he would. "Praise God," exclaimed Pastor Bowers.

"Look around you," Macumber wrote in a letter to his parents. "Look everywhere you can. See the skies and the mountains, the hills and the valleys. See the trees and the oceans. Look at all the creatures of the land and those of the sea. Feel the raindrops and crystals of snow. . . . Feel the warmth of the sun. . . . What is the probability that all this randomly found its way into place? . . . What you see about you is creation."

In April, authorities transported Macumber back to the state prison in Florence, where the warden returned him to administrative segregation in Cellblock 2, the oldest section of the penitentiary. As before, that meant restricted recreation, limited visits and meals consumed alone in his cell. Besides his parents and brother, the "special woman" he'd spent time with while out on bond came down to Florence. During her second visit, Macumber told her not to return—it would be too painful for both of them. With tears, she agreed. He would never see her again.

CHAPTER 10

A Career in Prison

Bedford Douglass warned Bill Macumber that they had little chance of gaining another reversal. This proved to be the case. In June 1978, the Arizona Supreme Court affirmed Macumber's conviction. Judge Corcoran's strategy had worked: By allowing an offer-of-proof hearing, then ruling that the evidence lacked "sufficient circumstantial probability of trustworthiness," he'd addressed the concerns of the two justices who would have allowed Valenzuela's confession. Corcoran's finding of "insufficient trustworthiness" squarely met the conditions set by *Chambers* and Justice Holohan's minority opinion. Corcoran did this so well that the Arizona Supreme Court, in unanimously affirming his decision, now cited and effectively adopted the core of Holohan's argument: Yes, the justices ruled, sometimes the right to present a defense does trump the attorney-client privilege—but only with "trustworthy" evidence.

The language of *Chambers* also dominated Macumber's federal habeas corpus appeal. Both the state and the defense cited it to support their positions. The defense pointed to *Chambers'* insistence on the due process rights of the defendant, while the state pointed to the relative reliability of the confessor in the Chambers case—he, unlike Valenzuela, had still been alive. In August 1979, a U.S. district court dismissed the habeas petition. Bill Macumber had seemingly come to the end of the line.

At Florence, Macumber had by then spent more than two years in Cellblock 2. The conditions there felt like a dungeon to him—dirty, unsanitary, cold in winter, withering heat in summer, rats and roaches everywhere. The first winter, as he recalled, he nearly froze to death. In September 1977, prison officials removed half the roof for repairs, but they didn't replace it until the next June. Snow fell into the cellblock. Reaching out from his cell, Macumber could catch snowflakes. He and the other inmates slept with their clothes on, still shivering. In the morning, they had to break the ice in the toilet with a broom handle.

In the summer of 1979, just as the courts were rejecting his last appeals, the prison warden summoned Macumber. If we transfer you to North Unit, he wanted to know, will you try to run? Bill thought that funny—where or how would he run? Of course not, he told the warden. No, he wouldn't.

A week later, a guard stopped at his cell and told him to pack up. North Unit, a medium-security annex located across the street from the main prison, had once been the women's prison, before they shifted the female inmates to Perryville. Macumber was shocked as the guard drove him through the gates leading into the annex. Everything was green, with flowers all over the place. The annex had no cells; the inmates lived in three dorms. The guard stopped the van at Dorm 3, Macumber's new home.

He sensed the old fear creeping in. The less-confining conditions were nice, but without a cell, he'd lack protection. He'd be accessible to all the inmates. He had no choice, though. The dorm had a central dayroom and two wings, each with a bathroom and two rows of thirteen beds. Macumber dropped his possessions on his bunk—Bed 13, in the first row—then went to the clothing room to pick up blankets, sheets, a pillow and towels. He began to unpack, keeping a wary eye on the dorm's inmates. A slender man in his early thirties had the bed next to his. After half an hour, he turned to Bill and introduced himself. He went by the nickname Coyote. "You shouldn't worry here," he told Macumber. "We all make a point of getting along because it's such a small unit." True enough, Bill thought. The annex housed only 146 men. After nearly a thousand sometimes hostile inmates in Cellblock 2, this felt like heaven.

At lunch call, Coyote walked with him to the kitchen. Macumber couldn't believe his eyes when they stepped inside: Every table had a tablecloth with a napkin holder, salt and pepper shakers and a bottle of hot sauce. The windows had blue curtains. The room looked bright and clean. Most striking, it was quiet, with none of the screaming and yelling Bill had heard daily in the cellblock chow hall. After being "in the walls," learning to live like an animal, he was amazed that a place like this existed in the prison system.

Coyote took him on a tour after lunch. Though small, the annex had tennis courts, a volleyball slab, a weight-lifting area. Prisoners could be outside the dorm all the time except for count, which took place at 11:00 A.M., 4:00 P.M., and 8:00 P.M. They didn't have to return to their dorms until 9:30 P.M., when the yard closed.

Macumber wished he could regard this vast change in surroundings as a turning point for him. Yes, he had more freedom, a better environment, safer conditions, fewer worries. Yet he still faced life in prison without his sons, without his freedom. So all the improvements made little difference to his mood. He wrote his parents and brother anyway, reporting on his new home. They promptly came to visit, expressing astonishment at the change from Bill's life in the walls. They could meet with him now in a large visitation room, and from there go outside to sit at picnic tables. Rather than hassling everyone, the guards were courteous and helpful. Bill could see how much this setting raised his family's spirits, so he did his best to maintain a cheerful attitude. He never again wanted to cast shadows.

Then came an event that would prove a turning point—that would, in fact, trigger a transformation in Bill. During the fall of 1979, several members of the Phoenix Jaycees visited Florence on a recruiting mission. At the North Unit annex, they spoke to a large group of inmates about starting a prison chapter of the Arizona Jaycees. Neither Bill nor the other inmates knew about this group, but they listened. The Jaycees (originally short for Junior Chamber of Commerce) was a civic- and community-oriented organization active in all fifty states, with chapters in hundreds of cities, devoted to raising money for charities by staging events. They'd first ventured into the criminal justice system in 1962, with a chapter formed in the state penitentiary at Moundsville, West Virginia. The Arizona Jaycees initially got involved with prisoners in 1968, and by the time the Phoenix contingent came to visit Macumber's unit at Florence, they had some five hundred inmate members in twelve prison chapters. This organization sounded appealing to Macumber. If Florence started a prison chapter, they could be a part of the Arizona Jaycees and could participate in programs offered by the United States Jaycees. Macumber, with his degree in business administration, could imagine all sorts of possibilities.

During a break after their visitors' presentation, the inmates conferred on their own. Let's give it a try, they decided. Why not? We have nothing to lose.

The Phoenix Jaycees, genuinely delighted, began handing out documents and paperwork. Then, to Macumber's surprise, the Jaycees selected him to be the interim chapter president, to serve until the prisoners could get organized and hold a regular election. The Jaycees would come down every week, they promised, to guide him through the start-up process.

So it began. Macumber's life did not shift from dark to light, but the new home and the sudden presence of the Jaycee program had an effect. He forced himself to face up to his situation. He came to realize that he'd lost the life he'd once known, lost his sons, lost all else he'd once held dear. He began to feel the need to get himself back on track, to apply his spirit and talents not only for himself but for the peace of mind of his parents, brother and friends. It would not be easy, he knew that. But he aimed to stay with it.

The inmates named their Jaycee chapter the Roadrunners and held their initial meeting two weeks after the visit by the Phoenix members. Choosing officers was their first order of business. One of the inmates moved to elect Macumber by affirmation, and half a minute later Bill became the chapter's president, a position he would hold for four years. The group, about thirty men at the start, began meeting regularly, discussing possible goals and projects. With Macumber using the Jaycee president's manual as his guide, they set up prison classes on such topics as financial management, public speaking, personal dynamics, family living, communications and spiritual development—anything that would help inmates prepare for their eventual release. When the Phoenix Jaycees came to visit again after one month, they were astonished at the progress; they'd never seen a new chapter get off the ground so quickly. After two months, the Roadrunners had grown to sixty members.

As one of their first activities, the Roadrunners proposed to construct and operate a snack bar for inmates in the North Unit, something usually allowed only in minimum-custody yards. Yet Macumber won approval from the warden and central prison authorities in Phoenix. He located an old trailer, converted it to a working grill, stocked it with food and hired inmates as cooks. Next Macumber convinced the warden to let them expand the snack bar into the visitation area to replace a row of vending machines. The Roadrunners' snack bar opened just before Christmas 1979, serving steaks, chops, fish, complete breakfasts, hamburgers, sandwiches, burritos, pizza, popcorn, soft drinks, coffee and ice cream. They entered 1980 on a roll, full of energy, now redesigning the North Unit's entire visitation area. Macumber's parents noticed the change in him before he did, and his brother mentioned it when he visited early in the new year: Bill had become too busy to think of where he was.

Members in free-world Jaycee chapters around the state soon petitioned the prison administration, asking permission for Bill to attend the monthly meetings of Jaycee chapter presidents in various Arizona cities. Macumber learned of this when the warden called him in to report that central administration had approved the request. The news stunned him, for it broke all precedent. The Roadrunners celebrated, as did Macumber's family. The first meeting he attended, escorted by a North Unit guard, took place at the Jaycee chapter in New River, Arizona. On the drive there, Bill felt some misgivings, not knowing how he, a convicted murderer, would be received. But his reception in New River turned out to be gracious, the Jaycees regarding him not as Bill Macumber, a prisoner, but as Bill Macumber, president of the Roadrunner Jaycees. He struggled to hide his joy and gratitude. He would never forget that night.

In June 1980, the newly elected Arizona Jaycees president, Ron Walker, befriended Macumber and appointed him his presidential adviser on prison Jaycee chapters. The Roadrunners kept busy all through that year and the next two. In the summer of 1981 they built an annex softball field, making it one of the finest in the prison system. Using income earned from their snack bars, they built a large racquetball and handball court at the annex as well. Their snack bar income also funded donations to groups such as the Make-a-Wish Foundation and Special Olympics. One day, the Arizona Department of Corrections director himself, Ellis MacDougall, appeared at Florence to present Macumber and the Road-runners with commendations.

Years later, thinking back on these accomplishments, Macumber would chuckle particularly over how they built the softball field. The North Unit captain of security, a fellow named Gilbert, had said absolutely no, they couldn't do it. "I don't want to see you building a ballfield," he'd told Macumber. So the Roadrunners built it when Gilbert went on a six-week vacation. On Gilbert's very first day away, Macumber had the Roadrunners start clearing the field. They'd finished by the time he returned. Macumber heard his name being shouted over the unit's intercom that day, Gilbert summoning him. What the hell, Gilbert sputtered, didn't I tell you not to build this? No, Macumber replied, you told me you didn't want to *see* me build it. Later, after Gilbert retired, he happened to spot Macumber in downtown Phoenix, on Jaycee business. Gilbert crossed the street to greet him and shake his hand.

In June 1981, when the Phoenix Jaycees hosted the annual Arizona Jaycee awards dinner, they invited Macumber and allowed him to bring his parents. As the Jaycees handed out awards for their various programs, Macumber heard the Roadrunners name called time and again; that year, their chapter ended up the third most awarded in the state. Finally the moment came to bestow one last honor, the President of the Year Award, chosen by the chapter presidents and the state board of directors. Ron Walker announced the winner: Bill Macumber, selected unanimously. Macumber walked to the podium amid a standing ovation, accepting there a plaque and a shining silver belt buckle. He looked out at the crowd, first seeing his beaming parents, then the warden of the

Florence prison, smiling and clapping with everyone else. Never before in the history of the United States Jaycees had an inmate chapter president won this award.

During these industrious years with the Jaycees in the early 1980s, prison authorities changed Macumber's "home" several times, but he remained the Roadrunner chapter president and continued his monthly trips to Jaycee meetings. He often made a second trip each month, for Ron Walker had appointed him to the Arizona Jaycees Awards Committee. He enjoyed the long drives, especially since he and his escort would usually stop for a good meal before returning to Florence.

Eventually, prison officials moved Macumber to the Outside Trustee Unit, a minimum-custody section at Florence. Macumber had not thought it possible for anyone with a natural life sentence to see OT, but there he was. They gave him a bed in the warehouse, a large hall with some three hundred inmates. On his second day, they assigned him to work as a Florence Complex plumber, under the supervision of a civilian named Charlie Dumar—who promptly drove Bill to the nearby town of Coolidge so he could take a driver's test and get a current Arizona state driver's license. Macumber's surprise over this doubled when Dumar, the next morning, told him to take their truck to Phoenix and pick up a load of gas pipe from Phoenix Pipe and Steel. Bill assumed there would be an escort, but Dumar said no, go on your own. Macumber drove alone to Phoenix and back that day—a type of freedom he thought he'd never see again. He stopped at a Jack in the Box on the way home, since Dumar had handed him lunch money. He never considered running; that, he'd explain later, would deny everything he wished to prove. Besides, he'd given the guards his word. When he pulled into the plumbers' yard that evening, Dumar greeted him with a big smile.

From then on, his various trips to Phoenix and other places were sometimes escorted, sometimes not. The escorted trips usually came about because one of the guards, Jim Piekarz, a Jaycee member, enjoyed the outings. When going together, they took Piekarz's personal car; when alone, Bill drove a prison pickup. Macumber also started visiting other prisons in the state, reporting on and recruiting for the Jaycees. On a few evenings, he and Piekarz even stopped to visit Macumber's parents and have dinner, the guard right there at the table with his family. Things were quite relaxed back then—that's the only way Macumber could explain the situation years later.

The Outside Trustee Unit had its own Jaycee chapter, ASPOT Jaycees, headed by Paul LaBarre, a onetime civilian Jaycee in Phoenix, now a prisoner with five consecutive sentences for robbery. He asked Macumber to join his chapter as well, and Bill agreed. LaBarre also asked Macumber to come work with him at the Florence Complex's TV studio, which he ran. Bill jumped at the opportunity; after a year on the plumbing job, he'd had his fill of cleaning plugged sewer lines. LaBarre began teaching him the TV business—installation and maintenance and the technical aspects of transmission over a closed circuit. For Macumber, it felt like going to college all over again.

LaBarre had yet another project for Macumber. The Florence prison ran the Outlaw Rodeo, an annual three-day event attended by both free-world and inmate cowboys. The prison administrators had staged this themselves in 1983 and 1984—and had lost money both years. So they handed it to the ASPOT Jaycees in 1985. Working together, LaBarre and Macumber pulled it off, showing a profit of more than $36,000, most of it donated to charities such as Special Olympics, the Make-a-Wish Foundation and the Jerry Lewis Muscular Dystrophy Association telethon. By the next year, LaBarre was gone, released, and Macumber found himself serving as president of the ASPOT Jaycees, director of the Florence TV studio and chairman of the 1986 Prison Outlaw Rodeo. He knew he could run the Jaycees and the TV studio—in fact, that year he designed and implemented a new state-of-the-art closed-circuit satellite television system for Florence. But he wasn't certain about staging a profitable three-day rodeo on his own.

He began by making a number of trips to Phoenix to sell advertising for the rodeo magazine, something that had not been done before. Then, using a stray truckload of forty-foot-long steel pipes, he saw a way for the Roadrunners to install lights on the Florence prison rodeo grounds, so they could have an evening performance as well as the afternoon rodeos on Friday, Saturday and Sunday. Over a weekend, a crew of forty Jaycee inmates, working around the clock, assembled the pipes into ten tall poles equipped with crossbars, lights and wiring. Inmate ingenuity, they called it. With an evening performance and magazine advertising to go along with the usual entry fees, ticket sales and snack bar proceeds, they cleared just over $70,000—all but $2,500 again donated to charities.

When Macumber finally stepped down as president of his Jaycee chapter, he became editor of the Arizona Jaycee newspaper and special adviser to the state Jaycee president. In that role he traveled throughout Arizona, speaking and teaching at street and prison chapters, civic groups and high schools. He also took a job, for Arizona Correctional Industries, overseeing the two inmate crews that installed ACI-produced furniture in the Peoria school district. In his spare time, he converted a reach of high desert outside the prison into arable farmland and taught inmates how to grow their own crops. He arranged, as well, for a local sundry store in Florence to sell inmates' artwork and handicrafts. Newspapers in Arizona were now publishing feature articles about him.

Macumber eventually realized he was earning a PhD in people. In prison, he met so many types. He learned to evaluate rather than judge, focusing on how people spoke, what they said, their expressions and tone. He could goof around with anyone. He could kid, challenge, give them trouble. As time went on, he became a kind of counselor and mediator for the younger inmates, parenting and teaching and policing, as needed. Some of the teaching took place in the yard and the dayroom, some in formal classes—among others, he taught courses in spiritual development, planning techniques and management development, offering each class several times, with nearly four hundred inmates participating overall. The mediating and settling of disputes among inmates often happened at the request of the warden. Prisoners and guards alike came to venerate him. During visitation hours on Sundays, inmates at other tables would bring their families to meet Macumber, explaining to their relatives how much Bill had changed their lives, how much they cared about him, how much they'd do for him. Macumber would always beam and shake hands and toss a line to their parents: *I give him trouble, but he deserves it.*

When alone, Macumber would write—pages and pages of poetry, essays and fiction. Over time, the pages became books: twenty-four novels (mysteries, adventures, westerns), four children's novellas, a nonfiction history, a collection of poems. The poems kept coming, twenty-six hundred in all. Sixteen won poetry contests; eleven made it into anthologies.

A good deal of Macumber's writing stayed as typed pages, but *History's Trail*, his collection of poems about the Arizona desert, was published in a limited edition in 1984. It sold more than five thousand copies at the Florence store he helped establish, and remains available at various Arizona public and university libraries. Macumber included a dedication page: "I dedicate this work with pride and love to my three sons, Scott, Steve and Ron Macumber." At the time, he had not seen or heard from his boys in nine years.

Despite all his activity and achievement in prison, Macumber had never stopped trying to win his freedom. With the legal appeals to the courts exhausted, no funds for a lawyer and no possibility of parole, he looked to the Arizona Board of Pardons and Paroles for clemency, filing an application in the early summer of 1983, when he was forty-seven. This panel did not concern itself with questions of guilt or innocence; it assumed that verdicts were correct, sentences fair. Its purpose, rather, at least in cases such as Macumber's, was to recommend commutation of sentences when the board members saw mitigating circumstances—usually a prisoner's demonstration of remorse and rehabilitation. They were, in other words, dispensers of grace and mercy—to those who repented.

Macumber, though, could not seek mercy based on remorse and rehabilitation, since he, as always, maintained his innocence. He filled out the form as best he could. Asked in one section to explain why he felt entitled to a change in sentence, he wrote, "First, because I was in no way involved with the crime for which I was convicted, and secondly because additional incarceration will have no positive bearing on my future actions and only inhibit the positive contributions I could make in the free world. Finally, I pose no threat whatsoever to any member of society." Asked to describe his involvement in the crimes that had put him in prison, Macumber simply wrote, "I was not involved with or in the crime for which I was convicted."

Mainly, he documented all he had accomplished in prison over the previous four years. Macumber's prison counselor added a confidential progress report: "I have only seen this resident once, his file is exemplary. His file reveals and substantiates his writing capabilities. He is calm, courteous and cooperative during interviews." In further support, Macumber enclosed copies of two newspaper feature articles written about him; a pile of glowing letters from Arizona Jaycee officers and members; another pile from former neighbors, friends and colleagues; copies of his awards, commendations and certificates; samples of his poetry and a list of the prizes they'd won; and an inventory of all the writing he'd completed so far. One particularly compelling letter came from a fellow inmate in North Unit whom Macumber had recruited to be a Roadrunner vice president. "It has been my privilege to know Bill Macumber since September of 1979," wrote Cleatus G. King. He continued:

> Over the years Bill and I have become close personal friends. Bill and I come from two entirely different worlds. He from the stable, citizen-type world and I from a totally criminal kind of environment. I have never, in all my life, been involved in any type of activity even remotely resembling the Jaycees. I would have thought such a thing to be extremely funny had someone even suggested such a thing. I was finding it difficult to stay out of trouble for two days at a time let alone get involved in something as straight as Jaycees.
>
> In 1979, Bill moved from the Central Unit to the North Unit and I followed a few months later. Not long after I arrived there the Roadrunners Chapter was chartered and Bill managed to talk me into joining. Bill became our first President and I, somehow, managed to get myself elected to the Internal Vice President's position.... Bill has a management and business background and he began to school me in both management and his personal philosophies. Strangely enough, I began to notice a change in myself. Slowly but surely I was

stepping away from the outlaw and towards the kind of man who was my friend and that I was learning from. . . .

Now we are into our third year and I again find myself on the Board as Internal VP. . . . I have managed to become a model convict by the administration's description and I attribute this directly to Bill Macumber. The difference between myself now and what I was a few years back is like night and day, and the same applies to many men in this Chapter. . . . Myself and many others can clearly attest to the interest and faith that Bill Macumber has placed in so many of us. . . . I would respectfully like to submit his name to you for your consideration.

In the final sections of his application, Macumber spoke directly on his own behalf. "I was in no way involved in the double murder for which I was convicted . . . ," he wrote. "I did not know either of the victims nor did I have any motive for committing these crimes. A man by the name of Ernest Valenzuela confessed to this crime in front of four different witnesses and had a motive for this crime. There are also signed statements from an eyewitness who was present when the crime was committed. All of this information is a matter of public record . . . however it was never heard or known to be in existence [by] the jury. . . . I realize that the vast majority of people convicted of crimes make this same statement, yet the fact remains that some of them are telling the truth, and that truth has been supported in later years. . . . I firmly believe the same thing will happen in my case."

Macumber pointed out that he had never been in trouble with the law before his conviction, not even a traffic ticket. He invited the board to compare his activities and efforts to help others before and since his incarceration: "You will see that my interests and motivations have not changed . . . I am the same man I have always been. . . . My lifestyle and personality has remained constant since my teens." He also invited the board to consider certain assumptions.

Assumption No. 1: "If I am in fact guilty of the crimes for which I have been convicted, then you have to believe that for a few short seconds out of my forty-seven years I became a totally different man and for no known reason murdered two people that I did not know. I would have then had to immediately change back to my former self and continue my life for twelve years until my alleged crime was uncovered."

Assumption No. 2: "If I am in fact guilty of these crimes then I have managed to totally fool everyone including my family, friends, associates and members of the staff of D.O.C. for a total of twenty-one years, because these crimes were committed back in May of 1962."

Assumption No. 3: "That I am in fact not guilty of the crimes for which I was convicted, sentenced and incarcerated and that I was (a) a victim of circumstance or (b) a victim of a concentrated effort to get me out of the way by my ex-wife and her associates."

With that, Macumber concluded his petition by thanking the board "for taking the time to look through all of this information as well as the supportive documents that are included."

Whether the board in fact looked through all the information cannot be said. Following usual procedure, the board held a preliminary Phase I commutation of sentence hearing, without the prisoner present, to decide whether to advance to a Phase II personal hearing. That decision, as conveyed to Macumber: "To DENY and NOT to pass you to a Phase II personal hearing at this time."

Macumber tried again in November 1988, filing a second application for commutation of sentence. This time his letters of recommendation included enthusiastic paeans from the chief security officer for the prison's North Unit ("He was traveling throughout the State of Arizona teaching personal development and attending various meetings. . . . Not once was he ever involved in a problem"); his ACI job supervisors ("He has had a major impact on the Florence Complex. . . . His leadership abilities have aided him in training other inmates, giving them a sense of worth and responsibility"); Charlie Dumar ("On many occasions I have sent Bill by himself to do various jobs. I have no problem with him leaving this facility alone. . . . If I was in business I would hire Bill without a second thought"); and the president of the Arizona Jaycees ("I consider it a privilege to write a letter for him and wish that I could do more. . . . If Bill was released today he would be welcome in my home or as my next door neighbor. I consider him to be a very special individual who cares a great deal for his fellow man"). Macumber included as well a formal commutation of sentence proposal, prepared by a professional criminal justice consultant hired by his father. "Mr. Macumber has maintained his innocence in this case from the very beginning," the consultant wrote at the end of his proposal. "He is not asking the Board to rule on that issue. . . . Rather the issue is whether or not Mr. Macumber has satisfactorily demonstrated his ability to return to the community with minimum danger to others."

Once more, the board rejected Macumber's petition without advancing to the second stage: "It was the decision of the Board at your Phase I Commutation of Sentence Hearing on February 1, 1989, to DENY and NOT to pass you to a Phase II personal hearing at this time."

Macumber tried yet again, filing a third application in 1992, along with an updated proposal from the criminal justice consultant. Bill was fifty-six now and since his second conviction had been in prison for fifteen years. He well understood the difficulty of his particular situation. Because the Scottsdale murders occurred in May 1962, he'd been sentenced under Arizona's 1956 criminal code, making him one of the few remaining "old-code lifers." Lifers sentenced under the newer 1973 statute were by law automatically eligible for parole after twenty-five years, but the older statute didn't specifically address parole eligibility—old-code lifers were entirely dependent on clemency for release. "As it currently stands," Macumber wrote in his application, "I am faced with no hope for the future in that I have no possibility for parole. I am therefore requesting that my sentence be given a bottom number such that I will have some light at the end of the tunnel, regardless of what it might be." The consultant recommended that he serve twenty years, which would put that light five years in the future.

If nothing else, the board remained consistent: In December 1992, for the third time, it denied Macumber's application without passing him to a Phase II hearing.

Even while Macumber sought mercy during those years, he and his father also looked once more to the justice system and the prospect of reopening Bill's case. In July 1983, just as Macumber was filing his first clemency petition, Bedford Douglass received a phone call from a former

Maricopa County Sheriff's Office evidence technician named Dave Brewer. The Macumber case had always troubled him, Brewer told Douglass. There'd been lots of funny business in the department back then. He wanted to talk.

Douglass explained that he didn't represent Macumber anymore. He advised Brewer to contact Bill or his father. So on August 30, Brewer called Harold, who two days later summarized their phone conversation in a letter to his brother-in-law: "He told me . . . he would tell us everything that he knew and would testify in court for us if it would do any good. He said that he knew Carol and what she was up to at the sheriff's office, that she had had affairs with several of the officers and had tapes to hold over their heads if they didn't help her when she wanted them to. . . . That the shell casings were kept in the desk drawer of a Mr. Hart and were available to her at any time. . . . If it can be proven it should bust things wide open and bring about his release very soon."

After talking to Brewer, Harold had called Bedford Douglass, relaying what he'd heard. He reported that conversation to his brother-in-law, as well: "Douglass told me Bill should write him and he would get into it again. In fact, he sounded rather eager to do just that. . . . I suppose we will be in the thick of it very soon. I believe that once we get going on it again that several ex-sheriffs will be stepping forward with what they know so it is hard to tell just how much it will snow-ball. It looks like the best chance Bill has had since he was arrested."

Bill Macumber wrote to Bedford Douglass in early September. Yes, he affirmed, he certainly would be interested in having Bedford look into this Dave Brewer matter, though "I do not have any income, so whatever is to be done will have to be by your office. . . . For seven long years I have been putting together bits and pieces of information given to me by former members of MCSD that now work for the Department of Corrections, but it was never enough to do anything. Thank God I think things have finally taken a turn in our favor. . . . The only question left then is, are you willing to take me on again . . . ? I have waited so long, Bedford, for something positive to happen and I truly believe that the time has finally come. If you can agree to take this case again I would be forever in your debt."

It took Douglass a while, as he had many open cases, but he finally called Dave Brewer late that year. They arranged to meet on December 8, 1983. That morning, they talked for ninety minutes, Douglass tape-recording the conversation, with an investigator for the public defender's office, Warren Granville, also present. Brewer began by describing the Maricopa sheriff's department in the 1970s as a place where evidence—for the Scottsdale murders and other cases—was readily available in unlocked drawers to everyone who worked there. Shells, latent finger-prints, files, everything. Brewer then turned to a conversation he'd had with Corporal Richard Diehl on Saturday morning, August 24, 1974—one day after Carol gave her statement to deputies and four days before Bill's arrest. They were alone together in the department's ID room. Diehl had some latents from the Scottsdale murders he wanted Brewer to compare with Bill Macumber's fingerprints. First, though, they fell to talking. Brewer recalled their conversation for Douglass.

"This was at the time they were breaking the case . . . ," he began. "Macumber, I'm not sure if he was already charged but they were prepar-ing to charge him. And as I remember [Diehl] was in internal affairs at the time. . . ." Diehl told him that they had "done an investigation on Carol." They were going to fire her. They found out that she had been "involved with several deputies and Phoenix police officers," that she "had tape recorded some of the meetings." So they "made a deal." Carol kept her job and "she turned Macumber on the homicide."

"This conversation . . . ," Douglass asked, "it was around the time he was first arrested?"

"Yeah because Diehl told me about it and then brought the latents in for comparison. I ran the comparison, as I remember it was a two finger sequence of fingerprints. They weren't Macumber's."

DOUGLASS: How long after you had the conversation with Diehl did he bring the prints in for you to compare?
BREWER: Same morning.
DOUGLASS: And he told you that Internal Affairs had been investigat-ing . . . Carol Macumber?
BREWER: Carol, that's right. . . .
DOUGLASS: The sheriff's office had to make a deal?
BREWER: Right. . . .

DOUGLASS: So Carol agreed to make a case against her husband for
not being fired and being allowed to keep her job?

BREWER: Right.

DOUGLASS: And what happened to the tapes?

BREWER: I don't know.

DOUGLASS: Did Diehl say that the sheriff got the tapes from Carol?

BREWER: No I don't remember him saying that. . . .

Warren Granville, Douglass's investigator, here joined the conversation, drawing Brewer back to his comparison that morning of Macumber's prints.

GRANVILLE: Can I just interject here. . . . Who presented those to you
for comparison, was that Diehl?

BREWER: Diehl, yeah.

GRANVILLE: Do you recall where he got those latents for a comparison?

BREWER: He went down the hall and came back with them.

GRANVILLE: And when you did your comparison you found out
there was no comparison. . . .

BREWER: There was no identification.

GRANVILLE: No identification. Did you tell Diehl at that time and
what did Diehl say to you?

BREWER: He said thank you.

GRANVILLE: Did he come back with an additional set of prints?

BREWER: I never had any more to do with it.

Douglass and Granville then turned the conversation back to Bill
and Carol.

DOUGLASS: You mentioned that you were not convinced that Macumber committed the murders, or that the casings introduced at
trial were the casings actually found at the scene of the homicide?
Why are you not convinced?

BREWER: Well, I knew Macumber. . . . I'd known him for awhile at
parties and stuff and he was active in the Sheriff's Posse and he

didn't seem to me like he was a homicidal maniac or anything, and then they were having a lot of marital problems.

DOUGLASS: He and Carol?

BREWER: He and Carol . . . I just, I just never was convinced that Bill would have done anything. . . . And with the casings. . . . Because there was no chain of custody and I always wondered if those casings could have been handled by anybody. . . .

GRANVILLE: Did you know Carol Macumber personally?

BREWER: I worked with her, you know. . . . I knew enough to stay away from her.

GRANVILLE: Well, what do you mean by that?

BREWER: I didn't care for her. She was very abrasive. I didn't trust her.

Long ago, Bedford Douglass had heard similar reports about Carol from sheriff's department sources. It was these reports he'd vainly tried to confirm by seeking Carol's personnel file at a hearing months before Macumber's second trial. Yet now, in 1983, he saw little use for Brewer's account, which likely involved hearsay. Douglass never followed up with Brewer, and many years later could not recall taking his statement. The public defender's office just was not going to reopen and reinvestigate a closed case. For that, Bill Macumber would need an innocence project.

PART TWO

QUEST FOR JUSTICE

CHAPTER 11

Arizona Justice Project

By the time the Macumber case came to Larry Hammond's attention, he was both an icon and a lightning rod in the legal world—at least that part of the legal world concerned with such matters as public interest, civil liberties and criminal justice. He'd accrued his outsized achievements by fighting hard, which meant offending others when needed. In fact, he'd had to battle even to become a lawyer. Born in Wichita, raised in El Paso by religious Episcopalian parents—his father a wholesale druggist, his mother a music teacher—Hammond as a child suffered from asthma and a crippling stutter. The stutter hampered him as a student, the asthma as an athlete—he instead became a fanatic baseball fan.

He came to regard his stuttering as a sign of intellectual inadequacy. While attending the University of New Mexico, though, he noticed that his stutter abated when he spoke in a foreign language—so he majored in Russian. Then he enrolled at the University of Texas law school, forcing himself to stand and stutter before large lecture classes. He flourished there, becoming editor of the law review, a job that required research and writing, not speaking. As he liked to put it, he'd "never knocked over an idea and looked at it" until law school, but now, encouraged by an older student, he came to see that the fun of law school was pondering and debating big ideas. He hadn't really done that before; he'd never read or argued deeply. He didn't transform overnight—even in the political and cultural tumult of the late sixties, he mainly remained closeted in his studies. His incremental evolution continued when, upon graduating in 1970, he was selected to clerk for a renowned U.S. Court of Appeals judge, Carl McGowan, who in a gentle, unpretentious way urged him to devote part of his time to pro bono work. Then Justice Hugo Black picked Hammond to clerk for him at the U.S. Supreme Court, and when Black died months later, his replacement, Justice Lewis Powell, kept Hammond on. Hammond's evolution continued: While researching and writing drafts for Powell in the landmark capital punishment case *Furman v. Georgia*, he privately came to believe the death penalty unconstitutional, at least when imposed in an arbitrary way. (He kept this view to himself, for it conflicted with Powell's thinking.) After his Supreme Court clerkship, Hammond took a position as assistant Watergate special prosecutor under Archibald Cox, serving on a task force prosecuting former U.S. Attorney General Richard Kleindienst, accused of lying to Congress to protect President Nixon. He quit in late 1974 when special prosecutor Leon Jaworski approved a lenient plea deal for Kleindienst, and ended up at an elite ten-lawyer firm in Phoenix where half the attorneys were former U.S. Supreme Court clerks.

When he arrived there, Hammond still had no clear idea of what he wanted to do as a lawyer. He knew only that whatever path he chose, he'd have to talk, and this terrified him. Then his firm assigned him to serve as co-counsel on a school desegregation case in Tucson, where his clients were a group of black children who'd been deprived of resources and dumped into the district's poorest schools. Because of a judge's mandate, he first spent a full year working on written witness statements, something he could do easily for it involved no public speaking. When the trial began, Hammond felt his old familiar terror, for now he'd have to talk in a courtroom—a capacious one at that, fitted with a microphone at the podium. But as he began to cross-examine his first witness, a statistician for the school district, Hammond could hear his own voice booming from the speakers, resonating across the room—and he found he could speak clearly, his stutter gone.

This trial would prove pivotal to his development as a lawyer. Hammond not only gained his voice, he won the case. It was classic NAACP fodder: black children, intentional discrimination, a school district assigning blacks to all-black schools, busing patterns that bypassed white schools, uneven allocation of resources. Hammond thought the case great fun—living in a Tucson hovel of an apartment for months, fighting for something important instead of plodding through the usual boring practice of law. Everything he did *mattered*. Everything he did had an impact. Hammond came to see how bad things could be if lawyers like him didn't volunteer to help. That's how it started for Hammond, that's how he found his calling.

Later, during the Carter administration, he returned to Washington to serve as first deputy assistant attorney general in the Office of Legal Counsel. In that job, death penalty issues once again drew his attention, for President Carter asked his team to prepare a white paper about capital punishment. He also once again had to talk—in fact, he often had to testify before Congress. As before, he discovered that when he spoke into a microphone—when he heard his voice resonating through the room—his stutter receded. By 1980, he was back practicing at his small, exclusive law firm in Phoenix and speaking without hindrance in the courtroom.

His firm handled mainly civil litigation, often representing plaintiffs on a contingency basis. Hammond was doing what he thought right, his clients often powerless victims of malfeasance. But by now he had an urge to develop a criminal law practice and tackle death penalty cases. He got his chance at a backyard barbecue in early 1981, when a deputy public defender, John Foreman, struck up a conversation with him and his law partner, James Scarboro, who had clerked for Justice Byron White. Foreman described the challenges of representing people on death row. Scarboro, intrigued, suggested that Foreman give them a call if he ever needed help. Well, Foreman said, we need help right now.

The defendant was John Henry Knapp, a Mesa taxicab driver. He'd been convicted in the arson deaths of his two young children and sentenced to death by Judge Charles Hardy on the very day before Hardy started presiding over Bill Macumber's first trial. Foreman thought the case involved reasonable doubt, but Knapp no longer had a lawyer. The clock was ticking, his execution fast approaching.

A complex civil case just then consumed Hammond—he was representing a group of homeowners whose community had been destroyed by floods when a panicked dam operator opened the gates at a lake above their houses. The entire firm, for that matter, had an overload of civil cases. They'd even had to turn down a lucrative lawsuit involving the collapse of a public auditorium's roof. Nonetheless, Hammond and Scarboro decided to visit Knapp at the state prison in Florence. When they returned, they called their eight partners into a meeting and urged them to lift the moratorium on taking new cases—they wanted to represent Knapp. Sitting in the firm's conference room, Scarboro presented their reasons, saying he considered it their obligation, as lawyers practicing in a state that had the death penalty, to understand it firsthand. Hammond agreed: If we're going to practice law in this state, he argued, we need to get our hands dirty. A corporate partner asked, Do you think he's innocent? Scarboro said, I don't know. The partner asked, Could we give him a lie detector test? Scarboro said, Good idea. We'll do it at the same time we give all our corporate clients tests.

That ended the meeting—and started not only Hammond's pro bono defense of John Knapp but his path toward becoming one of the best-known death penalty lawyers in Arizona. He would spend more than ten years on the Knapp case, taking over as lead counsel when Scarboro moved to Colorado in September 1984. He would win a stay of execution and then a new trial for Knapp. He would hire fire experts to conduct "flashover" arson tests, challenging the core forensic evidence against his client. He would lure Tom Henze—the prosecutor in Macumber's first trial, now a prominent criminal defense attorney—to serve as his co-counsel. He would level prosecutorial misconduct charges, in a motion to dismiss, against the deputy county attorney who'd handled Knapp's first trial. He would, in December 1991, see Knapp's new trial end in a hung jury, the prosecution costing Maricopa County's indigent-defense fund more than $450,000 and Hammond's law firm more than $1.5 million in donated time. Everyone wanted to settle except Hammond—he was ready to go to trial again. Instead, in November 1992, Knapp entered

a no-contest plea to a reduced second-degree murder charge and, for time already served, walked free.

Hammond also won reversal of another arson-murder conviction: Ray Girdler, found guilty in 1982 of killing his wife and young daughter, gained release in 1990 after Hammond once again established that what state experts called arson had been a spontaneous "flashover" fire. He played an advising or secondary role in the exonerations of other prisoners as well—among them Paris Carriger, who faced execution for a murder and robbery, and George Peterson, a mentally disturbed veteran who'd falsely confessed to a rape and murder. He successfully pursued a mammoth pro bono case on behalf of state prisoners opposing involuntary transfer from protective segregation to the general population. He joined the board of a newly formed group meant to serve as backup support for lawyers handling capital cases. Hammond had become the go-to lawyer for victims of manifest injustice in Arizona.

This did not sit well with all of his partners. Hammond's law firm split up in 1995, in good part because of his and some like-minded colleagues' inclination to take on consuming unpaid criminal cases. The Knapp and Girdler cases in particular caused the split: With $3 million in donated time and $500,000 in expenses—the expenses a bigger issue than what they didn't earn—Hammond could see how some of the older partners might object. They had more than eighty lawyers in the firm now, and they'd come from varying cultures and cities, so did not hold a common view or mission. Hammond and a few of his closest colleagues decided to leave the firm—but they then learned that twenty-five lawyers wanted to join them. So they elected instead to stay and to invite the others to depart. In this fashion, Hammond in 1995 presided over the founding of his current law firm, Osborn Maledon, a boutique practice with forty-five lawyers, three working full-time in criminal law.

Over the years, Hammond would handle his share of lucrative civil litigation, enough to be offered membership in the prestigious American College of Trial Lawyers. The invitation, he liked to say, represented a testimonial to a fraud—though he'd handled several high-profile civil cases, he chafed at doing so. He prayed that the legal community would continue to see him as a civil attorney, for it made his firm a lot of money, but in his soul he was a civil liberties and criminal defense attorney,

representing the indigent and disenfranchised. He and his closest founding partner, Bill Maledon, who'd clerked for Justice William Brennan, billed the most hours for Osborn Maledon—about 2,500 to 3,000 each a year—but their compensation differed substantially, since Maledon collected every dollar he billed and Hammond had to write off about a third of his hours. That was fine with him. After all, he had by far the better deal: He had the ability to do exactly what he wanted.

What Hammond most wanted was to launch the Arizona Justice Project. For some time, the Arizona Attorneys for Criminal Justice (AACJ) had been urging the creation of such a group in the state. In 1992, Barry Scheck and Peter Neufeld had founded the nationally renowned Innocence Project, the nonprofit legal clinic affiliated with the Benjamin N. Cardozo School of Law at Yeshiva University in New York. By 1998, four other such clinics had started around the country. In Arizona, AACJ lawyers weighed how to proceed. As criminal attorneys, some of them argued, we don't defend just the innocent. To call something an "innocence" project demeaned what they did.

On Sunday, January 18, 1998, at the AACJ annual convention in Prescott, a half dozen members were standing in a hallway. Tired of hearing the same debate again, someone said, Why don't we call it a justice project? That solved the problem. Yes, they'd use that name. Their mission would not be to defend any and all criminal defendants. Their mission would be to handle "innocence and manifest injustice" claims. And unlike Scheck and Neufeld's group at the Cardozo law school, which focused solely on cases with DNA evidence, they'd take cases that involved any credible evidence that might firmly establish actual innocence or significant injustice. But they wouldn't take death penalty cases; they wanted to represent inmates who couldn't get help elsewhere, and prisoners sentenced to death already drew the cream of the capital defense bar. After everyone finally agreed to these terms, the Arizona Justice Project came to be in January 1998—with that "innocence and manifest injustice" language in their literature, and Larry Hammond as founding chair.

They had no money, no infrastructure at all. The AACJ itself had an office and director, but nothing for the project. Hammond's law firm,

Osborn Maledon, agreed to provide some pro bono assistance: a paralegal part-time, space for files, postage and printing. Hammond's administrative assistant, Donna Toland, would essentially have to run the Justice Project out of her hip pocket. Hammond's biggest fear was that someone would find out they existed. Then they'd be inundated. So they had to move slowly and quietly. AACJ members and the local criminal defense bar would stand by, provide support, handle the individual cases. The Justice Project would just be a clearinghouse. We'll get cases, Hammond reasoned, and refer each to a lawyer.

That's not how things worked out, though. Hammond found it difficult to farm out cases—lots of lawyers in AACJ had promised to volunteer their time, but few did. In fact, lawyers all around the state started sending not just their most troubling cases to the Justice Project but all their mail from prisoners, all the pleas for help. Very soon, the prisoners themselves discovered the Justice Project and began writing directly to it. Within months they were inundated, just as Hammond had feared.

Then he discovered, to his horror, an entire room of unopened letters at the AACJ headquarters. He thought they at least had a system for managing the onslaught. The AACJ lawyers hadn't even told Hammond about the letters, which had gone unanswered for months. Hammond decided to get a truck and move the whole room of files to Osborn Maledon. He and Donna Toland took it over, the entire operation, with a small handful of other lawyers helping. They would be the hub. If you wrote to the Justice Project, your request would come to Osborn Maledon, to Larry and Donna and the firm's paralegals. They would respond to each letter within one month, and with a personal message, not a form. Hammond didn't want inmates getting identical letters that suggested they weren't respected. He set up a dedicated Justice Project mailbox at his law firm. Donna referred the emergencies right away, while other letters piled up, Hammond tossing them into a big cardboard banker's box he hauled around with him—to his home, to his office on Sundays, and often to his cabin up in the national forest near Diamond Point, a hundred miles north of Phoenix. When the pile of letters reached the top of the box, Hammond knew he had at least eight hours' worth of work. He'd punch his tape recorder on and start dictating his responses. It became a big part of his practice, all listed as pro bono hours. He felt compelled to treat these letters as diligently as he did Osborn Maledon's paying clients. Yes, more than 90 percent of the letters had no real merit, and only 5 percent called for a detailed examination. At best, they'd take on 1 percent. But Hammond couldn't know which 1 percent without reviewing all of them. He had to make sure there wasn't a rattlesnake hiding in the pile.

The Benitez case had been just such a rattlesnake. Steven Benitez, an inmate who had a prison gang contract on his head, was supposed to be in protective segregation but ended up in the general population. There, in his cell one night in late January 1998, Mexican Mafia members stabbed him to death. Benitez's mother, Mary, called Hammond to report the news. You should know his name, she said, because he wrote to you a couple of times. Hammond went back, looked at their files. They hadn't screwed up, they had responded—but they hadn't done everything they could. Hammond didn't feel at all good about it. From then on, he vowed, they'd open every piece of mail from inmates. They'd at least have a paralegal evaluate every single letter.

The Justice Project was just nine months old, still more a notion than an organization, when, on September 18, 1998, Hammond received a phone call from Judge O'Toole. At the time, O'Toole had been a Maricopa County Superior Court judge for fourteen years, including a stint as presiding criminal department judge. He had before him the letter he'd received from Macumber's cousin Jackie Kelley. He had the Supreme Court's Vince Foster decision. He had Steve Wilson's column from the *Arizona Republic*. Most important, he had his abiding memories of Ernest Valenzuela and the irksome hearing in Judge Corcoran's courtroom.

Now that he was a judge himself, O'Toole could see clearly what Corcoran had done. He'd so smartly bypassed the attorney-client privilege, once the defense effectively addressed it by getting a waiver from Ernie's mother. Instead, Corcoran had hung his denial on the hearsay rule and that "insufficient trustworthiness" language. He was sharp—O'Toole, like Bedford Douglass, had to give Corcoran that much. He'd seen the hole in Holohan's minority Supreme Court opinion and had driven right through it. But O'Toole thought that Corcoran's ruling displayed a narrow sense of justice. In his own years on the bench, he always preferred to let the jurors hear the evidence, to let them decide. Then again, he didn't share Corcoran's kind of ambition—Corcoran had aspired to rise to the Arizona Supreme Court, so he'd made sure to not get reversed. O'Toole knew him quite well: Though a bright, even nice guy, Corcoran, he thought, was full of himself, with a kind of smirk to his smile and what O'Toole considered a tedious, deliberate manner. Corcoran had surely used the notorious Macumber case as a springboard. Four years later, in 1981, he won appointment to the state court of appeals. Eight years after that, in 1989, he reached his goal: a seat on the Arizona Supreme Court, where he replaced, of all justices, William Holohan.

O'Toole, looking back with the perspective of time and experience, objected not only to Corcoran's decision but also the Arizona Supreme Court's affirmation. O'Toole fumed particularly at how the court characterized his testimony at the evidentiary hearing: *The attorney indicated that the murder confession was simply a passing comment as he and his client were concerned with the defense of another wholly unrelated charge.* The justices had deliberately minimized his account. They had essentially said he should have stopped and chronicled Valenzuela's confession—conduct that would have been utterly unethical.

O'Toole couldn't be certain of Macumber's innocence; really, no one could without DNA evidence. But he'd seen Macumber convicted for murders that Valenzuela had convincingly confessed to. On top of that, he could find no motive for Bill Macumber, nothing in his life to suggest a hidden homicidal rage. Things didn't fit. This case didn't pass the smell test.

That, in essence, was what Judge O'Toole told Hammond on the phone in September 1998. I am aware of this case, he said. I represented the man who confessed to the murders. They had a hearing, Corcoran wouldn't admit my testimony. Look at Corcoran's ruling in light of the Vince Foster case. I'm concerned. I think this man Bill Macumber is innocent.

On the same day he talked to Hammond, Judge O'Toole wrote to Jackie Kelley: "I am belatedly responding to your June 27 letter concerning your cousin, William Wayne Macumber. . . . I am not able to directly assist you regarding your cousin. However, I have contacted the following attorney, who has vast experience and is highly qualified in representing people who are in situations very similar to your cousin. . . . Larry Hammond has graciously agreed to review the matter and offer what direction and assistance he finds appropriate. I suggest that you contact Mr. Hammond to discuss your concerns. By copy of this letter, I am sending him a copy of your letter and the column written by Steve Wilson. I wish you the best of luck."

When Jackie received this letter, she wept and praised the Lord. Sitting at her kitchen counter, looking out a window at her rambling New Mexico property, she believed her prayers had finally been answered. Ever since her cousin's arrest, she'd been fighting for Bill. He had no fiercer champion—she could knock back whiskies with the rowdiest of the good old boys in her region and didn't mind passing them on the curving country roads, even on days full of sleet and snow. Though a devout Christian who played the organ every Sunday morning at the First Baptist Church of Ignacio, a twenty-two-mile drive into Colorado, she'd resisted advice to "trust the Lord" and "leave it in the Lord's hands"—she thought the Lord might need some help from a good appellate lawyer.

She and Bill had grown up together in Iowa, both born in Davenport. Her family moved eighty miles north to Cedar Rapids when she was three, but being an only child, she often visited relatives during the summers. Jackie's mom and Bill's mom were sisters, and Jackie just adored her Aunt Mimi and Uncle Harold. She'd spend weeks on end at the Macumber house, playing games with Bill and his brother. They grew up in a time and place when young children could be out on the streets during the evening, on their own, with no one worrying. Halfway between Bill's house and Jackie's grandparents' was Castles Ice Cream, with its crenellated roof; when the cousins could talk a grown-up out of a nickel, they'd buy two dips of ice cream on a cone. For five cents, they could also see movies every Saturday night during the summer, on the giant outdoor screen set up at the redbrick school across from her grandparents' home. Either Aunt Mimi or Jackie's grandmother would serve a big bowl of popcorn. They'd sit on folding chairs, watching comedies and horror films. They'd never miss that. Bill was lots of fun. Jackie never once had a fight with him.

They stayed close as teenagers and young adults, even after Jackie married and had her first child. When her husband, Lee, a navy medic, got sent to Korea in 1952, she moved into the Macumber home and lived there for a year and a half. Bill, in high school then, would take her to the movies and ice skating. He'd also pick her up from where she worked, at International Milling on the Mississippi River, to go hunting in the late afternoon. They hunted for squirrels, mainly. Back then in Iowa, everyone had guns, everyone hunted. They'd grown up with guns. Jackie's dad had taught her to shoot when she was eight. In her time, she'd owned some dozen or so guns, and on her New Mexico spread, she still had four or five. By itself, Jackie liked to say, a gun has never killed.

Once during her sojourn with the Macumbers, late on a night in 1953, Bill came home quite tipsy. He and Harold worked then as plane spotters for the Ground Observer Corps, part of the national civil defense system. Bill had earned a couple of prestigious awards, and two air force officers had traveled from Chicago to present them. They'd taken him out for a nice dinner, then ended up at the VFW hall, where the beer began to flow. At home in bed well past midnight, Jackie heard pebbles being tossed against her upstairs window. Seeing her wobbly cousin tottering on the driveway, she scrambled down the stairs. If his parents caught him, she feared, they'd skin him. Sakes alive, it was hard to drag that drunk six-foot-seven teenager up a flight of stairs, he giggling and she shushing him, but Jackie managed.

As the years passed and they all went off into their lives—the Macumbers moved to Arizona, Jackie had two more children—the cousins saw each other less often, but they still wrote, and visited whenever she got to Phoenix. Jackie was living in Ramona, California, working as a secretary for professors at the Scripps Institution of Oceanography, when she learned Bill had been arrested on a murder charge. Her father informed her as she arrived home from work one day—he'd heard from Harold. "I tell you," Jackie would say many years later, sitting in the kitchen of her New Mexico home, "if Saint Peter were looking at me through this dirty window, I would not be any more nonplussed." She didn't believe it, not for a second. Absolutely no way. They'll discover their mistake, they'll see he's innocent. Jackie could imagine no other outcome.

Yet there had been quite a different outcome. She didn't know what to do after the trials but pray and go visit Bill. The first time, she went to Florence with Aunt Mimi and Uncle Harold. She walked in bug-eyed, never having been in a prison. They sat at a long table with Bill across from them, behind a midlevel glass partition. To see her cousin there left her nearly speechless. Then and at her later visits, Bill always put on a cheerful face. She knew he didn't want others worrying about him. Still, she worried all the time. On the morning she received Judge O'Toole's letter, she'd been worrying and weeping and raging for more than twenty-two years.

"I received your most welcomed letter yesterday," she wrote back on September 27. "I cannot begin to thank you enough, not only for your letter, but for your time in reviewing my cousin's case, and for contacting Mr. Lawrence Hammond on our behalf."

That same day, she wrote to Hammond: "Yesterday I received a most welcomed letter from Judge Thomas W. O'Toole. . . . In the judge's letter, he suggested that I contact you, which I am now doing." She wanted Hammond to have her address and cell phone number—both out of Colorado, she explained, because there were no landlines or post offices in her remote corner of New Mexico. "We are short on money, but long on time and persistence. If you would like to have me come to Phoenix, Arizona, to visit with you, I think I can arrange, somehow, to do that. Both my husband and I are retired, so time is our forte. If there is anything you can do to help me obtain my cousin's release from prison, I would be eternally grateful."

An Osborn Maledon paralegal handling Justice Project matters responded in early October, advising Jackie that "Larry and I" had taken "a look" at her letters and the attachments sent to Judge O'Toole in June. As part of the Justice Project, he explained, "we donate our time to conduct post-conviction research in cases where there is a suspicion that a significant injustice has occurred." The first was an "initial review." For that, he'd appreciate getting from Jackie copies of "any and all documents" related to Macumber's case, particularly transcripts, investigative reports and appellate briefs. "We will contact you after our initial review is complete. At that time we will let you know as to whether or not Mr. Macumber's case is a matter that the Justice Project would be interested in handling."

Jackie had no such documents, but she felt sure that Bill and his brother, Bob, would. She quickly contacted them, asking that they provide everything they had. In mid-October, Bill Macumber shipped off what little he possessed. Bob, it turned out, had much of the second trial's transcript and various other documents. His wife, Clara—known to the family as Toots—was then working less than a mile from the Osborn Maledon law offices in Phoenix. One late October morning, she drove there, the boxes piled in the trunk of her car. She rode the elevator to Hammond's floor, where she found someone to follow her back down and load the boxes onto a cart.

The Justice Project began to look through the documents. Hammond, at first glance, just did not see how the Vince Foster case provided a way to reopen Macumber. One issue in Foster had concerned the waiving of attorney-client privilege in extraordinary circumstances, such as when a dying client confesses to a crime for which another person faces charges. That's why the Macumber rulings had colored the debate in the Foster case during oral argument and in written decisions at the Supreme Court. The discussions about attorney-client privilege there and in other legal forums all addressed the same question: Should the constitutional rights of the accused outweigh the expectations of a dead client? A compelling question, but in the end, Hammond concluded that the Foster opinion didn't answer it—the justices merely raised it as a consideration before ruling in favor of Vince Foster's lawyer. (Only in a powerful dissenting opinion by Justice Sandra Day O'Connor, citing *Macumber*, did the defendant's interests trump the dead client's: "In my view, a criminal defendant's right to exculpatory evidence . . . may, where the testimony is not available from other sources, override a client's posthumous interest in confidentiality. . . . Extreme injustice may occur . . . where a criminal defendant seeks disclosure of a deceased client's confession to the offense. See *State v. Macumber*.")

What was more, given how shrewdly Corcoran had handled the matter in 1976, it didn't initially appear to Hammond that attorney-client privilege represented the key issue in Macumber's case. Corcoran had allowed a full hearing, essentially waiving the attorney-client privilege to do so. He'd heard from various witnesses, then decided that their testimony lacked "sufficient circumstantial probability of trustworthiness."

This was a hectic time for Hammond. Most weeks, without the expected help from volunteer attorneys, he found himself alone, reviewing dozens of letters from desperate inmates. Cases piled up at his law firm. Life became a blur. Years later, he would not even remember the letter he wrote to Bill Macumber on November 16, 1998.

The Justice Project could offer him no help, Hammond reported. "Under the circumstances we do not believe that a petition for Post-Conviction Relief can be filed, as the [Foster] decision does not constitute a change in law applicable to your case. There is much to suggest that the trial court erred in excluding Valenzuela's statements, but the issue has been litigated and we see no way to re-open that topic. Please advise as to the arrangements you would like to have made so that we can return your trial transcripts. I am sorry that we are unable to offer any kind of assistance."

Hammond would look back at this letter with regret and puzzlement. The Justice Project staffers knew of Judge O'Toole's concerns, they knew Macumber had always protested his innocence, but apparently they didn't, at the start, grasp the importance of this case. In hindsight, it appeared to Hammond that they hadn't been paying attention. "Not very flattering," he groaned.

And yet, Hammond did not return the transcripts. Why? Something about the Macumber case still gnawed at him, he realized only later: an enduring echo from his past. *Chambers v. Mississippi*, the most important case he'd ever worked on. Reading through the trial record, he couldn't help but notice that the judges' rulings in *Macumber* all cited *Chambers*, over and over. The judges' rulings, in other words, kept quoting language he'd helped Justice Powell craft back in 1973.

No, Hammond didn't want to let go of Macumber, at least not yet. In 1999, rather than return the transcripts, he asked a Phoenix attorney to give the file a "final review." That attorney, however, turned out to be another of the volunteer lawyers who promised but did not deliver. He held on to the Macumber file for much of 1999, only to return it in

December with a note saying his schedule simply did not allow him "sufficient time to look at the matter in depth."

Then came Jackie Kelley. In December 1999, polite but impatient, unaware of Larry's letter to Bill, she lobbied Hammond from her New Mexico ranch:

> I first wrote you on September 27, 1998. On October 5, 1998, I received a letter from you, requesting copies of all information available on my cousin's case. On October 24, I sent you all I had. I also told you Robert Macumber, brother to William Macumber, had a great deal of material that he would bring down to you personally. Now, of course, I do not know just when he got all this material down to you, nor do I know just how much material there was to go through. . . . I was wondering if it would be at all possible for you to give us an idea of your thinking on this case. I realize that you undoubtedly have a lot of material to go through. I can also well imagine that this is not the only case on which you are working. And I know this is a service you are graciously donating. But, if you could give us any idea of your thinking, it would be greatly appreciated by all of us.

Jackie's letter caught—commanded—Hammond's attention. This would not be the last time she pushed him; they were only beginning their complicated relationship. Hammond wrote back quickly, apologizing for the delay, assuring her that they were looking for a qualified volunteer to review the file. They had also recently forged "very positive relationships" with law schools in Arizona, and "law students in conjunction with faculty members have agreed to review a number of our cases." They might very well assign this file to such a team. Hammond had *Chambers* on his mind now, and more. "The Macumber case remains high on our list," he advised Jackie. Macumber's case was "a disturbing one, to be sure."

How to tackle it, though? With limited resources, Hammond considered his options. On his desk sat a phone message from the Phoenix lawyer Earl Terman. Do you have anything? Terman had inquired. He wanted to volunteer; he wanted to help the Justice Project. Okay, Hammond decided. On January 4, 2000, he wrote again to Jackie: "After my last letter to you, a happy coincidence occurred that will allow us to take a closer look at Mr. Macumber's case. We have been contacted by a senior member of the Arizona Bar, Earl Terman, who has expressed an interest in volunteering time with our Project. He not only has considerable criminal defense experience, but has taught in the criminal law field at the law school. We have asked him to take a first look at Mr. Macumber's file."

Terman was sixty-six, a veteran attorney on the road to retirement, still handling cases but eager for new challenges. He had moved to Phoenix from Virginia in August 1974—the very month of Bill Macumber's arrest. Terman remembered the case hitting the newspapers just days after he'd arrived in town. Now he tore into the Macumber file. He had only partial transcripts and a scattering of other documents. Where were the trial exhibits, where the sheriff's reports, where all the evidence? So much seemed to be missing. Reading through what he had, searching for what he didn't have, Terman began burrowing into the past, laboring to reconstruct a thirty-eight-year-old murder, a twenty-six-year-old trial. On January 5, just one day after getting the file, he fired off an e-mail to Hammond, asking questions, making requests, mapping strategies. *Was there procedural due process? . . . Where's the police report? I didn't see it. . . . Did you get cooperation from the public defender or prosecutor? . . . How much help can I get re investigation?* On his checklist: *Get newspapers articles of the event . . . Speak to the attorneys and to Tom O'Toole . . . Speak to the defendant, wherever he is . . . Talk to the jurors . . . Talk to the original witnesses . . . Check to see if there is any DNA evidence . . . Get info on the deceased Valenzuela . . . Research the Vince Foster case . . . Look at Arizona dicta about how to reopen a case.*

"This really does require investigatory staff," Terman concluded. "As you might tell, I am excited and hope to be able to get something done."

Hammond weighed Terman's enthusiasm against his need for staff support. At the start of the Justice Project, with a reputation still to cultivate, Hammond wanted to be careful with their first few cases, choosing genuinely righteous ones. "I think we should talk by telephone before you invest more serious time in the case," he e-mailed Terman. "This is a good outline and we can work from it in thinking what tasks can be performed productively. Thanks for jumping on this so quickly."

A week later, Terman again reported to Hammond. By then, he'd spoken to Judge O'Toole and from him had learned there existed substantive "corroborating evidence" for the Ernest Valenzuela confession: the statement of an eyewitness at the murders. "In reading more of the trial transcripts," he wrote, "it's hard not to get excited about this case. . . . I believe you have a winner here."

Hammond liked winners. "This does sound promising," he replied. "Keep up the good work."

They were under way. By mid-January 2000, Terman had constructed an ambitious "working status checklist," listing thoughts, people to interview, things to do. He wanted to speak with Paul Prato and Bedford Douglass. He wanted to talk to James Kemper. He wanted the police file, the court file, the Valenzuela file, old newspaper clippings and all of the physical evidence ("where are the exhibits?"). He wanted to find Linda Primrose ("this is definitely something I need help on"). He wanted to find Dave Brewer. He wanted to find Frieda Kennedy. He wanted to visit with Bill Macumber. He wanted to speak to Tom O'Toole, Ron Petica, Dr. Erickson, Dr. Rubinow. What about the tire-track evidence? What about Valenzuela's fingerprints? What about all the missing police reports? What about that probation officer's presentencing report—how could he conclude "no possibility of a frame-up exists," how could he refer to Bill's "violent temper" and bizarre Army CID stories when the only evidence came from Carol? What about Corcoran finding Valenzuela's confession untrustworthy? "Let's make it trustworthy with more evidence," Terman declared.

That last item drew his particular focus. Reading through the Macumber file, Terman believed he saw much evidence supporting the legitimacy of Valenzuela's confessions: everything from Linda Primrose's corroborating statements to the psychiatrists' evaluations and Valenzuela's fantasies. Valenzuela had a violent record and Valenzuela had a motive, his two victims in the way of a drug-stash retrieval. What they now needed, Terman suggested: more people from that night in the desert turning on Valenzuela and more details of his confessions to those not under attorney-client privilege—his cellmate, his girlfriend, the sheriff's deputy. And what of all this, he asked, could they frame as "new evidence"—the threshold to reopen the case? What about the discovery that the sheriff's department had failed to connect Primrose and Valenzuela in 1964?

They had to do some fundamental legal research, Terman decided. How much new evidence did they need? "Do we really have to get evidence there was in fact a conspiracy in the sheriff's department amongst a few persons . . . that caused the statement from the wife, the bullet casings evidence and the palm print evidence?" he jotted in his notes. Here Terman pointed to their central challenge: "It is one thing to hint there was access to doing the forgery work but how do we prove it was in fact done without getting certain co-conspirators to confess?"

Terman also turned to the Justice Project's potential new client. On January 18, in a brief letter, he reached out to Bill Macumber for the first time: "I have been assigned by Mr. Larry Hammond of the Justice Project to review your file to determine if there has been manifest injustice. I have been given all the transcripts from your second trial. I wonder if you can obtain a secure line to speak with me. Please get in touch when you are able. I look forward to hearing from you."

CHAPTER 12

A Case Worth Pursuing

The note from Earl Terman did not startle Bill Macumber. He'd learned about the Justice Project review of his case back in September 1998, when Judge O'Toole and Larry Hammond first wrote Jackie. One morning that October, for fifteen minutes—all the prison would allow—he'd spoken by phone to Steve Wilson, the *Arizona Republic* columnist. He'd shipped to Jackie what transcripts and depositions he had. He'd held off typing up his latest novel because he had only two ribbons left and thought he'd better save them for possible correspondence with the Justice Project attorneys.

Then came Larry Hammond's letter in November 1998, saying they couldn't take his case. Macumber moved on. Even when Jackie wrote him in early January 2000, with news that the Justice Project had assigned his file to Earl Terman, he paid little attention. He was sixty-five now, with a bad heart and emphysema. The religious resurgence he'd experienced in the Maricopa County Jail had long ago ebbed, then evaporated; over so many years of unanswered prayers, he'd lost faith in God's existence, or at least His ultimate powers. He doubted anything could or would be done for him at this late date.

His situation behind bars had changed drastically since his industrious period in the 1980s. Throughout that decade, life, even in prison, had become a pleasure for him as he threw himself into his activities, building and teaching and leading. He'd been able to do this not least because of Ellis MacDougall, director of the Arizona Department of Corrections during Macumber's early time in prison. MacDougall, introducing innovative management techniques, greatly reduced prison violence not by power but by distributing perks. He allowed prisoners to wear personal clothing. He developed a wide-ranging recreation program for inmates. He actively supported prisoners' involvement with the Jaycees, the Lifers' Club, Toastmasters, and the rodeo. He actively supported Bill Macumber as well.

They had the opportunity to meet and talk on several occasions, once at a state Jaycee convention held at the Grand Canyon. There they sat together for two hours, discussing ways to expand the Jaycee program within the prison system, a conversation that eventually led to new Jaycee chapters at the Tucson and Perryville prisons. McDougall came to trust Macumber, enough so that he gave him express approval to travel all over the state to teach at Jaycee chapters, speak to civic organizations and represent the Outlaw Rodeo at other state rodeos.

Then, at the end of 1982, MacDougall retired. His replacement, James Ricketts, made few changes, so MacDougall's departure wasn't felt at first. After Ricketts came Samuel Lewis, who took over as director in April 1985. Lewis, an ex-Marine and former deputy director of the Arizona Department of Public Safety, had once called an ACLU lawyer a "cocksucker" at a public hearing, thereby flummoxing *Arizona Republic* editors wishing to include accurate quotes in their coverage. Still the MacDougall era legacy continued—at least for a while.

The first hint Macumber had of coming changes was word of the Outlaw Rodeo's demise—the 1986 rodeo would be their last. Sam Lewis cited staffing and security concerns as his reason. Next Lewis eliminated tennis from the inmates' recreation program, explaining that he did not want the public to view the Arizona prison system as a "country club." Macumber loved to play tennis almost as much as he enjoyed running the rodeo, so the double loss felt like personal blows to him. Yet he knew this was only the beginning, that Sam Lewis had an agenda. Colonel Lewis—the title a carryover from his tenure at the Department of Public Safety—did not believe in "coddling" inmates.

In the fall of 1988, Lewis ordered elimination of the prison dairy. Next he ordered elimination of the hog ranches, the prison slaughterhouse and, finally, the prison farms. This particularly rankled Macumber's business sense, for now so much of what made the prison system self-sufficient had to be purchased from outside contractors. It rankled Macumber further when Lewis, in late 1989, ordered the confiscation of all taped movies at the Florence prison TV station. At the time, Macumber had some two thousand films on the shelf there, films the station showed nightly based on inmate requests. Prison officials told him to box them all up, place them on pallets and get them ready for shipment. He refused; he knew this would be a hard blow to the inmate population, and he wanted no part of it. As a result, he lost his job at the TV station. (Two weeks later he found another one, overseeing inmate crews for Arizona Correctional Industries.)

Then, in early 1992, Lewis began to severely limit inmate travel outside the prison. This affected Macumber more than any other prisoner. Bit by bit, he was losing the freedom and responsibility that had become a way of life for him. The final jolt came in the summer of 1995, when Lewis ordered the shutdown of all inmate clubs, explaining that he was simply making the Arizona prison system "what a prison system should be." At the time, Macumber was president of both the ASPOT Jaycees and the Lifers' Club. Getting advance word that Lewis intended to seize the Jaycee and Lifers' bank accounts, Macumber wrote checks to Special Olympics, clearing both accounts.

By the time Lewis ordered the elimination of all inmate snack bars, Macumber was reeling. In his lifetime, he'd tell others in later years, only his arrest, trial and incarceration exceeded this systematic destruction of everything he'd built. "To be totally honest," he wrote to one correspondent, "I never truly recovered."

In 1996, Macumber's father fell ill with bone cancer. Harold continued to visit Bill in prison when he felt up to it; the two remained close, the father never ceasing to believe in his son. One day Bill's brother,

Bob, called to report that he'd just taken Dad to a hospice. He put Harold on the phone. Hearing his father's terribly weak voice brought tears to Bill's eyes. I love you, he told his dad, and Harold said the same. Those were the last words they exchanged. Five days later, Harold died. When his mother had passed away a decade before, Bill had been allowed to attend her funeral dressed in a suit, without handcuffs or guards. But now prison officials said he could go to his father's funeral only in prison garb, shackled to two guards. Bill declined—he would not debase his family or his father's memory in that manner.

By then, Sam Lewis had retired, but the dismantling of Arizona prison life continued. Lewis's replacement, Terry Stewart—dubbed "Son of Sam" by the inmate population—maintained Lewis's approach. His greatest impact on Macumber came in the spring of 1997, when he ordered the removal of all lifers from minimum-custody units. Macumber ended up in East Unit, after years in the Outside Trustee quarters. The only job he could get there involved sweeping basketball courts, which took him fifteen minutes a day and paid ten cents an hour. He refused to do that, so for the first time in more than twenty years, he was unemployed.

In mid-October, authorities transferred him again, this time to another state prison entirely—the Mohave Unit at the sprawling, low-rise Douglas Complex, set on a barren reach of high desert in the far southeast corner of Arizona. There Macumber received a warm reception, for he knew a number of the inmates from past years in the prison system, and he knew the Mohave Unit warden as well, from their time together at Florence. But Bill still couldn't get a good job. He started initially on the yard crew, then became a clerk for the yard crew's supervisor, which at least occupied his time. In early 2000—just as he first heard from Earl Terman—Macumber went to work for the Mohave Unit library. That truly kept him busy and engaged, for he soon set out to overhaul its inventory system and checkout procedures.

He was now many years older than most of the inmates. Both staff and prisoners at Douglas had taken to calling him "Pops," the younger inmates accepting him as a sort of surrogate parent—or grandparent. The prison guards, too, treated him with a genial, affectionate respect. Yet life among youngsters could be trying at times, especially given his ten-by-seven-foot "home" in a large dorm room, an open bathroom off to one side. He could never truly be alone, with the younger inmates, so full of energy, always hollering. He had a small personal TV in his cubicle, which he listened to over headphones, favoring the news and sports, but to hear he sometimes had to yell for the others to quiet down. On occasion, Pops couldn't help it, he came across as the old cuss parent. He had not heard from his own sons in twenty-five years, since they last came to see him in the spring of 1975.

After reaching out to Bill in January 2000, Earl Terman kept working. Poring through all he could find about the Macumber case, he began to identify the chief issues and assemble, step by step, a coherent ten-page, single-spaced "Macumber Narrative." He focused first on the murder scene, recording in his notebook a number of relevant facts: no evidence of theft; a thatch of human hair sixty feet from the bodies; tire track impressions never cast; the Impala towed downtown before being dusted for prints, the route taken not established, "nor were the times the truck left and arrived at the downtown sheriff's station." Terman scoured the newspaper and TV coverage from thirty-eight years ago, noting, "It did not appear that there was any mention of the hair. . . . Also there was no clear mention that the shooting had occurred in a rhythm, whereby the first shot fired into each victim was at a distance . . . followed by execution bullets to the head." He saw that Linda Primrose's statements— judged truthful by a polygraph and a psychiatrist—reflected those unreported facts: Terry screaming and yanking her hair, Ernie shooting the running girl then shooting again up close to her head. "She also led them to the scene of the crime and successfully pointed out the positions of the cars and the people on the ground, in detail which was not in the newspapers," Terman wrote. He thought it "noteworthy" that "the sheriff's people did not connect" Valenzuela with Primrose. He thought it "noteworthy" as well that the defense at Macumber's second trial "did not strongly argue the corroboration" that Primrose's statements provided for the Valenzuela confession. "If there could have been a stronger emphasis on the Linda Primrose corroboration, and additional instances of Valenzuela's confessions which occurred outside context of a privilege, such as his confession to cellmate Richard Green, or his confession to the sheriff's officer, these may support an argument that the Judge abused his discretion. Neither the officer nor Richard Green were contacted. Thus it is not 'new' evidence, but instead it is the attorney's failure to get it into the record."

Terman, even as he made these arguments, recognized certain troubling issues in the Macumber case. Though these issues gave him pause, they did not deter him. After studying and pondering, he saw reasons to dismiss each of them, reasons to believe Macumber innocent.

The defense at the second trial, he had to allow, "did not appear to have any affirmative evidence that Carol had pulled the switch of evidence." But now they had Dave Brewer's 1983 statement. Terman had found a transcript of this interview within weeks of opening the Macumber file and had promptly scribbled a note to Bedford Douglass: "I am getting deeper into this case. I work with Larry Hammond and the Justice Project. Attached is an interview in 1983 with Dave Brewer. Can you tell me what follow-up action resulted, if any? This reads like terrific and explosive new evidence potential. Please call." Douglass had never responded but Brewer's reference to an "internal investigation" of Carol, and his revelation that Macumber's fingerprints initially didn't match the latents, continued to intrigue Terman. Brewer, he thought, "relayed two significant facts which might justify a new trial."

Ernest Valenzuela's confession, Terman acknowledged, was "short on details." But Terman believed that could easily be explained by his history of hard drug and alcohol abuse. What details Valenzuela did provide remained consistent from confession to confession, and dovetailed with Linda Primrose's statement. Ernie had mentioned getting a .45-caliber gun from his nephew, Terman noted, and that nephew didn't deny it when questioned by deputies. The nephew, in fact, thought Ernie "certainly capable" of such a murder.

Terman knew that Macumber came home one night around the time of the murders with a bloody shirt. But he saw that Bill had both an explanation—a fight with teenagers—and what Terman considered a "corroborating" witness: Soon after it happened, Macumber had told Phoenix police officer Robert Kimm about being in a fight "up in the northern part of the city near the freeway." Studying the transcripts, Terman found that Kimm, who patrolled the area around the Macumbers' gas station, had confirmed this at Bill's second trial. Kimm testified that Macumber told him "he had stopped to help two or three kids, apparently having some car trouble, and that as he helped them, they jumped him and a little fight ensued. . . . As I recall we discussed the thing. . . . There didn't seem to be any serious injuries involved or anything like that and I think he asked about a police report. It didn't look like it would really do that much good. It was a mutual type combat. . . . If he got the best of them, they probably would just as soon forget it too." So that, Kimm said, was the advice he gave Bill: Forget about it.

Terman turned finally to the murky issue of just what Bill and Carol said to each other during their pivotal exchange in the spring of 1974—and what Bill then said to sheriff's deputies during his interrogation on August 28. More than one sheriff's deputy, Terman saw, testified that Bill admitted he'd confessed to his wife, just as Carol claimed. And the Arizona Supreme Court, in affirming Macumber's conviction, said, "In essence, Macumber admitted that he had told his wife that he had killed the two victims." Terman bridled at that "In essence." He looked instead to Macumber's own account of his conversation with Carol that night in the spring of 1974.

She'd come home from her community college class at around 3:00 A.M., he testified at his second trial. They'd argued angrily over the terms of a divorce, he threatening to "bring up all your boyfriends," she saying, "I will kill you first." He retreated to their bedroom, and she followed him in sometime later.

> She lay there a little while, maybe for 15 or 20 minutes, then she rolled over and said, "Do you remember the kids in Scottsdale? . . . The kids from the telephone company . . . the ones they checked your gun on?" . . . I said, "What about it?" And she said, "Well you know they were shot with a .45 and you have got a .45." I said, "Well, so do a lot of other people." And then she said something about me coming home with blood on my clothes and I said, "Yes you know about that. I told you about the night it happened. . . ." She said, "You know, there were fingerprints on the car." I said, "Well if that is the case, if my prints are on that car, they can damn sure match them." . . . I was mad. I said it facetiously.

Terman's conclusion: "Somewhere in this quarrel the sheriffs said that Bill admitted to his wife something about his having killed the two in Scottsdale. But Bill denied under oath that he ever told this to her. . . . The police did not take or have their notes available nor did they tape record this interrogation which lasted from early morning until midnight. Bill doesn't deny saying something to this effect but he said it was in the context of the quarrel and that he was just upset with her. Carol even testified that she did not believe him."

In early February 2000, Terman sent Bill a copy of his ten-page Macumber Narrative, a document punctuated by animated passages written in all caps, signifying issues Terman deemed particularly telling (such as THE SHERIFF'S PEOPLE DID NOT CONNECT THIS "ERNIE" WITH THE ERNEST MENTIONED BY LINDA PRIMROSE). In a cover note, he wrote, "Enclosed is a narrative to date on your case. Please read and comment (additions, corrections, thoughts)." His Macumber file being incomplete, Terman also had a few questions: Did the original set of fingerprint tips match yours, or just the palm print? Was your second conviction ever appealed on the federal level or in a post-conviction relief petition? Were you previously aware of the 1983 Dave Brewer statement? What was done as a result of Brewer's comments?

In his cubicle on the evening of February 8, Macumber read through Terman's narrative, then reached for pen and paper, eager to respond right away. "I would first like to thank you from the bottom of my heart," he wrote, "for the time and effort you have already expended in my behalf. I had begun to believe that any thoughts of the truth ever being known was all but impossible. Whichever way this goes I want you to know I truly appreciate what you're attempting to do."

Addressing Terman's questions and requests for comments, Macumber advised that "only the palm print matched," not his fingerprints. He knew of no action other than the appeal to the Arizona Supreme Court—"if there was, I was never told nor did I ever receive a brief, transcript or results." (In fact, there'd also been an unsuccessful federal habeas corpus

petition.) Yes, Macumber was "made aware of the Dave Brewer statement" shortly after Brewer gave it to Bedford Douglass. "As soon as I
received a copy I immediately wrote back asking if that would be enough
to possibly get us some kind of hearing. The reply said . . . that Brewer's
statement, in and by itself, was not grounds to reopen the case. My father
also went down to Bedford's office on the same errand and was told the
same thing. To my knowledge, nothing was ever done about it." As far as
he knew, no one had ever attempted to find Valenzuela's 1964 cellmate,
Richard Green. Nor had Bill seen any real effort to connect the thatch of
hair to Primrose's statement. At no time, he wrote, "did I ever make a
statement to Carol saying that I killed anyone." He didn't have "any idea"
what night he came home with a bloody shirt after the fight with three
boys, but "I did attempt to report the fight as you already know." He
found "the rest of the narrative to be pretty straightforward and correct."
He was "probably missing and overlooking some things but twenty-five
years is a long time." He hoped his comments helped, and he'd do his
best to answer additional questions. He concluded, "Mr. Terman, thanks
again for your interest and your energy. I hope it leads to some daylight
on down the road."

Terman kept pursuing leads through that first half of 2000. He read Bill
and Carol's divorce file. He talked to Dave Brewer. He confirmed that Ed
Calles had attended classes with Carol at Glendale Community College
and "apparently got her a job with the sheriff's office." He located Carol,
living with two of her sons up in Washington State. He located former
sheriff Paul Blubaum up in Idaho. He located former sheriff's fingerprint
technician Jerry Jacka. He located former sheriff's deputy Charles Ford,
who'd matched Macumber's palm print on the day of his arrest. He compiled a list of Carol's "alleged" and "possible" lovers and started trying to
reach them.

Terman came to suspect a strong connection between Carol and Ed
Calles. He also came to suspect that Carol back then "had a hold" over
the sheriff's department, though he recognized that Dave Brewer's statement was "hearsay as of now." He thought it interesting that Carol gave

her August 23 statement soon after being "brought in as a suspect" in the kitchen-window shooting. Despite some initial misgivings, he grew ever more convinced of Macumber's innocence.

The passage of so many years, however, presented sizable obstacles. Terman was trying to excavate the distant past. He still couldn't find any of the physical evidence—no exhibits, no original fingerprints, no shell casings, no crime scene photos, nothing. He couldn't find Frieda Kennedy or Linda Primrose. Richard Diehl had just died. So had Jack Watson, who'd picked up the shell casings at the murder site. Terman couldn't get his hands on Valenzuela's federal prison file—the feds were resisting. He also couldn't track down the "Terry" in Linda Primrose's statement. "She may be a Yaqui or Pima Indian according to Dave Brewer," Terman reported to Hammond on May 9. "Brewer remembers seeing her around the Courthouse in the early 1980s."

Terman also faced the problem of the Justice Project's limited resources. He had no substantive support, no staff or investigators. "Since I wrote my report in early February," he advised Macumber in an update on May 10, "I was hoping to get help to track down the numerous players from the past. I have some help now but I am essentially making the contacts myself."

Yet he had located Carol and two of the boys. That's what Macumber most focused on in Terman's report. He would have dearly loved to ask where his sons were, but he suspected it probably best that he didn't know. They had made no attempt to contact him over the years, and he imagined they had no room in their lives for him now. He could not—would not—interfere with them at this late date, however much he wanted to. "They have made it more than evident that they want nothing to do with me . . ." he wrote to Jackie in mid-May. "I would gladly die to change that, but of course it will not change."

In late May, the Justice Project finally found the means to provide Terman some much-needed help. Rich Robertson had been a journalist at the *Arizona Republic* for twenty-eight years, for a while serving as the city editor. Then he'd migrated to TV news, working as an on-the-air reporter. He'd discovered he didn't like that—he'd rather investigate than stand in front of a camera. He'd decided to switch careers, to become a private investigator for lawyers. Most legal investigators were ex-cops who couldn't write, he reasoned, but investigators needed writing skills. They had to figure out what was important, then convey it in a coherent way—the very definition of a reporter. In April 2000, Robertson hung out his shingle. The next month, Larry Hammond, who knew Rich from his work as a journalist, came calling. Of course, Robertson would have to work mainly pro bono, but it would get him started. Robertson readily agreed—he was full of piss and vinegar then and had time on his hands.

Hammond handed him two cases that May. One he'd get paid to handle, it involving a court-appointed death penalty case. The other was the Macumber file. Robertson began by reading a pile of documents and conferring with Earl Terman. The low, limited quality of the initial investigation caught his attention right away. The very nature of gathering evidence had changed since 1962; back then, the Maricopa County Sheriff's Office had been a small force in a medium-sized town, faced with a double murder committed far out in the rural high desert. If DNA had been used in those days, there'd be no mystery to resolve. They could still do a DNA analysis today—if only they had the handkerchief or the thatch of hair from the murder scene. But those items had gone missing, as had so many of the sheriff's reports. The few remaining documents were scattered about at various agencies, and the fundamental government filing system had changed. Trying to find everything was, Robertson thought, like doing archaeology. Better if they'd sentenced Macumber to death. At least then everything would have been preserved for the endless appeals. Instead—as Robertson soon discovered, to his dismay—in September 1982, as part of a "housecleaning," the Maricopa County Superior Court had authorized the destruction of all evidence and exhibits in the Macumber case.

Robertson set out to find Linda Primrose. He started his search for her with a reverse-directory check, looking for Linda's father, then went to the county recorder's office to study property deeds. To locate women whose last names changed with marriage, you had to trace them through men, following the property records. Linda's father had owned a house in downtown Phoenix that he'd transferred to Linda's brother, who'd sold it. Robertson saw that the son had signed a deed notarized by a Durango, Colorado, notary. He dialed information there, got a phone number, and made the call. Linda had passed away in January, the brother told Rich—but here are the numbers for her daughter and twin sister.

Bingo—a lead, at least. Robertson talked to Primrose's daughter, Theresa Hay, on May 23. Before Linda died, Theresa said, she told her adult children all about her role in the Macumber case. But she stuck to her recantation: She'd been running around in a stolen car, she claimed, and had needed a cover story that would elicit sympathy from her abusive mother. Robertson didn't think that rang true, since Linda's mother (he'd found her in Redway, California) had told him that Linda never said a word to her about the murders or the statements to deputies. What Robertson thought more interesting was Theresa's reference to her mother keeping a file or scrapbook on the Macumber case. Theresa, who lived in Phoenix, promised to search for and share whatever she found.

The next day, Robertson talked by phone to Linda Primrose's identical twin sister, Glenda King, living in Houston. Glenda told him she'd been "terrified" by Linda's statements back in 1962, partly because the cops had "pestered" her about her sister and partly because she feared someone coming after Linda might get her instead. But bottom line, she had not believed Linda then and didn't now. She thought her sister had made up the story to embarrass her abusive stepfather, a top executive at Mountain States Telephone, where the two victims worked. Linda, she reported, had a history of weaving "outlandish and detailed lies." Everything Linda did from age thirteen to twenty came out of her desire to get even with her parents for all the abuse.

Robertson's next phone call proved more supportive of Terman's narrative—and Dave Brewer's statement. On June 2, he made preliminary contact with former sheriff Paul Blubaum, then living in Grangeville, Idaho. Blubaum was fuzzy on some details, but he did clearly recall that Carol Macumber had been investigated around then for having sexual relations with officers. Carol, attending class with reserve officers from all around the state, "was taking up with them after the classes," Robertson wrote in a report to Hammond and Terman. "Blubaum doesn't recall any formal discipline, but he remembers banning Carol from all training classes and ride-alongs with officers. He says Carol hired a lawyer who tried to get the decision reversed, but Blubaum says he stuck to it." Robertson suggested that Terman follow with his own phone call, "now that we've got him thinking about the case again."

Five days later, Terman did so. In this conversation the former sheriff remembered more, remembered particularly that control over evidence had been loose; he recalled hearing about the evidence being kept in Roger Hart's unlocked desk drawer. And he confirmed what he'd told Rich days before about Carol. "Yes, he remembers she was being investigated for sex activities with sheriffs from various counties," Terman reported. "She was found guilty apparently and her sanction was that she was suspended from the ride-along program, and suspended from attending classes at the Sheriff's Academy, and some other penalties like leave without pay. . . . Yes, they did have records kept of internal investigations but he has no idea if they would still be around. He does not remember any pressure being put on him directly from her to trade tapes to keep her job. But he does not rule out that this could have happened. He was particularly displeased that Carol would have hired an attorney to try and keep him from implementing any sanctions against her."

Blubaum repeated to Terman another memory he'd shared with Rich Robertson days before: that Macumber had been mentioned as a possible suspect during the initial 1962 investigation, that Jerry Hill had in fact asked Macumber to bring in his .45 pistol for testing. Terman thought this quite odd, since he'd seen nothing at all about it in the records. He thought it odder still when Blubaum recalled that at one time Macumber "had worked with" the two victims—something Terman knew to be untrue. Terman concluded that Blubaum "may have been kept out of the loop on this case." In fact, Blubaum allowed as much to him in their conversation. He'd become sheriff, he told Terman, just after a new law placed the sheriff's department into civil service. That meant he could hire and fire only two people himself: his secretary and his deputy chief. All others were grandfathered in, and Blubaum couldn't touch them. "This led me to ask whether he felt he was really knowledgeable about what went on in his office and he told me he wasn't," Terman reported. "He said it was very probable that underlings could have kept info from him (such as the threats made by Carol Macumber to keep her job)."

Terman's to-do list now included eight items, among them "find the internal investigative file on Carol Macumber." He knew that the defense had futilely looked for it during Bill's second trial, that without it Bedford Douglass could only "allude" to certain matters. This file, Terman believed, would "confirm that Carol had an incentive to take action on her behalf to get out of trouble." Equally important to him was the physical evidence. His last item, No. 8, remained as always: "Find the crime scene photos, fingerprint lifts, gun casings, etc. from this case."

Larry Hammond thought this report "very interesting." He suggested that of the tasks on Terman's list, "the most telling may be No. 8." As intriguing as Carol's activities might be, and the whole Valenzuela-Primrose angle, "the physical evidence will make the most difference here." They needed a gateway into the appellate legal system, and actual innocence wasn't enough; they needed rights denied or new evidence that would sway a jury. So often, that sort of new evidence involved the ever-evolving forensic sciences—Hammond had seen as much in his successful fight to overturn the Knapp and Girdler arson convictions. Alas, Hammond himself could not assist directly just then. He was burdened by his own legal work and preparing to leave that August on a five-month sabbatical. "I wish I had time to help in some meaningful way," he wrote Terman and Robertson, "but life is a total blur these days."

Rich Robertson—like Terman, working pro bono—kept going. In June 2000, he vainly combed through superior court and sheriff's department records, searching for physical evidence. He wrote reports about what had gone missing. Then, on June 12, he made what would be a pivotal phone call. He'd recognized the name of the sheriff's deputy who'd lifted the prints in 1962, for Jerry Jacka was now one of the most widely published photographers in the southwestern United States. Robertson had interviewed him while preparing a big report for the *Arizona Republic* on the theft of artifacts from Indian reservations—Jacka's specialties included photographing such artifacts for *Arizona Highways* and dozens of other magazines. Robertson had been to Jacka's Phoenix home and had spent time there with him, so he knew Jacka was a pack rat; he also knew that most cops liked to keep souvenirs. Robertson called him.

Jerry, he asked, do you remember this case? By some chance, did you keep anything? Do you have a file on this?

Yes, Jacka recalled the case, but he had no idea if he had anything. Just then he was packing up, preparing to move eventually to a new home three hours north of Phoenix. He'd keep an eye out for a file, he promised. If he found it, he'd let Rich know. Robertson hung up feeling satisfied: He'd planted a seed.

Robertson also managed to locate Carol's old roommate, Frieda Kennedy, even though he didn't know her married name. He called the personnel department at the Maricopa County Sheriff's Office. Someone—it must have been a new clerk—gave him Frieda's Social Security number and date of birth. He asked, the clerk gave—simple as that. You create your own luck, Robertson reminded himself. You don't edit your questions, you don't rule on your own motions. He went to see Frieda with a fellow investigator, Hayden Williams, an ex-cop. She lived out in Buckeye, a sparse farming community west of Phoenix that the freeway had bypassed years before, leaving a downtown composed of a few dozen decaying buildings. Driving into Buckeye, Robertson felt as if he'd traveled back into the 1950s. Frieda's house stood near the center of town, showing its age. They knocked on her door unannounced, with no call before—that would make it too easy to say no. She turned out to be nice and welcoming, letting them into a clean, homey living room, inviting them to sit down on a sofa covered with a blanket. They sank deep into that couch—the springs had given up long before. Hayden Williams did a double take: He realized now that he knew Frieda—she worked at the phone company with his wife, and they'd met a number of times at office parties. That connection helped break the ice. But in the end, Frieda remained evasive, denying knowledge of Carol's affairs; she knew only of her going out for "coffee" with various deputies and officers. She did know Carol had access to evidence in the sheriff's department. Nothing else. Robertson intended to return for another visit after she'd had time to think everything over. He never did, though. Why didn't I, he wondered years later. Why didn't I go back?

Of course, he knew why. In those days, he'd been trying to figure out how to make a living, how to blend journalism and private investigation into a paying job. So he was always scrambling. He'd just started out as an investigator and had no staff, no income. Working the Macumber case pro bono for the Justice Project took him away from paying jobs. He regretted this limit. He felt he could have done more, found more, helped Bill Macumber more. He didn't do all he could. But at least he shook the tree. When you shake trees, he reminded himself, you get fruit eventually. So much of investigating was serendipity.

In the summer of 2000, Earl Terman's efforts on behalf of Macumber also began to stall, as the Justice Project's dependence on unpaid volunteers took its toll. He'd grown increasingly convinced of Macumber's innocence. Yet on August 16, in a status memo to the Macumber file, Terman reported that "there has been little activity over the past three months." He'd learned nothing to rule out Valenzuela as the prime suspect, but he hadn't received all the records he wanted from the Federal Bureau of Prisons and the federal public defender's office. He and Rich Robertson intended to revisit Linda Primrose's relatives and try to see her scrapbook, but they hadn't yet done so. Although he'd discovered Carol Macumber's whereabouts, he wasn't "ready to confront her." His search for Primrose's companion Terry continued; following a lead from Dave Brewer, he now awaited a call back from an Indian reservation law enforcement official who might know her. He was also on the trail of a former deputy, Major Love, who'd apparently conducted the internal affairs investigation of Carol. He still needed to contact Ron Petica. Ditto for Ernie's old cellmate, Richard Green; Deputy Charles Ford, who'd made the palm print match; Officer Joe Rieger, who'd investigated the kitchen-window shooting; Sergeant Jerry Hill, the lead investigator; and Pat Ferguson, the Conciliation Court counselor. Terman also listed four men "alleged to have had an affair with Carol." He hoped to talk with all of them.

On the day he wrote this memo, August 16, Terman met for two hours with Larry Hammond and Rich Robertson. Hammond was about to leave on his sabbatical from Osborn Maledon; he and his wife would spend the rest of the year traveling through Europe and the Middle East. He thought the Macumber case warranted more support now, particularly since he'd be away for five months. He wanted to hand the Macumber file to a team at the Arizona State University College of Law—a team that by then had become a critical part of the Justice Project arsenal.

One morning back in the fall of 1999, Hammond had appeared at Professor Robert Bartels's door on the ASU campus in Tempe. Bartels, a Stanford Law graduate who held a distinguished post as the Charles M. Brewer Professor of Trial Advocacy, had spent ten years teaching at the University of Iowa—for two of those also serving as a special assistant attorney general, prosecuting bribery cases—before coming to ASU. In Arizona, he'd sat on the boards of various community legal services groups, the Homeless Legal Assistance Project, the Arizona Capital Representation Project and the Arizona Center for Law in the Public Interest. He'd also served a two-year tour of duty as deputy chief U.S. attorney for civil rights matters in the District of Arizona. He'd briefed and argued five cases before the U.S. Supreme Court and some fifty cases before other appellate courts. He'd handled eighty federal habeas corpus and state post-conviction cases, some two hundred civil cases, some one hundred criminal cases. Larry Hammond, for good reason, thought he'd make a superb partner. That's what brought him to Bartels's door. Donna Toland and I just took over the Justice Project, he told Bartels. We're having trouble finding help. Can we get law student volunteers and team them with volunteer lawyers?

Bartels didn't hesitate—the Justice Project fit well with his interests. He quickly started recruiting law students as volunteers, former students and ASU faculty as supervisors. That first school year, 1999–2000, sixteen students and ten faculty members from the ASU College of Law reviewed seventeen cases for the Justice Project. Bartels soon stepped in and started supervising a number of cases himself. So began Bob Bartels's and Larry Hammond's enduring partnership in guiding the Justice Project.

Hammond was fifty-five in 2000, Bartels fifty-six, both tall, lean and craggy. If not an unlikely pair—they shared deep-seated values, having come out of law school in the heady, activist 1969–70 era—they were certainly a study in contrasts. Where Bartels was careful and cautious, Hammond was impetuous and emotional. Bob spoke in a low, soft voice, almost inaudible at times, a tone that matched his considered manner. Larry spoke forcefully, and sometimes with irreverence. Bob focused firmly on the facts in evaluating a case; Larry relied more on his feelings. Bob thought Larry "unjustifiably optimistic" about the world in general, though he meant that as a compliment. Larry thought the Justice Project might go up in flames but for Bob restraining him.

Before leaving on his sabbatical, Hammond wrote a note to Bartels on August 17, 2000: "I hope to have spoken to you before I leave town, and I wanted to put into your hands a couple of documents about the William Wayne Macumber case. This is a case in which the Project has already invested a very substantial amount of time and volunteer energy (as you will be able to see from looking at the couple of documents I have attached). We have reached a point, however, at which it would be very valuable to have the help of a couple of students and a supervising faculty member to work with Earl Terman and Rich Robertson. If you think there are students who could be enticed, I would suggest that you be in touch directly . . . with Earl Terman."

In his office at the ASU law school—a cramped, crowded warren with two desks, both entirely covered with tottering piles of documents—Bartels looked through the attached documents, mainly reports by Terman. He appreciated how much work Terman had done, fashioning not legal analysis but a complex narrative. That complexity, of course, presented problems, as did all the elapsed years. Bartels had deep qualms. How could they investigate this? More challenging still, how could they ever convince a judge to reopen the case? Judges and the legal system wanted finality, after all. It was incredibly hard to win actual innocence cases, especially without DNA evidence.

Bartels did not see how they could prevail. Still, he recognized Larry's excitement, and he knew that Larry thought this worth pursuing. Okay, he told Hammond, if you want to do this, I'll help. And I'll get you a couple of students.

CHAPTER 13

Stroke of Luck

AUGUST 2000–JANUARY 2003

A stroke of luck—looking back, that's how Bob Bartels would describe finding the pair of law students who first took up the Macumber file under his supervision. One week after receiving Larry Hammond's request, Bartels wrote a memo to all second- and third-year law students at ASU. The subject: "Pro Bono Credits (and Possibly Academic Credit) for Work with the Justice Project." Bartels described the project's purpose—"to investigate selected criminal cases to determine whether there is credible evidence that establishes the defendant's actual innocence or indicates that a fundamental injustice has occurred." And he invited applications from "student volunteers who are willing and able to work on Justice Project cases during the Fall 2000 semester." Except during final exam periods, he noted, "student volunteers will spend a few hours each week on their cases," supervised by a faculty member.

Bartels's memo intrigued Sharon Sargent-Flack, then a second-year law student. Professor Bartels, after all, was legendary at the law school and had a national reputation. If you wanted to learn the rules of evidence, you studied Bartels; even practicing attorneys still consulted Bartels's famous evidence outline. She slipped her résumé into Bartels's mailbox. So did Karen Killion. Though only a first-year law student, so seemingly not eligible, she wanted badly to join this endeavor.

Bartels chose both of them as Justice Project volunteers—his stroke of luck apparently involving some judgment. Then, on September 21, he sent them a memo, assigning a case: William Wayne Macumber's. "I will be your faculty supervisor," he wrote. "Attached are copies of the few documents that we have in hand. The two of you should read the attached material, get together, and then call me or stop by my office." (Lest they get confused, he advised them that his office had the name "Yossarian" on the door, rather than Bartels.)

Sharon and Karen read through Terman's memos, focusing particularly on his ten-page Macumber Narrative, which they thought full of detail and passion. Then, at 10:00 A.M. on October 11, they met with Terman and Bartels. Sharon scribbled notes as Terman walked them through the story: *No motive for Macumber to kill. He denied what wife told sheriff. Macumber's interview not recorded or transcribed.* Terman talked on, telling Karen and Sharon about Primrose and Valenzuela, about Tom O'Toole, about Judge Corcoran, about Dave Brewer. He spelled out two potential tracks—"conspiracy" and "evidence to prove real killer." He mentioned a possible long-shot third track—a clemency hearing. He raised the idea that the Vince Foster case might support allowing the Valenzuela confession. Yet here, as in his written narrative, he had to allow: "Not enough conspiracy evidence to infer that wife framed husband."

After this meeting, Karen and Sharon kept communicating with Terman as they started to look through the files. They recognized his great investment in the Macumber case and soon began to share that feeling. Karen Killion, then thirty-six, had an especially personal reason: As a child, she'd lived on the same street as the Macumbers—West Wethersfield. She would have been in the same grade at Sahuaro Elementary School as Bill's oldest son, Scotty. In fact, she thought she spotted Scotty in one class picture. And Karen's father worked at Honeywell, just like Bill. She asked her dad—yes, he thought he remembered Macumber. But Karen's family had moved from the neighborhood in 1972, two years before Bill's arrest.

Besides reading files, Karen and Sharon went in search of missing reports and trial exhibits. They contacted a range of agencies; they visited the sheriff's department; they filed Freedom of Information Act requests; they sat one long day in a hot, un-air-conditioned basement at the federal public defender's office, going through boxes. They encountered obstacles wherever they went—so much was missing. So much, as well, was murky, the evidence conflicting and ambiguous. Initially, their take on the case vacillated. The sheriff's investigation seemed so inadequate—the leads the officers had disregarded, the issues they'd ignored, their failure to follow up with Valenzuela. Yet Macumber reporting shots through his kitchen window—that struck Sharon as odd, that left some discomfort in the back of her mind. Sharon also paused over Bill's puzzling "I suppose to keep her from leaving us" response, in the end concluding that "Macumber gave a speculation, not necessarily admitting that he *did* make a statement like that." Karen wavered over Linda Primrose's reliability. All the drugs and alcohol she used might have affected her memories. That she'd "cooperated" with Thomas Hakes after resisting Hill and Jones seemed peculiar. That she'd offered two versions of her story also tended to cast doubt. Still, there were plenty of elements common to both versions, and Primrose's account included details not in the newspaper reports. Two facts not in any of the news stories—the thatch of hair, the girl running—fit exactly with Primrose's statement.

Most important, the records documented no follow-up or evidence that investigators had ever connected Primrose with Valenzuela.

Linda Primrose had talked of being at the murder site with "Ernie." Ernest Valenzuela had talked of being at the murder site with "an unknown girl." No one had noticed this; no one had put the two reports together.

Both Primrose and Valenzuela had identified the killings as being in the desert north of Scottsdale. Both had described Joyce as running away. Both had said everyone in their group was drinking and smoking pot.

Primrose had described Ernie as being about five foot seven, twenty to twenty-two years old, with brown eyes and black hair. Valenzuela was five-nine, eighteen, with brown eyes and black hair.

Primrose said Ernie had "pulled time" for burglary. Valenzuela had five burglary convictions between 1963 and 1964.

Primrose's description of the killings showed Ernie to be a violent,

158 • BARRY SIEGEL

homicidal and dangerous person. Valenzuela had all of those character-istics.

Most striking: Primrose said "Terry" pulled her hair "as if in a fit," and the deputies had found a thatch of hair at the murder scene.

In the end, the cumulative record, layer upon layer—the deputies disregarding the Valenzuela and Primrose leads, the evidence kept in an unlocked desk drawer, the Latent Lift 1 print never being sent to the FBI, Bill's very character—convinced Karen and Sharon beyond a reasonable doubt. Once they realized that Carol had access, had affairs, had taken fingerprint classes and was divorcing Bill, they felt certain about this case. Those fingerprint classes especially: Carol had earned an A and a B, getting practical training in taking prints, developing latents, interpret-ing patterns, preserving and photographing, considering chain of cus-tody, and preparing evidence for court testimony. Then there was Valenzuela repeating his confession six times, something the jurors never had before them. Knowing what they knew—more than what any jury heard—Karen and Sharon saw plenty of reasonable doubt.

So did Jen Roach, when she joined them on the Macumber team. After her first year of law school, Bob Bartels hired Jen as a summer research assistant, giving her the Macumber case as one assignment. The next school year, she signed up for Bartels's criminal justice seminar, where again he assigned the Macumber case. She considered it a remarkable opportunity for a second-year law student: to work for Bartels and Ham-mond, two great lawyers with towering reputations. She thought Bartels a flat-out genius, and she liked being around geniuses. She also liked help-ing people, especially underdogs. She shared Karen and Sharon's dismay at what they all considered a gross injustice.

That judgment only deepened as they kept discovering more trou-bling elements. The shoddy police investigation—the deputies failing to secure the murder site, losing the hair and handkerchief, never typing the blood. Richard Diehl's and Ed Calles's memory lapses on the witness stand. Judge Corcoran mocking Bedford Douglass, accusing him of manufacturing reasonable doubt—what did that mean? The parallels between news media speculation back in 1962 and Carol's 1974 story to the cops: An LAPD officer's conjecture in one article had the victims caught in Bill's headlights, the boy reaching for his billfold, Bill thinking it a gun—exactly what Carol claimed Bill told her.

Carol's statement, they noticed, also seemed to parrot details in the Sterrenberg-McKillop murder file—one 1966 sheriff's report in there concerned a young man (Lester McFord II) who posed as a military CID agent looking for AWOL soldiers. They saw also an obvious coziness between Carol and the investigating deputies. Richard Diehl, for example, saying to Carol during her August 23 interview, "In talking to you about other situations, Bill is subject to dreaming . . ." Why would Diehl have occasion to speak to Carol regarding her husband's dreaming in "other situations"?

Diehl. Diehl and Ed Calles. Sharon, Karen and Jen kept going back to these deputies' memory lapses on the witness stand, their lapses and their failure to record Macumber's sixteen-hour interrogation. That kind of police work, they saw, had not gone unnoticed by Macumber's defense attorney. In the courtroom, Bedford Douglass had challenged both Diehl and Calles about the August 28 interrogation. Diehl first:

Q: It was on the 28th that you talked to Bill?
A: Yes.
Q: And it was on the 23rd that Carol had made the allegations?
A: Yes, sir.
Q: Did you take notes on what Carol said?
A: No, sir.
Q: Did you tape record it?
A: No, sir.
Q: Did you get it down word for word somehow?
A: The secretary first took it down and then transcribed it.
Q: So your secretary knew shorthand?
A: Yes, sir. . . .
Q: She serves the same function that the court reporter is serving here, correct?
A: That is correct. . . .
Q: Now, when Bill gave his statement on the 28th . . . who was the stenographer then?

A: We did not have one.

Q: Nancy Hallis [Halas] wasn't there?

A: No, sir.

Q: Then I presume you taped the conversation?

A: No, sir.

Q: Then I guess you took voluminous notes?

A: I didn't, no, sir.

Then Ed Calles:

Q: Did you videotape this conversation with Bill?

A: No, sir.

Q: Now, getting a statement down accurately, of course, is very important, is it not?

A: Yes, sir.

Q: And as a matter of fact, Detective Diehl, who took Carol's statement, took pains to get it done accurately by bringing in a stenographer, correct?

A: He took a statement, yes, sir.

Q: Did you then bring in a stenographer to take down what Bill was telling you?

A: No, sir.

Q: Now, the Sheriff's Department does have tape recorders, does it not?

A: I would assume they have, yes.

Q: Well, you have used them on occasion, have you not?

A: On occasion I have used my own personal tape recorder, yes, sir.

Q: But in addition to the one that you have, the Sheriff's Department has a tape recorder?

A: I believe so; yes, sir.

Q: They are fairly easy to use, correct?

A: That is also correct, sir.

Q: Why then didn't you tape record the statements you took from Bill Macumber during that five-hour interrogation on August the 28th, 1974?

A: Simply because I didn't have a tape recorder.

Q: Well, let's see. This interrogation, it took place at the Maricopa County Sheriff's Office, did it not?

A: That is correct, sir.

Q: It took place in room 10, correct?

A: That is also correct.

Q: And is there at the Maricopa County Sheriff's Office [a place] that they store who knows how many tape recorders?

A: Well, I assume there are tape recorders there, yes.

Q: You did not record it on tape, you did not record it by a stenographer, correct?

A: That is also correct.

Q: Then could I see the notes that you took during the process of the interrogation?

A: When my departmental report was transcribed I destroyed the notes.

Q: How many notes did you take during the interrogation?

A: I can't recall, sir

Q: As a matter of fact, you made no notes at all, did you?

A: I can't recall, sir.

Q: Referring to the preliminary hearing transcript . . . do you recall the following questions and the following answers being given by you: Question—Did you make any notes for yourself during that five-hour period? Answer—There was no notes made.
Do you recall that?

A: If that is what the answer is, it is a true answer.

If not an overt conspiracy—a long reach—this at least seemed to Jen Roach a failure of critical thinking. Carol had training and motive, Bill had an exemplary history but just went out and killed. Jen—who would later become a Maricopa County public defender—found it interesting to sit alone and go through the entire file, spotting all the discrepancies. No motives, no reason for the murders—it just didn't make sense to her. It looked like collective cowardice by the investigators and prosecutors: expediency over accuracy. Exchange your failure to solve these murders for this—for Bill Macumber. Instead of proper, rigorous thought, just assume. Even with all Jen's later experience, her exposure to the vagaries of the criminal justice system, this case remained particularly troubling to her. The raw injustice of it stood out. A case where the system had failed.

Earl Terman remained involved, but a meaningful handoff had now been made to Bob Bartels and the ASU law students. Terman advised Macumber of this in mid-December 2000: "I wanted you to know that I am still with your case but that since October the file is being studied by a small team of volunteer law students and their law professor, to see what they could add. In January 2001 the head of the Arizona Justice Project, Larry Hammond, will return from a sabbatical and we are expected to staff your case."

To "staff your case" would represent a significant commitment by the Justice Project. They were not a general-purpose criminal defense firm, ready to represent anyone who hired them. With limited volunteer resources, and a focus only on cases involving actual innocence or manifest injustice, the Justice Project had to be highly selective. Innocence and manifest injustice by themselves weren't enough; the project staffers had to pick cases where they believed they could accomplish something, where they could prevail. They had no time for tilting at windmills. So they had to assess legal issues, not just read compelling narratives. Did they have new evidence that would sway a jury? Did they have denial of due process rights? Most important: Could they persuade a judge to reopen this case? Could they win?

First Sharon Sargent-Flack and Karen Killion, then Jen Roach as well, set out to answer those questions, filling the Macumber file with their own reports. Sharon focused initially on the firearms evidence trail, while Karen addressed the fingerprints. Jen added a second memo about the ballistics and the ejector marks. The match of Macumber's gun to the murders looked dubious to them. They saw a broken chain of custody right from the start, with no report documenting how the shells moved from the homicide scene to the sheriff's property room. They saw as well that the shells eventually ended up in Sergeant Roger Hart's unlocked lower right-hand desk drawer. They saw that the barrel, extractor and firing pin marks on these shells didn't match Macumber's gun. Bill, they knew, had changed the barrel on his automatic several times—but he'd kept all the worn-out barrels and had given them to the deputies when they took his gun.

After their initial survey of the evidence, Jen assembled a comprehensive, chronological seventy-five-page "Macumber Outline." Sharon compiled a fifty-page spreadsheet inventory of all the case files. In a "Top 10 Action Plan" memo, Karen mapped out their overall strategy. She considered two courses of action: immediately speak to people who might know and talk about a possible frame of Macumber or do everything but talk to those people. Because "MCSO [Maricopa County Sheriff's Office] stands to lose a lot on this case, and William Macumber is basically at the mercy of the state right now," she chose to emphasize "a course of action that does not immediately announce the Justice Project's interest in Macumber's case." Instead, she proposed that they first dig for physical, tangible evidence: missing police reports, FBI files, fingerprint latents, photos and negatives. What about locating the victims' Chevy Impala, or at least getting a picture of it? What about locating Macumber's .45 automatic, which the county had auctioned during its 1982 court-authorized housecleaning? Seeking hospital emergency room records for the juveniles Macumber fought with one night around May 1962? Accessing telephone records to verify the reported calls between the Macumbers' service station and Mildred Lunsford, the woman who insisted she spoke to Bill all through the evening of May 23, 1962?

Following in Terman's footsteps, Karen Killion compiled her own Macumber narrative, at sixteen pages even more detailed and comprehensive than his. She readily acknowledged weak spots in their story: She recognized Linda Primrose's erratic conduct and two conflicting accounts; she saw that Primrose's sister didn't believe her statements; she allowed that "obviously the jury did not buy" the defense argument about Bill's palm print being planted. Yet the many failures and irregularities in the case file shocked and educated her. This was Karen's first exposure to a murder prosecution, her first X-ray look at the insides of such a high-stakes case. She found the initial investigation by the sheriff's department fascinating—how they chased down leads or didn't, how they handled Macumber's sixteen-hour interrogation, how everyone had open access to the evidence. How contradictory testimony existed as to whether the Impala driver's door was open. How no one could "recall" whether the driver's window was up or down. How so much of the record had gone missing: On October 26, 1965, Karen saw, the local newspaper printed a photo of Sergeant Jerry Hill standing by the case file and a cabinet containing 325 supplemental reports, inventoried by an indexing system the deputies had created to handle the overwhelming number. But by 1974, the indexing system and many of the reports had "disappeared."

The roundup and test-firing of .45 pistols in 1962 also drew Karen's attention. At his second trial, Macumber recalled that Sergeant Roger Hart had picked up his gun at the service station, something Hart denied, testifying that he worked in ID, so wouldn't have physically retrieved any guns. (Sergeant Robert Kimm, in a curious two-sentence sheriff's report drafted just before the first trial but never introduced as evidence, also denied picking up Macumber's pistol.) Yet by January 1963, Karen saw from news accounts, Sergeants Jack Watson and Roger Hart had test-fired over 350 guns, and none had delivered a slug that "even comes close" to those fired by the death weapon. Had Hart lied? And what did it mean that Hart and Watson made breech-face and firing-pin comparisons only, while in the 1970s, Robert Sibert relied solely on microscopic ejector marks, smaller than a human hair? The Macumber trial, Karen noted, was the first time Sibert had done this, even though he allowed that you could fake ejector markings without actually firing the weapon— you simply inserted a fired casing into the weapon, then ejected it.

More than anything, Karen focused on the fingerprints. The Maricopa County Sheriff's Office didn't even reveal the existence of fingerprints to the media until October 24, 1963, almost a year and a half after the murders. Then they released just four latents, the newspaper quoting Sergeant Hill as saying, "We've checked everyone and eliminated every print but these." Yet Jerry Jacka, Karen knew, had lifted a total of fifteen. She considered his methodology, which included dusting and photographing each print in situ before lifting it with Scotch fingerprint tape and placing it on a latent card. Four of these prints he submitted to the FBI for comparison (Nos. 2, 9, 13, 14), the same four the department released to the news media. Latent Lift 1, Macumber's palm print, wasn't among them. Karen could find no documentation regarding it until the day of Bill's arrest in August 1974. Jacka, she saw in the transcripts, testified that he'd lifted it from the chrome strip on the driver's door, below the window and above the handle. When asked during the trial if he could tell what the print was, a fingerprint or a palm print, he replied, "Well ... it is difficult to tell. . . . It is difficult to ascertain." He did not send Latent Lift 1 to the FBI because "lift number one being a partial print in my opinion was such that you could not determine or establish the type of pattern." He made similar statements to the *Arizona Republic* after the trial: "We had no way of knowing whether it was a palm print, part of a digit, part of a finger." By contrast, Sergeant Charles Ford testified that he, in 1974, charted twenty clear points of identification between Latent Lift 1 and Macumber's right palm print. In fact, Ford claimed he could have found at least three times that amount or more on what he considered a "good print" and a "large area with . . . lots of points of comparison." Were Jacka and Ford looking at different prints?

Karen noticed something else, as well: At trial, Ford produced two negatives that showed the print on a chrome strip with an identification card below it. But according to testimony, it appeared that the photos didn't reveal anything identifiable as the Impala. If only they had those lift photos, Karen thought. Instead, they had an empty evidence locker.

Looking at the evidence, she couldn't see Macumber being guilty. So who else might have committed the murders? Ernest Valenzuela, of course. But Karen saw other possibilities, lots of crazy folks in the Macumber file. One guy in Illinois had collected photos of Joyce. Someone else had followed her around, wanting to date her. In Joyce's purse at the murder scene, the detectives had found a slip of paper with only a license plate number written on it. The car's owner, it turned out, was a fellow worker at Mountain States Telephone—a woman who'd left by bus for California on the night of the murders. What was *that* about? People wrote down license plate numbers only when they sensed something suspicious, right? Karen spotted other odd things all through the reports, most unnoticed by the investigators. The deputies had written each report from an isolated perspective—just that particular officer at that specific moment, with no overview, no one to make connections and identify patterns.

Going into the Macumber case, Karen had wanted to be a prosecutor. Now she changed her mind. Prosecutions, she came to realize, could be full of political pressure, particularly in high-profile cases like this one. She wouldn't like working under those constraints. She decided she'd always be oriented to the defense.

On December 18, 2000, Rich Robertson received a phone call from Jerry Jacka. Here was fruit, falling from a shaken tree: Hey there, Jacka said. Guess what I found.

Six months after Robertson first contacted him, the fingerprint technician turned photographer had come upon a file. Among other documents—notes, reports, letters—the manila folder contained photos of the fingerprints from the Macumber case. The prosecution had given him this file to study as he'd prepared to testify at the first trial, in 1975. After testifying, he'd just walked out with it.

This was huge—until then the Justice Project had no physical evidence of any sort to look at. Now they at least had photos of the latents and lifts. Or, at least, *Jacka* had photos. On February 5, 2001, Robertson drove to Jacka's home in north Phoenix to see them. Jacka allowed him to look through everything piece by piece, twenty documents in all, Rich taking notes and constructing an inventory chart over the course of two and a half hours. Jacka wouldn't let Rich take the file, though—he thought the Justice Project should get a court order for that.

The next month, Bob Bartels made his own visit to Jacka's home, bringing Karen and Sharon with him. He thought Jacka's house was very Arizona Southwest, the walls full of beautiful Indian artifacts, Jacka's evocative photographs of landscapes and Native Americans displayed everywhere. Jacka, friendly and cooperative, showed them the photos, which included Polaroids both of lifts on cards and of latents taken directly off the Impala. He had a photo of Latent Lift 1, and he also had an eight-by-ten blowup of what Jacka believed to be Latent 1 from the dusted surface of the Impala chrome strip, before he lifted the print. But at the end of the visit, Jacka again hesitated to hand the photos over; he still thought the Justice Project should get a court order.

By then, Larry Hammond had returned from his sabbatical. Still reviewing, still assessing whether they'd commit to a formal appeal, the Macumber team—Hammond, Bartels, Robertson, Terman, Sargent-Flack, and Killion—held meetings, organized conference calls, wrote reports, combed through more boxes, and vainly made FOIA requests, seeking any extant FBI records about Macumber. Most important, they lined up what Bartels, in a letter to Macumber, called "an excellent finger-print expert."

Steven Anderson worked then for the Scottsdale Police Department but was transitioning to a private practice. "We are making arrange-ments," Bartels advised Macumber, "for him to compare Valenzuela's prints (and yours) to the images of the lifts."

In his cubicle at the state prison in Douglas, Macumber followed the Jus-tice Project efforts with cautious optimism, comforted by Professor Bartels's recent involvement. He also took comfort from visits paid by dear friends and relatives—a close Honeywell colleague drove all the way from Denver, his cousin Harleen and her husband, Jay, from Apache Junction, outside Phoenix. The visits distracted him from the deadening routine of life at Douglas.

No longer engaged by the Jaycees and rodeos, Macumber measured life now as best he could. There'd been a hard-pounding thirty-minute rain the other day, a welcome burst with everything so dry, and the ground thirstily sucked up the water. Welcome also: The prison dentist had finally filled the last of his cavities and would soon take impressions for the par-tial dentures he badly needed. The dentist had told him he'd get the sets four to six months after the impressions—a long time, but at least his teeth loomed on the horizon. Maybe he'd have them by Christmas—a nice gift.

In mid-May, Macumber felt compelled to write Bob Bartels a lengthy letter, raising familiar questions about some of the central issues in his case. How could they possibly connect his gun to the shell casings by the ejector marks when nothing else, not the firing pin or the breech or the extractor, matched? How could they not connect the black human hair found at the murder scene with Linda Primrose's account of a girl pull-ing out her hair? How could they not let Tom O'Toole and Ron Petica testify about Valenzuela? How could they not have a record of his .45 pistol being test-fired back in 1962? How could they keep all the evidence unsecured in an unlocked desk drawer?

Macumber apologized to Bartels for going on like this. "I have lived with these questions, Mr. Bartels, for 27 years now and I still have never received any satisfactory answers. . . . At any rate, sir, I didn't mean to bend your ear, so to speak, to this extent. I've had no one over the years except for family that has wanted to listen."

In his crowded, disheveled office at the ASU law school, Bob Bartels studied Macumber's letter, moving line by line through his questions. How to respond? Bartels certainly found it disturbing that the jury had never heard about Valenzuela or connected him with Primrose, but the Justice Project attorneys couldn't relitigate that now. Yes, they could bring it up in a petition, but they'd face a much higher burden of proof than at trial—they'd have to establish that no jury would find Macumber guilty beyond a reasonable doubt if they knew of Valenzuela and Primrose. That seemed pretty hard to Bartels. The prosecutor would say, Yeah, what about the shell casings and palm print and Carol's statement? So the Justice Project had to reinvestigate those three elements.

To Bartels, the forensic evidence, particularly the fingerprints, offered the best chance to reopen Macumber's case. He and Larry Hammond both had a good deal of experience in the ever-evolving forensic sciences; besides the flashover arson tests that had played such a huge role in the Knapp and Girdler cases, Bartels had considerable familiarity with fingerprints and ballistics. You could, he reasoned, attack the state's case through the prints and shell casings, rather than emotion or intuition or feelings for Bill. The shell casings evidence appeared basically worthless to him. The palm print also seemed suspect to Bartels—Karen Killion's narrative memo convincingly documented how a small, obscure, unclassifiable partial print in 1962 had evolved by 1974 to a clearly readable palm print. On the other hand, they had no direct proof of tampering, and no explanation for how someone could do it. They had doubts but no smoking gun—at least not yet.

Typing out his response to Macumber, Bartels followed the order of Bill's questions, his answers reflecting his caution. The points Macumber raised about the ballistics evidence "are interesting and we will review the materials we have regarding them." The Justice Project had also "noted the coincidence between Linda Primrose's story and the tufts of hair," and though "this point probably is not sufficient by itself, it is significant." Yes, Tom O'Toole and Ron Petica should have been permitted to testify, but "that issue may be precluded as a legal matter by prior proceedings." Carol's access to evidence in the case "is a point that may have some significance, although we will need additional evidence that she actually took advantage of that access." For now, Bartels concluded, "we are focusing our efforts on obtaining comparisons between (a) existing photographs of . . . the latent prints and (b) your prints and Valenzuela's. When those comparisons have been completed, hopefully in the near future, we will be in a position to decide what direction to take next."

"Hopefully in the near future" would prove difficult for the Justice Project, working as always with limited resources and unpaid volunteers. Weeks turned into months. Not until October were they able to conclude that Valenzuela's prints didn't match the latents lifted off the Impala. At a meeting on December 21, the Macumber team members discussed whether they should widen their focus and "pursue" Carol. That would involve approaching her directly after first learning as much about her as possible from friends, relatives, Frieda Kennedy and the various police officers she'd known back in the 1970s. "If we do this right," Earl Terman wrote in a memo, "we might still get leads to those who could add much more to the probability that the fingerprints were switched. That's the key evidence which must be surmounted. If the fingerprint evidence is neutered by the expert [Steve Anderson] and we show the 'doability' of the switch, then we just need to pile on the motives for doing the switch."

The palm print still remained their chief focus. Two months later, in February 2002, the Justice Project finally obtained a court order—signed by Thomas O'Toole, presiding criminal judge—instructing Jerry Jacka to turn over all records and photos of prints he possessed related to the Macumber case. As soon as Steve Anderson received Jacka's file, he began a close study of the critical Latent Lift 1 photo. Something soon caught his eye: a relatively faint diagonal line near the top of the photo. The portion of the lift tape above this line looked quite different from the portion below it, as if the part above was not on the same kind of surface. What did this suggest? Did this line exist on the Chevy Impala itself? Or did the line provide proof of a switch?

The Macumber team decided they needed to compare this photo to an actual 1959 Impala driver's door chrome strip. Which meant they needed to find one. Rich Robertson undertook the search.

In the spring of 2002, Larry Hammond stepped more directly into the Macumber case. Once again, the catalyst was Jackie Kelley. During a driving trip that included stays in Las Vegas, for a family reunion, and then Douglas, for a visit with Bill, Jackie and her husband spent one night in Phoenix, where they'd arranged to meet Earl Terman on the morning of Friday, May 10. But when they checked into their Motel 6 late Thursday night, the desk clerk handed them a message from Hammond, asking Jackie to call him. Terman had suffered a heart attack. So instead of meeting with Earl, Jackie talked to Larry on the phone for two hours that Friday morning—their first direct contact, and the first of many conversations.

She poured out her memories about growing up with Bill. She testified to his steadfast character. She spelled out her understanding of the case. Hammond, who'd been overseeing the Justice Project's investigation from one step back, listened raptly, gaining a new, focused perspective. He thought Jackie a fascinating woman, living out there in the New Mexico wilderness, clearly so devoted to Bill, convinced of his innocence. He admired her tenacity and already, during their first conversation, felt the pressure she would come to apply constantly on behalf of her cousin. She pushed Hammond on, she compelled him forward.

So much about the Macumber case bothered him. Judge Corcoran, as much as anything. Hammond *knew* Corcoran. He thought it unforgivable judicial conduct to essentially tell a defense attorney he should have taken a police report. He didn't believe Corcoran could sit up there on the bench after barring Valenzuela's confession and think he'd done the right thing.

Carol's August 23 statement also left Hammond shaking his head. Even Carol later allowed that her account, though true, "sounds . . . ridiculous," and he had to agree. What an incredible notion: that Bill would portray himself as an Army CID assassin; that Carol would forget and "let it drop" between 1962 and 1974, a stretch of twelve years during which she bore and raised three sons with him; that Bill would confess a twelve-year-old double murder to his estranged wife, who worked for the sheriff's department; that Carol would then move out of their house, leaving her three sons with Bill, and for months not mention his confession to her sheriff's department colleagues; that Bill would shoot into his own house, endangering his kids; that Carol would suddenly come forward to report his confession hours after being interrogated as a suspect in the kitchen-window shooting. She did not, Hammond noticed, even have her details right: Bill shooting through an open car door conflicted with the victims' contact wounds; Bill rifling the girl's purse conflicted with reports of it sitting untouched on the car seat. Carol initially said that Bill had come home one night with blood on his clothes "approximately ten years ago," the month unknown; then, at Bill's second trial, she testified unequivocally that this occurred on the night of the murders—and at 10:00 P.M., precisely the time when a model homes guard testified he'd talked to a very much alive Tim, letting him and a girl look around the John F. Long Homes while he locked up for the night. Carol also testified that "the purse had been gone through so I assume from that the door would have to be touched in some way." Hammond had to laugh.

Then there was that marathon interrogation of Macumber on the day of his arrest. Diehl and Calles had him from 8:30 A.M. to midnight and never once turned on a tape recorder, never once called in a stenographer. Larry Hammond had seen this kind of game all too often in criminal cases. He'd represented innocent people who'd falsely confessed, innocent people who'd failed polygraph tests, innocent people who'd ended up on death row. Sixteen hours they had Macumber, and no record made of the interrogation. Even as the deputies reported it, Macumber's statements didn't constitute a confession. Nor did Bill's testimony at the trial, despite those few ambiguous moments. The Justice Project had dealt with false confessions, but this wasn't one. Rather, you had Macumber being cooperative, trying to help, saying, Let's sort this out. The way Hammond saw it, August 28 just was not a damning day.

The bottom line for him: The cops had no recording, no transcriber. They knew how to record and transcribe; they did that with Carol. They made a deliberate decision not to record Bill. They shouldn't even have been allowed to testify, to put that day into evidence. It was all crap. The idea that Calles talked to Macumber from 7:00 P.M. to midnight in the sheriff's office, with tape recorders available, and never tried to record or take notes? Crap. Just crap. They had to go out of their way to avoid making a recording. Or maybe they did record. There may very well have been a recording. Hammond had seen that game played as well. You had a room already wired. You put a tape recorder on the table, lay a cassette tape down on it. *Do you mind being recorded? But let's talk first.* . . . The conversation begins. Who knows what they were doing?

Once you find something wrong, Hammond liked to say, keep looking. Almost always you'll find more things wrong than you can see initially. There's always more. He didn't think the Maricopa County Sheriff's Office warranted a presumption of regularity. Either they didn't record their hours with Macumber for reasons that didn't serve the interests of justice, or they did record and didn't like what they got. If they want to claim that the defense attorney made these charges unfairly—well, fuck them and feed them cheese. If they don't want to be accused, then record. Make a record.

So: They allow a dubious statement by a divorcing wife but not Valenzuela's confession. That was crazy. As was the investigators' sheer incompetence, or worse. The criminal justice system failed here, Hammond believed, just as it had in other cases. When innocent people get convicted, then exonerated by DNA, you can look back at what convicted them—and often it involved flawed or inadequate forensics. These DNA cases pointed to a far larger pool of unrecognized false convictions, for in very few cases did you even have DNA. The Macumber case, for example. The lack of DNA made this one nearly impossible. Yet Hammond did not want to let it go.

On June 24, six weeks after Larry talked to Jackie, the Justice Project's Macumber team met again to consider the fingerprint evidence and discuss other angles to pursue. With Terman now sidelined and scaling back his involvement, the team included two lawyers (Hammond, Bartels), two investigators (Rich Robertson, Hayden Williams), a fingerprint expert (Steven Anderson), and two law students. Or, rather, two former

law students: Karen Killion and Sharon Sargent-Flack had recently graduated, but neither wanted to let go; the case by now consumed them.

Bartels brought to this meeting their fingerprint expert's report,
which contained pivotal news. Rich Robertson had managed to find, up
in Washington, a chrome strip from the driver's door of a 1959 Impala.
Studying it and Jacka's photos, Steve Anderson had concluded that the
critical Latent Lift 1—Macumber's palm print—could not have come
from such a strip.

Anderson's analysis confirmed that the Latent Lift 1 impression
indeed contained the right palm print of Bill Macumber—the print had
well over one hundred points of identity. However, Anderson didn't
think it came off the chrome strip. "Latent #1," he concluded, "contains a
distinctive size, and distinctive shapes, that clearly reflect the surface of
its origin—and it is possible to eliminate the chrome strip, and all other
similar strips, as the source of Latent Lift #1."

This news ignited the Macumber team. They began laying plans.
Rich Robertson and Hayden Williams would now try to talk to Carol,
revisit Frieda Kennedy and find Dennis Gilbertson. Bartels and Robertson would seek to reinterview Jerry Jacka. Rich would track down an
entire 1959 Impala driver's door for further examination—Anderson
had discovered that their chrome strip covered only part of the door.
Larry would seek another expert to review the ballistics evidence. They
were rolling. "I think," Bartels e-mailed Karen and Sharon, "we are
headed toward filing a PCR petition for Macumber."

Two days after their meeting, Hammond called Jackie Kelley to
report about their fingerprint expert's "gold mine" of a report. Jackie
scribbled notes as she listened. The next day, Bartels sent Bill Macumber
a similar report—uncommonly upbeat for him. "It has been a long time
since I last wrote you," he began, "for which I apologize. . . . The main
reason has been that there have been a number of developments in the
investigation of your case, and I have postponed writing to you several
times to see where the latest developments would take us." They had pursued a lot of angles, he explained, but had refocused most recently on the
fingerprint evidence—and their expert had told them that Latent Lift 1
"could not have come from the chrome strip" on the victims' Impala. "At
this point we are hopeful that we will be able to wrap up our investigation

in the reasonably near future. . . . Please let me know if you have questions. I hope you are doing well."

At the state prison in Douglas, Bill Macumber read this letter with growing hope. Maybe he still had a chance. Maybe they were heading somewhere. At the least, he sensed a change in the Justice Project's outlook: Now there were others besides his family and friends who believed in his innocence.

It took the Justice Project team members—then juggling dozens of cases, with twenty more arriving for review each month—the balance of 2002 to run down all the leads they wanted to pursue. In late November they held a meeting to discuss what still needed to be done. By January, they were ready for the final step before committing to file a petition. The time had come to meet Bill Macumber, to make the four-hour drive from Phoenix down to the state prison in Douglas.

On January 14, 2003, Hammond wrote to Macumber: "Well, we are at long last making some real progress on your case. We have a great many things to talk to you about. . . . We would like to come see you in two weeks. We have made arrangements through your counselor to come to the prison to meet with you at 10 a.m. on Thursday, January 30. We look forward to meeting with you and talking with you about the case. . . . We expect that it will be a fine day for us all."

CHAPTER 14

Journey to Douglas

In Phoenix on Wednesday, January 29, 2003, five members of the Justice Project's Macumber team piled into Bob Bartels's brand-new four-by-four Nissan Pathfinder for the 230-mile drive down to Douglas. Though they had worked closely for years, this would be Bob and Larry's first visit to a prison together. Their complicated schedules rarely allowed them to be in the same place at the same time. For both of them to make an overnight journey to Douglas, involving an eight-hour round-trip, had required weeks of planning. Yet if they meant to file something, to commit to a petition, they needed to meet the inmate. They wouldn't make their decision based solely on this visit, but it represented the next crucial step. They had to assess the man they meant to defend.

With them were Rich Robertson, Hayden Williams and Sharon Sargent-Flack, who'd started practicing law in northern Arizona. They left Phoenix in the early afternoon, with the goal of traveling in daylight and reaching Douglas in time for dinner. They drove southeast on Interstate 10 for the first two and a half hours, once past the Phoenix sprawl rolling through flat, open territory surrounded by the Gila, Maricopa and Papago Indian reservations. They made Tucson by midafternoon and kept going, Interstate 10 down to two lanes in each direction, the road winding through an empty stretch of Arizona that felt nearly uninhabited. Their turnoff came after 155 miles: exit 303, Arizona State Highway 80. This was more a trail than a highway—seventy-five miles of narrow curving country road, winding past barren desert flatlands dotted with sagebrush and sorrel, then gullies and gulches and low, rolling hills. Fifty miles from Douglas, they passed historic Tombstone, Arizona, with its billboard promising "Gunfights Daily!" and its lines of tourists waiting to watch costumed cowboys and lawmen reenact the bloody gunfight at the O.K. Corral. No matter that the 1881 shootout took place in a narrow alley, not at the corral, and no matter that Wyatt Earp and Doc Holliday weren't seen as heroic until later—authorities initially charged them with murder. Back then, as now, narratives shaped outcomes in courtrooms. Or as Bob Bartels liked to tell his students, there are no facts, just evidence. *Don't conflate facts with evidence.*

He and Hammond had seen—and tried to correct—their share of faulty narratives. Recently, in one case, they'd managed to do that even without DNA evidence. In the fall of 2000, at the same time Karen and Sharon first opened the Macumber file, another law student volunteer under Bartels's supervision, Michelle Dolezal, had opened the Lacy file. *State v. Lacy* involved a manslaughter and aggravated assault conviction. Reading through the court documents, Michelle decided that Lacy's trial attorney had done a terrible job of defending him, advancing a primary theory of the case that fell apart in the courtroom. What's more, the attorney had failed to recognize that the victim's fatal head wound could not have been made by the .45-caliber bullet in Lacy's gun—the hole in the dead man's skull was literally too small. Bartels and Dolezal filed a petition for post-conviction relief, which Bartels argued at a hearing in October 2002, calling Larry Hammond as an expert witness on issues involving ineffective assistance of counsel. Judge Silvia R. Arellano issued her oral opinion from the bench that same day: Lacy's defense counsel had been ineffective, she ruled, and "the totality of the evidence establishes that no reasonable trier of fact could have found the defendant guilty based upon the evidence presented." Lacy walked free in January 2003—just days before the Justice Project's journey to Douglas.

All through that afternoon, driving across the rolling Arizona desert, the Macumber team members talked about their case and their coming visit with Bill. They wanted to look Macumber in the eye and ask him about the shooting into his kitchen window; about why he occasionally changed the parts of his .45 automatic; about his conversation with Carol in the spring of 1974; about their deteriorating relationship and what he knew of her affairs and fingerprint classes. They also wanted to hear about his prison life—the Jaycees and Florence Outlaw Rodeo, the money raised for charities, his book writing and poetry. They wanted to gain a tangible sense of this man, and this case. They wanted their client to frame everything—to transform their welter of reports into a narrative.

Some twenty-five miles beyond Tombstone, the Macumber team passed another historic town: Bisbee, with its charmingly restored and brightly painted neighborhoods of Victorian and European-style homes perched improbably on hillsides, overlooking narrow gullies. On another day, another trip, they might have stopped there for a while—its allure far surpassed Tombstone's. But they were eager to reach their destination. The team arrived in Douglas late that afternoon.

Douglas, with a population of eighteen thousand spread over almost eight square miles, sat on the border with Mexico, across from Agua Prieta, a pueblo in the Mexican state of Sonora. Founded as an American smelter town, after the Spanish had earlier settled and then abandoned the area in the eighteenth century, it still felt abandoned in some ways, or at least eerily remote, tucked into the far southeast corner of Cochise County, 6,169 square miles of scrub brush, ranches and tiny towns. Yet it offered several prominent features, chief among them the venerable Gadsden Hotel. Opened in 1907, named for the Gadsden Purchase and now recognized as a national historic site, the dignified five-story hotel included a capacious main lobby featuring a white Italian marble staircase, four marble columns and vaulted stained glass skylights.

This is where the Macumber team dined and spent the night. Early the next morning, Larry Hammond went jogging down to the border crossing—he was an avid runner of marathons until his knees gave out. He watched the flow of pedestrians and cars passing through the checkpoints, something not everyone in this region bothered with; Cochise County had been an established crossing corridor since the mid-1990s for smugglers of both narcotics and illegal immigrants. Hammond turned finally and resumed his jogging. Back at the hotel, he showered and met his colleagues in the lobby. Their drive to the state prison took no more than ten minutes. A right onto Pan American Avenue, a left at Arizona 80, then a right onto Highway 191. Seven miles down that road, they saw the sign for the state prison.

The Douglas prison complex sat on a vast, isolated semiarid steppe, a sprawling collection of plain one-story structures surrounded by miles of chain-link fence. The Macumber team stopped first at a gated guardhouse at the complex's main entrance, which stood by itself far from the prison buildings. They climbed out of Bartels's SUV under a bright blue sky, with a brisk wind blowing in their faces. They had to produce identification, declare all possible "contraband"—including cell phones and laptops—and open the car's trunk for inspection. Back in the Pathfinder, they drove across the complex to the low-rise Mohave Unit, Bill Macumber's home. Sharon Sargent-Flack looked wide-eyed at everything. Hammond had prepared her, instructing her on how to dress: no brown, tan or khaki clothing (the shades worn by the prison security staff) or orange (the inmate's uniforms); all skirts and dresses at least knee-length; no spandex-like material; no sheer, see-through or open-netted fabric; no sleeveless tops, no tank, tube or halter tops; no necklines lower than the collarbone; no bare midriffs. They could bring in only their personal identification, prescription medicine, one unopened package of cigarettes, one engagement or wedding ring, one religious medallion, one wristwatch, one pair of earrings (or two observable body-piercing adornments), and two car keys (or one key and a vehicle's remote-control entry device). They could also bring in a maximum of $20 in coins, in a clear plastic bag—this to be used for the vending machines in the visitation area. It had been many years since Macumber's prison featured a snack bar.

One by one, the team members handed their IDs to the guard at the entrance to the medium-security Mohave Unit, then stepped through the metal detector and removed their shoes for inspection. A second guard arrived to escort them down a short hallway, which led into the large open visitation area, a big room filled with round tables, watched over by a single guard standing behind a counter. A door and windows on the far wall opened to an outside area featuring picnic tables ringed by a high chain-link fence.

The team first saw Bill Macumber as he stepped into the room through an interior doorway near the guard's counter, stooping a bit to clear his head. He wore a bright orange jumpsuit that didn't quite seem to fit his tall, lanky frame. They knew he stood six foot seven but were still struck by his height. With arthritis now in his knees and hip, he appeared to lope toward them, looking as if he had extra hinges. At sixty-seven, he was gray-haired, with a narrow, craggy face. He seemed genuinely happy to meet them, greeting the team members one by one, shaking their hands, his manner courtly, his voice deep and resonant, a baritone full of gravel. They chose to sit down at a table in the outside picnic area, to gain privacy away from the guard but also to allow Bill a cigarette—he'd been a smoker all his life. So, Macumber began, what do you want to ask me?

As they started to talk, Hammond studied the man. Macumber came across as uncommonly helpful and attentive. Like other prisoners, he had things he wished to address; he particularly wanted to express his objections to how the authorities ran this prison. The unidentified "sleeper" gang members, the prisoners not really protected in protective segregation—he didn't fear for his own well-being any longer, but he worried about other inmates. Hammond wanted to listen to these concerns, but Bartels, always the most organized, kept Macumber from straying too far off message.

Together, the two lawyers began asking Macumber questions. He responded in a slow, methodical way, not trying—as prisoners often did—to glibly fill in gaps if he didn't know something. They had him recount in detail the window-shooting event: where he stood, the trajectory of the bullet, how he could be in the line of sight. Macumber told them about the shattered window, the wobbly but climbable fence, the neighbors who heard the shot. They also asked him about his palm print on the Impala. Hammond hoped Bill would flat out say, No way I ever touched that car, and Macumber almost did, but in the end he declined to be so unequivocal. I guess it's possible the car came by our gas station that evening, he allowed, though he didn't think it likely.

What about earlier, another time? No, Macumber pointed out, the kids had washed the car just before leaving home. Rich and Hayden, knowing the most about guns, asked him about the ejector markings. Macumber explained the inner mechanism of pistols, why you couldn't use those markings to make a match. No, he said, he'd never changed out the firing pin on that gun. Yes, deputies picked up his gun for test-firing in 1962, within two weeks or so of the murders. Hammond asked about his fight with the three juveniles, the night he came home with a bloody shirt. Larry had some skepticism about that event, but his concerns eased as he listened to Macumber's response, his measured recollection of the encounter. It sounded rational, Bill being a mechanic accustomed to helping stranded motorists. Hammond believed him. They also asked him about Carol's fingerprint education. She had a fingerprint kit and would practice on him, he said. Yes, she took his prints. They talked to Macumber finally about Carol's statement, and about just what he said to her that spring night in 1974. Macumber didn't equivocate now: No, he most certainly did not tell her he killed the couple on Scottsdale Road.

The conversation continued for well over three hours, eventually evolving from questions to plans. They explained to Macumber their intent to focus mainly on the palm print and the shell casings. To that end, they told him, they'd recently secured an entire driver's-side door from a 1959 Impala and would be examining it closely. They also told him they had located Carol, along with his sons Scott and Steve, in Olympia, Washington, and would be making a trip up there to speak to her, if she would be willing. They told him as well to hang in there, that they would be doing their very best to compile enough evidence to support the filing of a post-conviction relief petition.

Macumber listened with mounting appreciation. His visitors' words and manner made him feel more confident than at any time since his arrest.

Macumber had read it correctly: The Justice Project team left the Douglas prison that day with a deeply favorable impression of him. Here, Hammond believed, was an innocent man who was somehow not angry or bitter. Macumber, always courteous and patient, hadn't raged at them or anyone. Understanding the complexities of his case, he'd avoided glib responses. If he had said things they couldn't reconcile, if he had caused them to doubt his veracity, they'd likely be at the end of the road. He hadn't, and they weren't.

Rich Robertson also believed that Bill had been truthful. Except for those represented by the Justice Project, most of his clients were guilty—if not of the actual charge, at least a modified one. Prisons just weren't full of innocents. When Robertson investigated what clients told him, he usually discovered it to be bullshit. Their stories kept changing as Rich found new information. But Bill differed. His story never changed—in fact, it had never changed over many years. He offered little to refute. Robertson had been around long enough to recognize bullshit, and didn't see bullshit here. Macumber wasn't like the other prisoners Rich had known. Rich instinctively, genuinely liked Bill. He wanted to help him. He couldn't imagine how Macumber had endured in prison for twenty-six years—how he'd endured in a place where only he knew himself innocent, where everyone else considered him a murderer.

The visit cemented Sharon Sargent-Flack's impression of Bill Macumber as well. She'd joined this trip to Douglas because she continued to believe in both the Justice Project and Macumber. Meeting Bill confirmed her belief. His character, his love for his sons, his involvement in the Jaycees and the rodeo and charities, his being allowed to leave the compound as a trustee—really, his whole life informed her belief. So did the elements of the case. How, she wondered, could any jury find Macumber guilty beyond a reasonable doubt?

On the long drive back to Phoenix, the team members shared their thoughts. The others, talking on, could not help but look over at Bob Bartels. Behind the wheel of his Pathfinder, he said little, his few words, as usual, almost inaudible. His law students had come to think his speaking style a manifestation of his intellect—those less intelligent might talk loudly and quickly to mask their uncertainty, but Bartels seemed to have something like three hundred well-ordered rooms lined up clearly in his brain, ready for recall. He spoke slowly and softly because he wasn't vying for people's attention or seeking approval. He stayed inside his mind.

Unlike the others, he had not been trying to assess Bill Macumber. He didn't have much faith in his intuitive ability to judge a person's innocence. He had, though, been trying to judge the appearance of credibility—in other words, how his client would do on the witness stand. Though even there, he had to be careful; how someone came across in a prison interview and in a courtroom might differ considerably. Yes, he also had been weighing whether Macumber was consistent or full of crap—but here he judged the content, not the person. That was Bartels's way, the only approach he trusted. People fell prey to thinking they could judge, that they could rely on what a person seemed to be. Studies showed otherwise. Still—even on Bartels's strict terms, nothing Bill Macumber had said was problematic or inconsistent. He found Macumber to be direct, steady and matter-of-fact—Bill had not been posing.

Should they put more into this case? The answer, shared by all: yes.

Ten days later, Larry Hammond expressed their commitment even more firmly in a message to the team: "I am convinced that we owe it to Mr. Macumber to go forward with his case. . . . We are in a position to tell the Macumber story in a way that it has never coherently been told. . . . As soon as we can, I think we ought to get to the business of drafting the petition. . . . Bob—I wonder whether it would be wise for us to go ahead and put together a team to begin drafting? . . . As I look at the Justice Project for the year 2003, I do not believe that we have a more important case."

First, though, Carol: Among the team's pressing tasks, none ranked higher than a visit with her. That March, some six weeks after their journey to the state prison, Rich Robertson and Hayden Williams flew up to Portland. They rented a car there and started the drive north on Interstate 5 through a forest of towering redwoods, heading toward Olympia, Washington. Williams, an ex-cop, now a private investigator who worked often for the federal public defender, had also paired up with Robertson to visit Frieda Kennedy. As with that mission, they planned to approach Carol without calling first. Better just to show up; it was a lot harder to say no to a face.

With the assistance of a local real estate agent—who offered to help solve the case with her psychic powers—they found Carol's house on a wooded Puget Sound inlet, at the end of a winding rural road. They saw no people or vehicles, so Robertson and Williams settled in to wait, huddled in their car with coffee and doughnuts under a light, misting rain. They left and returned a number of times throughout the day and evening, hoping to catch Carol. They eventually knocked on a few neighbors' doors. She's away, the neighbors explained, but is due home soon. So Robertson and Williams came back the next day, again huddling for hours in their car under what Rich would recall as misty skies. Finally, they saw a dark-colored van pull up sporting a Denver Broncos flag on the rear spare-tire mount. They watched as Carol and several family members climbed out and went into the house. They waited for them to get settled, then walked up onto the porch and knocked. When Carol opened her door, they introduced themselves. We're investigators for the Arizona Justice Project, Robertson explained. We're working on Bill Macumber's case. We hope you'll be willing to talk to us.

Carol was not willing, as she quickly made clear. She visibly tensed. She couldn't believe anyone was reviewing Bill's case, she said. She'd had it up to here—she pointed to her forehead—having to answer questions every time she turned around. It followed her everywhere she went. As Robertson would later recall at public hearings, she then said: Bill is as guilty as Saddam Hussein and get the fuck off my porch. Robertson and Williams didn't argue—they were trespassing, after all. Robertson left a Justice Project business card in her mailbox before driving off.

At a meeting one month later, in mid-April 2003, the Justice Project's Macumber team formally decided to file a petition for post-conviction relief. Hammond wrote to Macumber on April 22. "I hope this is good news for you," he began. "Our team had another meeting this past week and after years of careful evaluation we have come to the conclusion that, win or lose, we need to file a Petition for Post-Conviction Relief on your behalf. Between us all we have come to the conclusion that this is a case that needs to be pursued. It will take us some time to put all of the pieces together but that is what we intend to do. Please continue to be patient with us."

Hammond copied this letter to Jackie Kelley. She wrote back on April 27: "I cannot begin to tell you of the relief and joy with which I received your letter!"

Bill wrote back as well: "You cannot possibly understand my feelings after reading your letter. . . . It is the first real ray of hope I have had after twenty-eight years of hopeless existence. I am now an old man and yet I have an almost feeling of being reborn."

CHAPTER 15

Shaking a Tree

MAY 2003–APRIL 2005

Once again, Rich Robertson discovered the benefit of shaking a tree. First with Jerry Jacka, now with Carol Kempfert. They didn't get their interview with her, but the trip to Washington certainly yielded rich fruit.

In May 2003, Carol called her youngest son, Ron, to report about the visit by Larry Hammond's investigators. They knocked at her door, she explained. They're looking into your father's case, trying to get him out. She didn't talk to them. She demanded they leave her alone. She didn't want anything to do with them, and neither did Ron's two older brothers, Scott and Steve. She figured Ron felt the same. They're looking for you, too, she warned. But they don't know where you are.

Ron was thirty-five then, living in Colorado and going by the last name of Kempfert, his mom's maiden name. Twenty-eight years had passed since he'd last seen or communicated with his father; he'd been seven at the time of that final visit to Florence in the spring of 1975. Despite so much elapsed time, he had enduring memories of his dad. How he'd take his three sons to the desert for hiking and camping and hunting. How they'd go clamming at Pismo Beach and up in Oregon. How he taught them to race BMX bicycles and built them a bike ramp using neighborhood garbage cans. How he assembled that life-sized replica of the NASA *Apollo* space capsule, complete with working buttons, flashing lights and radio sounds. Every summer, his dad would set up an above-ground swimming pool. He'd also take them to Lake Pleasant; once Ron had drifted far from shore, his father swimming out to retrieve him. He made them belts and belt buckles, sometimes from snakeskins—he liked bringing snakes home in burlap bags, a habit that set their babysitter Donna screaming one day. Ron recalled those early years as a happy time, he and his brothers so close, all of them loving to be with their dad. When their parents separated and his mother moved out to live with Frieda Kennedy, they stayed home with him; he was the main person taking care of them and always had been. Ron had few memories of his mother from before Bill's arrest.

He didn't remember much about the split, either. Just vaguely, Dad sitting them down, June 1974 or maybe a little earlier, saying their mother was moving out. Nothing more. Oh yes, Ron did remember the shot through the kitchen window that August. Late that night, Dad burst into their bedroom; Steve and Ron had bunk beds. He woke them up, put them in the bathtub, told them to stay there until he came to get them. Ron recalled being set down in that bathtub, but not what happened next: when the police came or whether he fell asleep. The following morning, he saw a bullet hole in the kitchen cabinet. He vaguely remembered Dad saying someone had shot from the alleyway. He recalled nothing being said about who'd fired or why. He just knew his father seemed upset.

Then, days later, came his dad's arrest. Ron remembered arriving home from school, Mom there, saying Dad was at the police station. She took them all down to the sheriff's department, he in the backseat of their Gran Torino, Scott up front looking unhappy. Ron recalled someone running out when they got there, in the garage, saying, *Carol, the prints match, get the kids out of here.* She took them to "Denny's" house; Ron recalled that they were rear-ended on the way. Ron thought he'd met this "Denny" before, but he mainly knew of Denny because his mother talked about him a lot. They stayed there a few days, the boys and Carol. Only later would Ron figure out this must have been Dennis Gilbertson.

He had just a faint memory of seeing his father in the county jail. He remembered more clearly going back to school, having a lot of problems there, people making comments about Dad, Scott defending the family, Scott getting into a couple of fights. Ron also recalled the news media, the reporters and TV cameras camped outside their house, Mom being upset because the press wouldn't leave them alone, Steve and Scott even shooting their BB guns at the reporters. In the early going, Ron didn't remember ever being told why his father had been arrested. Yet he did recall Dad telling his boys how much he loved and cared about them, and asking them to believe him innocent.

Even after he'd been charged with the murders, the boys visited and stayed with him many times when he was out on bail. Ron recalled sitting at the table with his grandparents and father, being told by his grandma to eat his creamed corn. He remembered going to a shopping mall with his dad, and out to the desert. He recalled his dad writing a letter to his Desert Survival Unit buddies, saying he needed help, he needed money for bail so he could see his boys. But memories of his father began to fade after that—Ron could summon just bits and pieces. He didn't remember anything about the first trial or conviction; he recalled only something about a letter—his dad trying to get a letter to them through the judge, his mom being upset, the judge bringing all three boys into his chambers. This must have been after the first conviction, Ron figured, Dad just trying to talk to us. But they never saw that letter. Mom didn't want them to.

Only vaguely did Ron recall visiting his dad in the state prison at Florence, his grandparents taking him. On that last visit, just he and Steve went. Scott didn't want to go—maybe he was angry or scared, since he'd been closest to Dad, since Bill had coached his Little League team. In truth, Ron didn't remember the visit with Dad itself, just the drive there. That would have been in the spring of 1975. At the time, Ron didn't know this would be his last contact with his father.

His mom moved their family to Colorado that spring or summer. They were living there at the time of the reversal and second trial. Ron remembered more of that period: his mom finding out about the reversal, his dad getting out of prison, Carol eventually going to Phoenix to testify. Also, Bill's parents, Harold and Meryle, coming to look for the boys in Colorado. Carol spotted them in Colorado Springs and told her sons their grandparents meant to take them away. They began identifying hiding places—among them, a drainage pipe—in case their grandparents showed up. When they heard the court had reversed their dad's conviction, the boys felt scared, fearing they'd be separated from their mother.

They knew now what he'd been accused of, whom he'd killed. Their mom had told them: *Dad was driving out in the desert. At Bell and Scottsdale, someone ran a red light in front of him. He went after them with his bright lights on, got out of his car, went to the driver's side, asked for ID. The boy, realizing he wasn't a cop, challenged him, and Bill shot him. The girl started running, he grabbed and shot her, too. That's how he got blood on his shirt.* This didn't fit with the father Ron knew. But his mom told him, so it must be true. And the court did convict him. Ron wanted nothing to do with him. He began telling people at school his dad had died.

For Ron, that was essentially true. He grew up without a father. His mom had other men in their house, but none filled that role. One, a sculptor, stayed for a good while and treated them well, but he left after they moved from Colorado to Washington. Others came and went. Carol wasn't a bad mother; Ron would never want to bad-mouth her—she did her best, working a swing shift in the Aspen, Colorado, sheriff's department, leaving them most days just as they arrived home from school. Scott, almost five years older than Ron, played the role of father figure, with Steve in the middle, Ron a mama's boy. During this time, as Ron recalls it, he had no clue their father was writing letters to them. Only later did he come to understand that his mother had returned Bill's letters to their sender. So to Ron, his dad was not just a murderer but a father who'd abandoned them, who didn't want anything to do with them.

He first began looking into his dad's case while in junior high school. They lived in Eugene then, having moved there in the summer of 1979. Ron had no clear idea why; he just started reading some old newspaper stories, local coverage of the trials his grandma had given him. He learned now about the three key prongs of evidence, the prints and the shell casings and Carol's statement. He also learned about the dispute over the Valenzuela confession. Then, in July 1983, when he was fifteen, Grandma Meryle sent him a news article about Bill Macumber published that month in the *Phoenix Gazette*. "Jaycee Chapters in Prison Earn Recognition" read the banner headline across the top of the Metro section. Paragraph after paragraph chronicled Bill's leadership role with the Roadrunner Jaycees. "Jaycees are dedicated to community service," the article quoted Macumber, "and doing outside projects is our way of contributing to the society most of us will return to one day." It also, he added, helped dispel the misconception the public had about convicts: "All criminals aren't total anti-social animals. We're concerned about people too."

Ron studied the two photos of his father that accompanied the article. In one, a head shot, he was staring at the camera through dark sunglasses, his eyes invisible, his expression suggesting a tough old cowboy. In the other, he was sitting on top of a picnic table in the visitation area, one leg bent, that foot propped on the table's bench, the other foot—such long legs—planted on the ground. He wore eyeglasses in this one, his face turned to the left as he talked intently to another inmate about plans for their Jaycee chapter. Bill was forty-eight then, the wrinkles deepening in his drawn cheeks. Man, Ron thought, he sure is old.

Ron's view of his dad's case didn't change. He just wanted more information—he had curiosity, not suspicions. He spoke to his mom about contacting Dad. Okay if you want to, she said, but don't talk to him about the rest of the family. As he went on into high school, Ron kept looking through the news clippings and thinking more deeply about the case. He wondered why Ernest Valenzuela would confess. And why his father would keep a murder weapon for twelve years. Dad was smart, not a stupid person—Ron did remember that about him. He couldn't get Scott or his mom to talk about it, though. His mom's attitude was: They convicted him at two trials—that's it. Again, Ron brought up the idea of contacting his father—he just wanted to know him, maybe ask him, Why did you do it? This was in 1985 or so, Ron then a high school senior. Again his mom said, That's fine as long as you don't talk to him about the rest of the family. Still, Ron hesitated. He felt scared. And he knew his mom and brothers wouldn't be happy about it.

Ron's next conversation about Bill came in late 1988 when he started dating Deb, his future wife. Over lunch at a restaurant, Ron, growing serious, said, There's something I need to tell you. I'll understand if you don't want to see me anymore after this. Then he told her: His father was a murderer, in prison for life. Deb didn't blink. She asked, So what does that have to do with who you are?

They were all living in Vancouver, Washington, then, Ron still in his mom's house. His mother was not thrilled about Deb, thirteen years Ron's senior with two kids of her own. Carol had her say about it, but nothing more—until Ron proposed to Deb. Then matters grew tense. Ron moved out of his mom's home in May 1989, moved in with Deb, and they started planning their wedding. The divide deepened. Carol didn't attend her son's wedding. Nor did Ron's two older brothers. Over the years, there were strained efforts to mend relations. In the spring of 1995, Ron's family—they had their own daughter now, Megan—moved to Colorado, he looking for a better job market. Two years later, by himself, he visited his mom in Vancouver, and in 1999, Carol visited them in Colorado. That week didn't go well. It would be the last time Ron saw his mom.

Now, in May 2003, here was Carol calling him, saying Justice Project investigators had been out to the house. That news brought to the forefront some questions Ron already had in the back of his mind. Again those nagging thoughts about Valenzuela's confession, his father's gun. Maybe he wanted to build up hope about his father's innocence. Also, Deb had talked off and on about the case, saying things just didn't make sense. Once she'd even asked, What if your mom had something to do with this?

After hearing from Carol, Ron stewed. Why was someone looking into the case? Obviously, there must be a reason. This Justice Project sounded like a big deal. Still, he hesitated about opening communication with his father. He worried about the impact on his family if he let that man into their lives. He worried particularly about the impact on their daughter, Megan, just turning thirteen. He also feared a break beyond repair with his mom and brothers. On the other hand, if there was something to this, Ron wanted to know.

Indecision crippled him for a time. He couldn't sort it out, couldn't say what exactly he wanted. Still: There must be a reason for the Justice Project's extended involvement. A reason why they'd sent investigators to find his mother. A reason why they were looking for him now, too. A reason why they'd taken on his father's case despite two trials, two convictions.

In July 2003, some two months after hearing from Carol, Ron finally picked up the phone and called directory assistance in Phoenix—he had only Larry Hammond's name from his mother. Moments later, he punched in Hammond's number. At Osborn Maledon, Larry's assistant, Donna Toland, took the call, hearing a man identify himself as Ron Kempfert, Carol's son. Soon after, Hammond came on the line. Are you Bill Macumber's son? he asked. Yes I am, Ron said.

His mother had called him a couple of months ago, Ron explained. She'd told him that two Justice Project investigators came to their home in Washington and tried to speak to her, but she'd thrown them off the property. So he understood the Justice Project was investigating his father's case. Why, he wondered. That's what he asked Hammond: Why?

Hammond started by describing the Justice Project, who its workers were, what they did, their history. He walked Ron step by step through their involvement with the Macumber case. He said they had reason to think his father innocent. He tried to be careful here, saying that they expected to make certain claims in their petition but it would be up to a court, ultimately, to determine whether they had sufficient proof.

At moments in their conversation, Hammond found himself pausing, because he could hear Ron softly sobbing. Ron was alone in his home in Aurora, just outside Denver, his family away on vacation in Oregon. Larry's words shocked him. He'd been pacing when they'd begun to talk, but he'd had to sit down. Hammond offered to postpone the rest of their conversation, saying, I know this is hard to hear. But Ron urged him on and began asking questions: What do you have? Why do you think this? Hammond, concerned about client confidentiality, tried to be careful and noncommittal. Still, he told Ron about Valenzuela's confession. He told him more about the problems with the ballistics and the palm print—that print matching so perfectly, a virtual impossibility. He told him about his mother having access to the case file and the evidence. He told him about his mom's fingerprint classes.

Their conversation continued for forty-five minutes. By the end, Hammond, too, felt drained and deeply moved. Something in Ron's tone suggested an end or a purpose of its own for the Justice Project's endeavors, a purpose worth recalling when working other cases: Even if they couldn't gain freedom for Macumber, maybe they could at least open the door between Bill and his sons. That, in a way, represented one of the best things they did at the Justice Project, where so often their legal appeals met abject denial. They could make people aware that this man—Ron's father—merited dignity. They couldn't get every client out of prison, but they could give them back their self-respect, and a sense that someone cared about their situation. That, Hammond believed, was a major part of what they did at the Justice Project.

Before hanging up, Hammond gave Ron his father's address. Bill would love to hear from you, Hammond said. Whenever we speak to your dad, he talks about you. He talks about his boys all the time.

Later that afternoon, Ron called Deb in Oregon. Are you sitting down? he began. On her end, she only wished that he'd waited until she was there to make such a call to Larry Hammond. Hold on now, she said. She'd be home in three days.

Ron again agonized over what to do. He feared crossing Carol. He would be lying if he said his mother didn't intimidate him. If he made the next move, that surely would be the end of the road for any connection with his mother and brothers.

Deb's return helped him decide. No matter what he's done, she told Ron, Bill is your father. You should reach out to him. He's getting older, and you need questions answered.

One week passed. On July 14, steeling himself, Ron sat down to write his father a letter. He went through multiple drafts, trying to sort out what he wanted to say. He'd never been good at putting words on paper, so this took a while. Ron knew he didn't want it to be too long. At first, he started to write about all the things he missed, what he wished his father had been there for. Then he decided against that approach. Ron wanted his dad to know that once they opened a line of communication, it would stay open. But Ron also wanted him to know that he had questions, that he'd been looking into the case. The confession, the gun, the things that didn't make sense. He hadn't decided anything, didn't know whether his dad was guilty or innocent, but he wondered. So how to begin? Ron drew a breath. "Father," he typed. "This is very hard for me after 25 plus years and I know it has been hard on you too." He read those words. Yes, that sounded right. He'd keep going now, he'd finish this, he'd put it in the mail. A desire to hear his father's response drove him, at least in part. Yet at the same time, Ron feared that response. He feared that his father would reject him. He feared that his father would say, *Where the hell have you been?*

At the Douglas state prison early in the evening on Friday, July 18, Bill Macumber picked up his mail, a single envelope, and carried it back to the cubicle he called home. There he sat down on his bed. He'd taken his glasses off, so he had trouble making out the return address. He squinted and held it up to the light. Then he saw it, small letters in the top left corner: "R Kempfert." He sat still, hardly breathing, not quite believing, just staring at the envelope. He'd been prepared, at least: Four days before, he'd received a letter from Larry Hammond, reporting on his phone conversation with Ronnie. But after all these years, to hold in his hand an envelope bearing his son's handwriting! Macumber recalled that sparkling morning long ago, drawn from those memories of days now gone: the boys swimming across a lake, tied to inner tubes, Ronnie tiring and rolling over, Bill pulling him the rest of the way. Macumber hesitated, fearing the words he might find inside this envelope. He thought Ronnie might be lashing out. Carefully he pulled from the envelope one sheet of paper. He began to read the typed, single-spaced lines.

Father—
This is very hard for me after 25 plus years and I know it has been hard on you too. I've tried many times to contact you or to write but I just could not do it. I don't know if it was the fact that I never really got to know you or that I have thought of you as a murderer all these years, but the thought of talking to you scared me. I've gone over in my head time after time what I would say to you and now I find it difficult. I've missed having a father in my life. I missed being taught the things a father teaches his son. I missed the opportunity to share the important events in my life. My wedding to my wonderful wife. The birth of my daughter, your granddaughter. I want you to know that I think of you often. I have not forgotten you. I just did not know how to deal with it. Now all of that changes.

As you probably know by now I have been in contact with Larry Hammond. He has told me the basis of your appeal. I cannot say I am fully convinced, but the information he gave me confirms a few of my suspicions. I have only the newspapers and what Mom has told us over the years. But I wondered why a confession was never admitted and why would you tell of the murders to keep a marriage together. I think the thing that bothered me the most is that you would have been dumb enough to keep the gun for all those years. For some reason I just can't see you doing that. Something is very wrong with the way your case was handled. I have asked Larry to keep me informed as to any developments in your case. Mom has no idea that I have written you and for now it needs to stay that way.

Dad, as of right now I don't know whether you are guilty or innocent, but I need to know for sure. I am asking you to give Larry permission to allow me to see the evidence. I know after all these years I may not have the right to ask anything of you, but if you were framed I want to see you released from prison. I know this is a short letter, but I hope you will understand that this is very hard on me. I want to open a line of communication with you. To let you know that I am still here. Please write back. I promise the next letter I send will give you more information about my family and me. Also, I typed this because my handwriting is very, very bad and you would most likely have a hard time reading it. I would eventually like to talk to you on the phone or maybe even see you. I think for now that writing will do.

Father, I hope that this could be a new beginning for us. I know that mom, Scott and Steve will not speak with you, but I want you to know I am out here and thinking of you. I will write again soon and I look forward to hearing from you.

Your Son,

Ron Kempfert

Bill studied those last words, "Your Son," and the signature under it. *Ron Kempfert*. Yes, his youngest boy's handwriting, if not the Macumber last name. He held the sheet of paper lightly in his hand, reading and rereading. He had not thought he could feel such absolute joy. This was, he believed, the most important document he had ever received in his life.

Later that evening, Macumber sat down to write a response. He did not want to attempt a defense. Ron would have to arrive at his own conclusions, based on the evidence and his feelings. Mostly, Macumber wanted to convey his love. He also wanted to tell his son that he'd written him many times, every letter returned marked "Refused." Ron had a right to know that, ought to know that. "Dear Son," he began. "I had all but given up ever putting those two words to paper in my lifetime. Tonight a miracle took place in my life and made this day the happiest, most wonderful day I have known in the past twenty-nine years . . ." He continued:

> I guess some fathers might have a difficult time starting a letter to a son they have not seen nor heard from in almost thirty years. I have no problem with that whatsoever. I'll start it by simply saying I love you, Ronald Paul, as I have always loved you from those first precious moments I held you in my arms. . . . It has never changed nor will it change so long as I live. You always remember that, Son, no matter what the future holds. . . .
>
> I tried so very hard to stay in touch with the three of you after I came to prison. I can't even recall how many letters I wrote to you and your brothers. I do vividly remember each one of them coming back to me with "Refused" stamped across them. After a time they came back with a "Moved" stamp and no forwarding address. I had no idea where you were and I finally quit writing. . . .
>
> The years passed and the first knowledge I had of any of you came from Mr. Hammond's investigators when they went to talk to your mother in Olympia. They wouldn't tell me much, only that two of my sons were there and at that time they didn't know where you were. I wanted so terribly much to write to Steve because they mentioned him specifically. I didn't because I had no way of knowing how a letter from me would be received. Also I was very fearful of upsetting any of your lives. It was a terrible decision to have to make because I so desperately wanted to know how you were. Your wonderful letter changed all that. You called me Dad and you called me

Father. . . . I thought I would die without ever hearing such wonderful words. Thank God in heaven that will not be the case.

Son, you wrote that as of this point in time you don't know whether I am guilty or innocent. I can understand that especially in light of your only hearing one side of the story. Your father is not a murderer, Son. I told them I was innocent the day I was arrested and I've maintained my innocence every day of my life since.

He wrote seven pages in all, his handwriting sprawling from edge to edge of the sheets, leaving no margins or open space. He told Ron of his several commutation petitions, all denied because he would not admit guilt and show remorse: "If my freedom is dependent on my admitting guilt . . . then I will die here but I will die an innocent man, Ron. . . . Truth has been my strength all these years. . . . I am now an old man. I will be 68 next month. I still walk with my back straight and my head up." These words, he knew, provided no proof of his innocence, so yes, "of course you have my permission to see any and all of the evidence Mr. Hammond's group has gathered." Yet the attorneys might not be able to share this until they file their petition, so "please be patient as I must be." Bill himself had not been told much, "other than the fact that my palm print was forged."

Macumber shared highlights of his twenty-eight years in prison and couldn't help but beam a little—so openly wanting his son's regard. "I am the only inmate in the history of the United States Jaycees to be chosen President of the Year. . . . I am a fortunate man in many respects. I have managed to achieve a great deal even though I've been in prison. . . . I don't want to ramble on forever. I just wanted you to know that I could not sit idly by and let the years pass. . . . I am well respected by inmates and staff alike and I have walked through these years with honor and with pride."

He could have kept writing for many more pages, but he made himself stop. This represented a new beginning for them, and one of the happiest moments of his life. He felt like a father again after so many years of living with only memories. He had just one request: Could Ron send him a picture of his family? "I will close this by telling you once more that you and your letter have made me a very happy, proud and grateful man. I love you Son, with all my heart."

Days later, at his home in Aurora, Ron heard a knock on his door. The mailman had a certified letter for him—really, a thick, bulging package. He sat in his living room chair for one hour, trying to get up the courage to open it. Like his father, Ron worried what words he'd find, what response. Was his dad telling him it's too late, get lost? That would be rough, after he'd reached out. Ron kept staring at the package. From the kitchen, Deb kept calling out, *Just open it.* Finally, he did. His eyes fell first on "a miracle took place," then on "I love you." Words written by his father. Ron struggled to continue reading.

Bill had enclosed some of his poems and essays, and a few letters he'd received from the Justice Project. Ron looked through everything with mounting wonder. He found his father's overall attitude extraordinary. No bitterness or rage, such incredible faith and conviction—it flat out amazed him. How could someone be so positive and upbeat in his situation? How could his dad have accomplished all he had while in prison? Even more now, Ron wanted to determine the truth about his father. He wanted to see the evidence.

Father and son continued to exchange letters that summer and fall. Ron wrote about his family: Deb and Megan, thirteen now, "the light of my life"; his two stepchildren, James and Sara, who called him "Dad"; and Sara's two-year-old daughter, Taylor Ann—Ron's granddaughter. He wrote about his job as a delivery truck driver—"put me behind the wheel of a car or big rig and I am happy as a clam." He wrote also about his estrangement from his mom, her not approving of his marriage, not attending his wedding, "barely acknowledging" her granddaughter—"I pretty much have given up trying to fix things. With Mom it's her way or the highway." He told Bill he wanted to hear his father's voice. Could Bill send him the needed forms to complete, could they arrange to talk on the phone?

Macumber wanted to hear Ron's voice, too, but he asked if they could wait just a little while. He didn't want to cry in front of the other prisoners. "I still find tears in my eyes just thinking of the miracle that has taken place. . . . There is no privacy when we use the phones here and right now I don't trust my own emotions so please bear with me for the time being." He didn't yet have the photos Ron had sent because they'd arrived inside of an album, judged "contraband" by the prison authorities. He had, though, received a letter from his granddaughter, Megan, the first of many she'd send him. ("Hi! It's me, Megan! How are you? I would like to congratulate you on all the books, novels and poetry you have written! I am a typical teenager! I love music, I love boys, I am obsessed with clothes! I love junk food! I would really like to know more about you!") The letters from Ron and Megan had opened "a whole new wonderful world for me. I now have a family. People who care." If Ron wanted to read any of his books—Ron had asked—he could get copies of the manuscripts from Bill's cousin Jackie Kelley. Meanwhile, here were photos of Bill's parents, Ron's grandparents. "They loved you three boys so very much. Your grandpa helped you land your first fish. It was a rainbow trout and a real monster. Your grandmother used to feed the three of you homemade chocolate chip cookies all day and then wonder why none of you were ever hungry at mealtime."

By late September, Ron was holding in his hands one of Bill's books. His admiration deepened. "Most people might have just given up, but you have done so many special things. I have read your letters over and over and am just blown away by them. The love and caring that you have shown means more to me than you will ever know. You are my Father. I am proud of you. I respect you and I love you. Regardless of the outcome I love you, Dad." He had, as well, come to a conclusion: "Could my mother do something like this? I believe that she could. . . . I do not trust my mother. . . . Finally to the big question. Do I believe my father is a murderer? NO. I believe an innocent man is now sitting in prison. . . . There is too much pointing to that conclusion. The confession of Ernest Valenzuela is the biggest piece of evidence. Also, Mom had access to the files, the cards and to the shell casings. . . . You should not be there and I will do everything I can to get you out." Ron wanted his father to know one other thing: "I do have memories of you. I remember hunting in the desert for dove and quail. I remember jasper hunting and the belt and belt buckles you made for us. I remember racing BMX and the time I split my finger in the sprocket of the bike. You patched me up and I went back to racing. I remember the space capsule you made for us. I remember a lot. I have never forgotten you."

Macumber, flooded that fall and winter of 2003 by letters from Ron, Megan and Deb, walked through the Douglas complex's Mohave Unit as if on a cloud. Later, he wrote: "I had suddenly gone from a lonely old man to once again being a father, with the wonderful addition of being a grandfather. I can honestly say that even though I was still in prison, I had to be one of the happiest men in this world."

He and Ron finally heard each other's voices on December 7. As arranged, following prison protocol, Bill called collect. They had only fifteen minutes to talk, the prison's limit. Later, Ron would not remember much of what they said, other than "hello" and "I love you." He recalled the feelings, not the words, and the sound of his father's voice, so oddly like his own deep baritone. Mainly, he recalled trying to hold it together. He hadn't felt nervous ahead of this call, as he had with the first letters, but he had wondered, What will we say after all this time? In the end, it didn't really matter. Happiness, the eerie voice just like his, the struggle to not break down—that's what filled the fifteen minutes.

On his end, Bill, despite delaying this first call to prepare, could not hold back his tears. "I have not cried many times in this place," he wrote Ron and Deb that evening, "but I did today. . . . Megan, never in his life has this old man ever heard a sweeter voice. . . . What a wonderful day this has been."

It took a good while, but there came another, even more wonderful day. After exchanging letters and phone calls regularly all through 2004, talking at least once every two weeks, Ron finally made plans to visit his father in the spring of 2005. His work schedule and the family's budget had presented obstacles, but he'd fixed on a weekend when he could make the long drive from Colorado. Deb would stay home to take care of their menagerie of animals, which included two dogs and two cats. Megan, fourteen then, would join him. He and his daughter left on Thursday, March 31, with plans for a two-day journey, Ron stopping to show Megan Phoenix, Tombstone and Bisbee. That first night, they stayed at a Super 8 motel in Phoenix. When they reached Douglas, late in the afternoon on Friday, they drove out to the prison just to make sure of its location. They did not want to get lost the next morning.

On Saturday, April 2, they rose early in their room at the Douglas Motel 6, Ron feeling impossibly nervous. They followed the same route the Justice Project team had taken two years before, back up Arizona 80, right on Highway 191, then seven miles winding through a barren reach of desert. Going through the initial gates and security process only tightened Ron's nerves. In the entry area, where they had to show identification and pass through a metal detector, he grew even jumpier. A guard led them down the hallway, into the large visitation room full of round tables. Five steps into the room, Ron heard someone call out his name: "Ronnie?" He turned to see a man he did not know. "I'm your Uncle Bob," the man said. This was Robert Macumber, Bill's brother, who'd driven down from Illinois with his wife, Toots. With them were the Macumbers' cousin Harleen and her husband, Jay, from Apache Junction. They'd all been visiting Bill regularly over the years, often taking their RVs, parking them ten miles from the prison in Double Adobe Campground, staying a whole week there so they could see Bill on two consecutive weekends. Jay and Harleen had even attended the Outlaw Rodeos. Bob Macumber was sixty-seven, two years younger than his brother, a bit shorter and stockier—closer to Ron's size and build. Apparently Bill had arranged for everyone to meet this weekend. Ron felt weird at first—he didn't remember these people—but soon they were making introductions. *This is Megan. This is Toots.* Bob told Ron, "You can't imagine how long we have been waiting for this moment." They began talking, catching up, sharing reports about their families. Ron had his back turned to the interior door where prisoners entered the visitation area. Megan put her hand on his arm. "Dad," she said. "He's here." She had not seen a picture of Bill; she just knew. Ron turned around. Holy crap, he thought. He's tall. At six foot four, Ron couldn't remember ever looking up at anyone. He did now. Father and son said nothing at first, just hugged. Bill was crying, Ron was crying, Megan was crying. Finally, everyone sat down at one of the big round tables. Ron had only an entire lifetime to review for them. The others explained how they'd tried to find him and his brothers. Bill, a natural storyteller, recalled things he and Ron used to do together. He also spoke of his own childhood, his and Bob's, growing up in Iowa. Bob pitched in with stories, as did Toots and Jay and Harleen.

Eventually, they started talking about the case, started to go over the many questions Ron had. Issues about Carol and her family. All the elements of what had happened. Ron learned about his Uncle Bob dating Carol before Bill. He heard more about the kitchen-window shooting and his mom's relationship with the sheriff's department. Bob told of how sheriff's deputies had picked up both his and Bill's .45 pistols for testing back in 1962. Sitting and listening, Ron thought, They can't possibly be here *concocting* this stuff on Bill's behalf. It had to be true. He'd grown ever more convinced of his father's innocence. He regretted thinking of his father as such a horrible person for so many years. Ron dreamed of the day he'd be freed.

By Sunday afternoon, the talk had turned back to memories and tall tales. Bob told Ron he had a lot of Bill's stuff—drafts, writings, photos of great-grandparents, army mementos—that they wanted to give him. Everyone made plans for future visits. Ron vowed to try to get back to Douglas twice a year—at least until they gained Bill's release. That prospect sounded a gratifying final note. When visitation hours ended at 4:00 P.M., they all rose and hugged.

From the visitation area patio, looking through a chain-link fence, Bill Macumber watched Ron and Megan walk across the parking lot toward their car. Then he turned back to his cubicle. He thought he saw a great deal of himself in Ron, and a great deal of both of them in Megan. To him, reconnecting with Ron made everything else shrink to insignificance. He'd be seventy soon. If he died in prison, if he never got out, so what, it didn't matter. These two days had been the finest and most wonderful he'd known in the past thirty years.

"My friends here have been kidding me for the last two days about coming back down to earth," he wrote Ron on Tuesday. "I suppose I have been walking a foot off the ground since our visit, but it's hard not to. I am happier right now than I have been for many, many years, and I'm sure it shows."

CHAPTER 16

Playing Long Shots

JUNE 2003–JULY 2008

Since launching the Justice Project, Larry Hammond had watched class after class of volunteer law students go from failure to failure, despite their marvelous minds and energy. Innocence projects, by their nature, were often about failure. The legal obstacles they couldn't get over, the injustices they couldn't fix. They were always playing long shots. That they needed newly discovered evidence with verdict-changing capacity was tough enough. To accept non-DNA cases, as the Justice Project did, made it even tougher.

If only the Justice Project had paid professionals at the helm who could truly *own* the Macumber case. But they didn't. Larry Hammond had his consuming private practice at Osborn Maledon, as well as various death row cases—appointments from the county and federal courts. Bob Bartels, besides his position at the ASU College of Law, served as a special assistant United States attorney for the District of Arizona. Rich Robertson had a private investigator's firm to run, having added several PIs to his staff. The Macumber case, like the others at the Justice Project, depended on volunteer pro bono forensics experts and a steady influx of law students, who kept graduating and moving on. The Macumber case also depended on two Justice Project supervisors with distinctly different modes and outlooks. They revered each other, but Bob Bartels's measured caution at times conflicted with Larry Hammond's impetuous optimism. Where Hammond, far less skeptical, invariably wanted to run to court with a petition, Bartels often favored further investigation. Facts drove Bartels, feelings Hammond. The tension between these impulses now began to affect the Justice Project's handling of the Macumber case.

In late June 2003, Bartels decided that he needed to interview Jerry Jacka once again—his third visit, the team's fourth, to this fingerprint technician turned famous photographer. Jacka had moved from Phoenix and now lived on a 120-acre ranch near the remote town of Heber, three hours to the northeast. On June 26, Bartels drove up there alone. Since his earlier visits with Jacka, he'd had time to think about matters and carefully examine the print photos they'd obtained by court order. Despite Steve Anderson's "gold mine" analysis the year before, Bartels still had questions. How much did Jacka really remember about this particular case? How exactly had he lifted the prints? What kind of paper card had he placed the print on? Why hadn't he sent Latent Lift 1 to the FBI? Most important: Exactly how had Macumber's palm print ended up on the Chevy Impala?

Bartels chewed on these issues as he drove north on Arizona 87, the Beehive Highway, then east on Highway 260 toward Heber. Gradually the scenery changed from low to high desert, then, just past Payson, to primarily ponderosa pine forest. The elevation shot up abruptly at the Mogollon Rim, the highway a steep climb now, the view at the top spectacular. Jacka's ranch, set in a forest filled with towering pines and verdant meadows, sat at the end of a dirt road north of the highway. Bartels found the hard-to-spot spur and turned onto the property. Jacka emerged from his home to welcome him.

The photographer had preserved the historical ranch house as he added on. Bartels was impressed: the remodeling first-rate, lots of glass and views, everything rustic, the open kitchen–family room built around a big cedar tree. They settled in that room to talk, Bartels's eyes on the tree's thick trunk, its higher branches spreading through the twenty-foot-high ceiling. Jacka, friendly and cooperative as before, tried to answer all his questions, though Bartels's inquiries, in 2003, concerned a job he'd done one day in 1962. Often, the best Jacka could say was *My standard procedure would have been* . . .

They started by looking at the small Polaroids of Latent Lift 1. Jacka confirmed what he'd said before—he must have taken or been given these, to help prepare for the first trial in January 1975, as they bore the date "8-23-74" and someone else's initials. No, he did not remember how he oriented the lift tape, in relation to the chrome strip, when he lifted the print in 1962; he could only say that he probably applied the tape parallel along the length of the strip, rather than across it. He didn't know what would have caused the relatively faint diagonal line they both saw near the top of Latent Lift 1. He couldn't tell whether the print card represented the same latent print he'd lifted from the chrome strip in 1962. Looking at the Polaroid photo of LL-1 and one of Steven Anderson's blowups, he couldn't be sure whether it was a finger- or a palm print—it looked like a palm print, but sometimes you can be fooled. He had not sent LL-1 to the FBI because in the early 1960s, it wasn't the sort of print they could characterize for purposes of searching the FBI database. He wasn't sure why they hadn't included LL-1 in the prints reproduced on the flyer they distributed nationwide—he might just have concluded that the other latent prints were better for comparison purposes.

Bartels next asked Jacka if he remembered whether he'd photographed Latent Lift 1 while it was still on the chrome strip, before lifting it. Jacka had no specific recollection of doing so but said that was part of his standard operating procedure. Together, they looked at the blowup from Jacka's file, which seemed to show the same palm print as in LL-1 but in an unlifted state on a shiny surface. At Macumber's first trial, a Phoenix Police Department technician, Joe Garcia, had thought them identical, "one and the same." Jacka, studying the enlargement now, agreed that it probably was a blowup of the photo he'd taken of Latent Lift 1 before lifting it. Again, though, he didn't have a specific recollection; he'd possibly been given the blowup before the first trial in 1975.

Toward the end of his visit, Bartels shared with Jacka some of what bothered the Justice Project about the Macumber case, including the Primrose statements, the Valenzuela confessions, and Carol's history and access to the sheriff's file. He also told Jacka about their fingerprint expert's opinion that the version of Latent Lift 1 used at trial, as depicted in the Polaroid photos, could not have come from the chrome strip. As best he could, Bartels explained why, emphasizing the faint diagonal line near the top of LL-1. This information appeared to energize Jacka. He knew that Bartels had a 1959 Impala's chrome strip in his truck. Earlier he'd passed on inspecting it. Now he suggested that they take a look.

In Jacka's garage, they studied it and the LL-1 photo, with Bartels pointing out how the portion of lift tape above the faint diagonal line in the photo appeared different from the portion below. Jacka, testing theories about the line's provenance, put his own fingerprint on the chrome strip, but his decades-old lift tape crumbled, keeping him from completing the experiment. As they played around with his fingerprint kit, Jacka brought out some small squares of paper-thin plastic-like material, similar to photographic film. He'd sometimes used that material to make lift cards, he said. He again studied the Polaroid photos of LL-1. In fact, he added, it's very likely he'd used this plastic-like material for LL-1. Bartels thought that significant; from experience, he knew it wasn't hard, using Scotch tape, to lift prints off any kind of paper, but photographic paper made it easier still—a piece of cake.

After more than an hour together, Bartels thanked Jacka, loaded the chrome strip back into his truck, and drove off. Winding his way through the ponderosa pines, Bartels weighed what he now understood about the palm print evidence. Looking at Latent Lift 1 today, Bartels saw an obvious and distinct palm print, yet back in 1962, Jacka hadn't. To Bartels, it seemed logical to conclude that the current Latent Lift 1 wasn't what Jacka handled in 1962. But maybe Jacka hadn't paid close attention back then. You could say much the same about why Jacka hadn't sent Latent Lift 1 to the FBI, especially given the limited classification system at the time. Still, everything but the palm print pointed to Macumber's innocence. Bill's background and lack of motives, Valenzuela's confession, Carol's role—these elements combined seemed to increase the likelihood that someone had fabricated LL-1.

But *how*? That question remained unanswered after Bartels's visit to Jacka's ranch. Steve Anderson's opinion that Latent Lift 1 couldn't have come off the chrome strip was obviously quite favorable to Macumber.

So, too, was Jacka's surmise that he'd used plastic-like material for his LL-1 lift card. All the same, Bartels saw potential problems. Though he had confidence in Anderson, the primary basis for his opinion—that no explanation for the diagonal line existed consistent with LL-1 being lifted from the chrome strip—might just mean that Steve couldn't *think* of any explanation. They also had to address that blowup photo of what appeared to be Latent Lift 1 on the chrome strip, before Jacka lifted it. If that's what it was—possible but not certain—then they needed to develop evidence, or at least a theory, about how it, too, could have been falsified. They had to figure out how someone could make not just a switch but a double switch. Such a switch was doable, but it wouldn't suffice to simply raise disturbing suspicions, to show how the print metamorphosed between 1962 and 1974. They had the burden of proof: They had to demonstrate exactly *how* Macumber's print ended up on the Impala's door.

Steve Anderson's analysis provided a powerful defense, for it suggested that *something* was not right about the trial version of Latent Lift 1. Now, though, in the summer of 2003, Bartels decided they needed to get a second fingerprint expert's opinion. He wanted confirmation of Anderson's judgment.

The public defender's office in Mesa suggested John Jolly, then a fingerprint examiner with the Arizona Department of Public Safety. Larry Hammond knew Jolly, too—Jolly had come forward in 1991 to provide important testimony on behalf of John Knapp. Hammond called him on September 5, asking for help, explaining they wanted a second look as a "sanity check." It would not only have to be unpaid but also more or less low profile; though in transition to a private practice, Jolly still did some work for the state police, and his supervisor there bristled at Hammond for his frequent critiques of forensic lab work. Jolly nonetheless agreed, with enthusiasm—he had high respect for both the Justice Project and Steve Anderson. A month later, he picked up the Macumber fingerprint binders.

What did the faint diagonal line on Latent Lift 1 represent? Was it possibly a reflection from Jacka's camera flash? Was it a line on the Impala's door itself, where the car window and frame met? Or was it an edge of some sort that might suggest a planted print? Steve Anderson had reached one conclusion. Now Jolly would study the matter as well, though at his unavoidably slow pace: He was an unpaid moonlighter, after all.

Weeks slipped by. Jackie Kelley grew impatient, nearly frantic. Winter, fierce as ever, had blown into the New Mexico highlands. She watched the snowstorms from her kitchen counter, smoking Marlboros and, when the chill set in, sipping Canadian Hunter whiskey. She'd always tried to balance being polite with getting what she wanted. She'd worked ten years for professors at Scripps Institution of Oceanography, two years for the CEO at a big computer-information company in Washington, D.C., and then—after moving to New Mexico—ten years as secretary to the principal at Durango High School, over the border in Colorado. She'd found it fascinating but frustrating to get an inside look at the public education system, where teachers couldn't much discipline the kids, given all the rules. Where Jackie came from, men took their hats off when they entered a room, but these students sailed into the principal's office with snugly covered heads. At least they did until Jackie went to work there: They learned soon enough to remove their cowboy hats. Jackie didn't mind that she had a reputation at Durango High for being strict.

Early that December, she called Larry Hammond, urging him on, expressing concern about the delay, warning about Bill's declining health. Larry and Jackie had never met—all their communication had been by letter or phone—yet they'd acquired the complicated dimensions of a relationship. Though he thought her more apologetic than pushy, he by now very much felt her pressure. Apparently, it got to him during that phone conversation. Two weeks later, Jackie wrote to him: "I want to thank you for talking with me when I last called," she began. "I think I got your message, however, which is not to call you again. That's why I am writing this letter to you." She felt concerned now "about what I perceive as a loss of interest in this case." She appreciated the pro bono nature of their work, she understood all the difficulties, she remained eternally grateful. However, she was also "confused over what I am sensing as a change of heart on the part of the Justice Project." She suspected that "this change took place about the time Professor Bartels went north to visit with the retired deputy [Jacka] about the fingerprints." She was "at a loss to understand just why." She remained grateful to everyone, all the same, and wanted "to wish you and the team a very Merry Christmas and a Happy New Year."

Hammond, regretful and chastened, wrote back within days: "You are such a sweet and thoughtful person and I now feel guilty about discouraging you from calling me. To whatever extent my remarks imposed an embargo on communication with you, I wish to lift it." He assured her that he remained "very concerned" about Bill's case. He had, in fact, just e-mailed Professor Bartels, expressing his worry that "nothing—or at least very little—appeared on the surface to be happening." He had not heard back from Bartels directly, but he had some assurance to offer Jackie. The delay came not from waning interest but because "we are extremely concerned about making sure that we do the right thing and it was with that in mind that we took the extra steps of seeking a second opinion on the fingerprints." The delay stemmed, as well, from "the sheer volume of work that the Project has under way." (At the time, they had some twenty cases in court, thirty to forty more in an intense level-two evaluation, and twenty new files arriving each month for review.) Most cases, Hammond explained, had a private volunteer lawyer as supervisor, but with Earl Terman falling ill, the Macumber case didn't, leaving Bartels and Hammond directly in charge, a situation they tried to avoid because of their many commitments. Yet their roles, if limiting, also reflected their abiding interest: "The Macumber case has been different because we care so much about it. I can only make you this promise. This case is one of my highest Justice Project priorities. We will see it through."

In truth, the Justice Project was finding it difficult to push Jolly's progress along. Late that December, Jolly told Bartels he had reviewed all the material once but wanted to go back over it more carefully. Months then passed as they waited to hear from him again. At the start of June 2004, Hammond felt obliged to provide Macumber with a candid update. As Bill knew, they had obtained "a very favorable opinion" from Steven Anderson, "a fingerprint expert who knows all the players and is quite impressive in his insights. He believes the palm print must have been planted and he makes a pretty good case for it." However—this pained Hammond to write—"honestly, his analysis is not perfectly airtight. Professor Bartels believes, correctly I think, that we should get a second opinion, and to that end we have given all the materials to another respected fingerprint person, whose name is John Jolly. Jolly offered to do the work for us on a pro bono basis but it has taken him a great long time to get back to us with his opinions and reactions. Professor Bartels is following up with him and we hope to have a final answer very soon." Meanwhile, Jackie Kelley—Hammond must have grinned and grimaced here—"has been very good about continuing to encourage us and to keep us focused." As usual, Hammond ended on a note of optimism: "Our hope is to finish our work and get on to the filing of the petition this summer."

At the state prison in Douglas, with the summer heat closing in and no hint of rain—only wildfires off in the distance—Macumber struggled to see the positive in this letter. That they were going to try to submit a petition this summer surely represented the most significant news. Yet this Justice Project process had been under way now for more than five years. One way or the other, Macumber wanted to see the end of it. "I have tried to not let it wear on me," he wrote to Ron that month, "but to tell you the truth that has been impossible. I can never totally get it out of my mind and that has not been a good thing either mentally or physically. It takes a toll. Hopefully it will turn out as we would like it to. If not, then we shall have to abide with that and deal with it as best we can."

At the start of July, Larry Hammond e-mailed the team with a promising update: "I spoke to Steve Anderson this week. . . . He told me that he and Jolly both believe that Steve's opinions with respect to the fingerprint evidence in the Macumber case are airtight and cannot seriously be questioned. . . . Steve went to some extent to tell me that he was as confident of his opinions on this matter as he could possibly be. He thinks that both he and Jolly would be good witnesses in any hearing."

Days later, however, Jolly weighed in with a quite different report, reaching Hammond at his mountain cabin. "I spoke at length this afternoon with John Jolly," Larry advised the team on July 5. "He is dubious about our claims and wants to look at the [Impala] door and go over the whole thing one more time. He is coming to my office to discuss his findings a week from tomorrow—July 13—at 8 A.M. His negative reaction was exactly opposite to Anderson's, so this is likely to be an important meeting. Are any of you able or interested in attending?"

Rich Robertson joined Hammond and Jolly at this meeting. Rich had called all over the country, haunting auctions and the Internet, before finding a 1959 Impala door on sale, for $300, in a Washington State salvage yard. They'd had it shipped down to Larry's office at Osborn Maledon. It had arrived in a huge box, the window shattered, something of a rusting mess. They now pulled it from the box and laid it out in one of the law firm's tony twentieth-floor conference rooms, where large picture windows gave sweeping views of Phoenix and the Superstition Mountains to the east, Camelback and Mummy Mountains to the northeast. A few of Hammond's partners, walking by and glancing in, appeared puzzled, if not perturbed. Larry, Rich, and John Jolly had their reasons, though. Among them: They wanted to see if it was physically possible for the palm print to have come from the chrome strip, given the strip's size and shape. "I think it was a very productive meeting..." Hammond reported to Macumber on July 21. "We inspected the Impala door and Jolly went through a long series of issues that have been on his mind. We are hoping that we will be able to give you a final report on where we stand very soon."

By early August, though, the Justice Project had enlisted a third pro bono fingerprint expert, Bob Tavernaro, a former colleague of Jolly's at the Department of Public Safety, now doing private work. They wanted yet another opinion because Jolly had come up with an "innocent" explanation for the diagonal line on Jacka's photo: Someone, while making a comparison, might have folded the original card to place the fingerprint image next to a known print. On August 9, everyone once again gathered around the Impala door. They had the core team there—Hammond, Bartels, Robertson, Karen, Sharon and the three fingerprint experts. They spread out the photos of the prints. They took their own photos, using the same kind of old box camera employed back in 1962. They studied and pondered and brainstormed. "The beat goes on," Hammond reported to Bill on August 12. "We had another 'Macumber meeting' this week to bring together the now enlarged group of three fingerprint experts. . . . They have made some great progress." They would be convening again later in the week to finalize their recommendation, "but I believe they will say that they are now all convinced that the palm print did not come from the driver's side door."

Hammond's expectations weren't realized. Rather than "finalize" their recommendation at this second Macumber meeting, the experts eventually came to see they couldn't reach a provable conclusion. Instead, they would have to keep studying this matter—they would have to reassess the whole fingerprint issue. Hammond decided that one of these experts needed to own it, rather than all three participating in a one-day think tank. Bob Tavernaro volunteered. It would be a huge undertaking, but he was game.

All through the fall and winter of 2004, the Justice Project associates labored to get their hands on additional fingerprint evidence they'd located in the sheriff's department. They exchanged constant e-mails with the experts. Hammond and Bartels met to talk "about the long-range future of the case." "Professor Bartels said he would really like to take some time over the next month to draft his basic core thoughts for the petition," Hammond reported to Jackie. Once Bartels had done this, "our hope is . . . we will be able to turn it into a petition that could be filed sometime early in the next calendar year."

Rereading this letter at her kitchen counter in late December, Jackie Kelley found her eyes continually going back to "we talked about the long-range future of the case," rather than Hammond's "hope" to file a petition. Long-range? Really? She turned to her computer keyboard, newly acquired after a lifetime with her typewriter. "This has somewhat upset me," she wrote to Hammond. "I keep hoping that it won't be necessary for any LONG-RANGE efforts on Bill's case, that things can come to a head without too much time elapsing." She realized the great number of difficulties, she realized all their work on this case had been pro bono. "But oh me, next month it will be five years since Mr. Terman first started in on all this." She didn't want Larry to think her ungrateful, but "for both Bill and I the wait has been most excruciating. Both Bill and I are getting to be what some people call 'ancient'—and Bill's health is deteriorating." All the same, she was just "venting a little of my frustration," not meaning "to criticize any of the efforts you and the team have been making." She wanted only to wish the whole team "a very MERRY CHRISTMAS AND A HAPPY NEW YEAR." She would "keep praying that 2005 will see Bill's release from prison."

That Christmas season, Bill Macumber prayed as well. He tried to imagine Ron's home in Colorado, everyone busily involved in preparing for the holiday, the mood hectic yet buoyant. Quite a difference from the prison, where you'd never even know the season—they had not a single decoration or observance of any kind. "You probably don't remember," Bill wrote to Ron four days before Christmas, "but our last Christmas together, we all went up north in the snow and cut our own Christmas tree. You and your brothers went sledding and had a ball. We all managed to get wet and cold but we had a great time nonetheless and the tree we cut was just beautiful."

Ron had asked about his paternal grandparents—Bill's mom and dad. "Words alone could never do them justice," Macumber wrote. "Your grandfather was a very wonderful and unique man. . . . He was for me more than just my father. He was my teacher, my guide, my confessor and most important, best friend. He taught me so much. The importance of truth, the satisfaction of pride in oneself. . . . Dad taught me to love the land and every creature." Harold met Bill's mom on a blind date. She was "simply and wonderfully a woman of her time, wife, mother and homemaker." He was writing this "with tears in my eyes, Ronnie, because I still miss my father so very much." He hoped the day would come when "you and I can sit and talk of them in greater detail."

As for his case, Macumber had no report. "There has been nothing at all from the attorneys and I don't know where we stand or what the time frame might be. Jackie is writing Larry Hammond a letter so we'll see what comes of that."

Hammond, though in the midst of a trial, took the time to write Jackie back on January 10, 2005: "I have your letter of December 26, and I know it must have been difficult for you to write it. Obviously you wanted very carefully to balance your concern about the pace of the case with your genuine gratitude for the pro bono work." He, too, was "concerned about the pace of this case." And yet: "I do think some good things are happening." On December 28, the team had been able to review and inventory the remaining evidence at the sheriff's office. The fingerprint experts "have done some further research and they are very near providing to us their final opinion that the palm print could not have come from the 1959 Impala." Professor Bartels, the chief "overseer" of the case, had now returned full-time to the law school and his supervision of Justice Project work, after a tour of duty at the U.S. attorney's office. By "long-range," he meant only that once they filed the petition for post-conviction relief, "some time" would inescapably pass before they got to a hearing. "I hope all of these things will happen in 2005."

Despite Hammond's obvious desire for things to be going well, progress had slowed even further. The days and weeks kept slipping by, the fingerprint experts stopping and starting, stopping and starting. The Justice Project's dependence on volunteers and rotating generations of students, however helpful they were, sometimes frustrated Hammond. So did Bob Bartels's caution, though Bob remained his cherished, esteemed colleague. The tension between thoroughly investigating and running to court—the competing impulses—represented one reason they weren't getting this concluded. Hammond, left to his own devices, would have filed a petition by now.

On March 9, he e-mailed Bartels, asking what steps needed to be taken to move the case along. In response, Bartels, Robertson and the fingerprint experts exchanged a volley of messages, making plans to dig out whatever fingerprint evidence still remained in sheriff's department boxes. In early April, Bartels collected and sent this evidence to Bob Tavernaro, for what Hammond called "one final review." He hoped "that this summer will be the summer that all of this comes together."

But things did not come together that summer. They lost contact with Bob Tavernaro; they could not get in touch with him. Hammond's frustration mounted. Also his concern: The legal system mandated due diligence—they couldn't string out the appellate process endlessly, they had to demonstrate they'd moved at a suitable pace. "I have received renewed inquiries from the Macumber family," he e-mailed the team on June 11. "Have we made any further progress on the fingerprint work?" Hammond messaged the team again on August 2, sharing a letter he'd just received from Jackie (*Now, of course, my question is—what is happening? At the risk of being a real "pain in the b——" could you please give us an update?*). He received these letters periodically, he explained, "and they cause me increasing pain and embarrassment. I would very much appreciate any thoughts you may have about how we can best and most honestly respond. I continue to think that the Macumber case should be at the top of our list."

Rich Robertson finally reached Tavernaro on August 3. The apologetic fingerprint expert explained that he had undergone surgery five weeks before, then had been in recovery, so now was playing catch-up on his paying jobs. He and Steve Anderson, in fact, were both in Dallas just then on another case. They'd be there until mid-August. He'd jump back into the Macumber file as soon as he returned.

Hammond huddled early that month with Bartels and Robertson. "We need to hire an expert," he said. "We need to pay someone." For a while, they weighed that option, even though it would cost at least $10,000. In the end, they did not hire an expert—a choice Hammond would later rue. Instead, Robertson volunteered to get on Tavernaro, to really track him and bug him.

"We are pushing the experts as hard as we can push people who are volunteers," Hammond advised Macumber in a note on November 1. "I feel confident that they are going to come together to the conclusion that there is no explanation here other than the substitution of your palm print for the actual lift. . . . I do believe they will have an answer for us very soon."

All through November, Hammond kept after everyone, bird-dogging Tavernaro, proposing phone conferences, asking Rich to coordinate directly with the experts. But the holidays came and went. They were into 2006 before the experts finally gathered, in mid-January. They discussed the lines they saw in the photo of the palm print on the chrome, still unable to reach concrete answers. They considered issues of film size. They made plans to tackle the Impala door yet again—they would attempt to replicate the various reflections in Jacka's photos by taking multiple lifts off the door's chrome strip. With all the messy powder involved in that process, they would need to do this somewhere other than the Osborn Maledon conference room, so Jolly would pick up the door at Rich's house. Jolly would also search for a smaller fingerprint camera, so he could duplicate Jacka's photos. If possible, they would study sheriff's department lifts and photos from the early 1960s, just to see what methods were used in that era. All this sounded fine and good to Hammond when Jolly put it in a memo, but Larry still wanted to know when they'd reach the finish line.

Early that April, with a third generation of law students now on the case, he again prodded the three fingerprint experts: "Gentlemen, I met with our students last night who are working on the Macumber team. The end of the semester is rapidly approaching and our goal had been to see if it was at all possible to get our petition in order so that it might be filed sometime this spring. I know you are all working on this. Could you please give me an update and, if you think it would be useful, help us schedule a time to get together to talk about your findings." Jolly responded in mid-April, saying they hoped to finish their work by the end of the month. "I am not sure they will," Hammond advised Macumber, "but we are working very hard now with the team of students on drafting the petition and trying to finalize the work on the fingerprints and ballistics."

Hammond was right—the experts didn't finish. The semester ended and yet another round of law students graduated. Even Hammond now had trouble sounding optimistic. "Well you must have just about given up on us," he wrote to Macumber on July 31. "I sometimes wonder if we will ever get to the bottom of this. . . . It appears to me that we have now gotten to where we have exhausted just about everything there is to exhaust on the 1959 Impala. I can understand why the fingerprint people are being so incredibly cautious, but at some point this all becomes just too much." Still, the fall semester would be starting in two weeks, with a new crop of students available to help. "I know I have said this before, but I really believe that we are now finally getting close."

Larry Hammond surely meant that, surely believed they'd get there. He and the entire Justice Project team retained their faith in Bill Macumber's cause. If only they could stand and tell their story in a court of law. But the appellate legal system wanted concrete new evidence, not compelling narrative. The Justice Project didn't have that yet. Hammond couldn't stop, but he also couldn't move forward.

At the turn of the year into 2007, Jackie Kelley resurfaced. A cold wind howled outside her window on January 5. Nature's fury matched hers now as she began to type her latest note to Hammond: "It has been quite some time since I last wrote to you. As always, I want to thank you and the 'team' for all your efforts. . . . I fully realize that all your work has been done free, gratis. But I am also painfully aware that it has been over six years since we first contacted the Justice Project. What I am really trying, graciously, to ask is—WHEN? My cousin is not guilty of the crime for which he has been paying for over 27 years. His only crime is that he is poor and in prison. Unfortunately, my crime is that I'm just poor. Is there nothing that can be done, in the name of justice, when one isn't rich?"

Jackie's question stabbed at Hammond. He'd made justice for the disenfranchised his highest priority. He derived great pride and satisfaction from his law firm's involvement with the Justice Project and death penalty cases. His relentless zeal on behalf of indigent prisoners—his belief that they merited the same high level of representation corporate clients received—had tried the patience of adversaries and colleagues alike over the years. Yet Hammond had to admit it: In this country's legal system, the wealthy could afford more justice than the poor. *Is there nothing that can be done, in the name of justice . . .* Hammond reread Jackie's words. Okay, he decided. Let's try to answer that question.

On February 9, he convened a master meeting of the entire Macumber team. At this stage, it included Hammond, Bartels, Robertson, the fingerprint experts and the third round of law students. They gathered in a conference room at the ASU College of Law, Room 109, in the rotunda— where Hammond and Bartels had once taught a Factual Investigation class together. They talked about the case's status and whether they had reasons to go forward. Did they have enough to file? Or should they close the Macumber file? John Jolly and Bob Tavernaro spread out their reports and put the Impala chrome strip on the conference room table. The experts went on at some length, explaining about the print cards, about the way Jacka had taken his photos in 1962. But in the end, they had to admit defeat: They were unable to say Latent Lift 1 definitely had not come from the Impala door. Nor could they explain exactly how someone might have planted the print.

The experts' report disheartened the Macumber team. Waves of energy drained from the room. Rich Robertson felt deflated. Bob Bartels saw no reason to continue. Yet they all kept talking, still exchanging ideas, considering issues they should explore. They weren't ready to stop—at least, Hammond wasn't ready. Robertson reviewed what he'd been doing, what he might still do. Hammond proposed drawing up another to-do list, a battle plan of additional tasks. They didn't reach a conclusion that day—not one they articulated, at any rate. Instead, they ran out of time. Their scheduled two hours elapsed.

Hammond, as promised, composed a "10 Items" memo—which became 11 items—summarizing what they'd discussed about possible tasks. They would seek a court order instructing the Maricopa County Records and Identification Bureau to run all identifiable but unmatched prints. They would seek a court order instructing Linda Primrose's daughter to turn over her mother's scrapbook. They would review Dave Brewer's taped statement from 1983 and reinterview him. They would review Sharon Sargent-Flack's summaries of the trial transcripts. They would review the divorce and custody file. They would review again Judge Corcoran's decision to ban Valenzuela's confession, in light of *Chambers* and the Vince Foster case. They would review again the ballistics evidence and the newly evolving science in this field. They would review again the public defenders' file, searching for sheriff's reports they still didn't have. Finally, they would write to Bill Macumber, updating him and scheduling a conference call.

This last item proved a hard task for Hammond. Despite his usual attempt at optimism, Larry's letter to Macumber on February 21, copied to Jackie Kelley, could not obscure the bad news, so contrary to all his earlier reports and predictions. "Over the last few months, we have had a large number of meetings with the fingerprint experts who had donated their time to your case, but in the end they could not reach the conclusion we had anticipated. The belief that we have had for the last couple of years that the palm print could not have come from the handle and chrome strip area of the driver's side door just does not pan out. It does not mean that the palm print was not planted, it just means that if it was planted, it was planted so well that we could not prove that it had been fabricated." Hammond wanted to make one thing clear: "This does not end the case for us." They had reassembled their student team, adding Ty

Jacobson and Pete Rodriguez from the undergraduate ASU Justice Project Practicum. They had held a team meeting. With the help of Rich Robertson and his colleagues, "we are trying to make sure that we have looked at every issue." They would like to "set up a telephone call with you as soon as we reasonably can to talk about these open issues."

In his Mohave Unit cubicle on the evening of February 25, Macumber reread this letter a number of times. He found the news hard to fathom, considering that just a year before, the fingerprint experts were sure the print had been planted. Now they had changed their tune. Whatever the reason, Macumber believed he knew well what this meant. He would have to notify Ron right way. He reached for paper and a pen. "This is the hardest letter I have ever had to write," he began, "because I know you are already overburdened with problems up there. Still, I have no choice because you most certainly have a right to know what is happening or has happened. By the enclosed letter from Larry Hammond, you can see that effectively the work on my case has come to an end and with negative results. . . . This does end any hopes for me proving that I am innocent. There is nothing else that we could take before a judge that would carry any real weight. . . . The question is, what now?" The answer seemed obvious to Macumber: "Life goes on. We put this behind us. . . . We have no real choice." He was just sorry "to have to bring more problems and more sadness into your lives."

The Justice Project's conference call with Macumber and Jackie Kelley took place on March 14. Hammond led the conversation, with the student volunteers also talking to Bill, explaining the inability to eliminate the palm print. They couldn't avoid conveying their sense of frustration and disappointment. Macumber, as always, tried to cheer them up.

That evening, Macumber did much the same when he talked on the phone to Ron and his family. Following up, he wrote to them the next day: "I heard the hurt, sadness and dejection in your voices last night and frankly, it all but tore my heart out." He wanted to tell them something to ease the pain. "That something is the fact that regardless of all else I am innocent and that will remain so until the end of time. No court, no jury, no judge can change that. We can hold that truth in our hearts. . . . This is what I want you all to remember."

Hammond, as he promised, did not stop. On March 20, he sent the

Macumber team a fingerprint guide from the *Criminal Practice Reporter*, "in light of our effort to make sure we have thought about everything." Weeks later, at the end of the semester, he stopped by the ASU Justice Project Practicum with a question for the students: Did anyone want to continue on their Justice Project cases after the course ended? Pete Rodriguez raised his hand. So did Ty Jacobson. They would stay with Macumber, they said. They'd do whatever they could.

But what more could they do? The Macumber file stayed open at the Justice Project, yet the weeks passed without any progress. On August 8, Jackie wrote Hammond once again, begging in all caps: "IS THERE ANY WAY HUMANLY POSSIBLE TO FREE MY COUSIN FROM PRISON?" Hammond replied on August 29, almost out of words now: "You know that this case plagues us almost more than any case we have ever had. We are still looking at a few of the open issues. I wish I could give you more comfort but I will stay in touch."

Months later, on March 18, 2008, Hammond sent an e-mail to the Macumber team, asking for "thoughts to go forward or to come to a final decision." He attached the "11-part" task memo developed at their meeting a year earlier. The team gathered once again.

This session felt depressing to Hammond—all long silences and lack of energy. No one had anything to say or do that could make a difference. Yet Hammond asked, Don't we owe it to Bill to file, whether we win or lose? Maybe filing can bring attention and publicity, can draw people out of the woodwork? Bob Bartels was skeptical: What do you think you're going to find? Hammond countered: Who knows. We don't know who might be reading about it, who's alive from back then. You can never tell.

Then Rich Robertson joined in. He usually deferred to the lawyers, but not now. We have nothing more to do, he said. We can't go further. Lost evidence, missing witnesses, years elapsed, the palm print unexplained. Yes, maybe filing a petition would draw Carol out, or maybe one of the sheriff's deputies. But how do we make a decision based on something as ephemeral as that?

Bartels willingly played the bad cop, offering the voice of doom. He realized that he had an easier time doing difficult things than Larry did. Yet his attitude just now reflected more a lack of faith in the judicial system than in the Macumber case. The palm print represented only the second-biggest obstacle to him—number one was the courts' reluctance to grant relief in these kinds of cases. The team had to be realistic. They had put in an enormous amount of time. To keep going, to assemble a petition, would be a huge undertaking. And to what end? What were the odds of getting a superior court judge to agree with them? Extremely low, Bartels believed. The Justice Project had too many other cases and deadlines. He had some twenty on his own plate, with twenty to thirty new files coming into the office every month for review—at least three hundred a year. He felt guilty, really, devoting so much time and so many resources to this one case. They had to go where they could prevail, they had to be selective. Bartels believed Macumber innocent, but he didn't believe he could convince a judge.

Survival of the fittest, in other words—a Darwinian outlook on the judicial process. In the end, Hammond had to agree. We just can't keep telling Jackie and Bill we're progressing, he realized. All his positive letters to them bothered him now, and he didn't feel comfortable continuing that way. They weren't closing the case, but they needed to acknowledge they were at a standstill. They weren't abandoning Bill, but they weren't going forward.

The Justice Project might have stopped, but not Jackie Kelley. In the spring of 2008, after not hearing from the Justice Project for months, she persuaded her cousin to write to another legal-aid agency, Centurion Ministries in Princeton, New Jersey. On April 27, he did so. "My name is William Wayne Macumber and I am seventy-three years of age," he began, "and I have, for the past thirty-four years been an inmate within the Arizona Department of Corrections. . . . I pleaded my innocence at the time of my arrest, at the time of my trial and every day since. . . . I am innocent of this crime and innocence like truth never changes." Over five single-spaced typed pages, he laid out the facts of his case and the history of the Justice Project's representation since 2000. He believed the Justice Project's investigations "continue even to the present," but "I have heard nothing for over a year now." He had but two wishes: to "spend some time with my son and granddaughter as a free man" and "to end this life proved innocent." Perhaps that was asking too much, "yet I am hopeful that you might be able to do something on my behalf." If so, "I shall be eternally grateful." If not, "then I shall continue on as I have over these past 34 years as best I possibly can."

A Centurion Ministries director responded on June 17, politely declining. "It appears that your case is in good hands with the Arizona Justice Project.... You noted that you have not heard anything from them in a year. I would suggest you contact the Arizona Justice Project unit and see what the status of your case is. Our own experience is that these investigations do take a long time."

Heeding this advice, Macumber wrote to Larry Hammond that July. If they didn't have enough for a post-conviction relief petition, he wondered about the possibility of filing instead, with the Arizona Board of Executive Clemency, a petition for commutation of sentence. He'd tried that three times, so many years ago, but perhaps it merited another effort?

Macumber received no response to his inquiry. Larry Hammond had just departed on a six-month sabbatical, this time to teach a college course in North Carolina. The Macumber case, at any rate, was off the Justice Project table. The quest appeared to be over, the Macumber file closed, left to yellow and gather dust in the basement of the ASU law school library.

PART THREE

LAST CHANCE

CHAPTER 17

A Futile Affair

DECEMBER 2008–MARCH 2009

On its face, the spare, three-page document that arrived at the Arizona
Board of Executive Clemency in late December 2008 looked to be an
entirely futile affair. Here was yet another prisoner's petition for a commutation of sentence. Only 5 percent of these even made it to a Phase II
hearing, and only a fraction of the Phase II cases earned a favorable
ruling from the board. That this particular petition came from a convicted murderer serving a life sentence made success all the less likely.
Yet Bill Macumber, at the end of 2008—"with nothing better to do and
nothing happening in my case"—decided he might just as well file this
application.

He'd done so on his own, no longer in contact with the Justice Project. He had no hope whatsoever that his request would go anywhere.
He'd filed three such petitions in past years, after all, and had never
moved beyond a Phase I hearing. He'd been told he had to admit guilt
and express remorse before he'd get any consideration. He had no intention of doing that but figured he'd give it a shot anyway. At age seventy-
three, he was in declining health—arthritis in his left hip, emphysema,

prostate problems, chronic allergies, a heart murmur—and Jackie, as always, had been urging him on, asking if he could file yet another appeal.

He did, at least, finally have a real job again after years of little activity. In 2007, prison authorities had assigned him a position at the local Cochise College annex in the prison's Mohave Unit. There he worked as a computer technology clerk, creating and running a student enrollment and management program. He handled most of the student data collection, including attendance, assignments, and progress and term reports. This gave him a purpose and a routine, as well as a chance to work with good people in the college system. He rose now at 4:30 every morning—his aching arthritic hip kept him from sleeping later. He ate breakfast at 6:00, worked at Cochise from 6:30 A.M. to 3:00 P.M., then had dinner and spent most evenings watching TV, mainly sports. Just weeks before mailing in his latest commutation petition, he'd received an admiring letter of commendation from Charles Flanagan, then the director of the Correctional Education Division at Cochise, thanking him for his "personal investment in and commitment to the success of the Cochise College students and program." His efforts, Flanagan wrote, were "noticeable and valuable, as well as appreciated. . . . You can take pride in the positive impact you are having through your work."

Even without that letter, Macumber had no trouble filling up the section of the clemency application that asked for "positive accomplishments" he'd achieved in prison: chairman for two years of the ADOC Outlaw Rodeo, six-time president of the ASPOT and Roadrunner Jaycees, four-time president of the Lifers' Club, Jaycee President of the Year. He typed those lines, then handwrote a couple of additions: "Received a commendation from Director Ellis MacDougall for the realign of the Florence CCTV system. Appointed as Arizona Jaycee Delegate to the Jaycees Natl Convention held in Phoenix."

The next section asked why he believed he was entitled to a change of sentence. Macumber typed a two-sentence response: "I stated my innocence at the time of my arrest, throughout my trial and each and every day for the past 34 years. I am innocent of the crime for which I was found guilty and I shall always remain innocent because innocence as well as guilt is infinite."

A third section asked him to describe his involvement in the crimes that landed him in prison. Again he typed a two-sentence response: "I had no involvement in the crimes whatsoever. To my knowledge I never knew or met either of the victims."

A fourth section asked about his plans upon returning to society. "I would probably go to live on my cousin's ranch in northwestern New Mexico," he wrote. "I would also visit my son and his family in Aurora, Colorado, and my brother in Rockford, Illinois."

A final section extended what would prove to be a fateful invitation: "Give any other information you believe the Board of Executive Clemency should consider." Macumber thought this over. It had been many months since he'd heard from the Justice Project, but he didn't feel entirely abandoned. "The Arizona Justice Project and the ASU Law School have been working on my case for the past seven years [eight years, in fact]. If you need any information as to their findings you can contact Larry Hammond at the Justice Project or Dr. Bartels at the law school. They would be more than willing to talk to you."

At the Board of Executive Clemency offices on West Jefferson in downtown Phoenix, Macumber's application received routine processing in early January 2009. The five-member board, appointed by the governor, considered all parole, pardon and commutation requests in a two-step process. On January 13, the board sent Macumber notice that his first step, a Phase I hearing, had been scheduled for February 12. As these were in absentia sessions, Macumber would not be present, but his friends and family could attend, as could legal counsel "provided at your own expense."

Duane Belcher, the board's chairman and executive director, signed this notice. Belcher, fifty-nine then, brought to the board more than thirty-two years of experience in the criminal justice field. He'd worked for years as a correctional service officer in Arizona, getting promoted through the ranks to his last Department of Corrections position as supervisor of the home-arrest program. Governor Fife Symington III had initially appointed him to the board in 1992, and he'd served there ever since but for a two-year break, sitting as chairman from 1993 to 1997, then resuming that position in 2004. An outgoing African-American with graying hair and a passion for riding motorcycles—he didn't mind weaving through congested freeway traffic on his Honda 1800, what he called an "old man's luxury motorcycle"—Belcher spoke frequently to community groups about his experiences in the criminal justice field. He was a member of the National Association of Blacks in Criminal Justice and, by most definitions, an advocate of law and order. Yet he'd worked in both probation and parole, sometimes with juveniles, so he'd worn two hats, both policing and supporting convicts.

Macumber's petition caught his attention for a particular reason: the reference to Larry Hammond and the Justice Project's years-long involvement. Belcher knew Hammond and deeply respected him. Hammond, as it happened, had been piling up the honors recently, adding to an already distinguished résumé. In 2008 alone, he'd been named to the Maricopa County Bar Hall of Fame, won the John J. Flynn Lifetime Achievement Award from the Arizona Attorneys for Criminal Justice, and—most lustrous of all—received the 2008 Justice Award from the American Judicature Society, the AJS's highest honor. The AJS had presented this award to him at a special ceremony in his honor, held on the evening of April 24 on the baseball diamond at Scottsdale Stadium, with more than 325 people in attendance, including his wife and three children and his former client Ray Girdler, whose release he'd secured after nearly a decade in prison, wrongly convicted of arson and murder. Family, baseball and the fair administration of justice being Hammond's chief passions, he could not have had a better night.

Following the dinner, a series of distinguished speakers had risen to praise him. Judge John R. Tunheim, the AJS president, described Hammond as "a man of great intellect with a strong passion for justice" who has "contributed to a much better America" and is "one of the foremost criminal lawyers of our time and one of the finest gentlemen I have ever known." H. Thomas Wells Jr., then the president-elect of the American Bar Association, thought Hammond "richly deserves to be recognized for his contributions to improving our justice system—particularly for his work in representing indigent defendants in capital and other criminal cases." Janet Reno, the former attorney general of the United States, recalled the frigid day in January 2003 when she first met Hammond, they joining to plan the 2003 National Conference on Preventing the

Conviction of Innocent Persons: "It was exciting. He was after progress and reform. He wanted it, but he wanted it with an intensity that was low-key and compelling, and it made a difference." Then Tom Henze, who'd been the prosecutor in the first Macumber trial, and later Hammond's co-counsel in the Knapp case, rose to present the Justice Award to Hammond. "Tom Henze brought the house down with a remarkable adaptation of the classic baseball poem 'Casey at the Bat,'" an AJS *Bulletin* later reported, "delivered with great gusto and without notes, in which Larry Hammond comes to the plate in the bottom of the ninth for the hometown team—but does not strike out." Henze also announced the establishment of the endowed Larry A. Hammond scholarship at the University of Arizona College of Law and presented Hammond with both the crystal Justice Award and a customized number 08 Arizona Diamondbacks jersey bearing his name.

Duane Belcher knew of this honor, and also of the Justice Project's many achievements. In the eleven years since Hammond founded it, the project had grown and gained increasing recognition as one of the first and most effective innocence projects in the country. Belcher was familiar with the work of Justice Project volunteers on dozens of cases and thought it notable that the project had been working on Macumber's case for so many years. Yet something puzzled him: The project didn't have a hand in this petition for clemency.

On February 12, when the Macumber petition came before the board at a Phase I hearing, Belcher brought to his colleagues' attention the Justice Project connection—and its lack of involvement with this application. He recommended that they postpone action, as he wanted to talk to Larry Hammond first. The board agreed to continue the hearing for a month "for sentence clarifications." On the recommendations line of the action report, a board member wrote, "DB to contact Justice Project."

The Justice Project that Duane Belcher planned to contact no longer operated out of Donna Toland's hip pocket in a corner of the Osborn Maledon law offices. By then, the project had gained not just increased recognition but also two good-sized federal grants, expanded resources, its own office, and—for the first time—a pair of invaluable full-time staffers. Katherine Puzauskas had joined the project in early September 2008, after graduating from the Howard University School of Law. Lindsay Herf had arrived in November, after graduating from California Western School of Law. Both had backgrounds that drew them to the Justice Project: Katie had been involved in the Federal Capital Litigation Clinic at Howard, Lindsay with the California Innocence Project, where she'd witnessed one client's exoneration after nineteen years in prison for a wrongful murder conviction. Both had decided they'd found their calling in innocence projects and post-conviction relief efforts. They wanted to help the wrongly and unjustly convicted.

Katie began as an administrative assistant to Hammond, operating out of the Osborn Maledon law office, opening and screening mail from inmates. In early January 2009, the Justice Project—using grant money for the build-out—moved into its own quarters in the basement of the library at the ASU College of Law. There, besides reviewing inmate mail, seeking grants and recruiting law student volunteers, Katie also began an inventory of all Justice Project cases, aiming to assemble the information in a detailed spreadsheet. In late January, during the course of this inventory, she came across a case file she had not seen or heard of before, a file whose status seemed unclear. On the morning of January 27, she typed an e-mail to Larry Hammond and Bob Bartels: "I'm writing to get the status of William Macumber's case."

What to say, what to tell her? In his office at Osborn Maledon, Hammond considered Katie's troubling inquiry. They'd had no real contact with Macumber for almost two years, yet Hammond, in his mind at least, had never let go. Should he now? He just didn't know. On February 3, he wrote back to Katie: "I am very sorry to say that we really have no answer to the status of the case that is in any way satisfying. The Macumber case is one of the very first looked at by the Justice Project. . . . We have had a very large number of attorney supervisors, as well as a very long string of student participants. Bob Bartels and I have remained 'involved' in the case since its inception as a Justice Project matter a decade ago. We had come reluctantly to the conclusion that there was little, if anything, that we could do for Bill Macumber because of our lack of success on the fingerprint front, but Bob and I have both been reluctant to close the file." There was, he explained, "a great deal of conflicting evidence" and "lots of reasons to think that this man may not be guilty." But "honestly, Katie, I do not know what we can do about this case. I suspect that we should close it, but for all of the reasons that have prevented us from closing it so far, I hate to do it now." He would copy this letter to Bartels "to see if he has any other reactions."

Two weeks later came Duane Belcher's unexpected phone call to Larry Hammond. We have a petition here, Belcher began, from your old client. The news that Macumber had filed a clemency application startled Hammond. He did not think that a prisoner insisting upon his innocence could even seek commutation, so it had not occurred to Hammond ever to file such a petition on Macumber's behalf. In truth, he had little faith in clemency boards. He'd gone before them with last-minute entreaties and seen his clients and their families treated like dirt. He'd had two clients executed after such pleas. Still, here was Duane Belcher, calling about Macumber. On the phone, Belcher asked, Do you think this guy is innocent? And do you want to get involved, do you want to represent him?

We think he's innocent, Hammond said. And of course we'll get in. But did Belcher realize that Macumber had never admitted guilt, had never expressed remorse? Yes, Belcher understood that. He didn't care, it didn't matter. Inmates can say they're not guilty, he explained. The board recognized that there were some cases where nothing more could be done inside a courtroom. Especially when you didn't have DNA evidence. The board members believed it part of their role to look at such cases—to correct errors when all remedies in the courts had been exhausted. Hammond, still skeptical, started to emphasize Macumber's exemplary record in prison. Belcher's focus remained on the innocence question. The board, he told Hammond, will consider Macumber's application.

Hammond felt anguished now over the Justice Project's failure to file anything on behalf of Macumber. He feared that Bill would die in prison before they resolved his case, and that prospect began to haunt him. He regretted again his competing tug of impulses with Bob Bartels, the facts

Page 232.

versus feelings, the investigating versus filing. That was part of why they'd never concluded the case, he believed. Maybe now, though, they could cross some kind of finish line.

To Bartels, this development was bittersweet. The news that Bill had filed made him happy. Even better, the board had expressed interest—and in the actual innocence issue. At the same time, Bartels didn't exactly feel euphoric—he still doubted their chance of getting a commutation—but he thought they should help out with the petition and hearing.

On February 19, Hammond wrote to Macumber: "I recently learned that you have filed a commutation packet with the Arizona Board of Executive Clemency. I was contacted by the Executive Director, Duane Belcher, to see if the Justice Project would like to submit anything on your behalf to be considered at your Phase I Hearing. Would you like us to submit anything on your behalf? We are more than happy to, but wanted to get your approval first." Hammond added a request: "Would it be possible for you to send us a copy of your commutation packet?"

At the state prison in Douglas, Macumber read these words on the evening of February 21. So he had not been abandoned. At least not entirely, at least not irrevocably. Sitting in his Mohave Unit cubicle, he reached once more for pen and paper. "Thank you for your letter of the 19th," he began, "and of course you have my permission to speak in my behalf at the commute hearing." He would have let Hammond know he was filing, but having not heard from the Justice Project, "I assumed we had reached the end of the road." He didn't think anything would come from this petition, but "I felt I owed my family one last effort." Medical issues also drove him, he allowed: "Frankly I have slipped a long way down hill this past year or so. I am sick much of the time and require a lot of medical attention. Growing old in here is a tough way to go and to face ending one's life here is tougher still."

In advance of Macumber's Phase I hearing, the clemency board invited both the Justice Project and the Maricopa County attorney to submit letters. The one-page letter submitted by Robert Shutts, a deputy county attorney in the Homicide Bureau, infuriated Hammond. That the county attorney objected "to the hearing and possible early release of this defendant" didn't bother him. But Shutts's curt summary of the case did: The palm print matched, the shell casings matched—and "during a subsequent interview, defendant admitted he had killed the two victims." *The defendant admitted?* That was despicable, Hammond thought. Hammond tried to call Shutts but couldn't reach him. Later, he heard word of Shutts's explanation: *I was just reporting what I had been told.*

On March 9, Hammond submitted his own letter to the board. This is, he wrote, "one of those very troubling cases in which the *absence* of DNA has left a defendant without a clear basis for setting aside his conviction." This case "is a sobering reminder of the very high burden of proof placed upon the convicted defendant to prove 'actual innocence' as a ground for post-conviction relief." As the board knew, the "presumption of innocence" was gone now, the burden on the convict being to prove innocence by "clear and convincing evidence." While they had failed to find the evidence to meet that standard, "there is a great deal to suggest that this is an innocent man." He and Bob Bartels "have always been disturbed by our inability to find a basis that would clearly prove his innocence." This case, "possibly more than any other we have evaluated, is a daily reminder of the heavy burden that rests on a convicted defendant."

Both Larry Hammond and Bob Bartels attended the Phase I hearing on March 12, along with Larry's assistant Donna Toland—unusual representation for any convict at this stage. In a small, bare room at the Department of Corrections' Alhambra facility in downtown Phoenix, they sat facing the five board members. Besides Duane Belcher, the board included: Marian Yim, an attorney with more than twenty years of public law experience, including thirteen years as an assistant attorney general and a stint as staff attorney for the Arizona Supreme Court; Olivia Meza, with thirty years of experience in the criminal justice system as a senior federal court executive, a pretrial services officer and a probation officer; Tad Roberts, with more than twenty years of experience in the criminal justice system as a probation counselor, probation officer and prerelease officer; and Ellen Stenson, with ten years of experience as a member of the Legislature's Ombudsman–Citizens' Aide office. By state mandate, only two members of the board could come from the same background, the goal being to have a diversity of personalities and professional histories. The only requirement: an expressed and demonstrated interest in the state judicial system. The board, in this way, enfranchised the outlook of the citizenry, outside of and apart from the lawyers and the legal system.

As a courtesy to Hammond and Bartels, Duane Belcher had made Macumber's hearing the first of thirty they'd handle this day. Hammond's very presence had an impact on the board—that such a highly respected attorney would show up got their attention. So did the Justice Project's sustained involvement, the decade-long commitment by dozens of students and volunteers. The board members knew it was quite unusual for a case to claim the consuming, extended attention of these people. The board trusted Larry Hammond and the Justice Project. Hammond's impetuous, undying obsession provided its own kind of testimony on behalf of Bill Macumber.

By contrast, no one from the prosecutor's office had appeared. So before they started, Belcher read into the record the county attorney's letter, written by Robert Shutts. Then Hammond rose to present the Justice Project's perspective on what he believed "is probably the case we have had the longest in the Project"—one that "more than 30 people now have worked on in the last decade." He again walked through his narrative: Judge O'Toole's phone call, Valenzuela's confessions, Judge Corcoran's ruling, the ballistics and fingerprint evidence, Bill's personality and achievements. The ejector-markings shell-casing evidence, he said, "is highly doubtful" and "I think wouldn't even be admitted at a trial today." The palm print, he allowed, "is a mystery to us. . . . We have spent a lot of time looking at it." So with the burden of proof on the Justice Project lawyers and no DNA evidence available, they just couldn't prove innocence "to a reasonable degree of certainty." We "have been stuck with a case in which we have not been able to proceed. We have been convinced for a long time that it is one of the most worthy cases ever to come before the Project, but is not one in which we believe, if we went to court, based upon what we know now, that we would be able to establish a case of actual innocence."

For this reason, Hammond looked to the board for relief. "As you all know, historically, it's been a problem for any inmate who won't admit guilt . . . to come before the Board. I think your Board in the last few years has suggested that maybe somebody who has protested his innocence but doesn't have DNA might be able to have his case heard. . . . I think that this would be the case to do it in."

The board members responded with an extended run of questions—about the prints and shell casings, about Carol, about Valenzuela and Primrose, about O'Toole and Corcoran and attorney-client privilege, about the hair found at the murder site, about Carol's claim that Bill had told "wild stories" of working as an army executioner. The hearing continued for more than one hour, Hammond and Bartels serving up answer after answer—highly unusual at this preliminary stage. The board members weren't after a final judgment this morning, only an assessment. That they reached: After listening to the two Justice Project lawyers, they believed they had more than needed to move forward to a Phase II hearing.

"Actual innocence is something that is very important," Duane Belcher said at the hearing's end, "and people can apply for commutation because of claims of innocence." He looked around at his fellow board members. "I would like to talk to Mr. Macumber," he announced. Ellen Stenson said, "I'll second that." The others called out, "Agreed." Bill Macumber had never made it to a Phase II hearing before. Now he had.

CHAPTER 18

A Lot of Work to Do

MARCH–MAY 2009

The Justice Project staffers had a lot of work to do. They needed a new, expanded affidavit from Tom O'Toole. They needed to write a detailed, comprehensive memo summarizing the entire Macumber case. They needed to meet with Bill and prepare him for the hearing. They needed to round up his family. This is our game to lose, Hammond believed. This could really happen—why else would the board be moving to Phase II? He didn't want to raise everyone's expectations, though. The board might balk in the end, and even if it didn't, Governor Jan Brewer would have to accept its recommendation. Who knew about the governor?

Upon returning to his office after the Phase I hearing, he e-mailed the Justice Project team: "You all probably have already heard that the Board this morning voted unanimously to pass Bill Macumber on to a Phase 2 Hearing. . . . The Board was very interested in his story and not disturbed by his unwillingness to 'acknowledge guilt.' Bob, Donna and I came away feeling very optimistic about our chances before the Board." Now they had to prepare, and "we all think this would be a great project for a group of students." They might assemble a new group, "but it occurred to us that

Katie might enjoy working on this case and we have a lot of people who have worked on the case over the years who might also be interested."

Hammond—finally—could send positive reports to Jackie and Bill, as well. "We have been terribly disappointed that we have not been able to help Bill after spending almost 10 years on this evaluation," he wrote to Jackie, "but maybe now we can be at least of some help. . . . I would be happy to visit with you on the telephone. . . . At a time convenient to you, would you give us a call?" To Bill, he wrote, "Congratulations! . . . Bob and I on behalf of the Justice Project would like to help you in any way that you will authorize us to do." They had a number of ideas and questions, so he wanted to talk on the phone with Bill, too. "Donna will be in touch to set up a time. . . . Congratulations again."

In writing these two letters, Hammond assumed that Jackie and Bill had already heard the news. In fact, they had not. At the state prison in Douglas, Macumber felt shocked—"totally astounded"—as he read Hammond's words. After his three prior experiences with the board, he hadn't thought he had a chance of prevailing. He also had not realized that Hammond and Bartels would be attending the Phase I hearing. He rushed to call Ron and other members of his family. Then he sat down to write to Hammond: "First and foremost, let me express my deepest appreciation. . . . You all have my deepest thanks for attending the hearing and speaking for me." The Justice Project "most certainly has my authorization to act in my behalf in any way you see fit."

On her ranch in New Mexico, Jackie Kelley heard the news in two phone calls from Bill. He had written to her recently, dreaming of what they might do if he were freed. What do you think, he'd asked, of us running pack-train horseback tours through the Superstition Mountains? That had sounded great to Jackie—she did know horses. Another time recently, she'd sent him a photo of a big old coyote she'd spotted outside her kitchen window—way bigger than the norm. "Dear one," he wrote back, "your wily coyote is really Willy the Wolf—a gray wolf. The snoot is not nearly as peaked as a coyote's, and the chest is too broad." Damn—he did like to give her trouble.

She hadn't corresponded with Larry Hammond since August 2007. Since then—later that year—her husband had passed away. At age seventy-seven, she was alone now on her 160 acres, though her daughter,

Robyn, lived two miles up the road, her middle child, Mike, another half mile past that. She also had a handyman and a housekeeper, as well as Spec, her thirteen-year-old red heeler Australian cattle dog. So she didn't feel isolated. At any rate, she liked solitude. Solitude was fine with her, just sitting up on the mesa with the coyotes and deer and elk and only $300 in annual property taxes. She had a big library of taped movies and a nice collection of CDs; she liked classical music and everything that came out of World War II, swing and big band, especially Glenn Miller. She preferred instrumentals over singers, though Spec—short for Spectacular—often sang along with whatever she played. Just one old woman and one old dog. If she woke and got up in the morning, she was doing well, she was happy.

On Tuesday, March 17, before she'd received Hammond's letter—she had to drive five miles into Colorado to collect her mail—she sat down to write him. "My dear cousin has talked to me twice recently concerning his and your contact with the Commute Board. . . . Needless to say, I am overjoyed, and ever hopeful for success. . . . While it has been some time since you and I last corresponded, I most certainly do want to thank you for all your efforts. Perhaps the Good Lord will finally look favorably on all endeavors." Could Larry please, she asked, provide her some information about this "Commute Board"?

At the end of the week, after mailing this, she received Hammond's letter of March 12, with its invitation to give him a call. She did so on Friday evening. They still had never met, though their relationship had endured and evolved for ten and a half sometimes contentious years. They talked at length, sharing more than usual. Since their last contact, she told him, her husband had passed away, so she was alone now. She explained the living situation on her ranch, reminding him of her Colorado mailing address and lack of a landline. At least she had perfect cell phone coverage, she explained—an Alltel tower stood a mile from her house. She kept her cell phone with her at all times, so they could always reach her. And there might come a day when she'd be closer to them; she was trying to sell her land, though like many out there, she had received no serious offers. If she found a buyer, she'd move to Tucson. Wherever she lived, she would do anything within her power to help in the commutation process. After some discussion, Jackie and Larry agreed that she would try her best to attend the Phase II hearing, and there, before the board, she would offer to have Bill come live with her. "I would love nothing more," she told Hammond, "than to end my days sharing my home with my cousin Bill."

Three weeks later, in mid-April, Hammond and Bartels talked by phone to Macumber, with Katie on the line as well. This was Katie's first contact with Bill—"I had never had the pleasure of meeting this young lady," he would say later, "but she was to become a very important figure in my life." Hammond had thought Katie "might enjoy" working on this case, and she did indeed. Larry's letter to the board ahead of the Phase I hearing had galvanized her. She was twenty-six then, ready to tackle a worthy challenge. Ever since the Phase I hearing, she'd been recruiting law students, making assignments, and calling in the past generations of volunteers—Karen Killion and Sharon Sargent-Flack chief among them—to help prepare the Phase II memo. *My God*, she kept saying to everyone, *we need to do something*.

During the phone conference, she took copious notes. Hammond began by confirming to Bill that the Board of Executive Clemency had indeed passed him to a Phase II hearing—for some reason, Macumber had still not received official notice. The hearing, Larry explained, would be in Phoenix. They'd have Bill arrive a day before to talk to the Justice Project team. Or the team might instead travel to Douglas before he came to Phoenix. Hammond next recounted his conversation with Jackie, how she'd volunteered to assist throughout the proceedings and attend the hearing. They all talked, as well, about Bill's living arrangements upon his release, how Jackie had offered her home, how Jackie might move to Tucson. Macumber's preference, he let them know, would be to live at the ranch because he'd feel "free" there.

Macumber had another matter to discuss: his deep concern that the board might grant parole rather than release for time served. He worried mostly about how parole would affect his family. They had been dealing with his conviction and incarceration for thirty-five years, and he believed they had suffered too much already; he did not want to open the lives of his family to a parole officer, he did not want to sacrifice his relatives' privacy to gain his freedom. Bartels tried to ease his concern: Parole supervision might not be overly invasive, he pointed out. No, Bill said, he didn't want to risk even one visit to his family from a parole officer. Bartels suggested that Bill talk to his family members about this— they had stood by him for thirty-five years and might very well not mind the visits. Hammond added that the board might consider straight release for time served rather than parole; they could raise this with Duane Belcher. Okay, Bill said. He was willing to wait until the problem arose.

They were way ahead of themselves, of course, as Hammond pointed out. First they had to prevail at the Phase II hearing, where only a fraction of prisoners won a favorable ruling. That would require lots of preparation, both for the oral presentation and for the written letter to the board.

At the end of the conversation, as the others hung up, Katie found herself alone on the phone with Bill. Good-bye, take care, she told him. *Okay*, he said in his gravelly cowboy voice. *Okeydoke.* This phone conference left Katie fired up. They'd identified a number of factors that the board might look at favorably, including Bill's age, his stellar record, and the high regard other inmates and prison staffers held for him. But "the factor I see to be the most significant," Katie opined to the team in a memo that day, "is his persistent claim of innocence and the fact that a man by the name of Ernest Valenzuela confessed to the crime."

Valenzuela's confession represented a familiar dimension of the case, of course, but Katie Puzauskas brought fresh eyes to a file others had been thumbing through for a decade. She also brought her particular flair—she was a vivacious young woman with an efficient management style, unbounded compassion and an infectious spirit. Raised in Phoenix, she'd majored in psychology at the University of Arizona before enrolling in law school. Her mom was Italian, her father half Italian and half Lithuanian, making her, as she put it, "three-quarters Italian," with half of the three-quarters being Sicilian—"we like to think of Sicily as its own country." Her parents and assorted relatives—aunts, uncles, cousins, a grandfather—all lived in Arizona and always had food on the table: "We're Italian!"

She now threw herself into planning for Bill's Phase II hearing, Hammond having made her the Macumber case coordinator (she would later be named an overall Justice Project cases and programs coordinator).

She arranged meetings, she fielded calls, she counseled family members, she rounded up letters of support, she corralled relatives to attend the hearing. The Justice Project wanted to show the board members that Bill had a support network out there, that they wouldn't just be sending a lifer out into the world cold.

Hammond heard from Jackie on Saturday, May 2, six days before the hearing. She'd be coming in from New Mexico with her daughter, she reported in a phone call. Robyn had insisted on driving—*There's snow on the ground and you might hit a cow*, she'd told her mom. They would arrive in Phoenix on Wednesday. Bob Macumber and his son, Mark, would arrive that Wednesday as well, flying in from Illinois. Of the family, only Ron, it turned out, couldn't be there—work obligations would keep him in Colorado.

The generations of law student volunteers were coming as well. Karen Killion from up near Seattle, Sharon Sargent-Flack from Prescott; Jen Roach, Jenifer Swisher, Pete Rodriguez, Ty Jacobson—they'd all be there. Rich Robertson, too, of course, and Bob Bartels and Donna Toland and Carrie Sperling, who was then serving as the project's executive director. All the volunteers, from near and far. *What the fuck*, Larry thought. It had suddenly become, for him, just that: an amazing what-the-fuck moment. He couldn't believe it—hell, this case had been *closed*.

That week, calls from Macumber family members kept flooding the Justice Project and Hammond's law office. Jackie had the most questions. What should she say at the hearing? What should she do? Where should she stay in Phoenix? Are there freeways in Phoenix? She hoped not, she didn't like driving on freeways. She didn't really want to drive at all in Phoenix. Could Larry come get them at their motel, take them to the hearing? These weren't the sorts of tasks and issues high-priced senior lawyers usually handled, but Hammond found it all quite interesting. He decided everyone should meet at the Osborn Maledon law office at 1:30 P.M. on Thursday, May 7, the day before the hearing: the Justice Project team and the Macumber clan, together in person for the first time.

First, though, the project lawyers had to complete and deliver their all-important memo to the board, presenting an overview of the Macumber case. They'd blown past their Tuesday, May 5, deadline. The initial draft by Karen and Sharon, working off a core synopsis by Bartels, had come in at thirty pages, but Hammond thought it should be ten maximum—they wanted the board members to read it, after all. Katie, Karen, and Sharon went to work on paring it down, with everyone else contributing, Bartels and Hammond reviewing. They were still polishing it on Thursday morning, two days past the deadline. Not until late that morning did they hand their final version—ten pages, single-spaced, plus Tom O'Toole's two-page affidavit—to IntelliServe for high-priority delivery to the board's offices. The messenger gave it to the receptionist there at 12:46 P.M.—forty-four minutes before Jackie and her relatives were due to arrive at Osborn Maledon, she to meet Larry Hammond for the first time.

Larry wrapped Jackie in his arms, giving her a big hug, when he found her standing at the receptionist's counter. Jackie felt as if a slowly drawn circle had finally been completed. They liked each other instantly, despite all their difficult exchanges over the years. At 1:30, everyone filed into a conference room on the twentieth floor: Larry and Donna; Jackie and Robyn; Bill's cousin Harleen and her husband, Jay; Bill's brother, Bob, and his son, Mark. On speakerphone were Rich Robertson and Katie Puzauskas, who had remained at the Justice Project headquarters. As they began to talk, Katie suddenly thought, Wait, what about Ron? She'd just been on the phone with him, so she called him back and hooked him in. Listening to everyone greet him, she realized Ron was just now "meeting" some of his family—Jackie, Robyn, his first cousin Mark—for the first time since his early childhood. Then Hammond began walking everyone through what would happen the next morning. He and Bob Bartels would make the core presentation. Larry would offer a general overview, Bob would talk about the investigation and evidence. Everyone else would have a chance to speak, too. Karen and Sharon could explain how long they'd been involved with Bill's case. Pete and Ty could detail Bill's medical condition and his accomplishments in prison. Jackie could talk of Bill's plans upon release. Everyone could show their support for Bill.

Listening on the phone from Colorado, Ron grew increasingly restless and upset. Just three weeks before, in mid-April, he'd taken time off from work to visit his dad. Because of that trip, he couldn't take more time off this week. But he kicked himself now, listening to them all talk about the plans for the next day. He wanted to be there, he should be there. Across their living room, Deb studied his expression and listened to his tone as he spoke into the phone. In an instant, she turned to her computer screen and began searching for flights to Phoenix. Ron, seeing this, excused himself temporarily from the conference call, hanging up so he could phone his supervisor at Shamrock Foods and arrange for more time off. Deb found him a flight. Ron rejoined the conference call. "I'm flying in tonight," he announced. "I'll be there for the hearing." Around the conference room table, everyone started clapping. Whenever you land, Harleen and Jay offered, we'll pick you up, and you can stay with us. Bob Macumber said he and Mark would also greet him at the airport. Hammond, for once, tried to warn and discourage: It's such a long way to come, you might only get to talk for a minute or two. But Ron, determined now, didn't have time for discussion. His flight was taking off in two hours.

In the conference room, their conversation continued. Robert Macumber had a story to tell—a memory from just after Bill's arrest in 1974. He and his dad wanted to know more about why Bill had been arrested; they wanted to understand the evidence. So Bill's appointed lawyer got them in to see it all at the sheriff's department. When they arrived, the deputies took them into an open area. No red tape, no special arrangements. The evidence just sat there in a couple of short filing boxes. The deputies let them handle everything, including the prints and shell casings. The casings were in a three-by-five-inch box, the prints in one the size of a shoe box. Bob and Harold saw the fingerprint lifts on the cards. Not photos—the actual cards. They touched the items without anyone giving them a second glance.

Bob paused, replaying this moment in his mind, then continued. While looking at this evidence, he said, he noticed something odd: a difference between the palm print card and the other print cards. The fingerprints were mounted on dark tan paper that looked really old, while the palm print was on thicker, manila card stock that seemed newer. The fingerprints were all brown and dated; the palm print had no deterioration at all.

Bob shook his head at the memory. He hadn't realized the significance then. What a mistake. He wished he'd just slipped that card into his pocket. Sure, they would have arrested him. He would have had to serve two or three years. But he would have saved Bill from a life in prison.

Bob offered the Justice Project team yet another memory from back then. After looking at the shell casings, he suggested to Bill's lawyer that they view them under the scanning electron microscope at Motorola, where he worked. The sheriff's department had nothing like that, he pointed out. Maybe they could settle whether the shell casings truly matched Bill's gun. It took a while, but the sheriff's department finally said okay. They sent two plainclothes deputies out to Motorola. Bob checked them in at the gate and took them to the SEM lab, where they handed the casings to the lab director. Bob stayed in the lab with the director and the casings, while the deputies stood out in the hallway. The lab director put the casings through the SEM and took pictures. He and Bob could see something, but no distinguishing marks. When they finished, the deputies returned the cartridges and the photos to the department. Those photos were never used at trial, never even mentioned.

Bob Macumber looked around the Osborn Maledon conference room, again shaking his head.

Okay, Hammond said. This is something for you to tell the board tomorrow morning.

Ron's plane landed at 10:00 that night. A welcoming team—Harleen and Jay, Bob and Mark—greeted him at the airport. Ron had met everyone but Mark at the state prison during his first visit to Douglas. He and his first cousin, a doctor and assistant professor at the Northwestern University medical school in Chicago, had last seen each other when they were four years old. At the curb, Mark came up to introduce himself. Ron put out his hand to shake. Mark said, No, that's not good enough. They hugged instead. Back at Harleen and Jay's home in Apache Junction, Ron felt too jumpy to consider sleep. So he and Mark stayed up late, talking.

Mark had gotten to know Bill in a way Ron hadn't, because as a boy, growing up, he'd often visited his uncle in prison. He could tell Ronnie about the father he'd missed knowing all those years.

Mark had been six when the cops arrested his uncle. He visited him in prison whenever possible, first with his father, later with his own son and wife. The setting and locale changed from time to time. Sometimes Bill sat behind a screen, and Mark couldn't touch him even to say hello or good-bye. More often he met Bill in a kind of schoolyard, a fenced area with tables and chairs, and Mark could take a short stroll with him. Bill would try to scare Mark when he was young, but it never worked, because Bill would soon break into a grin and lift Mark high in the air, higher than anyone else in the family could raise him. Then he'd laugh and give Mark a big hug. He'd talk boring adult talk to Mark's parents, but he'd also always turn to his nephew and pay special attention just to him. He had an intense interest in Mark's life, and there was something about him that made Mark listen when he offered advice.

Sometimes, as Mark wandered around, playing in the dirt, other inmates would come up and talk to him directly—just him. These were scary, scarred, tattooed big-muscled men—at least they looked that way to Mark. But they all had the same message: They wanted Mark to know how much they loved Bill. They wanted to tell Mark what a great man he was, how he had changed their lives, how they would do anything for him.

Mark's account meant the world to Ron, but finally, near 3 A.M., his eyes closed. Drained of all adrenaline, he more or less passed out.

Katie also stayed up late into the night, working at the Justice Project offices alongside Karen Killion, the two preparing for the hearing and fielding e-mails from Larry Hammond. For Katie, this was a world of unknown. Would they be asked questions? What should she say? How to get Robert Macumber's new revelation about the fingerprint card stock before the board? At least they'd completed their memo in time, a huge accomplishment. And they had the whole family here, so unusual for this kind of situation.

"Wow," she wrote in a final e-mail to the team. "It was great talking to Bill's family. His overwhelming support will play a great role in tomorrow's hearing, especially with his son, Ronald, making the trip at the last minute to be at the hearing." She closed with a reminder: "The hearing is at ASPC Phoenix in the Alhambra Reception Unit at 8:30 A.M. We will be there at 8 A.M."

At home that night, reading Katie's message, Larry Hammond felt exhausted but exhilarated. A what-the-fuck moment indeed. He couldn't wait for the morning.

CHAPTER 19

Clemency Hearing

MAY 2009

The Department of Corrections' Alhambra Reception Center was a straight shot down Twenty-fourth Street from the Embassy Suites where Jackie Kelley and her daughter had spent the night, but they felt uncertain of their bearings, so wanted Larry Hammond to pick them up. Instead, after some negotiation, he drove to their hotel and led them down Twenty-fourth Street as they followed in their own car. That way, everyone could leave when they wanted.

At Van Buren, the two-car caravan turned right, then left into the Alhambra complex's large gravel parking lot. A crowd had already gathered. From the Justice Project, Hammond saw Rich Robertson, Bob Bartels, Katie Puzauskas, Karen Killion, Sharon Sargent-Flack, Pete Rodriguez, Ty Jacobson, Donna Toland and Carrie Sperling. From Macumber's family, besides Jackie and Robyn, he saw Robert and Mark Macumber, Harleen and Jay Brandon, Harleen's brother Henry Sanger, and a tall, husky man who had to be Bill's son Ron. There in the lot everyone greeted each other, Ron meeting not just the Justice Project team but Jackie Kelley for the first time.

Their dreary surroundings did not match this group's air of hopeful-ness. The Alhambra complex, a spare one-story brick facility, stood adja-cent to a state mental hospital, sharing the same grounds in a neighborhood of old motor hotels. After being sentenced, all state convicts initially came to this unit, where officials evaluated and assigned them a prison.

The Justice Project team entered the hearing room first. Inside, they found a cramped, uncomfortably spartan chamber, all cinder blocks and chicken wire. It reminded Rich of a bunker, while Larry thought of class-rooms from his childhood in El Paso. The walls were bare, the floor tile. Up front, the five members of the Board of Executive Clemency—Duane Belcher, Tad Roberts, Marian Yim, Ellen Stenson and Olivia Meza—sat behind a long laminated undraped table, a tape recorder before them, a microphone off to their left. Then came four rows of standard stackable plastic chairs, facing the board members. The place looked and felt like what it was: a prison.

The first row held just three chairs. Bill Macumber was already sit-ting there, in the middle; he'd been brought in first, by himself, coming face-to-face with the board members as they introduced themselves. Now he rose to greet the Justice Project team. He wore, as always, the inmate's bright orange jumpsuit. His hands and feet were shackled and tied into a belly cinch. He shuffled forward. At Hammond's request, the officers took off his handcuffs, leaving the leg chains. Moments later, Macumber's family members filed in. The Alhambra guards had emphat-ically warned that Bill could not touch or embrace them, but his eyes filled when he saw Ronnie—he hadn't known his son would be there.

After exchanging a few words with his relatives, Macumber sat back down, with Bartels on his left, Hammond on his right. The others took their seats behind them, Ron choosing a chair in the middle of the sec-ond row, Jackie sitting between Katie and Robyn in the rear. Someone rushed for extra chairs to handle the overflow—they had twenty-two people crammed into this small chamber, including two Department of Corrections guards from Douglas, who stood against the side wall off to the right. Near the guards sat one woman the others didn't know—a bystander likely there for a later hearing.

From his chair, Macumber could not see anyone in the room but the board members and his two lawyers, but he felt Ron's eyes on his back, right behind him. Bill and his two guards had left the Mohave Unit in Douglas just after 4:00 that morning under still dark skies. He'd felt excited beyond words. Four hours of driving hadn't diminished his emotions. Yet to others in the room, watching him, he seemed dazed—aged, quiet, slumped in his chair, as if worn out after all the years. On this morning, he listened more than he participated.

For a few moments, the board members studied the documents before them, provided by the Justice Project. Then the board's chair and executive director, Duane Belcher, looked up at Bill. "Good morning, Mr. Macumber."

"Good morning," Bill replied.

"First off," Belcher continued, "some information. You are serving a first degree murder conviction for life, and there is no possibility of parole on your sentencing structure, is that correct?"

"I believe it was called life without parole."

"Life—life without parole. Okay. And that was how many years ago, when the crime was committed?"

"Well, the crime was committed in May 1962."

Belcher turned through the pages of the Justice Project packet. The suggestion of a confession Bill had made to his wife stopped him. Belcher wanted to identify right off what they had here. "Okay now, with all the records we have. . . . You are professing your innocence in this matter?"

"From day one," Macumber said.

"From day one. Okay. And is that—is that still your statement?"

"It is forever."

The Justice Project's ten-page Phase II memorandum, sitting on the table in front of each board member, provided the road map to what would follow. Here the project team once again offered up its narrative about the Macumber case, this version more detailed and comprehensive than ever before. From an overview of the case, focusing on the handkerchief, thatch of human hair, tire tracks, shell casings and latent fingerprints, the memo moved to Primrose and Valenzuela and the confessions heard by Tom O'Toole. Then to Carol Macumber's statement, Carol who "certainly had motive to lie," Carol who "apparently suspected nothing" until after the couple's estrangement in the spring of 1974. The first trial, with a conviction based on an alleged "confession 12 years after the crime, a partial fingerprint and ejector markings on a bullet casing." The second trial, where, "despite Valenzuela's confessions to a cellmate, to his two attorneys and to a psychiatrist, the trial court refused to permit the defense to present evidence."

Midway through the memo, the Justice Project turned to its own involvement in the case since 2000. The missing sheriff's reports and empty evidence locker its staff had found. A ballistics comparison based solely on ejector marks. Fingerprint evidence full of questions "about Carol's role" and whether Latent Lift 1 was in fact the Lift 1 taken by Jerry Jacka on May 24, 1962. Carol and Bill's marital difficulties, Carol reporting the "alleged confession" during the divorce and custody proceedings, "at a time when she potentially stood to reap personal gain." Carol's access to the files and evidence, Carol's classroom training in lifting latent prints. The missing sources of potential DNA evidence—the handkerchief and the all-important thatch of hair. The lack of any motive—the murders a "drug deal gone south" and Bill with "absolutely no history of drug use or drug dealing."

Next the memo moved on to Macumber's personal accomplishments, his history of prison and community service, his role as an educator and author, his exemplary disciplinary record. His declining medical condition. His plans upon release—with no less than four families offering to take him in, all present at this hearing.

On these last matters, Bill's record and prospects, the project team sought to hang the case, still regarding an actual innocence claim as beyond the board's reach. "Respectfully, we urge the Board to conclude that commutation is warranted based on his exemplary record alone. We may all remain haunted by the injustice that may have been done to him, but we know that this Board cannot retry his case. Restoring him to liberty is a step toward justice that we hope the State of Arizona will take based on who this man is today."

In truth, Duane Belcher, at least, sounded perfectly willing to consider an actual innocence claim, even though the board could not "retry" Macumber's case. "Let me just explain a little bit about the commutation process . . ." he said, addressing Macumber. "Basically, the standard is, it's a mercy and grace issue, but the Board is looking at some specific things. The Board is looking at whether or not, number one, is the sentence . . . proportionate to the crime that was committed? We understand your statement to the Board that you're innocent of the crime, and that is perfectly a stand that you can take for this particular process. So, we'd look at—we'd look at, is the sentence clearly excessive? Now, obviously, if it's true that you're innocent, then one day in jail was clearly excessive." That was one of two chief factors the board considered. The other: "Would a person be law abiding should the sentence be commuted." *Clearly excessive* and *law abiding*—that's what the board needed to see, needed to find.

Hammond deftly responded. Bill was an "old-code lifer," he pointed out, not eligible for parole. Those convicted of first-degree murder under the newer code have generally been eligible for parole after twenty-five years. Only thirty-seven prisoners sentenced under the "no-parole old-code" policy remained in the state prison system. The board members well understood Hammond's point: This disparity could be a factor in determining if Macumber's sentence was "excessive" in relation to other cases.

Standing before the board, Hammond prepared to offer his opening comments. Normally he and Bartels let the students present, but for this hearing, they'd decided to do the talking themselves and have the students learn by watching. Staying true to their natures, Larry would go first, handling the emotional dimension; then Bob would follow with the facts and their investigation. Hammond began by introducing not only Macumber's relatives but also the entire Justice Project team, one by one, the volunteers reaching back to 2000, this being "one of the great glories to us in this project, that people who start, students have stayed with us." Larry here aimed not just to give his colleagues their due—more important, he wanted to underscore the project's decade-long commitment to Macumber. *Every person who touched this case can't let go*, he'd told the board at the Phase I hearing. Now he wanted the board to see these people.

Hammond next invoked Thomas O'Toole, so respected by the board members: "We have gone back to Judge O'Toole and he has very thoughtfully given us an affidavit, which we attached to the memorandum you all received this morning. I think it is very clear—and you all know Judge O'Toole—he was on the Superior Court bench here for 24 years and was presiding criminal judge several times—but he continues to feel very strongly that his former now deceased client, Ernest Valenzuela, was telling him the truth. . . . He believed it then and he believes it now, and he so stated in his affidavit."

Then Hammond sounded his most fundamental theme about this proceeding and Macumber's case: "I want to observe the challenge that Bill has and that we have in these cases. DNA has changed the face of the way people look at criminal justice in America, and we understand that and we are deeply invested in cases where there is biological evidence." But unlike Barry Scheck's nationally famous Innocence Project, the Arizona Justice Project also took on cases that lacked DNA evidence—such as Macumber's. "Because of the age of this case, and because of the loss of evidence over the years . . . whatever biological evidence [there] might have been . . . is long gone. And so we don't have the ability to look to biological evidence, and it has made our job over the last nine years a much more difficult one." This constituted one reason why they were so sincerely "grateful to have an opportunity to be heard by you." For the many people "who don't have the benefit of DNA, there's no place else to even be heard."

Bob Bartels followed, laying out the facts of the case and the Justice Project's investigation, underscoring and expanding on the first six pages of the memorandum. The prints, the ejector markings, Carol's statement—but now he added a claim not explicitly stated in the memo: That Carol "had been under investigation at that point for impropriety . . . that she had been involved in inappropriate relationships with a number of people in the Maricopa County Sheriff's Office . . . and this is something that we actually were able to confirm." He also added that "at least two family members, including her son Ronald, believe that she was capable of falsely accusing Bill of murder." And "one of the details in Carol's story"—that Bill said "he was acting under orders from the Army CID"—is "very similar to some information in a report in the Sheriff's file about another person."

The board members had to lean forward, straining to hear, since Bartels, as usual, was speaking in a near whisper. They asked him to talk more directly into the mike. He did, and continued. He thought the palm print doubtful because of Carol's classroom training in how to lift and transfer prints. Also because Jerry Jacka had taken Latent Lift 1 on photographic stock paper—particularly easy to manipulate—and had not, in 1962, sent that lift to the FBI "because he did not think it was a good enough print for comparison purposes." Another oddity, "which Larry and I just learned about yesterday": Bill's brother, Robert, allowed in 1974 to examine the latent prints in the sheriff's department, had noticed that the Latent Lift 1 paper backing looked much newer than the others. If only they had that print card now—but they didn't, making it "much more difficult for us to conclusively demonstrate that the palm print was planted." Bartels finished with a summary of the Primrose and Valenzuela statements, not dwelling long there because the board had heard much about them at the Phase I hearing. "Do you have any questions?" he asked the board members before sitting down.

They did. "Is Carol still alive?" Olivia Meza wondered. "I'm interested in knowing what she says now."

Rich Robertson rose to tell the story of his trip to Olympia, Washington, when, as he recalled it, Carol's only comment was "He's as guilty as Saddam Hussein and get the fuck off my porch." They had the board members' full attention now. Marian Yim would later say she put great weight on this testimony—the accuser revealed as a crude and hostile person.

Olivia Meza had another question: "I believe her son is here. Is that correct?" She wondered whether he'd grown up with Carol, and what had happened to him in their home.

Ron approached the microphone. He had no prepared remarks. He just began talking: "We were told that our father had committed murder and was guilty. It was constant." We were told "not to leave the house, not to go anywhere," that "our grandparents were going to come and take us away. That at the beginning of the second trial they came to find us in Colorado." It wasn't "until years later that I started looking into the case, when I was in high school." He discovered then "there were things obviously wrong." He decided "things did not make sense. . . . I mean, we heard all sorts of things from my mother."

Meza again: "Is that when you contacted your father in prison?"

"No. Um—I was afraid, you know, and it wasn't because I was afraid of my father. It was because I was afraid of what he thought of me. I was worried that he was going to be mad because he felt like we abandoned him." Only much later did Ron contact his father, after his mother reported that Larry Hammond's investigators had been up to see her. "And I took it upon myself to call Mr. Hammond and when I talked with Mr. Hammond things fell into place for me about what happened." Ron drew a breath, looked hard at the board members. "I have no doubts of what my father had done."

Hammond treasured Ron's testimony. To think he'd discouraged Ron from coming! Larry interjected now, wanting to explain how "serendipitous" this reassociation of father and son had been: "We were looking to see if we could find anyone in the family to talk to us. We had no expectations that there would be an opportunity for a father and son to reunite. But it happened. It happened without us urging it." Whatever else transpires in this case, he pointed out, whatever the outcome, they would always have that. "And the fact that he was able to get on a plane last night and get down here is for us in the room a definitely important gesture on his part. We're very grateful."

Marian Yim, changing course, had a quite different type of question: "We have in our packet a letter from Robert Shutts, Deputy County Attorney, Homicide Bureau. . . . In the last paragraph, there's a statement that during a subsequent interview, defendant admitted he had killed the two victims. I'm confused. What's this confession?"

Bartels answered, in a barely audible whisper: "The short answer is, the statement by Mr. Shutts is simply not accurate." He added, "Mr. Shutts had no prior involvement with this case."

Marian Yim studied her packet again. "Is this the testimony of Carol? Her statement that he confessed? Is that the so-called confession? . . . Because that's the only one I can figure . . . I don't remember reading that there was a specific admission . . ."

Bartels, again softly: "No, there wasn't."

Marian Yim had another question: Is this a mother capable of framing the father of her children? She looked at Ron, who returned to the mike. Listening to everyone else, he'd been preparing, thinking of what he wanted to say. He'd decided to reintroduce himself and explain his last name. "My name is Ronald Macumber," he began, speaking firmly, yet trembling, his eyes fixed on the board members. "I am Bill's youngest son. Growing up I was called Ron Kempfert. That was the name my mother decided to give us when my mom and dad divorced. . . . Now I am in the process of changing everything I have back to Macumber. But I would like to add about my mother. This really did not surprise me when Mr. Hammond told me what happened. . . . This does not surprise me. I have never—you would never think your mother would be capable of something like this, but when I was told by Mr. Hammond what they had found, all the evidence they had put together, it did not surprise me at all. She's capable of this. I have no doubt in my mind she's capable of this. She is one of the most controlling people I have ever met. . . . And what she has done to my father is inexcusable. And I just wanted to make you aware of that. She is my mother, yes, but I have no doubt in my mind she is capable, totally capable to do what you've been told."

A silence fell. Some in the room were blinking, wiping their eyes. Even the guards looked affected. None of them could see Bill's face, Bill's reaction. With his back to them, he held his head down, not looking around, as if he felt responsible for causing them all such pain. He'd not once made eye contact with his family members, or with anyone talking. "Okay," Marian Yim finally said to Ron. "Thank you."

Bill's brother, at Hammond's invitation, rose next. Larry invited Bob Macumber to "tell us and the Board what you told us yesterday about the ballistics back at the time of the trial."

Bob, at age seventy-one, struggled to gain control of himself, his voice shaky, tears in his eyes. "My name is Robert Macumber," he began. Then he stopped. "Excuse me, but we get emotional . . ." He drew a breath, started again. He recounted how sheriff's deputies had allowed him and his father to handle evidence and take the shell casings to the Motorola lab for testing. There, he explained, the lab director examined the cartridges for any discernible identifying marks—ejector marks, extractor marks, breech marks, firing-pin marks—but "couldn't find anything, and that's about as microscopic as you can get." What stood out even more for Bob was the strange difference between the backing paper for the fingerprints and the palm print. "The fingerprints that they lifted from the car were all—and again, this is 13 years after—they were all a little bit on the aged side, so the paper was a little bit brown from age. But that palm print was clear, crisp. . . . That's about all I can add on that."

Marian Yim thought Bob's testimony astounding. Apart from the differences in print backings, she considered it remarkable that deputies had let them handle and even cart off the evidence. Yim couldn't believe that the deputies would allow anybody, let alone the defendant's brother, to just mess around with the evidence. No chain of custody, no security—nothing. Yim, the only lawyer on the board, knew such evidence would be thrown out of court today. This, she thought, was a legal train wreck.

Larry Hammond guided the balance of their presentation to considerations more within what he considered the clemency board's realm. Ty Jacobson and Pete Rodriguez walked through Bill's stellar prison record and extended lineup of accomplishments. Most extraordinary to the board members, given their familiarity with inmates' histories, was Bill's single "minor" infraction in thirty years (for being "out of place" during a tense moment in the yard). Beyond even the Jaycees and the rodeos and his many novels, that stood out; the board members had never before seen such a pristine disciplinary history.

Duane Belcher, with years of experience in the state prisons, here fell into a casual conversation with Bill Macumber, prompted by the report that Warden Charles Flanagan had taken to calling Bill "Pops" and relying on him as a mediator. Since then, Flanagan had risen to be the deputy director of the Arizona Department of Corrections. "Did you have a C level clearance at some point in time?" Belcher asked Macumber—that being the highest level of trust clearance in the state prison system.

"It would have been called a C override," Bill explained. "It was an override given by the Director to inmates who couldn't normally get the override to minimum, okay?"

"And you couldn't get the override because of your sentencing structure?"

"Right. So Ellis MacDougall overrode and gave me a C override, which put me in OT [the Outside Trustee Unit], as well. First it put me in the North Unit Annex, then OT."

Belcher was leading Bill to memories of days long past, the years before Sam Lewis took over the prison system, the years when Ellis Mac-Dougall favored rehabilitation over punishment.

Belcher asked, "North Unit OT?"

"Yeah."

"Right. And this—were you able to participate in the furlough program, the 72-hour furlough program . . . ?"

"Not the furlough program per se, but you know, I made the final years of the Jaycees, I think I made 196 trips out of prison total. I never missed a rodeo. . . ."

Belcher smiled. "So we're talking a little bit better than North Unit OT, right?"

Macumber looked rueful. "Well, I hate to say this, but you know, back in those days, things were pretty wide open, Mr. Belcher. You know . . . inmates had it pretty decent back then."

Belcher nodded. "I got hired by the Department under Director MacDougall ten years ago."

"He was," Macumber said, "a unique individual."

The final strand in the Justice Project presentation involved testimony to Macumber's character and his prospects if released. One by one, project team members rose to endorse Bill, their words now more personal than legal. Donna Toland, Katie Puzauskas, Karen Killion, Sharon Sargent-Flack—all testified to Macumber's "positive" outlook and "extraordinary" accomplishments, and to their own steadfast commitment to his cause. So, too, did Bill's relatives, all offering their homes to him. Mark Macumber, overwhelmed by his memories of Bill in prison, of Bill's tender attention to him there, struggled when his turn to speak came. "Yes," he began, fighting tears. "Sorry, I hope I don't get choked up. I was five or six years old, I think, when all this transpired. I can only speak to knowing Bill as an inmate. . . . I'm very proud to tell people about this. It's a privilege for me to be here to speak up for him." Mark faltered. "I had written out a letter," he said. "I didn't think I'd get through it."

Belcher assured him, "I believe we do have your letter and we've had a chance to review it."

Mark tried once more: "You know, I owe my life to Bill. I hope that things work out well for Bill . . ." He retreated to his chair.

Ron again approached the mike, for a final tribute to his father. "I can't imagine what he had to endure over the past 35 years," he told the board. "I can only hope to be half the man he is. His positive attitude, you could never tell anything's wrong by talking to him. He's always the one propping me up when I'm upset about the way things have gone, what's happening to him. I just thank you so much for hearing this case. I greatly, greatly, appreciate it."

Then came Jackie Kelley. She spoke forcefully, so all could hear. "I am Bill's first cousin on his mother's side," she began. "I'm a few years older than he. I first met him when he was two days old in the Davenport Hospital, where he was born. And Bill and I have been more like brothers and sisters than cousins, along with Bob. The three of us were three peas in a pod, so to speak. I'm not the only one, but ever since this happened, I have been working in my own little ineffectual way trying to help, because I have always known he was never guilty. It's impossible. Anyway I do a lot of praying also and my whole church is behind Bill. If the good Lord sees fit to free him . . . I would love for Bill to come live with me."

Larry Hammond concluded their narrative. In his hand he held Macumber's book of poetry, *History's Trail*, published in 1984. "I want to end," he told the board, "with the mentioning of the book of poetry that Bill wrote. . . . It's called *History's Trail by William Macumber*. And I believe that Ron does not know that his father many years ago dedicated this book to him—to Scott, Steve and Ron." It was "very meaningful," Hammond felt, "that at a time when there had been no reconciliation between father and sons, Bill had done something like this." He thought it "powerful evidence." Not courtroom evidence, of course—but evidence all the same.

The board members now started to talk about the case among themselves. Jackie had been watching their faces all through the morning, trying to read them. So had Ron, so had Robert Macumber. In the back row, Katie had been holding her breath, thinking, *Do the right thing, do the right thing*. Jackie had worried most about Ellen Stenson, sitting to Belcher's left—her facial expression had stayed hard, never relaxing or warming. Ron had worried about her, too; her comments had been vague and noncommittal. He'd also worried about Tad Roberts, sitting on the far end of the board's table—nothing specific, just the way he came across. Katie, too, thought Tad Roberts might cause them problems.

The board members weren't just talking, though. It took a while for those watching to realize it, but the board members, following normal procedure, were deliberating—right then, right before them. Olivia Meza, being a relative newcomer to the board, began by asking Duane Belcher to go over the various choices between recommending release for time served versus making Macumber eligible for parole. Belcher reviewed the several possibilities: absolute discharge, general parole under supervision, home-arrest status, six-month reviews leading to eventual release, applications under Statute 414. "Those are all of the options," he concluded.

"Thank you," Meza said. "I appreciate that. Is it possible to submit alternative recommendations . . . or do we have to choose one to submit?"

Belcher explained, "There's nothing in the statute that ever mandates what the Board can recommend to the Governor." There was nothing, for example, that mandates commutation "is just mercy and grace." So "I think the Board can recommend whatever it chooses."

Katie could see Belcher trying to guide them, trying to show the board members how they might proceed. *Do the right thing, do the right thing.*

Ron wondered, Are they really deliberating right here, in front of us? He looked over at Sharon, whispering, *Are they making a decision now?* She just raised her eyebrows. He turned back to listen to the board.

Belcher kept going: "Now, I'll just add my little piece. . . . Now, if the belief of the Board is that Mr. Macumber is in fact innocent of this . . . then it would seem the logical thing would be to simply let him out of prison." But since he's been "down 35 years," parole might in fact "help with a period of transition." Or "the board could recommend both alternatives if it was inclined to do that."

Oh my God, Katie thought. She sensed now what was happening, what was coming. She couldn't yell out though, couldn't cheer, couldn't show anything. *Do the right thing.*

At the board's table, Marian Yim spoke next: "My feeling is that the facts that have been developed since the last trial cast significant doubt on his guilt in this case. I don't know that it firmly establishes his innocence, but you know, there's certainly more than reasonable doubt in my mind that he's in fact guilty."

Tad Roberts agreed: "Right . . . I'm sort of on the same line." To him, the only question was whether to recommend outright release or supervised parole.

Ellen Stenson, as it turned out, favored outright release. "Personally, I'm leaning toward the recommendation of time served based on his records. And there is evidence now to suggest that maybe he is innocent— I'm not willing to make that statement that he is innocent but there is reasonable doubt at this point. . . . So I am leaning toward a recommendation of time served."

Tad Roberts said he wasn't leaning at all: "I'm in favor of giving absolute discharge from this sentence."

Katie and Ron and Jackie tried to contain themselves. Ellen Stenson favored outright release! Tad Roberts, too! At least three of the board members were talking about actual innocence. Not mercy and grace but a miscarriage of justice. Incredible—unprecedented for the Board of Executive Clemency.

Indeed, Tad Roberts believed Macumber to be innocent. He'd worked in corrections for more than twenty years, and he'd also spent ten years as a coordinator for the Casa Grande Elementary School District, the first African-American in that role. He had a bachelor's degree in psychology and minority relations, a master's in education. He'd been around, he'd witnessed plenty. He only rarely saw reason to recommend a release, but he tried to be open-minded on this board. Over time, reading thirty files a week, he'd come to know which ones didn't hold up. He'd first reviewed the Macumber file for the Phase I hearing. Right away, he'd spotted inappropriate things. This wasn't at all a typical case. Bill Macumber, living in society, a neighborhood leader, then he wakes up one day and goes out to kill two young people? Then never again? In particular, he didn't trust the fingerprints, that one partial palm print—hell, once when he was a college student, he'd helped a friend push his stalled VW and got his prints all over it, then found himself accused by the cops when someone else stole the car. More than anything, Tad Roberts just had a sense about Bill Macumber; over the years, in the trenches, he'd learned what to look for, what to ask. Macumber, with all the freedom they gave him, there at the Arizona border, could have been long gone. El Salvador, Ecuador, Mexico—sitting on the beach, drinking piña coladas. Instead, every night he came back to the prison. Roberts felt inclined to recommend Macumber's release solely because of his prison record, though he in fact believed him innocent. Very seldom did he think this of a prisoner up for clemency. But he did now.

"I just strongly believe that there's been an injustice done here . . ." Roberts told the other board members. "If I was a judge he would be gone. He would be a free man."

Donna Toland had thoughtfully brought a box of Kleenex. Those listening, both team and family members, were passing it around now. Still they couldn't react, couldn't yell out. They had three board members for sure, Ron calculated. But they needed a unanimous vote.

Two hours into the hearing, Tad Roberts made the motion: "To recommend commutation for William Macumber to time served."

In his chair, speaking softly, Bill Macumber said, "Thank you."

For strategic purposes, to provide the governor with a secondary option of release on parole, Roberts added: "To time served and then as an alternative, to a sentence of 35 to life."

Marian Yim seconded the motion. One by one the others voted: "I agree." "Agree." "And I also agree." Unanimous.

They were all crying now, nearly everyone in the room—Jackie in tears, Katie, Sharon, Bob Macumber with his head in his hands, everyone still in their chairs but reaching out to hug their neighbors. In the corner, off to the side, the unknown bystander sitting alone near the guards sobbed as well—they learned only later she was there to attend the next hearing. This is like Santa Claus and the coming of the Lord combined, Jackie thought. Ron, though joyous, tried to be sure of what he'd just heard; his father had downplayed their prospects so much. In the first row of seats, Larry Hammond and Bob Bartels were patting Macumber on the back, their arms around him. The others still couldn't see Bill's face. Then he turned around, showing both tears and a grin. He looked lit up and buoyant—as if it were over.

The guards' mandate had been that family members could not touch him, could not embrace him. But the guards, too, were grinning broadly now and giving Bill the thumbs-up sign. They relented: You have ten minutes, they announced. "Better hug quick," Tad Roberts told the crowd.

Everyone jumped from their chairs and pushed toward Bill. Ron wrapped his arms around his dad. *You did it*, he whispered. Katie hugged him while introducing herself, this being their first meeting in person. Sharon Sargent-Flack embraced him, then Rich Robertson and Donna Toland. Jackie, coming from the back row, reached him last. *Bill, where are the words*, she said. He smiled: *I know what you mean, Jackie.*

As the guards led Bill away, the others poured out into the parking lot, everyone talking and hugging, Ron shouting, *He's going to get out*, Robert Macumber yelling, *No way they're keeping him in prison.* Party on, Ron suggested. What bar are we going to?

Family members and the Justice Project team ended up at Macayo's Depot Cantina in Tempe, ordering lunch and pitchers of margaritas, making plans for the day when Bill walked free. If only Bill could be here, they kept saying. Cell phones came out, everyone relaying the news to family and friends. Ron called home, asking Deb to get Megan on the line, too. "Unanimous," he told them. "Unanimous." Katie called her family as well, personally affected now, way past her role as Bill's lawyer. Jackie grew ever jollier, sipping margaritas and imagining the future. It's finally over, she thought. Bill will be out in a matter of weeks. He's coming home. What an amazing day—the most beautiful day in her life.

Some there understood they still needed Governor Jan Brewer to accept the board's recommendation. But how could she not accept? How could anyone say no? They had a unanimous vote, after all—and on the basis of injustice, not just mercy. The board got it, the board believed. Incredible and wonderful, everyone declared—and unprecedented.

As soon as Jackie arrived home late the next day, after a seven-hour drive from Phoenix to New Mexico, she and Robyn began cleaning out a closet for Bill. When she bought a new Ford Explorer the next month, she chose not to trade in her old car. Bill would want his own vehicle once he got there. Jackie thanked the Lord. All her prayers had been answered.

Bill Macumber's prayers, too. He'd started this clemency process without the slightest hope of success and now thought he stood a very good chance of seeing his days in prison come to an end. He believed, in fact, that his ordeal was all but over. The trip back to Douglas after the Phase II hearing was a blur to him. He recalled a final handshake with Larry Hammond, then being led out of the room by his two escorts, the Douglas guards who'd driven him to Phoenix. Before shackling him for the return trip, they shook his hand, wished him luck and talked of this "uplifting experience"—they no longer thought of him as a convicted murderer. Somewhere along the way to Douglas, they stopped and bought him a hamburger dinner. Though not quite the same as margaritas at Macayo's, Macumber savored the meal. Back at the prison, inmates and staff alike greeted him with joy and congratulations.

Four days later, on May 12, he wrote a letter to the Board of Executive Clemency, sending copies to each member. "Ladies and gentlemen," he began, "I fear that because of the emotions present at my hearing on May 8th I may have failed to properly express my deepest gratitude to each of you. If so, please forgive me. Know that my family and I are truly grateful beyond mere words." He had "hated to see the sadness" in his relatives' eyes, but on Friday "that sadness disappeared, to be replaced by joy" because of the board's action—which also "validated the extreme effort and dedication put forth by the Justice Project over the past nine years." He had "no crystal ball," no way of foreseeing the future, but "regardless of what happens now," they had all "witnessed the love, the faith and the dedication" demonstrated at his hearing. "That alone," Macumber concluded, "makes me unquestionably the most fortunate of all men."

That same day, Macumber wrote to the Justice Project—to "Mr. Hammond, Professor Bartels, Donna, Katie, Sharon, Rich and all other members." The past nine years "have taken us beyond that attorney/client relationship. In truth it has bound us together in a common cause. We have become friends and I do not use that term lightly." They had shared "frustration, a sense of helplessness and disappointment." Friday had given them "reason to set that all behind us." He recognized the limit: "True, what took place at that hearing does not prove my innocence. . . . We have been unable to prove my innocence to the world and perhaps never will." Still, "I saw the faces of the Board members and I listened to their words. Had they been polled as a jury, I know beyond all doubt their verdict would have been not guilty." He "later found that same thing to be true" of the Douglas prison guards present. "That fact alone lifts my heart beyond all possible words."

For thirty-five years, in the world where he dwelled, Macumber had been regarded as a convicted murderer. Now he wasn't, and this he treasured above all. He did not know what the future held, but "whatever happens cannot change what has taken place."

CHAPTER 20

A Corrective Role

Twice in his May 12 letter of thanks to the Justice Project, Bill Macumber recognized what hadn't happened at the clemency hearing: "What took place at that hearing does not prove my innocence. . . . We have been unable to prove my innocence to the world and perhaps never will." This was true, of course. The Department of Corrections' bare, cramped Alhambra chamber was not a courtroom, and the board members were not jurors. They had not heard from prosecutors, but for a one-page letter. They had not read through the full, thick court record. They were not agents of or operatives in the legal system.

That was just the point, however. They provided—consciously and intentionally—a perspective apart from the legal system. They provided, as well, an arena where the Justice Project could operate unshackled by the rules of evidence and the post-conviction appellate process. In this arena, Larry Hammond and Bob Bartels could transcend the role of lawyers in a courtroom, their words carrying more weight, more import. They could serve as substitute witnesses, in essence. They could select and order, distilling the complexities. They could stand before the board as narrators.

Bartels and Hammond valued this opportunity. Over the years, they'd grown ever more disenchanted with the nature and constraints of the legal system. Hammond saw a great disparity between lawyers' adversarial battles and the supposed search for truth—he didn't think the adversary system worked. Nor did Bob Bartels, for that matter. He had grown increasingly pessimistic about the willingness of courts to consider the project's appeals. In his experience, judges started with the absolute presumption that the Justice Project's petitions had no merit. Judges and the entire legal system were overwhelmingly concerned with clearing dockets, with getting cases processed. In his forty years of practicing law, Bartels had watched the system become progressively more resistant to looking at claims of actual innocence. The judges just weren't interested. So they made it almost impossible to get relief on appeal, throwing down burdensome obstacles and slavishly placing adherence to procedural rules above the possibility of manifest injustice. That wouldn't be such a problem if trial-level courts worked, but Bartels didn't think they did. All the DNA exonerations proved that and pointed to so many more miscarriages of justice.

Against that backdrop, Duane Belcher and his fellow clemency board members thought they could—should—play a corrective role. They could consider human nature, human behavior, the human dimension—elements not weighed in the legal system, where prosecutors didn't have to identify or prove a motive. (*You need motive in novels*, Marian Yim liked to say, *but not for conviction*.) Those operating in the system rarely admitted a mistake. Instead, they tried to block evidence of error. They tried, more generally, to keep such evidence from jurors. Come election time, the question was, How many convictions, how many got off? The legal system, Belcher knew, was not infallible—those DNA exonerations had affected him too, reminding him that innocent people do get locked up.

In seeing a "strong possibility" of Bill Macumber's innocence, the board members had responded, above all, to Valenzuela's confession and Primrose's corroboration—by far the most compelling elements to them, real attention grabbers. They'd also compared Bill's pristine thirty-five-year record in prison with Valenzuela's violent death in a prison brawl; they'd matched Bill's stolid cowboy personality to claims he'd braggingly fantasized about being an army assassin; they'd weighed Carol's account of an estranged husband's bedroom confession against the very boundaries of logic. This case just stood out—never had the board members seen one with so many dubious elements.

Still, they weren't insisting on Macumber's innocence. How could anyone really know for sure? That question always haunted them: Most cases involved ambiguous records, yet players in the courtroom were full of passionate certitude—on both sides. Belcher and the other board members knew how high the stakes could be, how murky the record. They also knew of the landmark 1993 U.S. Supreme Court opinion in *Herrera v. Collins*. "Clemency is deeply rooted in our Anglo-American tradition of law," Chief Justice William Rehnquist wrote in that decision, "and is the historic remedy for preventing miscarriages of justice where the judicial system has been exhausted.... Our judicial system, like the human beings who administer it, is fallible.... The traditional remedy for claims of innocence based on new evidence, discovered too late in the day to file a new trial motion, has been executive clemency." The board members took their *Herrera* role seriously. They felt they provided a kind of fail-safe protection, a way to catch errors in the legal system.

Just as a judge often asks the prevailing attorney to compose a working draft of the order he will issue, Duane Belcher now asked the Justice Project associates to prepare a rough version of the letter the board would send to the governor. He wanted something to work with. He'd provide them with comments from all the board members, and samples of previous such letters to the governor. Then he'd sit down with them to go over what he wished to see in the letter.

The team dove into the preparation of a draft. By early July, Duane Belcher was circulating it to board members for comments and revisions. It turned out the board members wanted changes; they felt the Justice Project's draft had not gone far enough in expressing doubts about Macumber's guilt. This surprised Hammond—he hadn't thought they could emphasize this in a letter to the governor. He'd pussyfooted around in the draft, thinking they needed to focus on Bill's age, medical conditions, and extraordinary prison record. But no—the board members made it clear now, they wanted to express their substantial doubts, they wanted to talk about a miscarriage of justice. They'd never done this before, and Hammond hadn't thought they'd do it now. Fine with him, though. A project team met again with Belcher, and once also with Marian Yim, the one lawyer on the board, with a law degree from Cornell. Then the project team happily revised, now underscoring the board's concerns. By mid-August, the board members had a version to their liking. Belcher signed the letter on August 25 and delivered it to Governor Brewer's office on September 2, along with a copy of Judge O'Toole's affidavit.

From any and all angles, this was an extraordinary document to issue from the governor-appointed Arizona Board of Executive Clemency. The unanimous board wasted little time before conveying its members' doubts, getting to them directly in the first paragraph. "We consider William Macumber's case truly unique," the board's letter began. "His record and accomplishments are extraordinary for any person, but especially for a man who has spent the last 35 years of his life in prison. That record is especially remarkable given that there is substantial doubt that Mr. Macumber is guilty of the crime for which he was convicted. Because we believe an injustice has been done in Mr. Macumber's case, the traditional remedy of executive clemency is appropriate and is Mr. Macumber's only avenue left for relief."

"Substantial doubt" and "injustice" were not terms usually seen in clemency board recommendations. But here they were. The board repeated "substantial doubt" three paragraphs later, then upped the ante, late in the letter calling Macumber's case a "miscarriage of justice." In five single-spaced pages, the board members explained why they thought so: Valenzuela's multiple confessions, Judge O'Toole's affidavit, Linda Primrose's eyewitness account, Carol's "motive, means and opportunity to falsely pin the murders on Mr. Macumber," Ron's "very moving testimony," and the "not reliable" ballistics evidence.

Bill Macumber, the board pointed out, had "no legal recourse other than commutation." There was no evidence left to examine, no DNA to test. His attorneys couldn't, in other words, satisfy the high threshold for post-conviction relief. In such situations, clemency was the "appropriate avenue for relief." Here Duane Belcher cited the U.S. Supreme Court opinion he so admired, *Herrera v. Collins*: "As Chief Justice Rehnquist noted in *Herrera*, 'our judicial system, like the human beings who administer it, is fallible.' And although a petitioner claiming innocence may not have a right to re-enter the judicial system to correct an injustice, 'the traditional remedy for claims of innocence . . . has been executive clemency.'" Macumber's case, Belcher argued, "is one in which the power of executive clemency should be used to correct a miscarriage of justice."

Only after laying down that argument did Belcher turn to the more traditional reasons to grant clemency: Macumber's stellar prison record and staggering list of accomplishments. Macumber, Belcher pointed out, "would have been eligible for parole almost ten years ago had he been convicted under the criminal code in effect at the time of his trial." Macumber "has already served more than fifteen years longer than the average person convicted of murder in Arizona." Prior to his arrest and conviction, Macumber had no criminal record, and he has been "a law-abiding citizen" in prison. Testimony from his family indicates he will, once released, have "the resources and support to live as a law-abiding, productive citizen."

Belcher's conclusion: "The evidence that now exists certainly casts serious doubt upon Mr. Macumber's conviction. The evidence presented to this Board leads us to believe that a jury presented with the same evidence would have reasonable doubt about Mr. Macumber's guilt. Based on this new evidence, his lack of legal remedy, and this Board's role under *Herrera v. Collins*, the Board concludes that Mr. Macumber's sentence of life is, today, no longer warranted." Therefore, the Board recommends his sentence be commuted to "time served" or in the alternative, "to a sentence of 35 years to life."

Never before had the Board of Executive Clemency done this. Never before had a unanimous board called for a prisoner's release based on a miscarriage of justice.

On September 25, seven members of the Justice Project team, including Hammond, Bartels and Katie Puzauskas, met with the legal counsel for

Governor Brewer, Joe Kanefield. They came to present and advocate. Hammond had known Kanefield for a long time; he found him this day pleasant but not responsive, other than to assure them that the governor's office would look at the file and take the matter seriously. But the decision, he reminded them, rested with the governor—it was not theirs to make. As Hammond put it to a colleague, he "heard nothing from Kanefield that indicated the governor had a pulse."

A month later, on October 23, Governor Brewer's office contacted Duane Belcher. Her people were still deliberating, and they had a question: Had the victims' families taken a position on Macumber's commutation? Did the victims' families wish to comment? This was, of course, a familiar issue in clemency proceedings, one often considered by politicians wary of potential backlash. That the Scottsdale murders had occurred almost half a century ago made the query more difficult than normal to address.

Belcher did some digging. No one in the McKillop family seemed to be around anymore—Tim had been an only child. But Joyce Sterrenberg's mother, sister and brother were still alive. At age ninety, the mother, Joan, lived in Chandler, Arizona. Belcher called the number he had for her. Joan's daughter Judy Michael happened to pick up the phone. With the mother listening in the background, Belcher asked if the family would object to the governor releasing Bill Macumber, following a board recommendation made after a commutation hearing in May 2009. The daughter—Joyce's sister—relayed the question to her mother, who, as Belcher days later reported to the governor'office, "stated that she understood and was alright with this information and was not objecting to any future release of Mr. Macumber. [The daughter] stated that she would 'prefer' that he not be released, however respected her mother's position of not opposing a Commutation of Sentence. . . . [The daughter] did not want to receive future notices of hearings on Mr. Macumber and only, respectfully requested, that I inform her by telephone if he was ultimately released on parole." (Later, to a local Arizona reporter, Joan Sterrenberg added that she wasn't consumed with the mystery of who'd killed Joyce, that she had "no way of knowing.") Belcher, after conveying this response to the governor's office, informed Larry Hammond as well.

All during the summer of 2009, Hammond had been uncharacteristically pessimistic about how the governor would respond. Despite their celebration on the day of the hearing, he and others at the Justice Project had recognized that governors didn't as a matter of course grant clemency to convicted double murderers. He'd talked to Macumber twice, in fact, warning him not to get his hopes up too much, with Bill always saying, *Sure, I know, I won't.* But this news of Governor Brewer inquiring about the victims' families raised Hammond's hopes. The question alone meant the governor was thinking about accepting the board's recommendation.

At the time of Bill Macumber's Phase II hearing in May 2009, Jan Brewer had been governor of Arizona for less than four months, and she had come to the job indirectly, not having been elected by the voters. That January, at age sixty-four, she was serving as Arizona's secretary of state, managing thirty-eight employees, when Democratic governor Janet Napolitano resigned to become secretary of Homeland Security in the Obama administration. In accordance with the state constitution, Brewer automatically stepped in as governor. A longtime state legislator and Maricopa County supervisor before becoming secretary of state in 2003, with a community college education in radiological technology, she'd forged a reputation as a fiscal conservative. But in her early months as governor, nothing was clear about her—not even whether she'd choose to run for election in her own right in 2010. Some in the Justice Project, at the time of Bill's hearing, thought she might not. That would be a good thing for them; it meant politics wouldn't affect her response to Macumber's clemency petition. The project team and the Macumber family had talked about this possibility at Macayo's on May 8, clinging to it as a reason for hope. Governors facing voters had strong reason to shy from releasing convicted murderers—there was little political upside to granting clemency but substantial risk, as more than one governor had learned when freed convicts attacked again. If Brewer didn't have an election to worry about, she just might be more willing to accept her board's unanimous recommendation.

Or, as an alternative, she could do nothing: State law specified that if the governor did not act on a unanimous recommendation for commutation within ninety days after its submission, the recommendation automatically took effect. Hammond had raised that possibility with the governor's legal counsel. No, not likely, Joe Kanefield had told him. She won't do that.

The waiting continued. On October 21, Katie made the eight-hour round-trip drive to visit Macumber at Douglas, along with Lesley Hoyt-Croft, a community college film student interested in producing a documentary about Macumber. This was Katie's first trip to the state prison. She and Lesley met Bill in his counselor's office and talked for ninety minutes. The aspiring filmmaker, feeling hopeful, asked what he'd do when he got out. Well, Bill said, my cousin Jay wants to take me fishing. And I'd sure like to eat some Dairy Queen.

More waiting. Word finally reached the project of certain internal differences among Brewer's advisers, the legal team at odds with the political team. This fanned some hope. But that hope lost most of its footing on Thursday, November 5: At an event in the Phoenix suburb of Glendale, where she lived, Brewer announced that she would indeed run for reelection. Bob Bartels thought that sharply reduced their chances. In the absence of actual hard DNA proof, they were now asking a conservative Republican governor, up for reelection, to go in the face of her base, her main constituency. Bartels proved prescient. Eight days later, on Friday, November 13, Governor Brewer conveyed her decision to Duane Belcher in a spare one-sentence letter: "The application for clemency for William Macumber, ADC #33867, is denied."

Belcher called Hammond with the news. Larry tried to shrug, to be stoic. As a lawyer, he needed to be the stable anchor; he needed to avoid making it about how he felt. After his many legal battles over the years, after seeing two clients executed, he just wouldn't let anything devastate him. Privately, though, he fumed. Katie, by contrast, didn't try to hide her tears. This hurt too much.

She consulted Hammond and Bartels, and Carrie Sperling. They all agreed Macumber had to be notified right away, that afternoon—they had to tell him before he heard the news elsewhere. Katie and Carrie would make the call.

Which one would lead, though? Katie shied from the task. "Carrie, why don't you tell him," she suggested as they put through their call. She knew, though, that she had to do it. She'd been the main contact with Bill and his family; she'd been the one talking regularly to him.

On the phone, she heard Macumber's usual cowboy baritone. Despite herself, she began to cry. We just got word, she said through her tears. The governor denied the petition, rejected the board's recommendation.

Macumber said little, mainly listening.

This is not the end of the road, Katie continued. There are other options. We will keep fighting. She didn't know if he even heard her, if he was listening, but she had to say it for herself. We can do a Rule 32 petition, she told him. We can file another clemency application. We can go to the news media. We can change the state law about old-code prisoners.

Macumber could hear her crying. That, on top of everything else, he'd say later, "just tore my heart out." Katie asked him if he'd like her to call his family members. No, he said, he'd do that. He appreciated her offer, but he had to handle this himself.

Early that evening, Carrie Sperling sent an e-mail to the entire Justice Project team:

We just received news from Duane Belcher, Chair of the Board of Executive Clemency, that Gov. Brewer denied Bill's commutation request. Of course, we wanted each of you to know the news. A personal phone call would have been more appropriate, but we also wanted to get the word out quickly—before you heard the news in some other way. Defeats are always hard, but they are near devastating when the person you represent has become a good friend, a person we all admire. Katie and I spoke to Bill today. He was, as always, stronger than we are. But I know this news must have been especially hard on him because we just couldn't fathom anything other than a commutation. So please remember Bill and take time to jot a personal note to him. Thank you for your countless hours of work on Bill's behalf. . . . After regrouping over the weekend, we intend to start strategizing our next steps to free Bill.

Macumber called Ron the following day. "I'm going to keep this really short," he said. "I have received the decision from Governor Brewer, and she has denied our petition." Ron started asking questions— *Why? How could this be? How could she?*—but Bill stopped him. He offered none of his usual wry banter—he sounded devastated. "I really can't talk now," Bill apologized. "I need to call Jackie, I need to call Bob."

Tears and anger informed his calls to those two. That bitch, Jackie fumed. Why couldn't Jan Brewer just wait out the ninety days and let the board's recommendation take effect on its own? Bob Macumber railed at the governor's lack of humanity. For her to snub her nose at her own board's unanimous vote appalled him. Why have a board at all then? He didn't think the governor had a moral bone in her body.

Two days later, Katie wrote to Bill: "Throughout the past several months, you have become a friend to us—a person we all admire—and it was our hope that we would finally see justice in your case. Coming to grips with the Governor's disappointing decision has not been easy for us, especially because we could not fathom anything other than a grant of clemency. As hard as it has been for us, I cannot imagine how hard it must be for you." Please know "we will keep fighting for your freedom, for as long as it takes." He still had all their support: "We have not given up hope."

Larry Hammond also wrote to Bill: "I started to write to you last Friday after we heard the Governor's ruling, but I was too angry. I started to write a letter to you on Saturday, but I was totally without anything comforting to say. I started to write to you on Sunday, but by then I did not know how you might be feeling and I called Jackie instead of writing to you." Jackie, as always, had provided him a "heart-warming visit." Her "determination to see this case through gave me some new perspective and new energy." They remained on his case: "We are entirely evaluating our position on your post-conviction relief petition." They would "stay very closely in touch."

Here was significant news: Hammond's reference to "entirely evaluating" their position about a PCR petition promised a possible reversal of the

2008 decision to close the Macumber file, to not seek redress in the appellate court system. The clemency board's unanimous recommendation had encouraged Bartels and Hammond to reconsider. Just maybe they could make an actual innocence claim under Rule 32 of the Arizona Rules of Criminal Procedure—the regulations that governed petitions for post-conviction relief.

In late November, Donna Toland sent a message to the project team. "Larry and Bob," she reported, "would like me to schedule a meeting regarding Bill Macumber's PCR. I am looking at the week of November 30. Can you provide me dates/times that might work for each of you?"

At 10:00 A.M. on Monday, December 7, 2009, the team gathered in the conference room of the Justice Project's offices, with others plugged in on speakerphone. Those participating included many who had been on the case from the start—Larry Hammond, Bob Bartels, Rich Robertson, Karen Killion, Sharon Sargent-Flack, Donna Toland—and representatives from the later generations: Carrie Sperling, Pete Rodriguez, Ty Jacobson, Jen Roach, Jen Swisher, Lindsay Herf, and Katie Puzauskas. They still wanted to do whatever they could for Macumber. How, though? What had changed, what might make action possible now? They began to consider.

The science of ballistics evidence had evolved, making it much easier to discredit the shell casing match from 1974. Forensic science reform in general had everyone's attention, having become the subject of assorted conferences and an extended new study by the National Academy of Sciences. Robert Macumber's revelation about the palm print card was new and compelling. Tom O'Toole's statements had grown ever more definite, detailed and insistent. The law and Larry Hammond's thinking had advanced about confessions from third parties—a central theme in both *Macumber* and *Chambers*.

Above all, they had the Clemency Board's unanimous recommendation, recognizing a miscarriage of justice. Rule 32 required the defendant, in claims of actual innocence, to demonstrate "by clear and convincing evidence that the facts underlying the claim would be sufficient to establish that no reasonable fact-finder would have found defendant guilty . . . beyond a reasonable doubt." *No reasonable fact-finder*—didn't they have that now? Didn't the clemency board qualify as a "reasonable fact-finder?" Yes, certainly. And didn't that give them a realistic chance of prevailing with a petition?

In the Justice Project conference room, all eyes turned to Bob Bartels. The team knew Larry's position, but what about Bartels?

Bartels weighed his response. Though as always inclined to caution, he couldn't deny that the board's action had affected him. After all, these board members were not wild-eyed liberals. They were, rather, fairly stern adjuncts of the state corrections system. The board's finding had changed Bartels's estimate of the project's possibilities. And something else had also affected him: He wasn't good at psychological analysis, particularly of himself, but he suspected he felt a bit guilty that the project associates hadn't filed a clemency petition themselves, that Bill had to do it on his own. That was a part of it, he had to admit—a part of why he now felt inclined to once again attempt a PCR petition.

One more thing, after nearly a decade on the case: Though he couldn't say there was no possibility Bill was a murderer—"The only person I'm pretty sure didn't do it is me"—he thought there was little possibility, and a lot more than reasonable doubt. He wasn't a gambler, but if he had to bet, he'd put his money on not guilty.

Yes, he told the Justice Project team. We have a chance.

That Bartels thought it possible carried a lot of weight. When the time came for a show of hands, the group voted unanimously to work on a PCR petition. They still weren't sure how they'd do it, though. Katie's message to the team later that day reflected the tentative agreement: "First, thank you for meeting this morning regarding Bill Macumber's case. It looks like we are preparing to move forward with a Petition for Post-Conviction Relief based on actual innocence and new evidence. At this point we are unsure about who will write the petition and argue Bill's case, but we will be talking in the next couple of weeks to make those decisions."

Eleven days later, on December 18, Larry Hammond rose to deliver the commencement address to the graduating class at ASU's College of Law. He chose to devote his speech to the Bill Macumber story and the Justice

Project's decade-long fight on his behalf, driven by "four generations of ASU law students." After reviewing the history of the Justice Project and its involvement in the case, he explained how on May 8 the Board of Executive Clemency had voted unanimously to commute Bill Macumber's sentence "on a ground never heretofore embraced"—and had done so "because of their significant doubt about his guilt." Four generations of law students were able to walk out of that hearing "with the knowledge that their efforts had contributed to righting an injustice." But just weeks ago—since Hammond had agreed "to accept the honor of speaking to you today"—Governor Brewer had decided to reject her board's recommendation, without explanation. Hammond looked out at the crowd: "What do you suppose happened next?"

He waited, savoring this moment. He hadn't told the Justice Project team he was going to publicly announce the reopening of the case. The team's decision had felt a bit tentative to him, as if some of them were still thinking it over. Hammond wanted to goad them, wanted to push them beyond thinking now. "This is what happened," he told the commencement crowd. "Last week, these four generations of present and former students gathered again and unanimously committed themselves to continue to work on Bill's case. Someday, these ASU students and graduates will be able to write a different end to this story."

CHAPTER 21

Attention Is Paid

DECEMBER 2009–JULY 2010

On the same day Larry Hammond delivered his commencement speech at the ASU College of Law, Katie Puzauskas sent a four-page memo to the Macumber team, outlining the battle plan for Bill's PCR. The petition, she advised, would include an argument of actual innocence—"which we must show by clear and convincing evidence"—and an argument "based on newly discovered material facts." Addressing how to make those arguments, Katie listed the issues they'd discussed on December 7 and the "things that still need to be investigated."

They would hang the actual innocence claim on Valenzuela's confessions and the affidavits from Tom O'Toole and Ron Petica; Linda Primrose's statements and the judgment of her truthfulness by Dr. Erickson and a polygrapher; Carol Macumber's conduct, access and ability to lift prints; Ron's testimony before the clemency board; and—above all—the clemency board's "entertaining Bill's innocence claim."

They would base the newly discovered material facts primarily on a new National Academy of Sciences report that discredited the type of ballistics and fingerprint evidence used in Macumber's case. They would try, as well, to cite the palm print backing paper—if they could ever prove it; Linda Primrose's scrapbook—if they could ever retrieve it; the sheriff's list of .45-caliber guns tested in 1962—if they could ever find it; and testimony from Primrose's friend Terry—if they could ever locate her.

Larry Hammond also wanted the team to consider questions about third-party confessions. He saw this as a growing issue in the legal system; recent cases had lowered the "reliability" threshold governing when the defense could offer testimony about such confessions. In 1987, the Arizona Supreme Court in *State v. LaGrand* had significantly altered the standard. After *LaGrand*, if a trial court believed that "a reasonable person could conclude from evidence in the record that the declarant's statement *could* be true, then [it] *must* admit the statement into evidence." And in 2010, the Arizona Supreme Court had applied the *LaGrand* standard to another case, *State v. Machado*, ruling that the trial court had erred in excluding an anonymous telephone call from someone who'd confessed to the murder. Attorney-client privilege remained in place, but if the Valenzuela confession came along now, Hammond believed it would be allowed under these new rulings. Hammond again pointed the team members to *Chambers*, writing a memo about its issues. He asked them to consider when and how third-party confessions were used. What most bothered him about Bill's case: If the State had charged Valenzuela with the murders, rather than Macumber, the courts would have relied completely on Primrose's statement and Valenzuela's confessions. But because they'd charged Macumber instead, the jurors could not hear this evidence.

Switch it around some more, Hammond suggested. If they'd charged Valenzuela with the murders, if he'd been on trial, Carol's statement about Bill would be absolutely inadmissible. Even if Valenzuela's lawyer sank to his knees and begged, no judge would allow it. Shame on you, the judge would tell him, for trying to blame a third party. Since lawyers employed this type of evidence all the time to convict, why not also to show innocence? Hammond proposed that the team research other cases where the prosecutor had depended on statements like Primrose's and confessions like Valenzuela's.

* * *

By April 2010, the Justice Project team had fully launched a renewed, expanded Macumber campaign. Associates had held several phone conferences with Bill; they'd created a Free Bill website; and they'd started screening a twenty-one-minute documentary, *Life: The Bill Macumber Story*, produced by Lesley Hoyt-Croft. They had also established a new ASU law school post-conviction relief clinic and had pointed that class at the Macumber case; Katie and Lindsay, its guiding spirits, attended every clinic session, working with the six enrolled students and recruiting others.

On April 30, the clinic left the ASU law school at 5:30 A.M., boarding a van for the four-hour drive down to Douglas. Katie and Lindsay joined the students and their instructor, Sigmund Popko, a former lawyer at Hammond's old law firm. They had assigned each student a particular aspect of Macumber's case, so they wanted the students to meet Bill and have a chance to ask him questions.

At the prison, they all gathered in the large visitation room. Katie greeted Macumber with a hug, then introduced the students and Lindsay. Macumber answered their queries for ninety minutes. Katie apologized as they went on, knowing he'd heard these questions many times in the past. Bill didn't care, though—he welcomed the company.

After they finished, Katie and Lindsay set up video equipment and prepared to show the *Life* documentary. Lesley Hoyt-Croft, whose good friend worked at Larry Hammond's law firm, had jumped at the chance to make the film after Lindsay and Jen Swisher presented the Macumber case to her Scottsdale Community College class. Macumber knew that Ron and Megan, who'd attended a screening in Phoenix, believed it might sway Governor Brewer. Bill doubted that, but he sat now in the darkened visitation room, watching. Near the end, he saw Ron on the screen, paying him homage: *He's an incredible man. . . . To endure, to keep his beliefs. He never backed down. He could have been out long ago if he admitted guilt, expressed remorse.* He saw also Ron's wife, Deb, imagining their future together: *I know him well. He'll look around our house, say this and this needs to be done. How much fun we are going to have. I've been telling him for seven years, you will get out of prison. This is not how you will finish your days. . . . Whatever power is out there will right this wrong.*

By the end of the screening, Katie and Lindsay were crying. Two guards standing against the far wall looked choked up as well. Macumber blinked hard, his eyes watering, his face reddening. When the documentary ended, he offered a big sigh, then said to Katie, "Please tell Lesley thank you."

The next day, Macumber wrote to Katie, thanking her first "for the nice hug when I arrived and again when you left. Old men really appreciate hugs from lovely young women and especially those they think a great deal of." He hoped the meeting with the students had gone well— he'd tried his best to "reach back in time," but "thirty-five years is just a very long time." He thought the documentary "an astounding piece of work" and "an emotional trip back through time for me." He'd found it "terribly difficult to hold back the tears." And "speaking of tears, yours and Lindsay's bothered me so much." He regretted that "so many people have shed tears because of me."

Over the next few days, several of the clinic students wrote him letters expressing their admiration and support. So did Lindsay Herf, who, like Katie, now held the title of case and programs coordinator for the Justice Project. "I want to tell you," she began, "how wonderful it was to meet you in person. All the students enjoyed meeting you as well and were so impressed by you." In her three years of doing innocence work, "I have never seen a case like yours—in that I have never been so convinced of a wrongful conviction as I am when I read your file." He should not consider the tears she and Katie shed as being a burden; "they are tears of frustration at the system." In prisons, "very few are innocent and it is those few who keep us going and give us strength to keep working." Lindsay urged Bill to "stay strong, as you have all these years." She offered her pledge: "The quest for justice is not over."

Next came a wave of news media attention. The narrative that journalists offered in the mid-1970s had largely reflected the story told by cops and prosecutors. The pendulum often swings in the press, though. Reporters embraced a new narrative that May, fueled by Governor Brewer's denial of the clemency board's recommendation—and also by the Justice Project's active prodding.

Besides preparing to draft a PCR petition, the Macumber team had started wondering whether they could ask Governor Brewer to reconsider her denial. As far as they knew, no formal mechanism existed for such a request—Katie had not been able to find any relevant case law. So she and Lindsay instead turned to the news media, thinking that perhaps public opinion would be the best way to persuade the governor.

A May 18 report on CBS's Phoenix affiliate, KPHO, effectively got the ball rolling. When reporter Sarah Buduson asked the governor on camera about her decision to deny clemency, Brewer said, "It's a very personal issue.... At this particular time, I'd prefer not to comment," then turned and walked away as Buduson continued to ask questions. Others filled the airtime instead. "I think one of the things that bothered us most is we don't know why it was turned down," Bill Macumber said during an interview at the state prison. "We strongly believe he did not commit the crime he was convicted of," added Katie Puzauskas. She and Lindsay pointed to Carol's access, knowledge, and motives—including the fact that she was "being investigated by the Maricopa sheriff's office for sexual misconduct at work." The most powerful comments of all came from Judge Thomas O'Toole, now retired and ever more willing to speak without qualification about Valenzuela. "There is no doubt in my mind when he told me about these murders he was telling the truth," O'Toole informed Buduson on camera. "He relished the murders, and that was his persona when he talked about it." Of Macumber's case, the judge said, "There is reasonable doubt. More than a reasonable doubt as to his guilt." O'Toole hoped the governor would reconsider her ruling. "I would think that the governor, even though she initially denied, would really be doing justice by granting clemency to this man who has been in prison for thirty-five years, who very likely is innocent."

The next day, P. S. Ruckman Jr., an associate professor of political science at Rock Valley College in Illinois, posted a report about the Macumber case—and Governor Brewer's refusal to discuss it—on his *Pardon Power* blog. Ruckman raised alarms and expressed hope that "the media will hammer this . . . on a daily basis until the topic is addressed appropriately." A Justice Project law student volunteer, Andrew Hacker, spotted Ruckman's post and relayed a link to Katie in an e-mail carrying the subject line "It's spreading . . ."

Indeed it was. Two weeks later, Adam Liptak, a legal affairs reporter at the *New York Times*, e-mailed the Justice Project, seeking information— he'd seen Ruckman's blog. Liptak's story ran in the *Times* on June 14, under the headline "Governor Rebuffs Clemency Board in Murder Case." Liptak quoted Tom O'Toole, Katie Puzauskas and P. S. Ruckman, who said, "I have been following state clemency for 30 years, and this is easily, easily, the most disturbing. It's borderline despicable." Liptak also quoted Carol Kempfert—one of her first public comments since the Justice Project reopened the case. She denied tampering with the evidence, and she called her former husband a dangerous sociopath and pathological liar. "I was in law enforcement for almost 20 years," she told Liptak, "and no one came close to being able to manipulate like Bill. This man could sell water to a drowning person."

After the *New York Times* story, Katie began fielding call after call from the news media: Phoenix TV stations ABC15, KPNX Channel 12 and News Channel 3; CBC Radio in Toronto; Citadel Broadcasting in Tucson; an NBC affiliate in Illinois; the *Arizona Guardian*. On and on. For a time that summer, Katie seemed to be working as Macumber's full-time press agent. One day, he sat for no less than four interviews. Then came a call from ABC's *Nightline*, in New York—its producers wanted to film a segment as well.

The competing narratives were now playing out in the media rather than in the courtrooms. As always, those following such accounts had to choose which story to favor, which to believe.

"This case has a stink about it," Judge O'Toole told one journalist.

To another, he said, "I represented the guy who committed the murders, and I'm convinced that he did. He told me in great detail how the murders were committed. Anybody who's been involved in looking at this case comes away saying this guy got screwed. I'm one of them. The legal system obviously got it wrong."

"Miraculously," Hammond explained to a third reporter, "out of the file jumped a palm print."

Ron had "no doubt my mother set my father up for the murders. . . . I firmly believe she lied. I firmly believe she planted the evidence. I firmly believe she framed my father for this."

Again, some of the reporters went to Carol as well. She had Googled

Bill from time to time over the years and so knew of his connection to the Vince Foster case. But she knew nothing of the clemency board hearing and recommendation until these queries from journalists. To them, she kept denying the charges against her: "He did tell me he committed the murders. He did come home with blood on his shirt. . . . I never lied." Most of the clemency board claims about her were false: "I had no access to evidence lockers. I did not manufacture or tamper in any way with evidence. There's a whole lot more to this story that has never come out."

Governor Brewer's spokesman now issued an expanded statement: "This decision was made . . . after very careful consideration and contemplation by Governor Brewer. This case involves the decision by not one, but two trials by jury. The Governor does not generally elaborate on issues related to her executive clemency power for multiple reasons. . . . Her thorough deliberation process takes into account all facts presented to her, including a thorough review of the application and testimony before the Board of Executive Clemency. In Mr. Macumber's case, this review included statements from Mr. Macumber, attorneys, witnesses, law enforcement officers, victims and trial transcripts from both jury trials that convicted him of murder. Every case is carefully scrutinized as the Governor balances the very real and important concepts of public safety, justice and mercy."

In the end, whatever else could be said, the news accounts undeniably stirred public opinion, just as the Justice Project had hoped. Katie felt the reports also vindicated their efforts, for despite offering competing narratives, the stories conveyed an underlying belief in Macumber and the Justice Project. Otherwise, why reprise this decades-old case?

The media attention culminated with the *Nightline* broadcast. The ABC program largely framed the story as a family conflict featuring Ron and Carol and Bill. Ron had his say—"I don't have any doubt anymore that my mom framed my dad for the murders"—and so did Carol, *Nightline* landing an exclusive on-camera interview with her up in Olympia. She again flatly denied fabricating her husband's confession. "Absolutely not. . . . I didn't wake up one morning and say, 'Oh gee, I think I'll go frame my husband today.' I did not and I will say this again, I did not manufacture nor did I ever tamper with evidence." Bill came home covered in blood the night of the murders, she insisted, and later confessed to her as their marriage was falling apart. "It sounds . . . ridiculous. But that's, in fact, what happened." As for Ron's charges, "Critical thinking is not one of Ron's better skills. If anyone was ever made for Bill to mold and manipulate, it would be Ron."

Nightline's cameras here cut back to Ron: "Let's say I'm gullible and my father is manipulating me, but please tell me how he's manipulating the Arizona Justice Project."

Nightline also pitted Ron against Governor Brewer, flying him to Arizona so he could confront her on camera at an unrelated news conference, asking why she'd denied his father's freedom. By then, Brewer had gained widespread national attention for having signed, in April, Arizona SB 1070, the controversial law that required aliens in Arizona to carry registration documents and police to question people about their immigration status if there is reason. SB 1070 had brought Brewer notoriety—but also a passel of conservative Arizona voters. When *Nightline* turned its cameras on her, she was just days away from trouncing her Democratic opponent in the gubernatorial election, 55 percent to 42 percent. "It's an unfortunate situation," she told Ron at her news conference, "that governors have to make difficult decisions regardless of what recommendations are made to them. . . . I know it's hard as a child that you're faced with this in your lifetime. But he was found guilty by two different juries, and I feel very comfortable with my decision. I appreciate your concern, but I've made my decision and it's final."

At the state prison in Douglas, Bill Macumber tried to make sense of all the attention being paid to him. The guards and other inmates approached him regularly now to say they'd seen him on TV. Never had he thought he'd be interviewed by so many TV stations. He hoped the exposure would help, and maybe even affect Governor Brewer. He particularly appreciated Professor Ruckman's blog postings and Adam Liptak's *New York Times* piece, since they'd kindled the media interest. "Perhaps I will remain in prison," he wrote to Professor Ruckman, "yet should that prove to be the case there are now countless people out there that believe in me and in my innocence. I find considerable satisfaction in that."

On July 23, Katie and Lindsay again made the four-hour, 230-mile journey to visit Macumber, this time with a young barrister from England, Sarah Cooper. Sarah, twenty-three, had first come to Arizona three years before to intern for Osborn Maledon and had returned now on a summer fellowship, eager to work with the Justice Project. They met Macumber in the big visitation room lined with vending machines. Bill was about to turn seventy-five. He found it astounding that he'd made it to that age, considering his situation. His hip hurt often now, and the emphysema had him coughing and clearing his lungs. But he'd survived. After the requisite hugs, they settled at one of the round tables in the otherwise empty room. Sarah led the conversation, reviewing their situation and plans. She expected to begin writing a draft PCR petition sometime in August—a task Hammond had assigned to her—but could not say when it might be ready to submit to the court. They'd also start assembling a new commutation package, as Macumber would be eligible to reapply for clemency next May, two years after his Phase II hearing. Bill's chances, they knew, might still be better outside of the courtroom.

Macumber listened with appreciation. Sarah seemed intense but self-assured, and he liked both traits. He particularly enjoyed her British accent. She, in turn, thought him impressive—so very articulate and straightforward, with a wry sense of humor. He paid attention, even as their conversation moved beyond the case, and he had all manner of insights about national affairs. As he had with every Justice Project team member, Bill made quite an impact on Sarah.

On the long drive back to Phoenix, Katie and Lindsay and Sarah couldn't stop talking about Bill Macumber. Early on, even they had wondered at times about his story. The bloody-shirt incident had troubled Katie when she'd first opened the file, though she knew that twenty-seven-year-old men did get into fights. The prints and ballistics had bothered Lindsay. The conspiracy theory had given Sarah pause. Yet they'd grown ever more convinced of Macumber's innocence. As they headed northwest on I-10, winding through barren reaches of high desert, they renewed their vows to do whatever might be necessary to help free him. Among other things, they told each other, that meant they had to try even harder to find out what had happened back in 1962 and 1974. They couldn't learn this, they now understood, just by sifting through the thousand-page record. They had to hit the pavement, go to the ground. They had to find the few people still alive who could tell them about the past.

CHAPTER 22

Going to the Ground

JULY 2010–OCTOBER 2010

We have a nonpresence when we go around questioning people. That's what Katie, Lindsay, and Sarah explained to first-year law school students early that September. *People talk to us. Maybe they think we're young, naïve girls. We're not a fifty-five-year-old cop or lawyer. That helps. That gets us in the door.*

They were recruiting for Sigmund Popko's Post-Conviction Clinic. Non-DNA cases, they and Zig told the students, required a lot of hard work—tracking down witnesses, document pulls, inmate visits, finding facts. You're reconstructing, trying to imagine the crime, factoring in human nature. Nobody knows what truly happened. You can't find it in the law books. This has nothing to do with the statutes and legal concepts you study in class. You'll be trying to learn things on the ground. You'll need to get out there, talk to people. "If that interests you," they told the students, "we invite you to join the Post-Conviction Clinic."

Katie, Lindsay and Sarah had by then been practicing what they preached for many weeks, trying to run down everyone they could from the time of Bill Macumber's arrest and conviction. They'd started with former Maricopa County sheriff Paul Blubaum, Lindsay driving out to the trailer park where they understood he lived. She looked in a window and saw no sign of him, so she dropped by a business address they had for him—only to learn he'd been dead for six months. A literal dead end, but they were hooked now, driven not just by their belief in Bill Macumber but also by their faith in the pursuit of justice. They consciously called themselves "the girls"—Sarah twenty-three, Katie twenty-seven, Lindsay thirty in the summer of 2010—which partly reflected their clever "Columbo" posture, partly their genuine hesitation. They shied from intruding; they had to force themselves to make calls, to get in people's faces about a long-ago double-murder investigation. Yet they realized this truly represented a last-ditch attempt. Being trained lawyers, they decided to regard each interview as if they were conducting the direct exam of a witness on the stand. Their goal: to collect a raft of sworn affidavits—newly discovered evidence—to attach to their PCR and clemency petitions.

With Blubaum gone, they turned next to Dave Brewer, the former sheriff's evidence technician who'd given his revealing statement to Bedford Douglass in 1983. Would he still be around twenty-seven years later? Would he still tell the same story? Would he have more to add? Lindsay, along with a law student, started looking for him. Online searches yielded three Dave Brewers in the Phoenix area. Lindsay struck out with the first two. One last Brewer to go, with an address listed on Ludlow Drive. Lindsay went casual that day, jeans and flip-flops, having been taught not to dress up on investigations—she didn't want to look like a cop or lawyer. Raised in Arizona, educated in California, she loved the outdoors and sports, especially swimming and distance running, and this showed in her open, sunny demeanor.

What she saw first, walking up the steps to this Dave Brewer's house, wasn't welcoming: A No Trespassing, No Soliciting sign and a political poster for a super-conservative Republican who'd run against Arizona's Senator John McCain. Lindsay knocked on the door. No answer. They started back to her car. Just then, a one-legged man came cruising up the street on a scooter. He looked at them; they watched him. He headed into the house they'd just knocked at. Lindsay turned, stepped toward him.

"Dave Brewer?" Yes, he said. "We're here to talk about an old case," she explained. "The Macumber case." Brewer didn't hesitate. "Come on in."

They talked for two hours. In his sheriff's job back then, he explained, he'd tagged, processed and photographed evidence, made fingerprint comparisons, and testified as an expert witness. He recalled being handed the latents and Bill's prints on the Saturday before Macumber's arrest, and he recalled the two not matching. He remembered contacting Bedford Douglass, giving him a statement in 1983—he hadn't realized nothing ever came of that. He didn't know if Bill was guilty or innocent, but there'd been shady things going on back then.

This first interview wandered all over the map, Lindsay letting Brewer go where he wished. He clearly enjoyed the chance to talk about old days. He seemed sharp, though, and lived in the present; she could tell he read newspapers, followed the news. And his account hadn't changed over twenty-seven years: His statements now were almost verbatim what he'd said to Bedford Douglass in 1983. Lindsay had brought a transcript of that taped statement, to jog Brewer's memory, but she didn't need it.

Weeks later, she returned to Brewer's home, her questions more focused this time, aimed at getting what they needed for a formal statement. She came back soon after with a draft affidavit, but he—careful and precise—wanted to make changes. Sarah Cooper joined Lindsay on the next visit, as she had her own questions. Finally they brought a six-page affidavit for him to sign in front of a notary.

Brewer's statement first addressed chain-of-custody issues, reinforcing what he'd told Bedford Douglass in 1983. All Maricopa County Sheriff's Office employees who worked in the Identification Section "could access latent print evidence and crime reports, even if the employee was not assigned to the case." He'd voiced his concern about this chain-of-custody problem but "was told that in Arizona a chain of custody was not needed." The shell casings from the Sterrenberg-McKillop case were kept in an "often unlocked" desk drawer that, when locked, could be "opened with a paper clip." One evening while he was in the sheriff's office basement processing evidence, "the officers who conducted a search of Mr. Macumber's house returned to the department with a bucket of shell casings." He asked what that was for—shell casings collected from Macumber's house, not the crime scene, were of no importance. As a result of all this, "I did not trust that the shell casings were properly maintained in Mr. Macumber's case." The latent print cards as well, kept in unlocked file cabinets along with the crime reports, "were accessible to anyone who worked in the ID Bureau."

Brewer turned next to his only direct involvement with the Sterrenberg-McKillop investigation, that Saturday-morning shift "when Det. Richard Diehl brought me latent fingerprints from the case and asked me to compare the latent prints to Mr. Macumber's prints, which were on file from Mr. Macumber's Sheriff's Posse application." He made the comparison and found that "Mr. Macumber's prints did not match the latent prints." This he reported to Diehl, after which "I was not asked to do any more work on the McKillop/Sterrenberg investigation."

Brewer finally focused on Carol Macumber, his account here unequivocal—and entirely consistent with his 1983 statement:

Carol Macumber was very abrasive and two-faced. I did not trust her. Carol Macumber had access to the crime reports, shell casings and latent prints in the McKillop/Sterrenberg case. In 1974, around the time Carol Macumber turned Mr. Macumber on the unsolved double homicide, I learned from Detective Richard Diehl that Carol Macumber was the subject of an internal investigation as a result of . . . sexual activities with other law enforcement deputies. . . . Detective Diehl, who at that time worked in Internal Affairs at MCSO, informed me that Carol Macumber tape recorded some sexual activities with other law enforcement employees and threatened to use the tape recordings to blow the whistle on the department. A deal was struck: Carol turned over the recordings, turned Mr. Macumber on the unsolved double homicide and kept her job until they worked out a transfer. . . .

I recall having coffee with Ed Calles right around this time. Carol Macumber was Calles's secretary at one point. Calles and I had a close professional relationship and I trusted that he would tell me the truth. I asked Calles, "How could you possibly help . . . Carol Macumber?" Calles responded that they had to save the department. I took this to mean that they had to stop the department receiving bad publicity about the sex scandal surrounding Carol Macumber.

In a courtroom, what Diehl and Calles told Brewer might be inadmissible hearsay, but the Justice Project could attach Brewer's sworn affidavit to any petition they filed. They weren't at an evidentiary hearing yet—they were just trying to get there.

Katie and Lindsay also began looking for Nancy Halas, the sheriff's department stenographer who took down Carol's statement on August 23, 1974. What happened in that interrogation room? Did Halas's indecipherable shorthand notes—which they had—possibly differ from the official typed statement? Halas had been twenty-five back then, so she'd be sixty-one now. Was she still around? Yes. They found an address for her in north Phoenix. Katie and Lindsay drove up there, as usual parking their car down the street. They knocked at her door. No answer. Over the next few days, they returned several times, never finding her home. They left a business card and on one visit talked to a neighbor. Still no response. They began to feel as if they were stalking this woman, but they didn't stop. Lindsay, with Sarah this time, drove out one blazing hot weekend afternoon. They sat outside Halas's home, across the street in the shade, composing a note to her. As they wrote, Halas's front door opened. They jumped up, darted over. "Are you Nancy Halas?" Halas, looking stricken, backed away, saying, "I'm not interested, I'm not interested, I'm not going to talk about it," before closing the door. This response shocked Lindsay. Nancy Halas obviously knew who they were. Why didn't she want to talk to them? Why didn't she just say, "What do you want?" or "I can't recall"? What made her so wary and resistant? Lindsay later wrote her a letter, but Nancy Halas never answered.

They struck out also in their efforts to interview Ernest Valenzuela's two sisters—Katie hoped that Valenzuela had confessed to them. She and a clinic student drove around for days, following address leads, checking with local churches, contacting the Pima and Gila Indian reservations. She found only dead ends, though. Or, rather, an empty lot. That's where the address for one sister led them.

They tried vainly, as well, to reach Thomas Hakes, the former sheriff's detective who'd taken statements from Linda Primrose. Calling him in Florida, they reached his widow.

Katie did manage to locate Theresa Hay, Linda Primrose's daughter. One weekday afternoon, without calling ahead, Katie and two clinic students drove out to her home. When they knocked, Theresa opened the door and nicely welcomed them in. No, she said, she didn't recall the visit years before by Rich Robertson. But yes, her mom had kept a scrapbook about the killings on Scottsdale Road. Katie explained the scrapbook's importance, and Theresa promised to look around. Theresa also asked them a good many questions about the case, their conversation lasting about forty-five minutes. Katie left thinking Theresa up-front and cooperative, but then weeks passed without a word from her, even after they followed up with a letter. So Katie drove out to Theresa's house once more, this time with Sarah, and left a note when they found her not there. Early the next morning, Theresa called Katie. She'd looked for her mom's scrapbook, she reported, but had been unable to find it. Okay, Katie said. If anything turns up, please let us know.

One summer afternoon, Katie and Sarah called Valenzuela's former attorney Ron Petica—retired and living in Bullhead City, Arizona—and took down his most detailed statement yet, which they then sent to him for notarized signature. That same week, they drove out to Judge O'Toole's house. O'Toole had already provided two affidavits but now they wanted him to drill even deeper. O'Toole obliged, leaning back in his chair, recalling the past, reliving his hours with Ernest. He filled five pages, his account not the least bit vague or uncertain. "I will never forget Valenzuela," he concluded. "To this day I could pick him out in a crowd. I have no reason to doubt that Mr. Valenzuela was telling the truth when he confessed to killing Joyce Sterrenberg and Timothy McKillop."

They found Dennis Gilbertson as well that summer. The Phoenix police officer had retired in 1999 after thirty-one years in law enforcement. They approached him through a former Phoenix cop turned private investigator, William De La Torre—they had De La Torre make the initial call, since he knew Gilbertson. Dennis agreed to talk, so Lindsay, Sarah, and Bill De La Torre met him at a Denny's in Peoria, where they spoke for a good two hours. Gilbertson had questions about the case, and comments to make based on his background in ballistics. Halfway through the conversation, Lindsay finally asked, Were you having an intimate relationship with Carol? Yes, Gilbertson allowed. But he hadn't known that she was married, with three kids. Something else he wanted to say: He had a clear memory of the shot fired from the alley through the Macumbers' kitchen window—because he was initially a suspect. The internal affairs investigators apparently knew of his connection to Carol.

They talked on, Lindsay taking notes. Days later, she and Katie met with Gilbertson again at Denny's, to have him sign a notarized affidavit; Lindsay's father, a notary public, joined them. Gilbertson wanted to talk more but had no changes to make to his statement. "In approximately 1972," it began, "I started taking classes at Glendale Community College. . . . I met Carol Macumber while attending school at GCC. Carol and I first became friends through a study group." Gilbertson continued:

> Sometime in 1973, Carol told me that she was divorced. She never talked about her husband and she never mentioned anything about having children. On a few occasions, our study group gathered at Carol's house around 35th Avenue and I never noticed any sign of a husband or children. In 1974, I separated from my wife and we were getting a divorce. During this time, I dated Carol Macumber. Carol and I had intimate relations on a couple of occasions, usually at my apartment. We were never intimate at her house.
>
> In 1974, around the time I was dating Carol, I was contacted by the Phoenix Police Department Internal Investigations Bureau. The investigators told me that someone had fired a shot into Carol Macumber's house from the alley behind the house and I was a suspect. I was shocked by the allegation for a number of reasons. The first was that Carol and I got along very well at that time. The second was that I had been working the night the shot had been fired. The investigators verified that I had been working that night and I was never contacted about the matter again.
>
> In 1975, Carol informed me she was moving to Colorado. It seemed to me that she just wanted to get out of Phoenix. In 1975, my divorce was finalized and Carol said she would help me find a job in

Colorado. I went to Colorado in the fall of 1975 for a visit . . . but ultimately decided to stay in Phoenix. I have not been in touch with Carol Macumber since 1975.

Katie and Sarah also talked twice to a former Maricopa County sheriff's deputy named Gerald Hayes, believing he'd also had an affair with Carol in 1974. Again Bill De La Torre made the initial call. Hayes had retired in 2003, after thirty-one years in law enforcement. He, like Gilbertson, agreed to sign a notarized affidavit. "The environment at the MCSO was best described as 'friendly,'" Hayes recalled. He met Carol Macumber in 1974 through a mutual friend, Mike Moreno, whose girlfriend, Frieda Kennedy, shared an apartment with Carol. One night, Mike and Frieda brought Carol on a patrol ride-along and introduced her. Being separated at the time, "I began dating Carol. Carol and I dated five or six times. . . . I stayed the night at the apartment with Carol a number of times. . . . She liked to party and she talked a lot." He had "absolutely no idea that Carol was married until our fourth or fifth date." As best he could recall, "Carol mentioned that she had one child," but "I did not think of Carol as a mother." He came to feel displeased about their relationship, suspecting she was dating other men; a guy came to the door looking for her during one of his visits. When he ended their relationship, before Bill's arrest, she had no reaction. He never talked to her again. "I was glad I had nothing to do with Carol when the allegations against Bill came about."

On the Macumber team's behalf, Bill De La Torre made yet another call: to Carol's old mentor Ed Calles. The sheriff's detective who'd interrogated Macumber and signed the murder complaint sounded wary. What's this about? he asked De La Torre. What's the evidence? By way of explanation, Katie sent him the clemency board's letter of recommendation. A week later, De La Torre tried again. No, Calles said, he did not want to talk. He now told De La Torre he had a serious illness, suggesting that such a discussion would cause him undue stress. De La Torre wondered about Calles's hesitancy. Why so uncooperative? In De La Torre's experience, the lead investigator always talked about a case.

Katie, Sarah, and Lindsay waited a month, then called Calles anyway. With the others listening on speakerphone, Lindsay took the lead—
she was good at keeping conversations aloft, keeping people on the line.
"We're looking back at the Macumber case," she began. "We're just trying to learn what happened. You can help us." Calles made it plain he
didn't want to help and didn't know why they were reopening the case.
He'd just say his piece and no more: He believed Macumber 100 percent
guilty because of the prints and the ballistics. Also because Bill had lied
about where he'd been the night he came home with a bloody shirt. If he
lied to them about that, what else had he lied about? Lindsay tried to
guide the conversation to Carol, but Calles resisted. Every time she mentioned Carol, he barked, *Are you recording this? Are you recording?
I'll know if you are.* His words sounded like a threat, quite gruff and
intimidating—Katie thought she would definitely not want to be interrogated by him. Lindsay didn't back off, though. She kept bringing up
Carol, and he kept asking whether they were recording him. He also
started suggesting he only vaguely remembered Carol. Then he indicated
he wanted to get off the phone. Only later did Katie think of what they
might have told him: No, we're not recording, but you should have when
you interrogated Bill Macumber.

One day, Lindsay happened to be up in Prescott, Arizona, researching
another case. She knew Joe Rieger lived there now—Rieger, the Phoenix
police officer who in August 1974 investigated the kitchen-window shooting, then attended the session where Carol gave her statement. Lindsay
had found an address for him, so as usual, without calling ahead, she
drove to his home and knocked on the door. No answer. She did not
leave a card. The next morning, she tried again: still no answer. Later that
day she called him, using a phone number that an Internet database
listed as being associated with his address. Rieger's wife answered,
sounding wary. They were on the road, it turned out—so Lindsay had
either called a cell phone or their home line had been forwarded. Rieger
finally took the phone. After Lindsay introduced herself, explaining she
had a few questions about "an old case," he peppered her for five minutes
about how she'd gotten his unlisted phone number. She explained that

she got it off a simple people-search database, but he didn't believe her. No, his number couldn't have just popped up on an online search. She promised him it had indeed. He asked for the database she'd used, and she offered to send him the search report, something he definitely wanted.

Finally, they moved on, Lindsay asking if she could meet with him for twenty or thirty minutes to talk about an old case—the Macumber case. No, he said. He'd talked to an investigator twelve years before— Hayden Williams, Rich Robertson's associate. He would not meet her, didn't want to talk. He'd discussed this case once and had nothing more to say. With that, Rieger hung up. The conversation had lasted some ten minutes. Lindsay followed with a letter, but he never answered.

First Nancy Halas, now Joe Rieger. People who'd been in that room when Carol gave her August 23 statement didn't want to talk. Why? And for that matter, why was Rieger—a Phoenix police officer—even there in a Maricopa County sheriff's interrogation room? That session with Carol, Lindsay noted, began at 6:45, but they didn't call in Nancy Halas until 7:45, an hour later. Then came that gap between August 23 and August 28. Very odd, Lindsay thought. Very odd.

If only they could find the jurors from Macumber's trials. Katie, Lindsay and Sarah had been searching for them ever since they'd gone to the ground. Rule 32 said they needed evidence "sufficient to establish that no reasonable fact-finder would have found defendant guilty . . . beyond a reasonable doubt." What better way to establish this than ask the original jurors how they would have responded to Valenzuela's confessions? They were reaching back thirty-four years, though. Were any jurors still around?

Katie tasked an undergraduate volunteer, Logan Mussman, with locating the jurors. Logan tapped the databases, working off the original voir dire lists from the second trial, in 1976. He started to get some hits. He narrowed those down by age, by location, by previous employment. He and Bill De La Torre began making cold calls. *Were you a juror . . . ?* They kept striking out. More calls, more misses. Finally they found one. Then another. In total, they reached four jurors still alive. One had

Alzheimer's, and one—a very elderly woman—just didn't see any reason to reconsider this matter. That left two jurors to interview at length.

The first, Sarah Elliot, welcomed the call from Katie and Sarah, for she had thought about Bill Macumber's trial often over the years. Two lives lost, another life at stake . . . it had been an emotional and draining experience for her. She'd always thought the jury reached the right verdict, but she would willingly discuss this—if she could first refresh her memory and be brought up-to-date. She asked that they send her the trial transcripts and other documents, including the clemency board recommendation, the Primrose and Valenzuela statements, and a transcript of the hearing before Judge Corcoran where O'Toole and Petica testified.

What she read in these pages greatly disturbed her. Sarah Elliot had been a forty-year-old real estate agent at the time of Macumber's trial, hoping not to be picked for the jury, since such a serious case involved a lot of responsibility. Now seventy-four and retired, she found the revelations about Valenzuela and Primrose startling and enraging. During her several phone conversations with Katie and Sarah, she kept asking, "Can you imagine how I feel?" Readily, she agreed to sign a notarized affidavit.

The palm print and shell casings, she stated, "were the most significant items of evidence to me because they placed Bill Macumber at the crime scene." In her opinion, "the palm print was the primary piece of evidence that convicted Bill Macumber. . . . I would ask myself, if he wasn't at the crime scene, how did his print get on to the car?" She recalled the state's expert testifying that the shell casings found at the crime scene matched Bill Macumber's gun. "Again, this was critical because it placed Bill Macumber at the crime scene. I would ask myself, if he wasn't at the crime scene, how did shell casings from his gun get there?" During the jury's deliberations, "we, as a group, could not get away from the palm print and shell casings." Whenever she thought about Macumber's case over the years, whenever she questioned whether they got the verdict right, "I always come back to the science. All we had was scientific evidence and I believe that's what convicted him."

Sarah Elliot did not have much of a take on Bill Macumber himself when she first saw him—she recalled only that "he had a mild demeanor." She also did not recall Carol Macumber's involvement being emphasized at the trial. But after reviewing the trial transcripts, "I strongly believe that Bill and Carol Macumber's pending divorce, Carol's alleged affairs with law enforcement co-workers and Carol's fingerprinting class at Glendale Community College raise serious doubt about the credibility of Carol's statement to the Maricopa County Sheriff's Office that Bill had confessed to her."

Most important, Sarah Elliot thought that knowledge of Ernest Valenzuela's confessions might have affected the jury's verdict. She thought it "terrible that the jury did not hear about Ernest Valenzuela's confessions because they are extremely significant." She had "no doubt that evidence about this man and his confessions would have impacted the jury's deliberations."

Sarah Elliot also saw great import in Linda Primrose's statement—and how it related to Valenzuela's. She only "vaguely recalled" Primrose at Macumber's trial, but after comparing Primrose's courtroom recantation with her original 1962 statements, "I strongly believe Linda Primrose was telling the truth about witnessing the murders. Her statement is legitimate. She told the same story and did not waver. Her statement accounts for the chunk of hair found at the crime scene." Sarah Elliot felt "very troubled by the fact that the jury did not hear Linda Primrose's story in detail" and wasn't "told about the hair found at the scene and who it did or did not belong to." Linda Primrose's statement, she believed, "is extremely significant."

Elliot directed some of her angriest comments at Judge Corcoran's decision to keep evidence from the jury. "I strongly believe that if a jury is tasked, by the state, to judge another person's actions and to have that person's life in their hands, that they should hear the whole story. All sides of the case should be presented." The great responsibility she now felt for Macumber's fate tormented her. "To think I may have played a role in convicting an innocent man is a terrible burden for me to carry. To not know the whole story is an injustice to everyone. It's an injustice to the criminal justice system. If a juror is to judge another's actions and to have a life in their hands, it is not fair for the juror to not be told the entire truth. To withhold such important evidence and statements from the trial is troubling."

There they had it: If one of the original jurors didn't qualify as a "reasonable fact-finder," who did? And for this reasonable fact-finder, the new evidence—or new to her, at least—indeed was "verdict changing."

The other juror Katie and Sarah interviewed did not even need such new evidence. When they called Lisa Piercefield, she readily agreed to talk. She'd been twenty at the time of the trial, the "baby" of the juror group, a college student and insurance secretary. She'd thought about Bill Macumber many times over the years, and in fact had researched his case in the newspapers and on the Internet. She had from early on thought Bill Macumber innocent. She'd sat in the jury box throughout the trial, giving the proceedings every ounce of her attention, only to be designated an alternate juror at the trial's end. So she didn't participate in the jury's deliberations, didn't get a chance to vote or share her views. The guilty verdict had stunned her.

This and much more she told Katie and Sarah when they visited her home one morning in the late summer of 2010. Lisa Piercefield was fifty-four then, with a husband of thirty-five years, children, and grandchildren. She was by no means a rebel or an iconoclast; she and her husband, Arizona natives, took being American citizens quite seriously. They strongly believed in abiding by all the government's rules and laws and had passed those values on to their children. She wanted to talk to Katie and Sarah—to give them a notarized affidavit—precisely because of her strong values, precisely because she believed in rules and laws. She did not believe they had followed the rules of justice at Bill Macumber's trial.

She didn't begin the trial thinking Macumber innocent. In fact, she thought him "really creepy" at first—so tall and thin, with his Coke-bottle glasses. Early on in the trial, he opened the courtroom door for her one morning and it "freaked me out." In her mind then, Macumber was a murderer, despite the innocent-until-proven-guilty rule. Then came the days of testimony. She never reached a "definitive conclusion" whether Carol "did or did not tamper with the evidence," but to her "it was always a real possibility," and for that reason, "I did not afford any weight to the fingerprint and ballistics evidence."

On the other hand, she thought the evidence about Valenzuela's statements—only now provided to her by the Justice Project—had great

import. She felt "disgusted that the jury was not told about Ernest Valenzuela and his confessions." To her mind, "this information would have
had a huge impact on the jury's decision." At the least, she was "sure that
it would have caused the jury to have reasonable doubt about Bill Macumber's guilt."

As the trial went along, her opinion about Bill Macumber quickly
changed. Rather than "really creepy," she came to think him "just a regular guy who was caught up in a set of very surreal circumstances." To
her, "he came across as a gentleman." He "sat straight up in court," with
no demeanor of a prisoner, no criminal history. She could not fathom
why such an upstanding member of the community would "go out and
shoot two young kids randomly without any reason whatsoever." In her
view, "people just don't do things like that on a 'whim.'" She had assumed
the other jurors shared her outlook, so she "was stunned with shock"
when she heard the verdict. She could not then or now understand how
the other jurors found him guilty—"I strongly believe there was reasonable doubt about his guilt."

Leaving Lisa Piercefield's house with a signed and notarized affidavit
in hand, Katie thought, "Too bad she wasn't on the voting jury." A simple
twist of fate.

Above all others, the person Katie, Lindsay, and Sarah most wanted to
interview was Carol's former roommate, Frieda Kennedy. Frieda had
given depositions before each trial and had testified at the second one.
She'd also talked once to Rich Robertson, a decade ago. But she'd always
been reluctant and vague, never forthcoming. Maybe now she'd talk
openly. Maybe she'd feel more comfortable talking to "two young
girls"—as Katie and Lindsay called themselves—rather than lawyers and
private investigators in suits. Frieda had been the person closest to Carol
back then. Frieda, they sensed, could be the key.

Working off Rich Robertson's old notes, Katie and Lindsay came up
with what seemed to be her last known address, still out in Buckeye.
Before driving there, they met at the Justice Project offices to pore through
Frieda's depositions. Then they climbed into Katie's Honda Civic. Buckeye sat some forty miles to the west of Phoenix, well beyond the urban

sprawl. Katie and Lindsay took I-10 west, passing the prison for women in Goodyear, then headed south on State Highway 85. Pulling into Buckeye, they drove past vacant lots interrupted only occasionally by a housing development or shopping center, rising in isolation. The address they had for Frieda took them to a dirt road amid farmland, then a moderate-sized home surrounded by a fence. They climbed out of their car into a howling wind, strange for Arizona. They both were dressed down, as usual—just jeans and casual tops. A guard dog started barking ferociously. That and the fence kept them from knocking on the front door, so they yelled out their hellos, hoping someone would emerge. A woman appeared. We're looking for Frieda Turner, they explained, using Frieda's married name. No, the woman said, she doesn't live here. The Turners lived down the road, last she knew, but she couldn't say if they still did.

Katie and Lindsay faced into the wind, fighting their way back to the Honda Civic. They drove to where the woman had pointed. There they found two well-sized homes on the same lot, one in front of the other, newly built. They went to the back house first and knocked. No answer. At the front house, the doormat featured a capital T, so they figured they might be in the right place. When they knocked, a woman opened the door. No, she said, Frieda Turner used to live here, in the rear house, but she moved. Last she'd heard, Frieda was living somewhere in Buckeye with a man named Boyd Pierce.

Back inside their car, they did an Internet search on Katie's Black-Berry for "Boyd Pierce + Buckeye." Bingo—a hit. They had an address. Lindsay guided as Katie drove slowly through an unfamiliar region. They missed a couple of turns and circled around for a while. This was an older neighborhood, not on a par with their first stops. The few small, worn homes out here looked to them as if they might be abandoned or harbor a meth lab. Pulling up to Frieda's home at the end of a cul-de-sac, Katie and Lindsay saw a ragtag lot with trash and toys scattered about. Neither of them wanted to get out of the car. Katie said, No, let's not. Lindsay said, Yes, let's. Even as they walked up to the house, they still debated. Maybe, Katie suggested, we should let Rich do this? With trepidation, they knocked. Frieda opened the door. Katie thought her kind of cute-looking—a fifty-six-year-old woman now, short and plump, with frosted hair—but a bit worn, with food on her shirt and a messy house behind her. She warmly welcomed them into her home.

During that first visit, they talked for one hour. Frieda wasn't always clear about things—she tended to say, "Maybe" and "Yeah, hmmm" and "I think I remember, but I don't know." But when they pressed her for specifics, she grew more precise. Frieda wasn't reluctant or guarded with them, as she had been with the men in suits. The passage of time possibly helped as well. Slowly at first, then more easily, she began to talk about her time with Carol. She told of working with Carol at the sheriff's department, together on the night shift in the identification department. She told of Carol, on several nights around the time of Bill's arrest, showing her the Sterrenberg-McKillop case file, which included the fingerprint cards. She told of becoming very good friends with Carol—Carol, in fact, had been Frieda's closest girlfriend at the time. Frieda was twenty then. Coming from a sheltered upbringing, living away from her parents for the first time, she looked up to Carol, thirty-one, "because she liked to have a good time and she had more life experience than me." In the summer of 1974, they became roommates, renting an apartment on Fifty-eighth Avenue, Frieda since she hated commuting from Buckeye, Carol given that she was "unhappy at home because her marriage to Bill had gone sour."

Katie wanted to go slow with Frieda, but had to ask: Did Carol have affairs during this time? Oh yes, Frieda said, with no hesitation, no searching of her memory. She named two men right off: Dennis Gilbertson and Gerald Hayes. They talked on from there, Katie taking notes, but once they had the outlines of Frieda's account, they began making plans for a return visit. They'd just been breaking the ice on this trip. They would bring Sarah Cooper with them next time.

When they arrived for their second visit, the vacant lots and tumbleweeds made Sarah feel way out on an edge, stranded in a wilderness. Yet when they stepped inside Frieda's home, they again were warmly welcomed. Frieda treated Katie and Lindsay as if she'd known them all her life. She poured them iced tea as they settled at the dining room table. She had cleaned up the house now and put herself together.

She had also, apparently, done some thinking, some recollecting. Before they began to question her, before she sat down, Frieda, unprompted, said, "Carol told me she 'went by the house and shot.'" That caught them way off guard. They'd been planning to ask her about the kitchen-window shooting, but later, easing into it. Now here was Frieda bringing it up herself, out of nowhere, at the top of the conversation. Katie asked, "Can you repeat that?" Frieda did, but then began to grow vague—her usual manner of speech. Such a process to get an affidavit, Sarah thought. Still—Frieda had volunteered this, she'd said it: "Carol told me she 'went by the house and shot.'"

For several hours that day, and over a series of later phone conversations, they walked Frieda through her memories, everyone taking notes. They didn't have to cajole her, though they did sometimes press her to be precise. She wanted to help. Eventually, Sarah collected all the notes and drafted Frieda's affidavit, distilling five hours of conversation into six pages. Katie and Lindsay, with Lindsay's notary public father in tow, made one more trip to Frieda's home. On October 11, 2010, she reviewed, then signed her statement.

In it, event by event, Frieda recounted her experiences with Carol. When they moved in together, Frieda recalled, Carol's three children stayed with Bill, and "she did not seem at all concerned about this arrangement." Frieda thought nothing of it herself, since "Carol had told me Bill was a good father." Besides, "I had seen it for myself. Before Carol and I moved in together, I had visited the house she shared with Bill and her three sons more than ten times. I also spent the night there on a few occasions. From what I saw, Bill was the one who took care of the kids; he would play with them and cook meals. He was the better parent. Carol didn't seem to care as much. Bill was a very nice man—courteous and kind. In no way, shape or form was Bill the type of man who would 'come on' to you, unlike most of the guys I worked with at MCSO. It was also clear that Bill loved Carol because he would do whatever she wanted. I do not believe that feeling was reciprocated by Carol." Frieda continued:

> It is my strong opinion that their marriage broke down because Carol wanted a man that was bigger and better than Bill. In my opinion this meant someone with more money, better physical looks and

who worked in law enforcement. Carol had affairs with men like this while she was married to Bill.

When I worked at the MCSO in 1973 and 1974, the environment was very friendly. A number of us would socialize and fraternize outside of the office. The office rules prohibited fraternizing with colleagues but most employees paid little attention to them. The MCSO was like a big playhouse. The deputies would hit on the girls that worked in the office, telling us we looked pretty and asking us to go out to coffee after work. . . . Going out for coffee was sometimes used as an innuendo for having a relationship. For a young woman like me, who was away from her parents for the first time, the MCSO was a fun place to be.

I believe Carol thrived in the playhouse environment. She knew a lot of people, mostly men, and she loved the attention they would give to her. To the best of my knowledge, Carol, while she was married to Bill, had affairs with Phoenix Police Officer Dennis Gilbertson and MCSO Patrolman Jerry Hayes. . . . I am confident that Dennis and Jerry did not know about each other, and I am sure Bill knew nothing about Carol's relationship with either of them.

I also suspect that Carol had a relationship with MCSO Sergeant Ed Calles. Carol had a crush on Sergeant Calles and the two of them would go out for coffee quite often. In fact, they seemed sneaky about it; only a few people knew they went out together. It is my belief that they were sneaky about their meetings because the MCSO prohibited fraternizing with colleagues and they were both married at the time.

It was an unspoken rule that I would not tell anyone about Carol's relationships. I believe the reason for this rule was because Carol was married. That said, I do not think Carol was fearful of Bill Macumber finding out about her affairs. I think Carol just saw Bill as a "country bumpkin" kind of guy. He was a nice, even-tempered man and Carol knew it. Carol was not shy at all. She was charismatic, persuasive, and wasn't very fearful of anything. She had a persona of a "come on" type personality. It appeared she could easily get the guys at work to do things for her.

Sometimes rumors about who Carol was sleeping with would

spread around the MCSO. I would say her reputation would be best described as "loose and easy." Around August 1974, Carol was called to Paul Blubaum's office. Paul Blubaum was the Sheriff of Maricopa County at this time. As an employee of the MCSO, you knew you were in real trouble if the Sheriff called you to his office. I remember standing in the hallway with her as she waited to be called in to the Sheriff's office, and she said that if she was fired she would "take twenty people down with her." I took this to mean that Carol would get those people fired too because she had something on those people. I suspected that "something" was the fact they had been fraternizing with her and other colleagues. Carol did not come across as scared when she said this to me—she would do whatever she needed to do in order to sort things out. . . . Carol always made shrewd decisions and was devious in her own way. She seemed to know what she was doing and most of the time she had a plan. . . .

In August 1974, when Carol and I were living together, and around the same time as Carol had been called into Sheriff Blubaum's office, I recall that there was a shooting incident at Bill Macumber's house. To the best of my recollection, Carol told me that she "went by the house and shot." I took this to mean that she had fired the shot into Bill's house. It also seems that she told me someone else was with her when the shot was fired. I suspect Carol would have done something like that because she wanted out of her marriage bad. . . . We trusted each other and did not keep secrets from each other. I told Carol everything. This is why I believe she told me about her involvement in this incident.

The same week as the shooting incident, while we were at our apartment, Carol said she wanted to talk to me about something she had not told anyone else before. She said "this is going to sound far-fetched" and then told me that, some time earlier, Bill had confessed to her that he had killed the two kids out in Scottsdale in 1962. I was shocked. . . . The story kind of came out of the blue, but Carol said she told me because she was scared that Bill would come and get her because he knew she had fired the shot into his house. I was petrified. Bill was an even-tempered person and I was shocked when Carol told me this story. . . .

After this I decided that it was not a good idea for me to live with Carol . . . I did not want to live with her anymore. I realized that I was in "way above my head." . . . Not long after Carol reported Bill to the MCSO, I moved back to Buckeye to live with my parents. . . . A couple of weeks or months after I moved back to Buckeye, I was in Phoenix and called Carol to meet for lunch. Carol was busy and could not meet me. I never heard from her again. To this day, I have not had any further contact with Carol.

They had possible new evidence now. Frieda, above all. The two jurors—reasonable fact finders, swayed by what they'd learned. Dennis Gilbertson and Gerald Hayes, undercutting Carol's credibility. Tom O'Toole, going deeper, reliving the past. But did they have enough to sustain a PCR petition? As Sarah Cooper began to pull together a draft for Larry Hammond's consideration, the Justice Project team weighed that question. Rule 32 posed such tough hurdles. They couldn't just collect all the impeachment evidence into a narrative. They needed new evidence that would kick out not one but all three pillars of the case: prints, shell casings, Carol's statement. They needed new evidence with verdict-changing capacity.

All through that summer and fall of 2010, Hammond had been consumed by a death penalty murder trial up in Prescott. Not until October did he review the partial draft and to-do list Sarah Cooper had left him before returning to England. He was impressed. Those affidavits—what a job they'd done, going out into the field, finding everyone, getting them to talk. But no, as much as he'd like to, he could not say they were ready to file a petition. They still didn't have enough.

CHAPTER 23

An Impossible Goal

As time went by, the Macumber PCR petition—and Macumber's exoneration— seemed more and more to be an impossible goal. Larry Hammond had told the Board of Executive Clemency that the absence of DNA left Macumber without a clear basis for setting aside his conviction, that they were deeply grateful for the board's interest because defendants without DNA evidence have "no place else to even be heard." Yet given the reality of politics in Arizona, the Justice Project could not count on clemency. However long the odds, they had to keep trying for post-conviction relief within the legal system.

This meant, Hammond decided, that they needed to more aggressively and thoroughly attack the ballistics evidence. That's what their partial draft petition lacked. They had to take full advantage of the National Academy of Sciences' 2009 report *Strengthening Forensic Science in the United States: A Path Forward*. Hammond loved it that the prestigious academy had actually held hearings into topics such as arson, bite marks and DNA. The resulting report, the first comprehensive review of the forensic sciences, had crystallized the shortcomings inherent in firearms identification, giving the team a significant scientific foothold—evidence that they could "newly discover." The Justice Project badly needed such new evidence. Hammond understood that a cloud had started to settle over the project's handling of the Macumber case, just as he'd feared. If they ever managed to get into court, a judge would surely ask, Has there been due diligence? Have you done everything you could, and within a reasonable time span? Hammond shuddered as he imagined how a judge might look at their performance over the years, even though they were a volunteer nonprofit operation with limited resources. All the delays, the cycling generations of students, their failure to hire a paid fingerprint expert, his own sabbatical at a critical moment. . . . That's why they needed continuous lawyers, people who could own a case.

The NAS report, Hammond reasoned, gave them an out. The NAS report represented new evidence not available at Macumber's trials or during the Justice Project's first decade on his case. The NAS report breathed new life into a possible PCR petition. Only now could they try to rebut FBI agent Robert Sibert's testimony at Macumber's trials, something the original defense had failed to do. Nine times the jurors at the second trial had heard Sibert call Macumber's gun the murder weapon "to the exclusion of all others in the world," and four times they'd heard the prosecutor echo those words. Hammond didn't think Sibert would even be allowed to make such an absolutist statement today. If he did, the NAS report—which considered firearms identification a subjective art form—would readily discredit him.

To craft an enhanced ballistics review, the Justice Project turned to Andrew Hacker, who'd just graduated from the ASU law school but remained involved with the project and the Macumber case. Hacker scrambled to educate himself about guns, even while preparing to take his bar exam. He reread Robert Sibert's trial testimony forty times. He parsed out the language Sibert used on the witness stand. He examined the 2009 NAS report. He pored through a pile of studies about firearms comparisons. Always, he looked at the footnotes, building a bibliography of further readings. Weekends, nights—he'd pick up another report whenever he had a chance. He liked doing innocence work whether paid or not, and beyond that, he liked working on the cutting edge of law and forensics.

Just as they'd once sought fingerprint experts, now the Justice Project associates looked for ballistics experts—which Macumber never had at his trials. Hacker first found William Tobin, a former FBI supervisory special agent and forensic metallurgist who, since retiring in 1998, had started questioning how the FBI matched bullets to crime suspects. Hacker also enlisted a firearms and ballistics consultant, John Nixon. He approached, as well, an ASU law professor, Michael J. Saks, a specialist in the field of law and science. Hacker carefully cultivated relationships with all of them. For a while the effort stalled: Tobin hesitated and withdrew—he felt uncomfortable criticizing Robert Sibert, a friend and former colleague. But he returned, galvanized, after happening to see the *Nightline* broadcast about the Macumber case. By the spring of 2011, the team had all three experts lined up, Tobin and Saks working pro bono. Three experts who unequivocally said Robert Sibert could not possibly have matched Macumber's gun to the shell casings by means of the ejector markings. Those ejector markings weren't a unique signature, they maintained: One weapon can make different marks, and different weapons can make identical marks. Sibert, they believed, should have eliminated Bill's pistol because the firing pin and breech face marks didn't match. Instead, he'd made a "selective search for marks" that supported his conclusion. Tobin's judgment: "The evidence does not support an inference that Macumber's weapon was, in fact, the murder weapon." With these three experts' affidavits in hand, Hacker went to work, writing his section of the PCR petition—what Hammond now considered the "linchpin" of their appeal.

In England, Sarah Cooper, Skype-conferencing for hours with Andrew, wrote the rest, focusing on all the familiar themes: Valenzuela and Primrose, Carol, Latent Lift 1, chain of custody. She also added a critical new dimension: the sworn affidavits they'd collected. Frieda Kennedy, Dave Brewer, the two jurors, Dennis Gilbertson and Gerald Hayes—she cited, quoted and attached every affidavit to the petition. The Justice Project still couldn't prove a frame-up, but by adding in the dubious circumstances, they hoped to reduce the value of the palm print.

With those affidavits and the emergence of new ballistics evidence, Hammond thought this to be "a very exciting, almost riveting time" in their eleven-year battle on Macumber's behalf. Section by section, drafts of the petition circulated among the Justice Project team, going through multiple rounds of editing. Simultaneously, the team pushed to complete and file a memorandum in support of a new clemency hearing for Bill—he would be eligible two years after the first one. They met weekly. They arranged a new analysis of the tire tracks, a new look at the fingerprints, another visit with Jerry Jacka. They assigned law students to research specific legal arguments. They tested their reasoning. They reassessed the petition's structure.

Yet now, in the spring of 2011, obstacles and distractions once again slowed their progress. Chief among them: Bill Macumber's health.

CHAPTER 24

Critical Condition

APRIL–JUNE 2011

Bill Macumber did not feel well when he came home from his job at Cochise College at 3:00 on the afternoon of Tuesday, April 19, 2011. In his Mohave Unit cubicle, he stretched out on his bed, hoping to improve. Over the next two hours his condition grew worse. Shortly after 5:00 P.M., he went to the prison's medical office. The staff took one look at him and promptly dispatched him to Cochise Medical Center in Douglas. Doctors there, after a brief examination, put him in an ambulance bound for University Physicians Hospital in Tucson. Larry Hammond's abiding fear had been that Macumber would die in prison before they could get him out. Now that outcome looked quite possible.

At the Tucson hospital, doctors determined that Bill had a blockage in his small intestine. On Friday, April 22, as they attempted to run a scope to observe the blockage, Macumber began hemorrhaging. They rushed him to the intensive care unit with major gastrointestinal bleeding and a blood clot in his stomach. Doctors there started plasma transfusions—eight pints in all—and hooked Macumber to a ventilator. His heart started beating irregularly. His left lung collapsed. The doctors decided to put him into a medically induced coma. Through multiple IV lines they delivered sedatives, antibiotics, painkilling narcotics and medicines to increase his blood pressure. They could not operate on the blockage, though—Macumber was too weak to undergo any type of surgical procedure. They did not think he would survive.

At his home in Aurora, Colorado, Ron Macumber received a call that Friday from the hospital's prison-ward medical director. Ron had been trying vainly for three days to get an update about his father's condition, ever since he'd first heard from a prison chaplain that they'd taken Bill to Tucson. The medical director now had grim news: Your father is in critical condition. We can't stop the bleeding. You might want to get down here.

Ron started spreading the word. He called Jackie. He called Bob and Toots. He called Jay and Harleen. He called Katie. She, in turn, talked to central prison medical authorities, arranging for powers of attorney, seeking permission for family visitation. Katie soon called Ron back with an update: Prison officials had opened visitation to everyone on Bill's list.

Once more, Macumber's relatives scrambled to his side. Ron flew into Phoenix on Friday afternoon and drove down to Tucson with Harleen and Jay. Early Saturday morning, Bob and Toots started driving from Illinois, Jackie and Robyn from New Mexico. At the hospital that weekend, Katie helped Ron with the paperwork. He felt scared when he finally saw his father. This did not look good. The doctors had Bill heavily sedated, on a ventilator, with all kinds of tubes running in and out of him. Ron had never seen so many IVs hooked up to a person. They were feeding him eight different medicines. The doctors told Ron that Bill, unable to breathe on his own, was essentially on life support. Seeking any kind of response, Ron took his dad's hand and yelled for him to squeeze. Bill did, slightly—Ron felt pressure on his fingers. But the nurse explained that he wasn't really conscious and probably didn't know who was holding his hand.

Then on Monday, April 25, Bill contracted pneumonia. More treatment, more tubes, more medicines. Jackie and Robyn arrived. So did Bob and Toots. Bob felt as shocked as Ron had. Bill's extremities were terribly swollen. A tube ran down his throat. He opened one eye when Bob hollered a greeting, but he couldn't know his brother was there. The relatives, all staying at a nearby Holiday Inn, shuttled back and forth, taking turns, waiting and hoping. They knew little for sure about Bill's condition—at the prison guards' instruction, the doctors wouldn't tell them much. This remained a Department of Corrections operation: Bill had one foot and one hand shackled to the bed's railing.

On Tuesday afternoon, as the doctors weaned him off the sedative, he began to rise out of the induced coma. Katie, alone with him just then, called out, "Bill . . ." He raised an eyebrow. "Everything's going to be okay," she said. "Ron is here." Bill opened his eyes, briefly, more than once. It seemed as if he was trying to speak. Katie leaned over him, waving, happy that she'd decided to drop by at this moment. She called Jackie at the Holiday Inn to report the news. Jackie and Robyn jumped into their car, heading back to the hospital.

Bill Macumber would remember nothing up to this point, nothing of the ambulance ride to Tucson or the visits by Katie and his family over the first week. He would only recall briefly waking up that Tuesday afternoon and seeing Jackie at his side, Jackie holding his hands and talking to him. He drifted back into a semicoma, the next several days as blank as before. When he finally came to again, he found himself alone in a room, surrounded by an array of IV bags, his ankle chained to the bed. He lay there for two hours, unable to move or call out, before a nurse finally appeared. Seeing him awake, she summoned a doctor, who examined and questioned him. You had a very close call, the doctor said. On two different occasions, I thought we'd lost you.

After a week, the doctors removed Macumber's IVs and arranged for his transfer to Rincon Unit House 9, an ICU ward at the Arizona State Prison Complex–Tucson. This, to his regret, put him back in the hands of the Department of Corrections staff, a far less caring and considerate group than the hospital medical team. Indeed, he did not find much to appreciate at Rincon. Led by a nurse, the guards installed him in a small claustrophobic cell, sealed by a steel door, that had room for only a bunk and a toilet. The guards left him sitting on the bed. He needed to use the toilet so tried to rise on his own. He made it to his feet but then lost his balance, falling and hitting his head on the concrete floor. Eventually a nurse found him there and lifted him onto the bed.

The next day a doctor came by and gave him a walker. With it, Macumber began to force himself to move. At first, it took all his strength just to push himself into a standing position. He practiced daily with the walker, shuffling back and forth in his cell, taking a few small steps, trying to get his legs to work. Then, at the doctor's order, the guards started letting him out of his cell twice a day for half an hour, so he could walk up and down the hallway. Slowly, his legs strengthened. After a week, he began using a cane. A week later, he discarded the cane.

Rincon remained an appalling place to him. He thought it a joke that they called it an ICU. He saw a nurse just twice a day, once in the morning for meds and vitals, once in the afternoon for more meds. The only other visitors to his cell were guards bringing his food, always cold—he never ate a hot or even a warm meal at Rincon. Rarely did he see a doctor. No human being, he came to believe, should have to live in a place like this, let alone someone recovering from a medical crisis.

On May 11, at least, he had a welcome visitor: Larry Hammond. Larry spent an hour with him. They would file the new clemency petition immediately, Hammond reported. And he hoped to soon complete the PCR petition as well. The Justice Project, he assured Bill, was still fighting on his behalf.

On that same day, Bill wrote to Jackie, "Well, love of my life, it appears as though I went off the deep end once again, but for the life of me I don't know what went wrong or why. One minute I was in Mohave Unit doing fine, and then next I was in some hospital in Tucson. Totally, and I do mean totally, out of it." He remembered only "a lot of pain and fear," but he did recall "you and Robyn being there." He was now over at the Tucson prison ICU unit, which "is not much—I can tell you that. . . . Being in this place is like being in solitary confinement, only much worse." He hadn't been able to take anything with him when he left Mohave, so "when I got here I had to buy things. Sweatpants and sweatshirt to keep from freezing to death. Shorts, t-shirt, socks and pants, just to have a change of clothes. It's very cool in these cells and they are cells, Jackie. They most certainly are not anything like a hospital room. One

bed and one stainless steel toilet and that's it. No TV or radio. Just terribly long days of just living here. If I can just maintain my sanity till I get
back to Mohave or wherever . . ."

Macumber, despite wanting always to present a positive face, couldn't
hide his despair. Those who came to visit in mid-May saw a dazed, weak,
clearly unhappy man, wearing a surgical mouth mask to protect others
from his germs. He had none of his usual witty verve. He had improved
but still felt deeply tired. Most of all, he longed for a return to Douglas.
He wanted to be back where he had friends, a routine and guards who
respected him.

On May 21, he wrote Jackie again, now making no effort to mask his
misery: "Quite honestly, I find it a wonder that I'm still alive. . . . I am
still very weak and especially so in my legs. . . . I have lost over 30 pounds
and I feel all worn out all day long. I don't get any sleep that is over an
hour and the time drags so terribly. I've never known days and nights
so terrible. If I don't leave here soon I don't know what will happen to
me. . . . Sorry this is so short but I am worn out. Know you are forever in
my thoughts and forever in my heart."

In late May, prison authorities told Macumber he'd be leaving the
Rincon Unit. Bill took that to mean they were returning him to Douglas.
Instead, they transferred him to another unit at the Tucson state prison
complex, Manzanita, which housed inmates with medical conditions
and "special needs." Not going back to Douglas pulled him into a deep
depression. He had to admit, conditions at Manzanita were better than
at Rincon—they even had a microwave, so he could heat the cold food—
but nothing like at Douglas. In his mind, Douglas constantly beckoned
now, looming as a kind of nirvana: the goal, the finish line.

Yet it appeared he would never get there. After two weeks at Manzanita, a doctor finally came to evaluate him. Given your age (almost
seventy-six now) and medical conditions, the doctor told him, you will
probably have to stay here in Manzanita's special needs unit, close to
Tucson's hospitals. With this news Macumber sank deeper into an anx-
ious depression. In certain relaxed moments before falling ill, he had
talked of what he "will do" when he got out—his writing and his life on
Jackie's ranch. Now he corrected himself: "No, I mean would do. . . .
Time is not on our side." On occasion, he thought back over his life, over

all that had happened, over what he might have done differently. "Well," he told a visitor, "I might have had less trust in law and lawmen." Though he'd never shown bitterness, he'd years before privately fixed on one abiding way to express his feelings: At the Cochise College graduation ceremonies each spring, he declined to recite the Pledge of Allegiance. "Show me where there is 'liberty and justice for all,'" he explained.

At the Justice Project, Katie, aware of Bill's suffering, swung into action. She worked the phone lines, she fired off e-mails, she arranged meetings with Department of Corrections medical personnel. The entire Justice Project team pitched in, pulling strings, lobbying hard for Macumber's return to Douglas. So, too, did the warden and deputy warden at Douglas—they wanted Bill back, they let it be known, even if he had to return in a wheelchair.

In the Tucson state prison's Manzanita Unit, Macumber engaged in his own form of lobbying. To the doctor who'd told him he'd have to stay there, Bill said: That's not going to happen. Well, the doctor replied, you really don't have a choice. Bill disagreed: I most certainly do have a choice.

They looked at each other. The doctor asked, How do you figure you have a choice?

Bill said, I'll refuse to take any of my meds.

That will kill you, the doctor pointed out.

Life has to have some quality as well as quantity, Bill replied. If I have to live here, I would rather end it.

Two days later, the doctor signed Macumber's release. At 4:00 A.M. on June 20, guards woke him and told him to pack up: They were transporting him back to the Mohave Unit at Douglas. "Words," Macumber would say later, "cannot even begin to express what I felt at that moment." Not long after, he found himself sitting in a bus bound for Douglas. They were taking an indirect route with intermediate stops, making it a long ride, but he didn't mind; he'd soon be among friends and people he knew. In an instant, the grave depression he'd been suffering for weeks evaporated. In its place came a feeling of hope, a feeling that "life might still hold something for this old man."

His reception at the Mohave Unit overwhelmed him. As he walked through the gate, a large crowd of inmates surrounded him, shaking his hand, slapping him on the back, asking how he was doing. Guards and other prison staff joined in as well, offering greetings and best wishes. When he reached his dorm, he found every inmate on his run lined up to welcome him. Turning to look at his "home," he saw that his buddies had repainted his cubicle and locker and put everything into top shape for his return.

For days, the steady parade of inmates and staff continued, everyone stopping to welcome him back. The warden came by, the deputy warden, the unit captain. More than two hundred inmates in all, and a good portion of the civilian staff. Macumber felt humbled, realizing how many people cared about him. He felt grateful as well, for they promptly gave him back his old job; he started working again at Cochise College on June 27, a week after his return.

Bill Macumber still prayed for the Justice Project to succeed, still dreamed of life with Jackie on her New Mexico ranch. Yet he felt at peace for the moment, he felt as if he'd arrived. You have no idea, he told a visitor late that June, how wonderful it is to be back here in Mohave. It was, he said, "almost like coming home." Home—a place where he never felt lonely, where he never cast shadows.

CHAPTER 25

A Second Clemency Hearing

JUNE 2011–MARCH 2012

In mid-2011, just as Macumber returned to Douglas, Bob Bartels had to step away for months when the U.S. Supreme Court agreed to hear his appeal of another Justice Project case, *Martinez v. Ryan*—which, as it happened, argued for a prisoner's right to effective assistance of counsel in post-conviction proceedings. At the same time, Larry Hammond fell seriously ill, sidelined for months by a devastating bout with a mysterious pneumonia of no known cause or cure. After thirteen days in an intensive care unit and repeated trips to hospital wards, he remained tethered to an oxygen tank. For help on the Macumber case, he eventually turned to an eight-hundred-attorney law firm, Perkins Coie, which took over the drafting of the PCR petition in October 2011. Within weeks, its lawyers, led by senior partner Jordan Green, completed the Justice Project's work.

On February 9, 2012—fourteen years after Judge O'Toole first called Hammond—attorneys for Macumber finally filed a post-conviction relief petition on his behalf in Maricopa County Superior Court. By then, another Justice Project petition had persuaded the Board of Executive Clemency to schedule a second hearing for Macumber, to be held on the morning of March 19. Both petitions included the sworn affidavits collected by Katie, Lindsay and Sarah. Both put all the Justice Project claims about Carol in the public record. Both offered a narrative and an argument.

Then, one morning in mid-February, Larry Hammond took a phone call from Deputy Maricopa County Attorney Vince Imbordino. We're going to oppose you at the clemency hearing, Imbordino told Hammond. We're going to call witnesses, we're going to argue the case. Macumber is guilty.

In the end, the Justice Project team knew, all criminal law was storytelling. They'd been the only storytellers for the past dozen years. Now they had company. From the moment he received Imbordino's call, Hammond understood that this second clemency hearing would be quite different from the one in 2009—not just for the Justice Project but for the clemency board as well. The board's members were used to getting no more than a letter from the county attorney. For the prosecutor to show up was pretty damned unusual. Maybe in a last-minute death penalty case involving a pardon or commutation. But not here, not over clemency.

Eventually, Hammond learned that the victims' families would also be attending and speaking to the board. So would Carol, on a phone link from her home in Washington. And a renowned ballistics expert, recruited by the county attorney. This hearing would, in effect, be an adversarial proceeding. Hammond realized it would be a challenge. The presence of Carol and the victims' families—whatever they said—would have an effect. How would the board handle competing narratives?

The Justice Project team members debated whether they should pull the hearing. All in all, they felt they had a better chance with their PCR petition. And whatever the board decided, it was quite unlikely that Governor Brewer would approve clemency for Macumber. So why risk a reversal of the board's 2009 recommendation?

For days, the team members thought it over. In the end, they decided they had to try—partly because of Bill's age and health, partly because of their own tremendous commitment over the last twelve years. How could they stop now? How could they forswear all they'd done, all they believed? The siren call still rang in their ears.

* * *

At long last, all the players in the Macumber case came together on the same stage. At 8:00 A.M. on March 19, a damp, misty Monday morning, some of them edged into a small, cramped conference room at the Board of Executive Clemency's headquarters on West Jefferson Street in downtown Phoenix, sitting knee to knee in three rows of chairs facing the board members, while others, in distant cities and states, pushed buttons on their phones, plugging into the board's conference system. Whether in the room or on speakerphone, they could not avoid each other now.

Macumber's family and the Justice Project team claimed one side of the chamber. Jackie Kelley and her daughter, Robyn, had once again driven in from New Mexico. Ron had flown in from Colorado. Jay and Harleen had come from Apache Junction. Representing the Justice Project were Larry Hammond and Bob Bartels, Rich Robertson, Andrew Hacker, Katie Puzauskas and Lindsay Herf (Katie and Lindsay now held the title of co-executive director for the Justice Project). Close by, across the aisle: the county attorney's team, led by Vince Imbordino; members of the victims' families, among them Joyce's brother and sister and Tim's cousin; and the state's ballistics expert, Lucien Haag, a former director of the Phoenix Police Department Crime Laboratory.

They all looked straight ahead, eyes fixed on the board members. Up front, Duane Belcher threw switches and checked lights, confirming the speakerphone connections: Bill Macumber at the state prison in Douglas. Bob, Clara and Mark Macumber in Illinois. Sharon Sargent-Flack in Prescott. And Carol, Steve and Scott Kempfert in Olympia, Washington. Bill Macumber had not heard their voices in thirty-seven years.

"All right, thank you," Duane Belcher began. "I think we're ready to go. We're going to do this in an orderly fashion. Everybody will respect everyone else. We're not going to get into a shouting match, we're not going to get into a debate. All of your comments, please address them to the Board. We won't want individuals talking to one another."

One more thing, Belcher added: While executive clemency is "mercy and grace" for prisoners who admit their guilt, it could also be granted for "a claim of innocence." Either way, today "we're not here to retry the trial."

This was not the same board that had heard Macumber's case in 2009; only two members remained from then, Duane Belcher and Ellen Stenson, and Stenson was absent that day, traveling out of state. Three new board members sat beside Belcher now: Marilyn Wilkens, with an administrative background in the Arizona Department of Corrections; Ellen Kirschbaum, with over thirty-one years in the Arizona criminal justice system, including two decades in the adult and juvenile correctional field; and Jack LaSota, a longtime Phoenix attorney, former state attorney general, and chief of staff to Governor Bruce Babbitt. With four rather than the usual five board members, just two could derail a recommendation, but that's how the clemency process worked sometimes. Before each board member sat a thick pile of documents. They thumbed through the pages.

The Justice Project's nineteen-page memorandum covered the familiar arguments, but now it also featured critical attachments—all the affidavits collected in 2010 by Katie, Lindsay and Sarah, including those from Frieda Kennedy, Dave Brewer, Dennis Gilbertson, Gerald Hayes and Rich Robertson on his conversation with Sheriff Blubaum regarding Carol. The sanctions imposed, her threat to "take twenty people down" if fired. Her affairs, her "job on the line." As the Justice Project's memo put it, her "motive to lie."

The board members, though, also had before them the county attorney's six-page memo in opposition to clemency, which argued that the fingerprints matched and so did the shell casings. Linda Primrose lied, her story was "fully explored and refuted." Valenzuela, too, Judge Corcoran finding his confession "unreliable and not supported by any physical evidence." Valenzuela's lawyers—Thomas O'Toole and Ron Petica—"were not equipped with any special truth-detecting abilities." The state's memo, like the Justice Project's, came complete with an arsenal of attachments, including sheriff's reports and pages pulled from the trial transcripts. There was testimony from sheriff's deputies that Macumber "admitted to police he had confessed the murders to his then wife." There was testimony from Macumber himself, offering his ambiguous, speculative "I suppose to keep her from leaving us" comment. There was testimony from Phoenix police technician Joe Garcia, saying that Latent Lift 1 and the photo of the print on the Impala were one and the same—so to tamper, someone would have to "fabricate a photo of the palm print *and* the latent palm print lift."

There also was a curious handwritten letter from Linda Primrose to Bedford Douglass from July 1976, begging him not to call her to the stand at the second trial, threatening to recant if he did. From the trial transcript, the Justice Project team knew of the threat, but they had never seen this letter before. In her seat, Katie studied it along with the board members. *I am guilty of making false statements in 1962 in an attempt to strike back at my mother. For all of this I am more than sorry. I am not guilty of being present at a murder. I was not there. All those lies I told at that time was just to hurt my mother who had hurt me. Since that time I have slowly put my life in order. I have married, I have two children. . . . I will not be used to cast doubt. I will make very certain the jury knows I lied in 1962. I am not a good person and I know it but God is with me. I would urge you to reconsider using me to cast doubt. If your man is not guilty, you should not need me. I've done enough wrong in my life—that I couldn't live with myself if a lie got a guilty man off on a murder charge. Enclosed is a little book for your man. Pass it on to him. No need to say where it came from.*

Interesting, Katie thought. She knew that Primrose had first claimed the Fifth at a pretrial hearing, refusing ten times to answer questions about the murders on the grounds that it might incriminate her. Only when that tactic failed did she write this letter. Katie wondered: What was that little book she wanted to pass on? Maybe a Bible?

Larry Hammond went first, invited by Belcher to open the hearing for the Justice Project. He was seriously ill at the time, frighteningly fatigued without knowing why. Later he'd learn he'd been suffering from hypotension—severe low blood pressure. His doctors had by necessity taken him off the steroid prednisone, used to combat his chronic pneumonia, and his own adrenal system had not kicked in. Belcher knew Hammond was ailing. "You can sit if you like," Belcher told him. "I mean, you don't have to—"

"I'm going to be brief," Hammond said, pushing himself out of his chair, stepping toward the podium and microphone. "So I'll stand up.

Thank you. If I had to stand up for more than a few minutes, I would take you up on it."

This time, so different from 2009, Hammond merely set the stage for his colleagues. Because three of the current board members had not been on the board in 2009, he explained, "we will want to briefly, this morning, summarize" the case. Andrew Hacker will provide an overview. Lindsay Herf will talk about Macumber's prison record. Katie Puzauskas will address Macumber's old-code lifer status. But first, "we will ask Mr. Macumber to speak to you."

Hammond leaned into the microphone, linked to the speakerphone. "Bill," he said, "this is your opportunity to address the Board directly and we'd like you to say whatever you think is appropriate for the Board's consideration this morning."

Address the board, yes. But Macumber knew that Carol, Scott and Steve could hear him, too. He sat alone at a table in the Mojave Unit at Douglas, a prison guard down the hall. He felt all of his seventy-six years. He understood he could better his chances for clemency by expressing remorse and repentance. Yet now, as always, he would not: "I told everyone that I was innocent on the day I was arrested, on the day I went to trial, on the day I was sentenced, and I'm stating my innocence here before all of you today because it is the truth. It was the truth back then, it is the truth now, and it will remain the truth forever."

Something else he wanted to say, now that he could, now that she was listening. "Accept this for what it is," he began. "My ex-wife, who I guess is on the line, has told a great many lies over the years, and she's hurt a great many people. But the worst lies she ever told, the most unforgivable lies she ever told, were those she told our three sons. She told them that I didn't love them, but she knew I— Those boys were my whole world and I loved them with all my heart then, and I do today. She told them that I didn't try to contact them, and all the letters that I wrote to my sons were returned to me as refused. My boys never knew I tried to get in touch with them to tell them I loved them. As a result, I have not heard from my two oldest sons in 37 years, but I'm very proud and extremely grateful to say that my youngest son, Ronnie, who is there with you today, didn't accept what he was told and went looking for answers. And he found those answers at the Justice Project with Larry Hammond. . . . I thank you, Mr. Belcher and members of the Board, for allowing me to say these words, and I assure you they come from my heart."

The Justice Project's presentation continued with Andrew Hacker, who walked once again through the chronology of the case and Carol's testimony, marshaling "some of the most important points supporting Bill's innocence." He'd been on the Macumber team for two years now, joining it just as he was graduating from the ASU law school. A fifth-generation volunteer turned Justice Project staff attorney, he filled the role Hammond had played at the 2009 hearing.

He called the confession story itself, Bill as army CID assassin, "preposterous." He pointed out factual errors—for instance, Joyce's purse was never rifled through. He noted that Carol supposedly heard this confession in April, then moved out in June, leaving her boys "with a double murderer." But beyond that, he held back. The Justice Project, Hammond had advised, should take "the high ground" at the hearing. So Andrew said only that at the time Carol reported this confession to sheriff's deputies, "both her personal and professional lives were in turmoil." Carol "was the center of a sensitive internal investigation at MCSO, was a suspect in a suspicious shooting at Bill's home, and she and Bill were in the midst of a contentious divorce."

Rather than identify the nature of the internal investigation, he asked the board members to turn to the documents sitting before them: "One last point on the alleged confession, and I do mean to be delicate here, but I would direct the Board to the affidavits from Dennis Gilbertson and Jerry Hayes describing the environment at the MCSO at the time of those arrests, and their particular relationships with Carol at the time."

The primary focus, Hammond had decided, should be on Valenzuela and Primrose. So that's what Andrew addressed in his concluding remarks, after first reviewing the forensic evidence and his three ballistic experts' affidavits. "It cannot be overstated how critical it was that Valenzuela's confessions were never heard by a jury," he told the board. "It is true that Judge Corcoran . . . ruled that the confessions lacked sufficient indicia of trustworthiness. What should be immediately apparent, however, is that Linda Primrose, the single most important person in this case, was not part of that hearing. The critical details she had provided to MCSO in 1962 corroborating Valenzuela's confessions were not considered." Andrew kept underscoring this theme: "The fact that in 1962, Primrose related non-public information about the murders, named Ernie as the killer, . . . and described a man who, two years later, repeatedly confessed to the exact same crime all strongly suggest that Ernie Valenzuela was the true killer, that Bill is innocent and he has spent more than half his life in prison for a crime he did not commit. Thank you."

The board members had questions for Andrew, some more pointed than those asked in 2009. Just what did Bill say to Carol at their home in the spring of 1974? Did the sheriff's department ever try to track down those juveniles who jumped Macumber on the night he came home with a bloody shirt? How much time passed between Bill's alleged confession and Carol's statement to the deputies? Hadn't Macumber used reloaded cartridges, like those found at the murder site?

Board member Ellen Kirschbaum finally zeroed in on the heart of the matter: What did Macumber tell deputies during the extended interrogation on the day of his arrest? "I heard Mr. Macumber say that he had never admitted to the killing. . . . Now I just wanted to clarify something, because I'm a little confused. In the report from MCSO, Sergeant [Barnby], part of it reads, 'Upon completion of the reading . . . Sergeant Barnby placed his hand on Macumber's shoulder and asked Macumber, Bill, did you tell Carol that you killed those people. Macumber hung his head for a moment and, looking at the door, said, quote, Yes, unquote.'" Kirschbaum eyed Andrew. "Can you explain that?"

Andrew did the best he could with a murky matter. "There is—I—there is disagreement in the departmental report. You know, Carl Pace, who testified at trial, said that he was present during the interrogation and Bill never confessed. There are sheriff's reports that say that Bill did. Bill himself has said he never did, and unfortunately the actual interrogation was not tape-recorded or video-recorded in any way so all we have are some of these after-the-fact recitations, which, as you point out, are conflicting."

*　*　*

By now, it was apparent to all how much this proceeding differed from the 2009 hearing. The mood and energy level, the sense of potential, were not the same. By necessity, the Justice Project presentations, though crisply efficient, suggested a distilled replay of the past. The board members' attention, so riveted on Macumber and the Justice Project two years before, turned this morning in multiple directions: to the piles of documents before them, to the victims' families sitting just inches away, to the county attorney's team. There was also the feeling that Governor Brewer would most certainly veto any recommendation to commute. All of this seemed to affect not just the board but Macumber's relatives. When their turn came to speak, their words were heartfelt but rushed, lacking the 2009 hearing's feel of dramatic revelation.

Ron spoke last, and only briefly. This time he delivered no ringing denunciation of Carol, no dramatic declaration that she was absolutely capable of framing Bill. "I will never leave my father's side," he said quietly. "My father is an innocent man convicted wrongly. . . . In the process of relearning who my father was, I have lost the rest of my family. It's a hard thing to live with. I love my mother. I love my brothers. But this is the right thing to do. This is what needs to be done. My father deserves clemency and I pray that he will see that granted to him. . . . I just pray that you do the right, pray that you—"

As he'd done with the others, Belcher hurried the exchange: "Okay . . ."

"—release my father. Thank you very much."

In 2009, the board had showered Ron and other Macumber family members with questions. This morning, they posed none.

Now came the state's presentation. Vince Imbordino, a thirty-year veteran in the county attorney's office, first called up his ballistics expert, Lucien Haag, for forty-six years a highly respected criminalist and forensic firearms examiner. Haag began plugging in his laptop, preparing for a PowerPoint presentation. Larry Hammond braced himself. He knew this would be difficult to counter, as the county attorney had provided him with an advance courtesy look at the material.

With the lights lowered, Haag began. Frame by frame, up on the screen, he pointed to various parts of a gun, moving his marker finally to the tiny ejector—"admittedly small, but that's why we used microscopes in the crime laboratory." He ran a high-speed video showing how the ejector in a semiautomatic pistol strikes and kicks out a cartridge. He offered a slide photo of a fired cartridge case, indented by "a plethora of marks . . . all of which could be used for identification purposes." He focused in on a welter of ejector markings, then enlarged the image click by click "to finally here. This is what makes it unique. . . . So it becomes an individual. . . . Then we have a means of matching the cartridge back to the gun that fired it. . . . Can ejector marks be matched? Yes."

Haag moved on to a second PowerPoint demonstration. He showed how by replacing the slide of a gun—"here's how easy it is to disassemble"— you can change the breech and firing pin marks. He showed how easily "you can get new gun barrels, you can replace the barrel." But the ejector was different: "It looks like a permanent part of the frame of the gun. . . . It's not obvious it could be removed. In fact, in 46 years as a firearms examiner, I've never removed or replaced an ejector." If you replace the slide and barrel, you can't match a gun by firing pin or breech marks. "But if you forget this ejector . . ."

Imbordino then asked Haag if he had "some personal knowledge" of the Macumber case and FBI agent Robert Sibert's match of Bill's gun to the shell casings at the time of the trials. Yes, he did, Haag said. He remembered this case "almost like it was yesterday." In between the two trials, "I was either at the FBI or for some reason saw Bob Sibert's photo micrographs"—photos of the shell casings taken through a special comparison microscope, used to examine ballistics evidence. "I could see a very compelling identification" based on "things called ejector marks." Sibert also "had his work reviewed by several examiners in the Bureau."

Haag had another memory, as well. A little while before the first trial, "a man showed up in my laboratory named Charles Byers." Haag "knew of him as a shooter, shooting enthusiast, and he wanted a tour." He "asked to see the comparison microscope." About a month later, "I got a call from the County Attorney's office saying Byers would be the expert [for the defense] at the first trial of Mr. Macumber." Later, in between trials, "I looked at what Mr. Byers had done and he deliberately, in my view, had taken cartridges . . . that didn't match very well. . . . Mr.

Byers, in my view, attempted to perpetrate a fraud on the first court." For the second trial, "I was listed as a potential witness for the prosecution." The defense attorney, Bedford Douglass, "called me . . . we were friends" and "interviewed me" about Byers. "I'd had an opportunity to see Mr. Sibert's comparison, I could see this was a nice identification. I explained that to Bedford Douglass." Douglass then "didn't produce" Byers at the trial—or any other expert. Haag "had reason to believe" that Douglass went to a "suitably qualified expert," but "I think you could conclude" that this expert "must have concurred with Mr. Sibert's original findings."

In his seat, Hammond fumed at this testimony. Nothing in the Power-Point material he'd seen ahead of time had suggested that Haag would say anything like this. Hammond thought such a tangent was beneath Haag, whom he knew to be a decent guy. The state could never introduce this kind of unsupported personal memory—a polemic, really—in a formal court proceeding, only here at a clemency hearing, when the county attorney knew there were no limits and no consequences. Hammond couldn't say that any of Haag's presentation was untruthful, but he believed it conflated issues and studies. Yet the board had no meaningful way to understand this.

Hammond could see that Haag's testimony obviously affected the board, particularly Ellen Kirschbaum—the way she listened, the direction of her questions, her focus on Bill's known use of reloads similar to those found at the murder scene. With a board limited to only four members this day—a fact Hammond deeply regretted—they could not afford to lose another vote.

How, though, to neutralize testimony from the victims' families? Their turn now. First, John McCluskey, Tim McKillop's cousin. His father and Tim's mother were siblings, he the last of the family on his aunt's side. "I'm really here to speak for her," he told the board: for Tim's mother. "You can imagine what she must have gone through during this whole ordeal. Her only son taken away from her." Based on what he'd read in the newspapers and heard from Vince Imbordino, he thought Macumber guilty. "But beyond that," McCluskey said, "with respect to his being in jail for such a long time and his poor health, I'd like to talk about . . . the 34 years that my aunt lived without her only child." She used to call Timmy "my youngster," and "she did that throughout the whole course of those 34 years." Imagine her shock "when she learned that her son at 20 was dead . . . executed in the desert for no apparent reason." How to describe "the loneliness, the emptiness of a situation like hers?" She ended up in a nursing home and died in 1996, "16 years alone as a widow . . . 34 years childless . . . isolated from the outside world." She was seventy-eight then—"that's about the same age as Mr. Macumber now. I don't think that I'm going too far to ask you to see that he continues the kind of life that she did, alone and isolated from those things that are important to her."

Judy Michael, Joyce's sister, spoke next. "We were, are, a very close family," she told the board. "It was very devastating to have my sister and Tim taken from us. And I can totally relate to how much the Macumber family wants him back into their lives. However, we were denied that opportunity to have Joyce and Tim back into our lives."

Then came Carol Sue McCluskey. Tim's mother, she explained, was her aunt through marriage. She'd spent much time caring for her. She'd known Tim and Joyce. "I just would like to say that these two kids were just so pure. They were wonderful, wonderful kids." The night of the murders was "the first time in his life Tim didn't come home without calling." The family thought the kids "had just decided to go and elope." So the next morning when the doorbell rang, "they thought it would be 'the youngsters' there to announce they were husband and wife." Instead, "it was the sheriff." They'd been a "very, very close family," but this "drove a wedge" between Tim's parents, Ann and Jim. "She grieved in her way and he grieved in his and they were never ever able to grieve together." After the murders, "Jim would eat his dinner in one room and she would eat her dinner in another room." Jim died "before they had a chance to re-bond." Ann said "that was two tragedies, the loss of her son and the loss of her husband."

In her chair, Katie started to feel woozy, as if she couldn't breathe. They weren't nearly finished, though. "Mr. Imbordino," Duane Belcher said, "maybe we should hear from some of the opposition that's on the phone, as well."

He turned to the speakerphone. "Ms. Kempfert," Belcher asked, "are you there?"

"Yes, I am."

"Okay," Belcher continued. "We're going to give you the opportunity to make some statements here. . . . What would you like to say today?"

Carol had sent Belcher a five-page letter ahead of this hearing, something the Justice Project knew nothing about and hadn't seen. She began to read from it, her voice clear and strong and unfaltering. "I welcome this opportunity to tell the story of the events that led up to Bill's arrest," she told the board, "and to defend myself from the accusations against me." This "may be a lengthy letter but I ask you to be patient. In order to understand what happened you must know the history."

She'd started dating William Macumber when she was sixteen and married him four days after turning eighteen. "During our courtship he told me that when he was in the Army he worked for the CID. He told me that this was a secret intelligence unit and that even though he was out of the Army, he was still active in the unit. He told me stories about the 'missions' he and his men went on. . . . Needless to say, my parents tried desperately to stop the marriage but I was young, immature, naïve and oh so sure I knew better."

At "about 10 P.M." one night in May 1962, less than a year after their marriage, Bill came home with "blood all over him." Since then, "many people have asked me why I was not suspicious over the coincidence between the Sterrenberg/McKillop murders and the events I witnessed" that night. "First, let me reiterate, I was young, naïve and believed everything Bill told me. Second, the newspaper accounts alternately reported the murders were the result of a drug deal gone bad or the work of a crazed random killer." Since "we were not involved in drugs and I certainly didn't believe Bill to be a random killer, none if it made sense." So "I put the matter to rest." Over the next ten years "we had three sons and life went on." But during those years, "I matured and came to recognize many inconsistencies in the stories Bill told about his exploits." By 1972, "our marriage was in serious trouble and I expressed my desire to leave." Bill said "he couldn't live without me and threatened suicide on several occasions." Then he said he was dying of cancer. Then that he had a heart condition. "I tell you these things because I want you to understand that after ten years of tales of wild army exploits, stories of how he was dying and pleas for sympathy, I had had enough. I simply did not believe anything he said."

From there, Carol turned to "an evening in April 1974." Here she once again walked through her account of Bill confessing the murders to her. "After telling me this story, Bill told me he had lived with this terrible thing on his conscience for all these years and that the only thing that kept him going was me and the kids. He said that with this on his conscience, he didn't know if he could go on if I left him." Yes, Carol added, "I know people are incredulous that I did not go running to the nearest police station to tell what I heard. Please understand—I DID NOT BELIEVE HIM." At the time, she was hoping to be hired as a full-time deputy sheriff. "I would have been greatly embarrassed to have to admit that I married and stayed married to a man who told such wild tales. And since I did not believe him, I could not see any good would be served."

Then came the kitchen-window shooting incident. "My immediate response was 'BS. He did it himself.'" Angry, thinking he was trying to implicate her, she gave her statement to deputies. Early the next week, "I was given a polygraph that related to the shooting at the house and I passed." Days later, "shortly after Bill was arrested, there were accusations that I had framed him. . . . I was given a second polygraph and questioned about tampering with the evidence. I passed that test too." Carol added, "The record of that I have here, and I assume that you have it also." (In fact, the board did not; nor did the Justice Project or the county attorney.)

She did testify at the second trial, Carol pointed out, giving the jury the chance to evaluate what both she and Bill said. And days after Bill's conviction, the foreman of that jury wrote her a letter. She'd enclosed it with her own letter sent to Duane Belcher, so "I'm not going to read the whole thing, but would like to read a part where he talks about how the jurors viewed the evidence and came to their conclusion. It says: 'Now as to the attacks on your reputation and the countless affairs, etc. etc., you should know that the overwhelming majority of the jurors could have cared less. The overwhelming majority of the jurors felt that this was completely immaterial. The overwhelming majority of the jurors felt that if the affairs were true, more power to you and you've had it coming.'"

Carol's conclusion: "In the end it boils down to this. Two people confessed to the murders but the physical evidence found at the scene points to only one of them—William Macumber. Since Bill could not explain why his palm prints or casings from his gun were found at the scene he came up with the story that I had framed him. I did not frame William Macumber. I did not tamper with evidence. William Macumber did, in fact, murder Joyce Sterrenberg and Timothy McKillop."

Carol had been more effective than Katie expected, not shaky at all. But Katie didn't think Bill the creature Carol made him out to be. The picture Carol painted did not at all resemble the one Katie had seen. Jackie thought the same—this was not the Bill she had known her entire life. Above all, he didn't lie. Bill told funny stories. But never anything about secret agents and covert missions.

Larry Hammond believed it significant that Carol had not directly denied or addressed their claims about a "sensitive internal investigation" of her. In fact, what she didn't say pleased him. Still, he knew she'd been effective before the board—at least those board members who wanted to vote no.

Effective, too, were Bill and Carol's two oldest sons, Scott and Steve, who spoke next. Both also had sent the board letters.

Scott, at forty-nine the oldest of the Macumber siblings, retired now after twenty-one years in the U.S. Air Force, began: "First thing I want to say is, this man put me through personal hell that no child and no family should ever go through." He is "flawed in character, flawed in integrity, and the man knows nothing of the word honesty." Though he insists "we have been brainwashed" by Carol, "I looked at the facts of this case for many years. . . . I've learned many things about my father, not only through my mother but through other people. The man is not credible, nor is he honest." This man "needs to remain where he is at." His exemplary achievements in prison are "to make Bill Macumber look important or special. He is not special. He did not do this out of the goodness of his heart. He does this to make Bill Macumber look like a great soul or a humanitarian. He is neither." In his letter, Scott had added one more thought, left unspoken now at the hearing: "Outside organizations are believing and listening to a twice-convicted murderer at the expense of my mother's name and reputation. I am tired of attacks and implications that my mother 'set Mr. Macumber up.' These organizations and Mr. Macumber need to provide proof of their allegations or shut up, apologize and retract their accusations." He concluded, "We have never been notified or been able to tell our side of this tragic story to the Board. In the past, your organization has heard only Mr. Macumber's side of the story. My hope is this letter will help the Arizona Board of Executive Clemency to arrive at a sound and informed decision."

Steven took the phone after his brother. At forty-six, he'd worked a variety of jobs, some in computer technology. If anything, he was even more vehement than Scott. "There's a couple things I'd like to hit right off the top," he began. "There were accusations made that my mother had never shown us the letters that my father had sent. . . . This is all blatantly false. . . . My brothers and I decided that they were to be returned without us reading them. . . . We did that intentionally. We returned those letters intentionally to him so he knew we wanted to have no contact with him." Also false: "That my mother told us that my father did not love us. . . . In fact, she said just the opposite." She said "sometimes good people do bad things but that has no bearing on whether he loves his sons." False as well: "That she told us he was a murderer." No, "we came to that conclusion ourselves." Steve had read the news articles and legal briefs, he'd done a lot of research, he'd even questioned his mother. "In a lot of ways I've been harder on her than most. . . . With the events of the last three or four years, I have pushed her more, Scott has pushed her more to defend herself than anyone else." His conclusion: "The lies that have been coming out about her framing my father are just astounding."

Above all, given Larry Hammond's "massive character assassination on her," Steve wanted to talk about his mother's character: "My mother took everything she had to support her kids. She was a single mother when, frankly, being a single mother was not the fashionable thing to do. She was a cop. She didn't make a lot of money. We lived on macaroni and cheese for a very long time. We didn't get to see her much because of the shift she worked. So it was very tough for us for a long, long time." He didn't know where Hammond or his brother Ron had come up with the idea that his mother was capable of framing Bill. Rather, "I'll tell you what she is capable of. She's capable of taking care of three boys, doing the best she can to raise them, sacrificing her own self." For thirty-seven years, he and Scott "have been quiet about this, and this is really the first opportunity that we've had to speak." He wanted to tell the victims' families how "very, very sorry" he is for their loss. "The only comfort that I can give you right now is that all three of us here—my mother, Carol, myself, and Scott—can assure you that the correct man is in jail for these murders. And he needs to stay there."

In his letter to the board, Steve had put it in even harsher terms: "What you have here in your midst is a killer and likely a sociopath who manipulates and lies to get what he wants. . . . Mr. Hammond, by repeating these lies about some big conspiracy, only fuels my father's need to be someone important enough for this to happen to." Mr. Hammond told Ron "we are SURE your mother framed your father." Steve thought that incredible: "Really? You're SURE? Where is your EVIDENCE? You don't have any, do you?" Steve directed his final comments to the board: "Please use your common sense and best judgment and realize this man is a manipulator. Understand everything he does is for himself and no one else. He is a liar and a killer and is where he deserves to be."

It was nearly noon now, the hearing about to enter its fifth hour. Duane Belcher called for a ten-minute break. The Justice Project team and Macumber family members rose from their seats looking subdued. In the lobby, Ron stood alone off in one corner, shaking his head. He'd known his mother would be on the phone but not his brothers. What his mom and Steve said, he'd heard before; it was nothing new. Steve had been living at home with Carol for more than twenty years, and Ron felt he was just repeating what she'd told him. But Ron had not known his more independent oldest brother also felt this way. They hadn't spoken in more than ten years.

Jackie sat in another corner of the lobby with Robyn. She'd gone into the hearing pessimistic, prepared for what the other side would say, convinced Jan Brewer would, at any rate, veto a clemency recommendation.

But still, she was shaken. Those two boys, Scott and Steve, were so young back then, nine and eleven, too young to have developed such a venomous attitude on their own. This *must* have come from Carol. How else could those boys so loathe their own father?

Katie had to walk outside the building, to the front landing, for fresh air. By the end, she'd felt seriously ill in the hearing room. Like all the oxygen had been sucked out of the chamber. It must have been so hard for Bill, so horrible, listening to his sons denounce him after thirty-seven years. It had been hard for her, too. She struggled with what she'd heard. Who knew? She wasn't there back then; she'd been on this case for just three years. Maybe Bill and Carol did talk about this crime at one time or the other. But even if Bill confessed to the crime to keep her, that didn't mean he committed the murders.

Ron, Jackie, Katie—they kept running everything through their minds. What Scott and Steve said about their father differed so greatly from Ron's memories, and differed also from all the independent descriptions of Bill as the devoted, loving primary caretaker of the boys. They'd seen those descriptions in Frieda's affidavit, in Pat Ferguson's Conciliation Court report, in the neighbors' testimony. *Bill was a good father, Bill was the one who took care of the kids, he would play with them and cook meals, he was the better parent, Carol didn't care as much. . . . All three boys expressed a great desire to visit with their father. Not seeing him is apparently very distressing to all of them. It is apparent that in the past, Mr. Macumber was the major parental figure for the boys. Witnesses state that they spent many hours together and seem to be very devoted.*

Then there were Bill's many letters. Pages and pages over the years to Jackie, more recently to Ron and Katie. Bill's journal as well, the four-hundred-page chronicle of his experience. Katie had read that journal, Ron and Jackie too. It did not seem possible to them for all this writing— all of *Bill*—to be false. If guilty, Bill Macumber had for fifty years delivered an extraordinary performance. In fact, his entire life—all day, every day—had then been nothing less than sustained masterful deception. Not just his public life in prison and the community but his private life on the page—all his writing a fiction, his journal, his clemency petitions, his dozens of letters to Ron and Jackie. He had to have devoted his entire existence to forging an alternative narrative—to fixing and denying one horrible, bizarre moment when he lost himself and murdered two strangers out in the desert.

To Katie and Ron and Jackie, this was flat-out unimaginable. Nothing they'd heard this morning had altered their assessment of the case. Katie remained convinced of Bill's innocence. Ron felt even more certain now. Jackie hooted at the question: "Heavens no, I haven't changed my mind. Not at all, not in any way, shape, or form."

Outside on the landing, with minutes to go before the hearing resumed, the Justice Project team huddled around Larry Hammond under cold, misty skies. Utterly exhausted, he could barely stand. He hadn't expected to be spending five or six hours at this hearing. Hammond seethed over everything they hadn't seen coming. The letters from Carol and her sons, plus the unexpected testimony by Luke Haag, his revelations about seeing the evidence, talking to Sibert, advising Bedford Douglass. Hammond, fighting his fatigue, exhorted his team, punctuating his points with repeated jabs of his finger, stabbing at the air. By then, though, he'd read the tea leaves. He thought they would probably lose.

At least they'd have one more chance to argue their case. After the county attorney made his closing comments, the Justice Project could offer a final rebuttal statement. Hammond hadn't planned to do this himself, didn't think he could physically, but his team implored him, saying they needed him up there at the podium. He agreed, asking only that Bob Bartels and Rich Robertson participate as well. One thing he knew they'd all have to do in those few moments: be less delicate about Carol.

First, though, Vince Imbordino had his turn. "It is not our intent to retry the case," he told the board when the hearing resumed. Yes, it "would be fair to say and honest to say" that if the case were investigated today, "there's no doubt that the crime scene would have been handled somewhat differently." And yes, in the years since this trial, "there clearly have been changes suggested in how experts testify in all the sciences." Yet the fact remained, "those casings were matched to that gun" by FBI agent Robert Sibert. As for Bill Macumber, when you read the record, "there's no question" he admitted to telling his wife he committed the murders. In his own short bit of testimony—*I suppose to keep her from leaving us*—he "is admitting to saying it, but trying to spin it if you will." Then Detective Ed Calles, in his testimony, confirms that Macumber admitted confessing to Carol—"unless you believe he is a part of the conspiracy." Yes, Macumber's fingerprints didn't match any off the car, but "his palm print wasn't taken until he was brought in for questioning." Valenzuela's confession was excluded by "a judge who ultimately became a Justice on the State Supreme Court," and now "here we are, forty years later, arguing about whether this confession was really valid." After reviewing all the evidence "there's no question in our mind that William Macumber killed these two young people." Yes, "obviously the people who are here believe that he didn't do it." But "if we believed that he didn't do it, we certainly wouldn't be opposing his release from prison."

By the time Larry Hammond approached the podium, the hearing was inching into its sixth hour. "Mr. Chairman," he began, "I know we all have been here a good long while today, and we are not going to restate and replow the ground that we have laid out before." He knew the board members "have looked carefully" at all the documents provided, all the statements and affidavits. Over the years, "we have come to respect your independent review of the materials." So we "are not going to stand up here and respond to each of the things that we heard today that we think you all know are incorrect." He would, instead, offer just "a very few points." Most particularly, about Carol Kempfert.

Here the gloves came off: Years ago, the Justice Project associates went "to considerable length to try to communicate with Ms. Kempfert." Above all, they had wanted to ask her about "the testimony she gave at trial with respect to whether she had any motive to lie . . . or to assist in the fabrication of evidence." We have "provided to you affidavits. . . . You have seen those affidavits." Ms. Kempfert "has not responded to those, nor has she responded today in all her remarks to the core question, whether she in fact was having affairs with members of the sheriff's office and, most critically, lied about that under oath at trial." Justice Project investigators had vainly "tried to interview her up in Washington" about this. Instead, they'd found others willing to talk. Hammond directed the board to Frieda Kennedy's affidavit: "There is no question—and we wanted to be delicate this morning—but there is no question that now we have multiple witnesses, all of whom say that Carol Kempfert lied at the time of trial about whether she was having affairs. She was having multiple affairs. And those affairs provided her the motive to do what she did." In her affidavit, "Frieda Kennedy also pointed out that Carol Kemp-fert told Frieda that Carol was the one who shot through the window. . . . We now have sworn testimony . . . that Carol fired that shot." Hammond left the rest unsaid, relying on the documents sitting before the board: "I'd like to say nothing further about that. I think that the questions about her credibility have been properly addressed in the papers we have filed."

He turned next to the suggestion that Macumber confessed to his wife. "This issue has gone on now for years," he pointed out, fueled by conflicting testimony. The police officers needn't be "lying or part of a grand conspiracy" to get it wrong. "Mr. Imbordino and I have been around too long to think that's necessarily the case. Police officers hear often what they want to hear. That's why we beg police officers to record. If we'd had a recording of the interview of Bill Macumber, we would know what he said and what he didn't say." Instead, "all we have are the various pieces of testimony." What we have "is total imprecision on that, and to suggest otherwise, I think, would be a false conclusion."

Hammond finished with a comment he'd later allow was "not kosher, normally." But he'd been so irritated by Vince Imbordino's claim that his office cared mightily about wrongful convictions, that his office had studied the case thoroughly before deciding on Macumber's guilt. "Mr. Imbordino has been involved in this matter for about five weeks," he informed the board. "He called me and we spoke—I think it was his first day having anything to do with this matter. And he told me he person-ally had no doubt that Bill Macumber had murdered these two people. I asked him what he had reviewed, and he very candidly told me, 'Noth-ing.' At that point he had not looked at the trial transcripts—indeed, he asked us to provide him the evidence—yet he had already made up his mind." Hammond understood well "why a prosecutor's office would want to stand behind a conviction," but for Imbordino to say to this board that he personally "after study" had decided on Macumber's guilt "I think is a little short of the mark."

Bob Bartels wrapped up the presentation for the Justice Project. He did his best to cast doubt on Lucien Haag's testimony, arguing once again that the millions of ejectors used in Ithaca .45 caliber pistols don't each produce unique marks on cartridge casings. He tried also to "cut through all the details and complications" by bringing the board's focus back to Valenzuela, Primrose and that thatch of hair. "Those seem to me to be the anchors," Bartels said in closing. Those are "what's necessary to look at whenever you're evaluating any other piece of evidence."

The board members had one more voice to hear before turning to their deliberations. "Mr. Macumber?" Duane Belcher asked. "Is there anything final you want to say . . . ?"

Little remained for Bill Macumber. After listening to the proceedings for six hours, after hearing Steve and Scott denounce him, he had nothing more to offer in his defense. He had only a question: "Are my sons still on the line?"

"Yes," Duane Belcher said. "I believe they are."

Macumber's voice ached, his one word an urgent plea. "Scott—"

"No, no, no," Belcher interrupted. "Mr. Macumber, . . . I said initially your comments are to the Board. Not talking to anybody, whether it's your sons or whatever. Your comments are to the Board."

"Okay . . . I'm sorry. I misunderstood that."

"Okay."

Macumber rushed his words now, warding off another interruption. "But I will comment to the Board that I love my three sons with all my heart. Regardless of how my two older sons feel, that will never change till the day I die."

"Okay."

"I can't say anything more than that."

CHAPTER 26

Nothing Quite Like It

They'd arrived at the endgame. "We are going to have some discussion," Belcher began. "You can stay right here, you can hear us. . . . The only thing we demand is you respect this Board, you respect our decision whether you agree or disagree with what we ultimately do."

Sitting next to him, Jack LaSota, the former state attorney general, took the lead. Hammond knew him well. They'd been friends since 1974 and law firm partners for ten years, 1985 to 1995. LaSota had been their firm's lobbyist, a power broker in the halls of state government. Hammond admired him and appreciated his great, self-deprecating sense of humor. He could tell LaSota had come to this hearing well prepared, more than Hammond had anticipated. He had really studied the case.

"Mr. Chairman and my fellow Board members," LaSota began, "this isn't an easy case. There's nothing quite like it. It's one of the most extraordinary I have ever seen. It has some of the stranger juxtapositions of facts and evidence that I've ever encountered in my 40-some years of serving in the legal business." Point by point, "in no particular order," he began to identify the elements that most intrigued him.

At the top of his list: testimony in the case file from the security guard at the model homes complex Tim and Joyce visited on the night of their murders. The guard was certain they'd come by shortly before 10:00 P.M., just as he was closing up. The guard's account seemed significant to LaSota for two reasons. First, the timeline: "He has them leaving there quite alive after 10 o'clock, and Carol has Bill arriving home at around 10, maybe even earlier. I have trouble squaring those two, what I'll call facts." Second, a particular detail that LaSota thought both "fascinating" and unexplored by either side—"maybe because it doesn't square with either the prosecution or defense's theory of what happened here." The security guard, he pointed out, noticed not one but two cars at closing time that night, the second either a Pontiac or Oldsmobile. "And he doesn't say much else about it other than that they left at the same time. Now, whether that's connected to the Sterrenberg car, whether it's hostile or it's friendly, we never again hear about it. And maybe it's impossible to hear about it. That's just another tantalizing element that makes this case unique."

Next on his list: "I wonder why Tim and Joyce were out there. And I don't mean that in any sort of salacious way. It's never really established why they're out there, which makes me wonder if they weren't out there at the behest of somebody else we haven't even heard about. Maybe the Pontiac or the Oldsmobile, I don't know, but what were they doing out there? It's never said. Highly unusual. They weren't in any state of disarray or undress or anything, and yet they were out there remote from either where he lived or where she lived."

For that matter, "why would Bill Macumber have been there, if he would somehow manage to get there and get back home before 10 o'clock? What was he doing there? And that's part of it . . . the lack of motive here that's bedeviled this case from day one."

Linda Primrose was "another unique feature. . . . She gives a detailed account, she talks about the thatch of hair that otherwise goes unmentioned. How could she have possibly known about that and what a strange thing to say, and then coincidentally to have hair found there."

LaSota pointed next to the latent palm print. "How could it be that it was so bad an example that at the front end you couldn't tell whether it was a palm print or a fingerprint?" LaSota held up his hand. "My, look at my palm. . . . Sure a lot bigger than any one of my fingerprints. And then it was so bad that it wasn't submitted to the FBI, and yet ultimately it becomes pretty clear that this is Mr. Macumber's palm print."

LaSota happened to know well both of Valenzuela's lawyers, Thomas O'Toole and Ron Petica. "Both of these men, who I consider to be of sound mind and discretion, were of the view that he was telling the truth. They are savvy individuals, and they never wavered in their belief over the years that this man had told the truth." What's more, Valenzuela ended up being sent to federal prison for a rape and murder on an Indian reservation. "It just strikes me that's another unique feature of this case. Ernie was probably sentenced for a crime similar to that which he confessed to."

Another "weird thing": The defense appeals the first case because its ballistics expert wasn't allowed to testify, then calls no expert at the second trial. "I can't help but agree with the prosecution's surmise that no expert testified because they couldn't find a reputable expert who disagreed with Sibert. But it's just strange that you base an appeal on something and you prevail, and then you don't do anything with it."

By now Hammond could see clearly that LaSota wasn't building an argument for or against Macumber's innocence—he was just outlining the details of a case that captivated him. Jack being Jack. On the one hand, on the other. He liked to think in an open way.

LaSota continued: "Another bizarre thing"—the polygraph exam given to Macumber on the day of his arrest. One of the questions—*Have you ever committed a serious, undetected crime*—was "pretty open-ended. I'm not sure how I'd answer that. I think I might say yes just not to err. . . . But what is a serious, undetected crime? It certainly doesn't implicate him necessarily in the vile murders of these two youngsters. . . . It's all open-ended. Who knows?"

LaSota wondered as well about FBI agent Robert Sibert's claim that "no other firearm in the world" would match the casings from the murder site—"that just sort of reeks of extravagance . . . that's a whole lot of assurance." Also: "The fact that all the evidence is gone, we don't have anything to look at now." And: "I'm just amazed at whether there was ever any effort to find out if Macumber's gun was cleared" during the 1962 roundup. Even more amazing: "Why would Macumber keep the gun? What's he doing hanging onto the gun 12 years later?"

Then there were the sons: two who "loathe him so much they would actually like to see their father stay in prison for the rest of his life." That's "a lot of emotion" and "they said it articulately and conscientiously," so "it means something to me." And yet, "on the other hand, the son who's here with us today feels 180 degrees different."

Finally: According to Linda Primrose, there were others out there that night, but they have never come forward. That didn't seem right to LaSota. "From what I've seen of conspiracies, eventually somebody blows the whistle. I would think over 50 years someone else would have come forward somewhere along the line, someone who may have been with Primrose and Ernie that night." It was "just stunning" that "no one has ever come forward to corroborate her account."

LaSota frowned, shook his head, studied the documents before him. "I don't know that anyone in human form is ever going to be able to discern exactly what the truth is. It's just totally baffling to me. I don't know quite how I feel about it."

Hammond took no offense at his former partner. He understood. Jack had no bile; he wasn't opposing them. Both narratives disturbed him. The unanswered questions, the things that didn't quite fit. The whole messy question of whether Bill confessed, what exactly he said to Carol and the deputies.

In closing, LaSota had a proposal: "I think we might well be better off to consider the question of guilt or innocence as sort of secondary to the question of whether someone who's been in prison for 37 years for two brutal murders might nevertheless warrant clemency." LaSota looked around at his fellow board members. "End of speech. Thank you for your time."

Marilyn Wilkens shared his puzzlement: "I'm left with more questions than answers, which makes it very difficult, which is why this poses such a problem for me today."

Ellen Kirschbaum, too: "For me it leaves so many gaps. . . . What was presented at the trials? What don't we get here?"

Duane Belcher tried to steer them back to LaSota's proposal, the notion of considering commutation rather than the question of guilt or innocence. In 2009, he reminded them, the Board had made two recommendations. One was to at least give Macumber a bottom number, when he'd be eligible for parole. Even if there was "a doubt or question" about guilt, "then at least make him parole eligible." Why not do that now?

LaSota seemed to agree: "I think I need to stop thinking about all the anomalies in this case." He'd rather discuss "with a little more specificity the situation of a 77-year-old inmate who has been in 37 years and has a virtually spotless record and has serious health conditions." On the other hand, LaSota added, "Macumber is unrepentant."

Marilyn Wilkens: "And I guess we do have a problem with that."

Belcher slumped in his chair, looking perplexed and frustrated. "Well, if he didn't do it, if he's innocent, I don't expect him to be repentant, don't you think?"

Macumber's unwavering claim of innocence, restated once again at the start of this hearing, served now as both his defense and his burden, an obstacle blocking his path to freedom.

LaSota began to read from the U.S. Supreme Court's *Herrera* decision, where Chief Justice Rehnquist wrote, "Our judicial system, like the human beings who administer it, is fallible." He thought those words relevant. "I don't know, I haven't heard enough to convince me that it's failed here, but there is sure a lot of strange goings-on. Enough to make me come to the conclusion that we really should consider whether this man merits the opportunity to in effect rejoin his family before his days are up."

Moments later, he offered a motion: "I will move to recommend not that his sentence be commuted to time served, but that he be given a sentence with a bottom number."

They started discussing what number, how many years. LaSota finally proposed "38 years to life," which would make him eligible within months.

Belcher agreed: "I will second the motion."

All eyes turned to the other two board members.

Ellen Kirschbaum paused, then shook her head. "I disagree."

Marilyn Wilkens looked down at her hands. "I'm going to disagree."

Belcher closed the file that sat open before him. "All right. . . . There is a 2-to-2 split. There is not a majority of the quorum of the Board, that would have to be 3 out of 4. So he's not recommended to the Governor at this time."

LaSota nodded. "We don't change the status quo with a 2-to-2 vote."

In his chair, Larry Hammond hung his head. He'd feared this; he'd feared a split ever since he learned Ellen Stenson wouldn't be attending. Ellen Stenson, who strongly believed in Macumber's innocence, who'd voted in 2009 for his immediate release. Ahead of this hearing, the Justice Project could have called Belcher and said they wanted to wait because Ellen wasn't going to be there. It would have put Belcher in a box, though, as the rules don't allow for such "board-member shopping." Of course, the Justice Project could have come up with a false reason instead—we're not ready, a family member can't come, someone's sick. Such dissembling would have worked, but given their relationship with the board, Hammond didn't think they should do that. Even though he'd lost twice before on two-to-two votes. Something changed when the board sat without a fifth member. They could decide by default.

Hammond had happened to bump into Ellen Stenson at a restaurant recently. In animated fashion, she'd started telling her lunch partner about the Macumber case. Hammond knew she would have been favorable to them today. *Would have.* Another simple twist of fate.

In the lobby after the hearing concluded, the Justice Project team and Macumber family members wandered about, as if searching for something they'd lost. Jackie, angry and depressed, felt certain Governor Brewer had urged the county attorney to oppose, felt certain Governor Brewer had somehow caused Ellen Stenson to be absent. Ron, frustrated that the board had considered innocence over clemency issues, also sensed Brewer's hand. Katie asked out loud, "Was this hearing worth it? Worth putting Bill through such a day, worth having Bill listen to his two older sons denounce him?"

In the weeks to come, they would all have even more to digest, more to process. They would, on the very day after this hearing, learn that the Justice Project, in another of its cases, had prevailed before the U.S. Supreme Court—in *Martinez v. Ryan*, on a 7–2 vote, Bob Bartels had successfully argued for a prisoner's right to effective assistance of counsel in post-conviction proceedings. "A very bittersweet 24 hours," Hammond e-mailed his team. Then they'd learn that Duane Belcher, Ellen Stenson and Marilyn Wilkens would be leaving the Board of Executive

Clemency—Governor Brewer had not renewed their appointments, Belcher being told she would like to see the board go in a "new direction." Soon after, they'd learn that Brewer had fired Duane Belcher before he could step down, having him escorted from the governor's office by capitol police officers after a heated exchange with one of her top aides. A day later, Ellen Stenson would publicly denounce this treatment of Belcher, telling a reporter she and Belcher weren't reappointed because they were the last remaining members of the board that in 2009 unanimously recommended commutation for Bill Macumber.

Through it all, Larry Hammond would tell those who asked that the beat still went on for Macumber. He would offer to discuss with everyone "what our next steps will be." He had lots of ideas. He'd learned things they could use at a post-conviction relief hearing. Things about Carol, things about the ballistics evidence, things about how to respond to the state. "New perspectives" he thought would be very helpful in the PCR process. Nothing had changed in his commitment or his fundamental assessment of the Macumber case. "Are we drinking Kool-Aid?" he told a visitor in early May 2012. "No. Absolutely not."

That spring, in his Mohave Unit cubicle at the state prison in Douglas, Bill Macumber could barely respond to the steady flow of letters and phone calls from his supporters. He couldn't pretend, couldn't hide his sense of devastation. The board's ruling mattered little to him. Only his sons' words had meaning, his boys' obvious hatred for him. On a notepad in his cubicle, he wrote, "We live in a sad world and for me it became sadder still as a result of that hearing." He stared at those words, a pen motionless in his hand. He searched for something better than that, a way to get himself through, a way to go on. Pen went back to paper. "Still, I did get to tell my two oldest sons that I love them," he wrote. "And I did get to hear their voices for the first time in 37 years. I will carry that memory to the grave as I'm certain I shall never hear their voices again."

CHAPTER 27

There Came a Day

After the second clemency hearing, Bill Macumber and the Arizona Justice Project had just one hope left, one last chance. The petition for post-conviction relief, filed by the Perkins Coie legal team headed by Jordan Green in February 2012, a month before the clemency hearing, was still winding its way through the legal pipeline. After requesting three extensions of the deadline to respond, the county attorney's office finally submitted a fifty-eight-page document in early July. Weeks later, Jordan Green countered with a last written reply. All the briefs then went to Maricopa County Superior Court judge Bruce R. Cohen, who would decide whether to grant an evidentiary hearing. The waiting began. If Macumber's lawyers somehow managed to get to a hearing—a longshot—they'd have the burden of proof, and the standard they'd face would be a "preponderance of the evidence," not just "reasonable doubt." Which is why Larry Hammond had turned with such hope to the clemency board, explaining that for the many defendants "who don't have the benefit of DNA, there's no place else to even be heard."

Many defendants indeed: Although the Macumber case is highly unusual, aspects of it reflect much of what transpires in courtrooms across the country. To learn the truth by means of a trial is surprisingly and uncomfortably difficult. Invariably, courtroom transcripts are full of complex and conflicting evidence. Certitude rarely seems justified, especially in light of what DNA testing now suggests about the legal system. It's impossible to say how many innocent people sit behind bars, only that the 300 DNA exonerations to date represent a small slice of the whole.

As with Macumber, in many of these DNA exonerations the case against the defendant seemed strong. As with Macumber, in many the defense could not find reliable forensics experts, could not locate crime scene evidence, could not sway reluctant appellate judges. Three reversals involved trial judges who suppressed evidence of third-party guilt.

Most attorneys, like Larry Hammond and Bob Bartels, acknowledge that criminal trials aren't searches for truth. In constructing stories, lawyers recognize only the evidence consistent with their theory of the case. So do the police, the forensic experts, the judges and—finally—the jurors. Everyone sees what they want, sees what fits their particular take.

I was reminded of this when, after Bill Macumber's second clemency hearing, I spent a day in Olympia, Washington, with Carol, Scott and Steve Kempfert. For hours, they eagerly served up their version of the Macumber tale, reprising all they'd said at the clemency hearing, sounding as convincing as they had on speakerphone. They pointed out that no one has ever offered hard proof that Carol tampered with the evidence or even explained how she might have done so. They denied the stories of Carol's affairs—"blatantly false" said Steve—but asked, "Where in the scheme of things does it matter anyway?" They challenged as well Rich Robertson's account of his visit to their home in March 2003—it was sunny and Carol didn't say, "Get the fuck off my porch."

In fact, weather records show light precipitation on the first day of Rich's wait for Carol and none the second, though there was "rain and / or melted snow" reported at times. Other differences are harder to pin down. Carol told me she'd "heard" she was the subject of an internal MCSO investigation but "never knew it back then, and if I didn't know, then I had no motive." Yes, Sheriff Blubaum called her in once and banned her from the academy and ride-alongs, but she understood this to be "because of my Macumber name association. . . . No one ever told me it was because of relationships." Yes, she brought her lawyer to

Blubaum's office, and yes, she threatened to sue, but still she "never heard this was about relationships." No, she never had a sexual relationship with Gerald Hayes, and she had one with Dennis Gilbertson only after leaving Bill. No, she'd had no relationship with Ed Calles; in fact, she couldn't clearly recall taking classes with him or getting a job reference from him. Yes, there'd been talk in the department about her having tapes that gave her leverage over various deputies—"a lieutenant called me in once and said, 'Carol, you know there's a rumor around that you've had relationships and have lots of tapes.' Whew, I didn't know they took that seriously." No, she didn't recall Dave Brewer. No, she never told Frieda Kennedy that she "went by the house and shot."

Steve and Scott portrayed their father—Scott constantly called him "Mr. Macumber"—as an angry, frustrated man who wanted to chase cops and be an authority figure; who always made it about himself; who took credit for Scott's accomplishments on the baseball field, though he himself was "nondescript with no exceptional skills"; who "lived vicariously" through his sons even while finding their efforts "never good enough." When I pointed out the striking differences between their description and all other profiles of Bill Macumber—reading from Ron's statements, Frieda's affidavit and Pat Ferguson's Conciliation Court report—they allowed there'd been many good times with their father. What Ron remembered was true and real, Carol added. They never claimed Bill was a bad father. Yes, he loved his sons. Yes, they all spent many happy hours together. Yes, the boys told Pat Ferguson they had a great desire to see their father.

Their attitude toward him changed after that Ferguson visit, Scott explained. Things happened after that interview. Most particularly, Bill carted off everything of value from their house—the tent trailer, the van, a gun collection, even their motocross bike. "He told us we're most important to him," Scott recalled. "Then he took everything. Once I realized I was less important than pieces of property, I lost love and respect." Steve didn't want to visit him at the prison in Florence—Judge Hughes made him, saying "your mother has brainwashed you." The boys, at ages twelve and ten, rejected their father's letters on their own; Carol left it up to them. The Scottsdale Road murders, Steve suggested, weren't necessarily a strange one-time event; Bill "very possibly killed several others." Scott and Steve didn't care to see their father's book of poetry, dedicated to them, or his journal, full of references to them. They didn't care that their father nearly died in April 2011. Get it done, Scott said, get it over. Scott hated him "with all my soul." Steve declared, "He's not my father."

Something in all this seemed out of kilter to me. Carol's denials came without her ever asking to see the underlying affidavits, except for Gerald Hayes's about their alleged affair. The sons' lambasting of Bill Macumber, so full of animated venom, lacked even a hint of conflict, longing or wistful curiosity. Their memories about rejecting Bill's letters conflicted with what Carol told a reporter in January 1976: "At first they answered his letters but I wouldn't mail back what they wrote. It was a message that in effect said, 'drop dead.'" Most important, the sequence of their recollections didn't fit: It was in fact Harold Macumber who carted items from their house soon after Bill's arrest in August 1974; their father didn't buy them the motocross bike until he was out on bail in late October 1974; their visit with Pat Ferguson didn't occur until March 1975, after the first trial, with Bill back in jail and the family about to move to Colorado. Affected by their intense feelings, I did not point all this out. They seemed to hate Bill Macumber too insistently for any such details to matter. Once again, as always, it finally amounted to what narrative you wanted—or needed—to believe.

Still—out of all the conflicting Macumber narratives, there came a day when one story prevailed, when one rose above all the others. Larry Hammond had not so much seen it coming as he had insisted on it coming. Don't we owe it to Bill to file a PCR petition win or lose, he'd implored his colleagues. You can never tell. Who knows what might happen?

What happened first was a courthouse conference—Judge Bruce Cohen, after reviewing all the pleadings attached to Bill Macumber's PCR petition, summoned the lawyers for informal oral argument in his courtroom at 2:30 P.M. on September 24, 2012. Judge Cohen, on the bench since 2005, wasn't well known to the Justice Project; he'd come out of a family law and mediation practice and had served as a volunteer coordinator for mentoring programs at the ASU Law School. He'd read all the submissions, he told those gathered before him, but had not made any decisions. He just wanted to get everyone together to clarify some details.

Three Perkins Coie lawyers sat at the defense table, led by the senior partner Jordan Green, whose practice focused largely on white-collar criminal defense. Gerald Grant, a deputy county attorney, represented the state. Present for the Justice Project, observing, were Katie Puzauskas and Andrew Hacker. There, too, were Bill Macumber's cousin Harleen and her husband, Jay, who'd driven into Phoenix from Apache Junction. Katie didn't expect much from this session, given the late afternoon scheduling. But then Judge Cohen started showering the lawyers with questions, all focused on the same matter: What's the new evidence? What was different if the trial were held today? What facts weren't before the jury in 1976?

Jordan Green rose to respond. He'd first agreed to take this case because Larry Hammond—"an amazing person, a buddy of mine for millions of years"—was ill and needed him. He also thought it would be a good experience for the younger associates in his firm who'd never been inside a prison. Then he'd met Bill Macumber and felt the same visceral reaction to him that so many others had. In his earlier years, Green had practiced criminal law, serving as defense lawyer in some twenty murder cases, but he'd never dealt before with a PCR petition. Only by mistake, he'd say later—a bit tongue-in-cheek—was he prepared when Judge Cohen started asking questions. He happened to have an outline with him titled "New Evidence," an outline written by the Perkins Coie team that focused less on Carol's alleged tampering and more on Valenzuela. He glanced at it and started talking. Harleen and Jay thought him organized and eloquent. Once again a lawyer for Macumber walked through the list, but with his own take: Ernest Valenzuela's multiple confessions, including some, Green pointed out, that the defense attorney didn't know about at the time of the trials—those to a cellmate and police officers. Linda Primrose's statement. The thatch of hair. Carol's denial of having affairs and of being under investigation, now refuted by several affidavits. The initial FBI ballistics report, which indicated the ejector marks matched only one of the four cartridges, not the three later identified by Robert Sibert—something else the original defense attorney didn't know about. Sibert's claim that the murder scene cartridges came from Macumber's gun "to the exclusion of all others in the world."

Judge Cohen appeared particularly interested in Valenzuela's multiple confessions and the ballistics evidence. Do you agree, he asked the prosecutor, that Sibert's "to the exclusion of all others" testimony wouldn't be admissible today? Yes, Gerald Grant said. He agreed.

Judge Cohen never indicated which way he was leaning, but Jay and Harleen thought he seemed impressed with the Perkins Coie lawyers. Cohen was surprised to learn they'd been involved with the case for only six months—he told them he would have thought they'd been on it for at least two years. Cohen also showed an interest in those sitting in the courtroom. He asked if there was anyone present from the victims' families (no). What about the defendant's family? Jay and Harleen raised their hands, Harleen explaining she was Bill's cousin. Judge Cohen thanked them for attending, then said he expected to make his decision within a week.

The waiting resumed, one week sliding into a second. Finally, on October 5, Judge Cohen issued his decision. At the Justice Project offices, team members blinked hard as they read it. Here was what they'd sought for a dozen long years: an order setting an evidentiary hearing into Bill Macumber's claims for post-conviction relief—specifically, his claims about "third party guilt" and the ballistics. The hearing would go for three full days, from November 7 through November 9. "This Court," Judge Cohen wrote, "is not yet in a position to determine whether relief is ultimately due to Defendant," but "this Court finds that on the identified issues of third party guilt and ballistics, Defendant is entitled to an evidentiary hearing."

Cohen's order represented a ringing validation of the Justice Project's extended effort but did not by itself promise Macumber's release. The burden of proof still rested with his lawyers, and even if they prevailed at the evidentiary hearing the State could retry Macumber or appeal the hearing decision all the way to the Arizona Supreme Court, drawing the matter out for many more years.

For that reason, Jordan Green began to push the state toward a deal. He didn't want to drag this out, especially not with a seventy-seven-year-old client with health problems. All along, he had suspected the state might fold its hand if the defense could force an evidentiary hearing. That's why he'd disclosed every witness and piece of paper he had. That's why he'd made clear how much he'd relish putting Judge Thomas O'Toole

354 • BARRY SIEGEL

on the stand. He had wanted to overwhelm the state, to scare it into walking away.

Two days after Judge Cohen granted a hearing, Green called Gerald Grant, ostensibly to talk about witness lists. Grant didn't yet have a list together. Green took that as an opening. Jerry, he said, are we just giving ourselves trouble? Why don't we find a way to resolve this dispute?

That led to a sequence of calls between the two. Both sides were checking their hole cards. Green worried how long Bill could survive. The state realized they'd likely lose everything if the judge ordered a new trial—with all the evidence destroyed, they couldn't put on a case. Most important, the lawyers could sense that Cohen was leaning toward the defense. PCR petitions always depended on which judge you drew. This judge seemed inclined to grant post-conviction relief.

Jerry Grant made Green an offer: If Bill Macumber pled guilty to two counts of second-degree murder, he could walk free for time served. Jordan Green didn't even take this to Bill—from the first time they'd met, Macumber had made clear he'd never plead guilty. That's not going to happen, Green e-mailed Grant. We won't talk to our client about a guilty plea. Green countered: If you offer a no-contest plea, for time served, we'll go talk to our client. A no-contest plea would allow Bill to maintain his innocence while acknowledging the factual basis for the case against him. He'd be sentenced as if he'd pled guilty—in fact he'd formally be found guilty in a courtroom—but he'd walk free still claiming he did not commit the Scottsdale Road murders.

In the Maricopa County Attorney's office, a committee of senior lawyers gathered, including Vince Imbordino, who'd so vigorously opposed Macumber's bid for clemency at the second hearing. Days later, Grant called Jordan Green once again. Okay, he said. We are willing to accept a no-contest plea.

The news electrified the Justice Project team members, though they knew this wasn't yet a done deal. Their joy mixed with their caution. Amazing, Katie thought, just incredible. "And quite a reversal," Larry Hammond pointed out. "Even Imbordino agreed!" Legal tactics often reminded him of a chess game. You never know why someone moved to PK4. You just know something's going on there.

On Thursday, October 25, Jordan Green and his law partner Lee

Stein, accompanied by Katie Puzauskas and Lindsay Herf, made the four-hour drive to Douglas to inform Macumber. To arrange this meeting on short notice, Katie had told prison officials it was an "emergency," and that seemed true enough—it all felt so urgent now. She tried to bank down her emotions. Once again, as so often before, the lawyers met Macumber in the Mohave Unit visitation area, empty but for them. Bill, as usual, hugged Katie and Lindsay and started chatting with them, unaware of why they'd come this day. Green cut him off. Hey, Bill, he said, we have serious issues to discuss. You want to get out of here?

Macumber listened without expression as they described the no-contest plea offer. He understood this to be big news, and it did raise his hopes. In fact, he was reeling. He clung especially to the thought that a no-contest plea was not an admission of guilt. That made it palatable. But he remained guarded, not allowing himself to feel or show emotion. Over the years, he'd built up a self-defense mechanism for this type of news. No way was he going to get worked up again over something that might not happen, something that—as these lawyers made clear—wasn't yet in writing. Instead, he asked process questions: What about my medications? What happens when they roll up all my stuff? How will I be transported? How will this happen? Jordan Green at first was puzzled, then believed he understood: Bill's response represented a way for him not to break down. Bill was holding himself together by focusing on the practical particulars.

After two hours, the lawyers rose to leave. Green pulled aside the single guard assigned to the visitation room, a woman who knew Macumber quite well. We just gave Bill positive but shocking news that he's getting out, Green told her. Would you watch over him and tell the night crew? The guard could summon no words. She started crying.

Justice Project team members kept quiet and held their breaths for days after that, fearful that the county attorney might get cold feet if word of the deal leaked and triggered a political backlash. Or if Governor Jan Brewer got hold of it. But by Tuesday, October 30, they appeared to have a done deal. In a conference call that day with his lawyers, Bill heard the news: The county attorney himself, Bill Montgomery, had signed off. They had a draft document. Discussions were under way for how to transport Macumber to Phoenix, where Judge Cohen would formally receive and accept the plea on November 7, at the start of the scheduled evidentiary hearing.

Now Bill let himself see this as a possibility, though it still felt more than unreal. Late that afternoon, from a desk in the Douglas warden's office, he began making calls to his family.

Ron Macumber's cell phone rang as he was standing in the aisle of a Target store in Grand Junction, Colorado, where a work assignment had taken him. "Are you sitting down?" Bill began.

"Dad, I'm standing in the middle of a Target. What's going on?"

"Well, they're transporting me to Phoenix next week and it looks like I'm going to be released."

Bill continued, explaining about the no-contest plea deal, but Ron couldn't process anything. Waking up the next morning, he tried to recall whether his dad's call had been real or a dream. Days later, he would still be trying to wrap his mind around the news. His father had sounded good on the phone but hesitant. Until Bill walked out of a courthouse a free man, Ron imagined, he'd be that way. Excited, but holding a lot back.

Jackie's phone rang next. By then it was early Tuesday evening. She knew something was up because Bill always called on Saturdays, following prison rules.

"Are you sitting down?" Bill asked again.

Jackie yelled so loud her dog, Spec, started barking at her. She stuttered, she gasped for air. Life stopped for her; the news took her breath away. Still, she could see Bill's big grin over the telephone. Bill, she managed to say, "This is one of God's miracles." Yes, she knew that much. Over and over, she murmured, *Praise the Lord*.

Next, Bill called his brother Bob. More yelling—Bob couldn't believe what he was hearing. Bob called his son, Mark, who told his wife. She sank to the floor, screaming.

Bill's final call that evening went to Jay and Harleen. Once more he asked, "Are you sitting down?" Jay said, "No, but I can be." He settled into a chair. Bill began by apologizing for calling them last. "That's fine," Jay said, "as long as it's good news." "Oh, it is," Bill replied. Yet again he offered his report. Jay and Harleen could barely respond. At the end, Bill said, "Kind of a shock, isn't it?"

Shortly after 4 A.M. on the morning of Tuesday, November 6, under still dark skies, Bill Macumber walked through the gates of the Mohave Unit, accompanied by two guards. He'd been visited all week by hundreds of well-wishers, a constant wave of inmates, staffers and wardens—the news had spread instantly at the state prison. Now everyone was asleep, farewells already exchanged. Or so Bill thought. Behind him, he began to hear loud yelling and screaming. All the prisoners were at their windows, shouting out their good-byes to him. He climbed into a prison van. The two guards, men he'd known for a long time, only lightly shackled him. They drove off, beginning their journey to Phoenix.

Macumber spent the next twenty-four hours housed at the Alhambra state prison complex in downtown Phoenix, the same facility he'd attended for his first clemency hearing. Jordan Green and Lee Stein, visiting him Tuesday afternoon, found him shaken up. To protect him from other inmates, the Department of Corrections had put him in the psycho ward, an environment he found unpleasant. Again, he wanted to talk to his lawyers about process—his medications and such. Bill's manner revealed both anxiety and joy.

After his lawyers left, Macumber spent the next hours as best he could, sleeping and waiting. Mostly waiting. The guards finally came for him late on Wednesday morning, to transport him to the Maricopa County Superior Court building on West Jefferson. Shortly after 1 P.M., a half hour before the hearing was to begin, they brought him into Courtroom 6B in the South Tower. He wore, as usual, the inmate's bright orange jumpsuit, with his hands and feet shackled and tied into a belly cinch. He had tears in his eyes as he fought to hide his emotions. Still, he perched almost jauntily on the defense table, his back to the judge's bench, looking toward the entry door. He wanted to see who was there, who was arriving. Already the courtroom was packed, with standing room only at the rear and side walls. Everyone, it seemed, had come: Larry Hammond and Bob Bartels. Katie, Lindsay, Andrew. Rich Robertson. Karen Killion from Washington, Sharon

Sargent-Flack from Prescott. Pete Rodriquez. Sigmund Popko and several former students from his ASU law school post-conviction relief clinic. Bill's family, of course: Jackie and Robyn. Ron. Bob and Mark. Harleen and Jay. Bill spotted, standing against the side wall, a man he'd not seen for thirty-eight years: Paul Bridgewater, the neighbor who'd put up his home for bond collateral. And he counted, sitting in the jury box, half a dozen reporters at least, from Phoenix newspapers and TV stations.

Hammond and Bartels edged their way to Bill, wrapping their arms around him. Waiting for the judge to appear, the three sat at the defense table, Bill telling them about his last hours at Douglas, all three smiling, though Bill still had tears in his eyes. Then Jordan Green and Gerald Grant emerged from the judge's chambers, where they'd been conferring. Larry and Bob moved a row back, sitting with Katie, Lindsay and Andrew. Bill asked Jordan, "Any surprises back there?" No, Green said. None.

Everyone stood as Judge Bruce Cohen entered the courtroom. Green's first request to him: Could they remove Macumber's shackles? The judge agreed. A deputy sheriff bent down to unlock the restraints around Bill's ankles, thinking that's all the judge meant. Jordan Green told the deputy, "Take the handcuffs off too." The deputy looked up at the judge: "Everything off, sir?" Cohen said, "Yes, if you would." The packed courtroom waited as the deputy fumbled with the padlocks. Seconds passed, seeming more like minutes. Then, at last, the chains and cuffs fell to the floor. Macumber sat down, unshackled. "Thank you," he said to the deputy.

Judge Cohen began the hearing. Before entering and receiving the agreement, he announced, he would allow members of the victims' families to address the court. John McCluskey rose to speak for his cousin Tim and for Tim's mother, as he had at the second clemency hearing, making clear that he "advocated that Mr. Macumber be incarcerated for the rest of his life." Judy Michael rose next, to speak once again on behalf of her sister, Joyce. "It's hard to be here, to sit through this," she said. "I loved my sister. I'm here to be her voice today. I want justice served for her. Mr. Macumber has had two trials, two clemency hearings, and now here he is today to get more justice for himself. Where is the justice for us?"

Judge Cohen responded gently: "I could never understand your loss.

It would be disingenuous if I said I know how you feel. I appreciate you being here. I appreciate that you are here speaking on behalf of the victims." Cohen looked next to the defense table. "I am sure there are people here on your behalf, too, Mr. Macumber."

Then he turned to the matter at hand: a two-page stipulation between the state and defense, providing for granting of Rule 32 post-conviction relief for Macumber in exchange for him pleading no contest to two counts of second degree murder. "I will accept the stipulation," Judge Cohen said, "and will enter on the record my findings." He began.

> It must be said that this matter relates to the tragic deaths of Joyce Sterrenberg and Tim McKillop. . . . They were both brutally and senselessly murdered. . . .
>
> This matter also relates to the life of William Wayne Macumber. . . . Mr. Macumber has maintained his innocence at all times. Despite that, he was twice convicted of first degree murder . . . and has been incarcerated for the last thirty-eight years.
>
> Lastly, this matter relates to the criminal justice system. Some will undoubtedly contend that justice was served almost four decades ago when Mr. Macumber was convicted for these crimes. Others will argue that these decades have served as a constant reminder of the injustice that at times occurs. While that debate would be as legitimate as the varying views of the participants, there is no opportunity to turn back time in a fashion that would ensure true justice, no matter which side of the divide one finds himself. . . . Therefore, the best that can be done at this point in time is what justice would now require.
>
> There is evidence to suggest that the verdicts from the 1970s were correct. There is also evidence to suggest that the evidence of alleged guilt is very much offset and perhaps exceeded by evidence that suggests otherwise. Despite the justice system being symbolically represented by the balancing of the scales, guilt and punishment are built on a foundation that requires not a mere tipping of the scales, but the elimination of all reasonable doubt.
>
> This judicial officer was not present at any of the original or second trial proceedings. It is therefore impossible to know what conclusion

would have been reached had those trials been conducted under the law, rules and analysis that now exists. Rather, this matter must be viewed in hindsight, and in so doing, there are significant questions as to whether justice was done when Mr. Macumber was convicted.

This leads this Court to the basis for the ruling entered this date. It is the view of this Court that this moment in time stands as a beacon for what is just in our justice system, even if it cannot remedy the past. . . . As Martin Luther King Jr. once said, "Never be afraid to do what's right. Society's punishments are small compared to the wounds we inflict on our soul when we look the other way." What we do here today under this very unique set of facts is consistent with the applicable law and does justice.

We will never know with certainty what happened on that May 1962 night in the desert in what is now North Scottsdale. And for that reason, justice requires that we do what is right. We do this not out of disrespect for the memories of Joyce Sterrenberg and Tim McKillop, but in honor of the principles under which our laws were created and developed.

Based in large part on the stipulations of the parties, it is the finding of this court that there is a legal basis for relief under Rule 32. . . . It is therefore ordered granting the Petition for Post-Conviction Relief and setting aside the first degree murder convictions entered against Mr. Macumber, conditioned upon the remaining terms of the stipulations of the parties.

With that, Judge Cohen invited Bill Macumber to rise and approach the podium. After an exchange aimed at establishing that Macumber understood the consequences, Cohen asked, "How do you plead, Mr. Macumber?"

"No contest," Macumber said, fighting tears.

Judge Cohen turned to the prosecutor, asking why he believed this no-contest plea was in the interest of justice. Jerry Grant ticked off his reasons: the loss of evidence, the risk of post-conviction relief being granted, the probable inability of the state to go forward with a new trial.

Cohen looked at Jordan Green, who said, "I agree the no-contest plea is in the interests of justice."

Cohen again addressed Macumber: "Sir, you understand that despite pleading no contest, you are sentenced as if you pled guilty. Do you believe this plea is in your interest?"

"Yes," Bill said.

The Court, Cohen concluded, finds the no-contest plea "knowingly made" and with "a factual basis." So "I accept the no-contest plea and find the defendant guilty of murder . . ." He paused for a moment. "I do want to say this notion of justice is one I have always wrestled with. . . . I wish we had a magical way to say just what is justice." Then he issued Macumber's sentence: "Not less than thirty-seven years, not more than thirty-seven years and eight months." Bill Macumber, in other words, would walk free for time served. Judge Cohen looked at Bill. "Mr. Macumber, good luck to you."

Two hours later, after final processing by the Department of Corrections, a metal mesh door at the Alhambra complex slid open and Bill Macumber, at age seventy-seven, stepped into the prison's lobby, free after thirty-eight years. Jackie hugged him, Ron hugged him, his brother Bob hugged him. Together, they walked through the prison's main entrance, Bill wearing a brown-checked flannel shirt, jeans and a bolo tie—clothes bought by Jay, who had in mind burning Bill's orange inmate jumpsuit in a backyard bonfire. Only Bill's white prison tennis shoes offered a reminder of his past wardrobe. He felt numb but waved and offered a thumbs-up to a crowd of well-wishers, including many from the Justice Project and Perkins Coie legal teams. Katie rushed to hug him, as did Lindsay. "It's a big day," he told a group of reporters and TV cameramen, "but it's a family day."

With that, his relatives hurried him to Jay and Harleen's car. On the drive to his cousin's home, Bill looked out the car window, wondering at how much Phoenix had changed. In Jay and Harleen's guest bedroom, he wondered also at a bedside lamp that turned on with a tap, rather than a switch. That first night there, he watched rabbits and quail scamper in the backyard, ate pizza with his family, and allowed himself one beer. "After thirty-eight years, I was a little bit hesitant to go beyond that point," he reported.

The next morning, he visited his parents' gravesite at a cemetery in north Phoenix, which he'd never seen before. Jackie gave him four hundred dollars in cash—and a billfold. He made plans to get his military and ASU records, to activate his Social Secruity and medical coverage, to buy more civilian clothes at a nearby Walmart, to go on a fishing trip with Jay. Then, at 3 P.M. that Thursday, he appeared at a press conference in the Perkins Coie law offices, sitting beside Jordan Green and Larry Hammond in a twentieth-floor meeting room that overlooked all of Phoenix. "The world has passed me by in four decades," he said tearfully, "but I will catch up to the degree I have to." Which included advocating "for elderly inmates and for the Arizona Justice Project." As always, he maintained his innocence: "I made that statement of innocence, I don't know, ten thousand times . . . and I'll take that statement to the grave." Before he left the state prison at Douglas, he reported, he'd left a quote posted on an inmate bulletin board: "Justice, however late, is still justice."

That evening, he, his family and the Justice Project team retreated to a Macayo's Depot Cantina for dinner in a private back room. This time, Bill allowed himself a scotch and soda with his combination plate, then another back at Jay and Harleen's home. Still, he remained on his feet.

Larry Hammond did not join them at this dinner. Instead, he started driving late that afternoon to Tucson, to attend an evening speech by Morris Dees, the celebrated cofounder of the Southern Poverty Law Center—who, as it happened, would be talking about the Macumber case. In his GMC Sierra pick-up truck, heading southeast on I-10, Hammond tried to sort out his thoughts. The Justice Project indeed had written a new ending to the Macumber story, a stunning and amazing end. Yet Hammond didn't quite know how to feel. It had been absolutely right to negotiate, to settle for a no-contest plea and time served, to have Bill walk out a free man. But, as a result, people would always be able to say he's guilty, not innocent. Which is what the county attorney Bill Montgomery had done at a press conference and in a press release after the hearing: "He's not innocent," Montgomery had declared. "He's guilty. . . . Had the evidence not been destroyed or lost, I have no doubt the State would have prevailed for a third time in convicting him."

Hammond understood that other people, including some who'd put enormous energy into this case, were less certain than he about Bill's innocence. This plea deal didn't resolve their differences, didn't answer all the questions. Still—almost everyone he'd talked to saw the Macumber case as a striking example of manifest injustice. Hammond focused on that. He thought also of the response from his long-time assistant, Donna Toland, when he shared the news about Bill. "Well of course," she'd said. "Why would you have invested so much time if this were not the way it was going to end?"

That was an idea he had not grasped. Hammond wondered, had he really thought success was inevitable? No, he couldn't say that. No, he hadn't known how it would end. Rather, he'd always thought this case just had to be pursued, win or lose. He'd always thought it the right thing to do. Hammond gripped the steering wheel of his silver blue pickup as he peered into the dimming sky. Yes. That is why he'd heeded the siren call of an impossible obsession. That is why he'd urged the Justice Project's ceaseless, quixotic campaign to free Bill Macumber.

A Note on Sources

This book is a work of nonfiction. It is based on a wide range of interviews conducted from June 2010 through November 2012. It also draws from a great wealth of documents: complete transcripts from both of Bill Macumber's trials and from a number of pretrial hearings; Maricopa County Sheriff's Office investigative reports from both the original 1962 murder investigation and the 1974 arrest of Bill Macumber; county probation and social workers' reports; Arizona Supreme Court opinions and decrees; complete records of both Arizona Board of Executive Clemency hearings; Arizona Department of Corrections files; legal petitions and appeals; depositions and affidavits; Justice Project memos and reports; internal Justice Project e-mail messages among Macumber team members; Justice Project correspondence with Bill Macumber and Jackie Kelley; correspondence between Jackie Kelley and Bill Macumber; correspondence between Ron and Bill Macumber; and Bill Macumber's four-hundred-page personal journal.

Over a span of two years, I traveled regularly to Arizona to visit with many of the characters who populate this narrative. I spent dozens of hours in the Justice Project's offices, then located in the basement of the library at the Sandra Day O'Connor College of Law at Arizona State University, poring over documents and talking at length with Katie Puzauskas, Lindsay Herf and Sarah Cooper. In person, via e-mail and on the phone, I spent many additional hours interviewing Larry Hammond and Bob Bartels. I spent an extended weekend with Bill Macumber at the Arizona State Prison in Douglas and another day with him at the Arizona State Prison's medical complex in Tucson; we also exchanged some twenty letters over the course of sixteen months. I spent a day with Ron Macumber at his home in Colorado, two days with Jackie Kelley on her ranch in New Mexico, and a day with Carol, Steve and Scott Kempfert in Olympia, Washington. In Phoenix I met Rich Robertson three times for comprehensive conversations. Twice I visited Bedford Douglass at his home in Mesa, Arizona, where we turned through the pages of the second trial transcript, reconstructing various scenes. One late afternoon, I met Robert and Toots Macumber at the home of Jay and Harleen Brandon in Apache Junction, where we all talked well into the evening. On another morning, Judge Thomas O'Toole welcomed me to his home for a wide-ranging discussion about Ernest Valenzuela and the Macumber case. By phone and e-mail I talked several times with Karen Killion, Sharon Sargent-Flack and Jen Roach. In the Justice Project offices I met with Andrew Hacker, Jenifer Swisher and Pete Rodriguez. At the Maricopa County Public Defender's Office, I talked to Paul Prato, Bedford Douglass's junior colleague at the second trial. In his downtown Phoenix law offices, I spoke with Tom Henze, the prosecutor at the first trial. Bill Macumber's neighbor Paul Bridgewater, who still lived in his Deer Valley house, drove me by the Macumbers' old home on West Wethersfield and showed me the Little League field—now a barren vacant lot—that Bill tended. In September 2010 I talked at length with four of the five Board of Executive Clemency members who in May 2009 voted for Macumber's release: Duane Belcher, Ellen Stenson, Tad Roberts and Marian Yim.

The documents—thousands of pages—provided the book's critical foundation. Using these records, I was often able to compare, clarify, question or confirm people's recollections. I could see whether events remembered now, years later, were also reported or described back when they actually happened, either in writing or conversations. Most important, by looking at the dates on the documents, I could build an accurate, unified chronology—an essential task in writing narrative and a difficult one, for people often blur and jumble time sequences.

The documents also allowed me to write from the interior point of view of various characters, including Bill Macumber. When I describe what they thought or felt at a particular moment, it often comes from what they told me, but it derives as well from what they wrote—at the time—in letters, journals and e-mail messages. By comparing different accounts and matching memories to dated documents, I was often able to corroborate a person's story. (For example, when Bill Macumber's journal says that his lawyer James Kemper informed him in early October 1974 about Ernest Valenzuela's confession, I can see that, indeed, Thomas O'Toole first wrote to Judge Hardy that very week.) Where memories diverged in critical ways that couldn't be resolved by documents or interviews—Bill's accounts versus Carol's, for example—I chose to identify the "competing narratives" rather than declare one to be the "truth."

Much of this chronicle relies on reconstruction. Again, the wealth of documents provided the foundation. Wherever possible, I supplemented the documents by interviewing those present at the scene of an event, seeking to weave multiple points of view into a unified, coherent account. That is how I chronicled Bill Macumber's first Phase II clemency board hearing in 2009, which I didn't attend (I hadn't yet started this project). Working with a transcript of the hearing, I talked to virtually everyone present that day, walking each person page by page through the two-hour session. I also persuaded Marian Yim, one of the board members, to scroll through the transcript, annotating and clarifying. Katie Puzauskas then drew me a detailed diagram of the hearing room, complete with a seating chart. I needed less help with the second clemency board hearing, which I attended, but afterward, again working with a transcript, I interviewed many present that day, seeking their perspective and memories.

Beyond the full court record and supplementary documents from both 1962 and 1974–77, I was able to draw from a range of internal memos and reports prepared by the Justice Project after its lawyers took up the case. Chief among them: Earl Terman's "Macumber Narrative" (February 3, 2000) and assorted e-mail summaries (January–August 2000); Sharon Sargent-Flack's spreadsheet summary (February 10, 2003); Karen Killion's

"Top 10 Action Plan" (January 30, 2001) and "Macumber Part I" narrative (January 31, 2001); Sharon Sargent-Flack's "Firearms Evidence Trail" memo (February 7, 2001); Karen Killion's "Summary of Fingerprint Efforts" memo (September 8, 2001); Jen Roach's seventy-five-page "Macumber Outline" (June 2004); Sarah Cooper's draft of the initial PCR petition (October 2010); and the Justice Project's memorandums in support of both clemency applications (2009 and 2011).

The affidavits collected by Katie Puzauskas, Lindsay Herf and Sarah Cooper in 2010 also added to my chronicle. So did Pat Ferguson's Custody/Visitation Report for the Conciliation Court (No. A-2956, March 26, 1975), Basil Wiederkehr's Presentencing Report (Case No. 83402, February 11, 1975), and the letters provided to the Board of Executive Clemency by Carol, Steve and Scott Kempfert in early 2012. I drew as well from the Arizona Supreme Court's two decisions in Macumber's case: *State of Arizona v. William Wayne Macumber*, 112 Ariz. 569, January 13, 1976, following the first trial; *State of Arizona v. William Wayne Macumber*, 119 Ariz. 516, June 9, 1978, following the second trial.

In recounting Larry Hammond's personal background and the genesis of the Justice Project, I found my interviews with Hammond helpfully supplemented by Roger Parloff's *Triple Jeopardy* (Little, Brown, 1996), an account of the John Knapp case that also informed me about Judge Charles Hardy. Because Hammond told Parloff and me the same stories, using much the same language, there is overlap between certain of our passages. I asked Hammond to review and confirm all biographical information in Parloff's book.

For my understanding of the DNA exonerations that provide one context for Macumber's case, I found helpful Brandon L. Garrett's *Convicting the Innocent* (Harvard University Press, 2011), which lucidly analyzes just what went wrong in the cases of the first 250 wrongfully convicted people to be exonerated by DNA testing.

Janet Malcolm's *Iphigenia in Forest Hills: Anatomy of a Murder Trial* (Yale University Press, 2011) provided me with yet another reminder—if I needed one—that lawyers are storytellers and courtrooms are venues for competing narratives.

A good number of law journal articles—some citing or focusing specifically on the Macumber case—educated me about the attorney-client privilege and its role in the Macumber trials. Among them:

Tyson A. Ciepluch, "Overriding the Posthumous Application of Attorney-Client Privilege: Due Process for a Criminal Defendant," *Marquette Law Review* 83 (1999–2000): 785–806.

Geoffrey C. Hazard Jr., "An Historical Perspective on the Attorney-Client Privilege," *California Law Review* 66 (1978): 1061–91.

W. William Hodes, "Executing the Wrong Person," *Loyola of Los Angeles Law Review* 29 (June 1996): 1547.

Brian R. Hood, "The Attorney-Client Privilege and a Revised Rule 1.6: Permitting Limited Disclosure After the Death of a Client," *Georgetown Journal of Legal Ethics* 7 (1993–94): 741–81.

Peter A. Joy and Kevin C. McMunigal, "Confidentiality and Wrongful Incarceration," *Criminal Justice* 23, no. 2 (Summer 2008).

Deborah L. Rhode and David Luban, "Confidentiality and Attorney-Client Privilege," in *Legal Ethics*, 3rd ed., University Casebook Series. New York: Foundation Press, 2001.

Paul Rosenzweig, "Federal Prosecution Policy and the Attorney-Client Privilege," testimony in February 2005 before the American Bar Association Task Force on the Attorney-Client Privilege, derived from Rosenzweig's "Truth, Privileges, Perjury and the Criminal Law," *Texas Review of Law and Politics* 7 (2002): 513.

66th American Law Institute Proceedings, "Illustration 4 [Macumber Case]," *66th ALI Proceedings* (1989): 332.

A number of pivotal appellate court decisions regarding the attorney-client privilege also helped me better understand the privilege's role in the Macumber case. Among them:

Swidler & Berlin and James Hamilton v. United States [the Vince Foster Case], U.S. Supreme Court, 524 U.S. 399, 141 L. Ed. 2d 379, 118 S. Ct. 2081 [No. 97-1192], argued June 8, 1998, decided June 25, 1998. Dissenting opinion by Justice O'Connor, joined by Justice Scalia and Justice Thomas. Transcript of Oral Hearing, June 8, 1998, 1998 U.S. Trans. LEXIS 48.

In Re: Sealed Case, U.S. Court of Appeals for the District of Columbia Circuit, 124 F3d 230; 326 U.S. App. D.C. 317; 1997 U.S. App. LEXIS 22814; 47 Fed. R. Evid. Serv. (Callaghan) 327; argued June 20, 1997, decided August 29, 1997.

Chambers v. Mississippi, U.S. Supreme Court, 410 U.S. 284; 93 S. Ct. 1038; 35 L. Ed. 2d 297; 1973 U.S. LEXIS 107; argued November 15, 1972, decided February 21, 1973.

In the Matter of a John Doe, Supreme Judicial Court of Massachusetts, Suffolk; 408 Mass. 480; 562 N.E. 2d 69; 1990 Mass. LEXIS 461; argued September 7, 1990, decided November 5, 1990.

Jose Morales v. Portuondo, U.S. District Court for the Southern District of New York; 154 F. Supp. 2d 706; 2001 U.S. Dist. LEXIS 10377; filed July 24, 2001, decided July 24, 2001.

State v. Doster, Supreme Court of South Carolina, 276 S.C. 647; 284 S.E. 2d 218; 1981 S.C. LEXIS 318, March 4, 1981.

State v. Valdez, Supreme Court of New Mexico, 95 N.M. 70; 618 P. 2d 1234; 1980 N.M. LEXIS 2725; September 15, 1980.

People v. Ernest Edwards, Supreme Court of Michigan, 396 Mich. 551; 242 N.W. 2d 739; 1976 Mich. LEXIS 270; 92 A.L.R. 3d 1149; argued September 12, 1974, decided June 3, 1976.

Arizona v. Pina, Court of Appeals of Arizona, 469 P. 2d 481; 1770 Ariz. App. LEXIS 623; 12 Ariz. App. 247; May 18, 1970.

U.S. v. Pena, U.S. Court of Appeals for the Fifth Circuit, 527 F. 2d 1356; 1976 U.S. App. LEXIS 12583; March 3, 1976.

The *Swidler* (Vince Foster) case before the U.S. Supreme Court in June 1998 drew widespread news media attention. Among the articles I consulted:

Walter Pincus, "Ken Starr Says Dead Men Should Tell Tales," *Washington Post*, May 24, 1998.

Tony Mauro, "Starr to Argue Privilege Stops at Death," *USA Today*, June 8, 1998.

Stephen Labaton, "Supreme Court Hears Case on Ex–White House Counsel's Notes," *New York Times*, June 9, 1998.

Simon Frankel, "A Confidence Better Kept," *New York Times*, June 9, 1998.

Ruth Marcus and Susan Schmidt, "Attorney Client Privilege After Death Is Upheld," *Washington Post*, June 26, 1998.

Stephen Labaton, "Justices Deal Starr a Defeat, Holding That the Attorney-Client Privilege Survives Death," *New York Times*, June 26, 1998.

The Arizona press extensively covered the Scottsdale Road murders in 1962. The news clips from those days, collected by the Justice Project, exist only as torn, yellowing sheets that often lack a date or even the name of the newspaper. The byline of Gene McLain at the *Arizona Republic* appears often in this file. Other stories come from the *Daily Progress* and the *Evening American*.

The arrest and trials of Bill Macumber in 1974–77 also drew much press attention in Arizona. Again the clips in the Justice Project file exist only as torn sheets that often lack identifying dates or names of newspapers. The bylines of Pat Sabo and Mel Foor of the *Phoenix Gazette* appear more than once. Two full-length magazine pieces stand out: Eddie Krell, "Death Hunted the Lovers in the Desert," *Front Page Detective*, September 15, 1974, and Robert Barrett, "How Do You Prosecute a 12-Year-Old Murder Case?," *Arizona*, October 12, 1975.

Governor Jan Brewer's November 2009 rejection of the recommendation from the Arizona Board of Executive Clemency triggered an extensive amount of press attention in Arizona and nationwide, starting in the spring of 2010. I cite and quote from these reports in Chapter 21, Attention Is Paid. Among the key stories and broadcasts were: Sarah Buduson, "Arizona Governor Refuses to Explain Clemency Ruling," KPHO TV, May 18, 2010; P. S. Ruckman Jr., "Arizona: Clemency Mystery," *Pardon Power* blog, May 19, 2010; Adam Liptak, "Governor Rebuffs Clemency Board in Murder Case," *New York Times*, June 14, 2010; Joe Dana, "Clemency Denial Frustrates Many," azcentral.com/12 News, July 12, 2010; Margaret E. Beardsley, "Group Fighting to Free Man They Believe Was Wrongly Accused of Murder," azfamily.com, July 26, 2010; Dave Biscobing, "A Life of Injustice? Governor Blocks One Man's Quest for Freedom," ABC 15 TV, September 7, 2010; Mary K. Reinhart, "Brewer Refuses to Reconsider What Clemency Board Calls 'Miscarriage of Justice,'" *Arizona Guardian*, October 21, 2010; Dan Harris, Steven Baker and Lauren Effron, "Did Wife Frame Husband for Arizona Cold Case Murders?," *Nightline*, ABC News, October 27, 2010.

Several months later, on June 5, 2011, a comprehensive three-part series about the Macumber case appeared in the *Arizona Republic*: "Arizona Murder Mystery: Guilt of Man in 1962 Killings Thrown into Question," by John Faherty.

My book, chapter by chapter, derives from a weave of the multiple sources listed above and below. For the most part, those sources are apparent in the narrative. Bill Macumber's thoughts and history, for example, clearly come from his letters, his journal and my interviews with him. Accounts of the Scottsdale Road murders draw from the sheriff's investigative reports, trial transcripts and local Arizona newspaper stories. I pieced together the Justice Project's efforts over the years through interviews with Macumber team members and from their many letters, memos and e-mail exchanges. My reconstruction of the trials came from transcripts, news stories and interviews with, among others, Tom Henze, Bedford Douglass, Paul Prato, Thomas O'Toole and Bill Macumber.

At the start of Chapter 1, I drew from Tom Henze's memories of partying on the Scottsdale desert as a youth. Bill Macumber's "memories of days now gone" in Chapter 2 came largely from his journal, as did the summary in Chapter 4 of his thoughts while in the Maricopa County Jail. The account of the jury's reasoning and vote in Chapter 9 derived from juror Sarah Elliot's September 8, 2010, affidavit and jury foreman Dick Adams's letter to Carol Kempfert, dated January 13, 1977. In Chapter 10, my report of Bill Macumber's life in prison drew in part from Arizona Department of Corrections logs and the supporting letters and award certificates in his clemency petitions; my own visit with Macumber in the state prison at Douglas allowed me to confirm directly the high regard inmates and guards have for him there. An interview with Gary Phelps, former deputy to Arizona Department of Corrections director Sam Lewis, provided confirmation of the account, in Chapter 12, of how life changed for Macumber under Lewis.

My reconstruction in Chapter 14 of the Justice Project team's journey to meet Macumber at the state prison in Douglas derived from interviews with Larry Hammond, Bob Bartels, Rich Robertson, Sharon Sargent-Flack and Bill Macumber. Sharon also shared with me the handwritten notes she took during the visit, and Bill Macumber reconstructed the day in a series of letters. My description of the team's drive from Phoenix to Douglas drew as well from my own journey to Douglas, following the same route the team took. The passage about the history of Douglas and the Gadsden Hotel derived in part from a Wikipedia posting and local newspaper accounts. My description of the team's entry into the prison drew from my own experience going through that security process.

My account, also in Chapter 14, of Rich Robertson's visit to Carol Kempfert's home in Olympia drew from interviews with Robertson, his testimony at two clemency hearings, and his written report to the Justice Project team dated March 9, 2003. I also talked to Carol, Scott and Steve Kempfert about this visit. Their memories differed from Rich's. In their version, Carol did not say, "Now get the fuck off my porch," though they allowed that Steve might have. And in their version, it was sunny. In checking the National Climatic Data Center Global Surface Summary of Day weather reports for Olympia, Washington, during the two days of Robertson's visit (March 1–2, 2003), I saw .17 precipitation, "rain and/or melted snow reported during the day" for March 1, and 0.00 precipitation, "rain and/or melted snow reported during the day" for March 2. Given the conflicting accounts, I chose to allow both parties to share their memories, Carol offering hers in Chapter 27.

In Chapter 15, the summary of Larry Hammond's first phone conversation with Ron drew in part from Hammond's written report to the team about that event. In Chapter 16, the story of Bob Bartels's visit with Jerry Jacka derived in part from Bartels's written report to the Justice Project team about that day. In Chapter 18, Mark Macumber's memories of his visits with Bill in prison drew from an account he wrote, "Bill's Story," and from his letter to the clemency board.

I attended Sigmund Popko's Post-Conviction Clinic on September 8, 2010, where Katie, Lindsay and Sarah recruited for the Justice Project, so I described this session from direct observation at the start of Chapter 22. Katie provided me with written timelines that helped in my reconstruction of their "going to the ground campaign" in the summer and fall of 2010. My discussion in Chapter 23 about the evolving world of forensic science drew in part from the NAS report mentioned there: Committee on Identifying the Needs of the Forensic Sciences Community, National Research Council, *Strengthening Forensic Science in the United States: A Path Forward* (National Academies Press, 2009).

I attended the second Phase II clemency board hearing described in Chapter 25, witnessing the six-hour session firsthand and taking extensive notes. I subsequently obtained a transcript of the hearing and, using it as a road map, interviewed Larry Hammond, Bob Bartels, Jackie Kelley, Ron Macumber, Rich Robertson and Katie Puzauskas. Bill Macumber and I exchanged letters. I spoke to Bedford Douglass by phone, confirming his contact before the second Macumber trial with the ballistics expert Lucien Haag.

In writing that chapter, I also drew on a number of key documents: Macumber's Petition for Post-Conviction Relief, filed February 9, 2012; the Justice Project's Memorandum in Support of William Wayne Macumber's Application for Executive Clemency, June 2011; State of Arizona's Memorandum in Opposition to the Application for Executive Clemency of William Wayne Macumber, March 2012; letter to the Arizona Board of Executive Clemency from Carol Kempfert, January 30, 2012; letter to the Arizona Board of Executive Clemency from Scott Kempfert, March 9, 2012; letter to the Arizona Board of Executive Clemency from Steve Kempfert, March 12, 2012; Linda Primrose's letter to Bedford Douglass, July 1976; jury foreman Dick Adams's letter to Carol Kempfert, January 13, 1977.

In Chapter 26, the reference to Governor Brewer's ouster of three clemency board members drew from several Arizona newspaper accounts: Gary Grado, "Dust-up Leads to Clemency Director's Firing," *Arizona Capitol Times*, April 24, 2012; Bob Ortega, "Clemency Board Faces Legal Hurdles: Brewer-Appointed Members' Training Called into Question," *Arizona Republic*, May 6, 2012; and Bob Ortega, "Arizona Prisoners Rarely Granted Clemency: Governor Seldom Uses Sentencing 'Safety Valve,'" by *Arizona Republic*, May 12, 2012.

In Chapter 27, my reference to what Carol told a reporter in January 1976 about Bill's letters comes from "I'm Terribly Frightened," an article in the *Phoenix Gazette* by Pat Sabo, published on January 14, 1976. My sources for the time sequence involving Macumber family members are several: In a letter to me dated July 3, 2012, Bill Macumber advised that Harold carted items from the house on West Wethersfield Road soon after Bill's arrest—Bill couldn't have done that himself, as he was in jail. Macumber's journal records his plan to buy the motocross bike for his sons on Friday, October 25, 1974, while he was out on bail before the first trial, and Ron Macumber confirms that's when his father bought them the bike. Judge Hughes didn't request a conciliation court report until March 1975, which is when Pat Ferguson interviewed Steve and Scott; Pat Ferguson's report is dated March 26, 1975.

My account in Chapter 27 about the post-conviction relief proceedings, plea bargain, evidentiary hearing and Macumber's press conference drew from court documents and interviews with all those involved, particularly Jordan Green at the law firm of Perkins Coie. I attended the evidentiary hearing in Phoenix on November 7, 2012, and also drew from local news stories, particularly two by Richard Ruelas in *The Arizona Republic*, "Ex-inmate Savors 1st Breaths of Freedom" (November 9, 2012) and "Man Convicted in '62 Murders Freed" (November 8, 2012).

I am acutely aware of how hard it is to get everything right in this kind of reconstructed nonfiction narrative. I realize also that as well as I may do my job, some players in the story may be unhappy about their depictions, feeling I have not represented them as they see themselves. That is inevitable and unavoidable. In the end, as harsh as it sounds, I am telling my story, not theirs.

Acknowledgments

Assembling a nonfiction chronicle such as this requires the cooperation of a great many people, to whom I am forever indebted. Most particularly, I thank Larry Hammond, who opened the doors of the Arizona Justice Project to me and then spent dozens of hours sharing his memories and insights. Without his gracious, patient cooperation, and his decision to urge the Justice Project's "full cooperation," my task would have been impossible. I am equally grateful to Katie Puzauskas, who provided a wealth of documents, constant guidance and invaluable support, fielding my unending flow of queries and requests over two years. She also proved to be a most considerate host, affording me use of the Justice Project conference room and a priceless copier-scanner.

I'm obliged as well to Bob Bartels and Rich Robertson, who spent hours guiding me through the Justice Project's decade-long work on the Macumber case, and to a number of others on the Justice Project team: Lindsay Herf, Sarah Cooper, Karen Killion, Sharon Sargent-Flack, Andrew Hacker and Jen Roach. I thank Ron Macumber and Jackie Kelley for serving up resonant memories and boxes of invaluable documents; Bedford Douglass for reliving the second Macumber trial; Judge Thomas O'Toole for recalling Ernest Valenzuela; Carol, Steve and Scott

Kempfert for graciously welcoming me to their home. I'm most grateful to Bill Macumber for his sustained cooperation and pivotal decision to provide me his journal and private correspondence.

A special thanks to Marc LaRocque, who as my research associate in the early stages of this project helped me navigate several complex topics. Marc holds a PhD in history from University of California–Irvine but proved to be equally adept at legal research, gathering a rich portfolio of articles and rulings about the attorney-client privilege.

Once the research is completed, the writing—and rewriting—begins. I am deeply indebted to Gillian Blake, the editor-in-chief at Henry Holt, for her superb editing advice, which ranged from meta-considerations to a rigorous line edit. Her close read of several drafts inspired me to keep revising my manuscript. So did the meticulous work by Bonnie Thompson, a gifted copyeditor. I'm grateful as well to Henry Holt's publisher, Stephen Rubin, for his continued support and faith in me.

My regard and appreciation for Kathy Robbins—after all these years still my agent, friend, mentor and scold—knows no bounds. Throughout this project she encouraged, championed and challenged all at once. She greatly improved both my spirit and my prose.

My wife, Marti Devore, and daughter, Ally Siegel, put up with me once again. Their love, support and tolerance make it all possible.

Index

Outlaw Rodeo and, 105
palm prints taken, 35
police interrogation of, and missing
    reports, 33–38, 135, 144, 147, 149–50,
    156, 158–61, 163, 165–66, 171–72, 326
polygraph and, 33–34, 343
preliminary hearings and, 42–43
prison life and, 70, 72–73, 75, 99–107,
    138–40
second trial and, 77–98, 142–45, 150,
    171, 250, 332–33, 329
second trial jurors and clemency
    petition of, 297–301, 307, 310
son Ron reunited with, 192–201, 212,
    218
sons and, 21, 24–26, 40, 43, 45–46, 54,
    69, 78, 107, 141, 185–92, 324, 340,
    347
Valenzuela confession and, 2–5, 51–54
victims' families and, 320–21, 329–30
visitation rights and, 56–60, 73–75
writing by, 107, 137, 336
Make-a-Wish Foundation, 103, 105
Maledon, Bill, 124
Maricopa County indigent-defense fund,
    122
Maricopa County Public Defenders Office,
    94
Maricopa County Records and
    Identification Bureau, 217
Maricopa County Sheriff's Office (MCSO)
    AJP investigation and, 147, 149–51,
        157–64, 171–72
    Bill arrested by, 35–37
    Bill's report of kitchen-window shot
        and, 27, 32–33
    Bill's second trial and, 80, 90
    Carol and, 26, 145–46, 149, 252, 282,
        291, 294–95, 304–7, 325, 349–50
    Desert Survival Unit and, 25
    murder investigation and, 10–18, 67,
        112–14, 163–65, 171–72, 290
    Valenzuela confession and, 18–19
Martinez v. Ryan, 319, 346
McCarthy, John, 16
McClusky, Carol Sue, 330
McClusky, John (Tim McKillop's cousin),
    321, 329–30, 358

McFord, Lester, II, 159
McGowan, Carl, 120
McKillop, Ann (Tim's mother),
    37, 329–30
McKillop, Jim (Tim's father), 10–12,
    14, 330
McKillop, Tim
    family of, and clemency, 270, 329–30
    model homes guard and, 171
    murder of, 9–20, 35–37, 342. *See also*
        Sterrenberg-McKillop murder
McKinney, Lieutenant, 53–54
Mexican Mafia, 126
Meza, Olivia, 233, 248, 253–54, 259
Michael, Judy (Joyce Sterrenberg's sister),
    270, 330, 358
Miranda case, 80
Moreno, Mike, 33, 295
Morris Dees Justice Award, xi
Mountain States Telephone, 10, 29–30,
    148, 165
Mulleneaux, Lawrence, 42
Mussman, Logan, 297–98

Napolitano, Janet, 271
National Academy of Sciences (NAS), 275,
    278, 308–9
National Conference on Preventing the
    Conviction of Innocent Persons,
    228–29
Nelson, Lamson, 49
Nelson, Salina, 49
Neufeld, Peter, xiv, 124
New York Times, 283, 285
Nightline (TV show), 283–85, 310
Nixon, John, 310

Obama, Barack, 271
O'Connor, Sandra Day, 2, 131
Orenelas, Loretta, 91–92
Osborn Maledon firm, 123, 125–26, 130,
    152
O'Toole, Thomas
    AJP and, 2–3, 135, 156, 167–69, 234,
        275, 278, 293, 298, 307, 319
    Bill's arrest and trial and, 48–53, 62–63,
        75
    Bill's second trial and, 81–87

About the Author

BARRY SIEGEL, a Pulitzer Prize–winning former national correspondent for the *Los Angeles Times*, directs the literary journalism program at University of California–Irvine, where he is a professor of English. He is the author of six previous books, including *A Death in White Bear Lake*, *Shades of Gray* and *Claim of Privilege*. He lives in Los Angeles with his wife and their daughter.